I0887903

Global Perspectives on Military Entrepreneurship and Innovation

Sanya Ojo
Nigerian Defence Academy, Nigeria

A volume in the Advances in Business Strategy and Competitive Advantage (ABSCA) Book Series

IGI Global
PUBLISHER of TIMELY KNOWLEDGE

Published in the United States of America by
IGI Global
Business Science Reference (an imprint of IGI Global)
701 E. Chocolate Avenue
Hershey PA, USA 17033
Tel: 717-533-8845
Fax: 717-533-8661
E-mail: cust@igi-global.com
Web site: http://www.igi-global.com

Copyright © 2021 by IGI Global. All rights reserved. No part of this publication may be reproduced, stored or distributed in any form or by any means, electronic or mechanical, including photocopying, without written permission from the publisher.
Product or company names used in this set are for identification purposes only. Inclusion of the names of the products or companies does not indicate a claim of ownership by IGI Global of the trademark or registered trademark.

Library of Congress Cataloging-in-Publication Data

Names: Ojo, Sanya, 1960- editor.
Title: Global perspectives on military entrepreneurship and innovation / Sanya Ojo.
Description: Hershey, PA : Business Science Reference, [2021] | Includes bibliographical references and index. | Summary: "The book is a collection of studies on military entrepreneurship, treating the subject with emphasis on metacognition, entrepreneurship that engages memory-monitoring and self-regulation, and meta-reasoning including knowledge about when and how to use particular strategies for learning or for problem solving"-- Provided by publisher.
Identifiers: LCCN 2020026659 (print) | LCCN 2020026660 (ebook) | ISBN 9781799866558 (hardcover) | ISBN 9781799866565 (paperback) | ISBN 9781799866572 (ebook)
Subjects: LCSH: Defense industries. | New business enterprises. | Veterans--Employment. | Entrepreneurship.
Classification: LCC HD9743.A2 G57 2021 (print) | LCC HD9743.A2 (ebook) | DDC 338.4/7355--dc23
LC record available at https://lccn.loc.gov/2020026659
LC ebook record available at https://lccn.loc.gov/2020026660

This book is published in the IGI Global book series Advances in Business Strategy and Competitive Advantage (ABSCA) (ISSN: 2327-3429; eISSN: 2327-3437)

British Cataloguing in Publication Data
A Cataloguing in Publication record for this book is available from the British Library.

All work contributed to this book is new, previously-unpublished material.
The views expressed in this book are those of the authors, but not necessarily of the publisher.

For electronic access to this publication, please contact: eresources@igi-global.com.

Advances in Business Strategy and Competitive Advantage (ABSCA) Book Series

ISSN:2327-3429
EISSN:2327-3437

Editor-in-Chief: Patricia Ordóñez de Pablos, Universidad de Oviedo, Spain

MISSION

Business entities are constantly seeking new ways through which to gain advantage over their competitors and strengthen their position within the business environment. With competition at an all-time high due to technological advancements allowing for competition on a global scale, firms continue to seek new ways through which to improve and strengthen their business processes, procedures, and profitability.

The **Advances in Business Strategy and Competitive Advantage (ABSCA) Book Series** is a timely series responding to the high demand for state-of-the-art research on how business strategies are created, implemented and re-designed to meet the demands of globalized competitive markets. With a focus on local and global challenges, business opportunities and the needs of society, the **ABSCA** encourages scientific discourse on doing business and managing information technologies for the creation of sustainable competitive advantage.

COVERAGE

- Core Competencies
- International Business Strategy
- Innovation Strategy
- Strategic Management
- Customer-Orientation Strategy
- Strategic Alliances
- Value Creation
- Adaptive Enterprise
- Strategy Performance Management
- Economies of Scale

IGI Global is currently accepting manuscripts for publication within this series. To submit a proposal for a volume in this series, please contact our Acquisition Editors at Acquisitions@igi-global.com or visit: http://www.igi-global.com/publish/.

The Advances in Business Strategy and Competitive Advantage (ABSCA) Book Series (ISSN 2327-3429) is published by IGI Global, 701 E. Chocolate Avenue, Hershey, PA 17033-1240, USA, www.igi-global.com. This series is composed of titles available for purchase individually; each title is edited to be contextually exclusive from any other title within the series. For pricing and ordering information please visit http://www.igi-global.com/book-series/advances-business-strategy-competitive-advantage/73672. Postmaster: Send all address changes to above address. © © 2021 IGI Global. All rights, including translation in other languages reserved by the publisher. No part of this series may be reproduced or used in any form or by any means – graphics, electronic, or mechanical, including photocopying, recording, taping, or information and retrieval systems – without written permission from the publisher, except for non commercial, educational use, including classroom teaching purposes. The views expressed in this series are those of the authors, but not necessarily of IGI Global.

Titles in this Series

For a list of additional titles in this series, please visit: http://www.igi-global.com/book-series/

Revolutionizing Institutional Theory Through Stakeholder Capitalism
Neslihan Aydogan-Duda (UC Berkeley Extension, USA)
Business Science Reference • © 2021 • 300pp • H/C (ISBN: 9781799844921) • US $235.00

Creating Social Value Through Social Entrepreneurship
Mine Afacan Fındıklı (Beykent University, Turkey) and Duygu Acar Erdur (Beykent University, Turkey)
Business Science Reference • © 2021 • 369pp • H/C (ISBN: 9781799847274) • US $195.00

Handbook of Research on International Business and Models for Global Purpose-Driven Companies
Rafael Ignacio Perez-Uribe (EAN University, Colombia) Carlos Largacha-Martinez (Fundación Universitaria del Área Andina, Colombia) and David Ocampo-Guzman (EAN University, Colombia)
Business Science Reference • © 2021 • 589pp • H/C (ISBN: 9781799849094) • US $345.00

Cases on Internationalization Challenges for SMEs
António Carrizo Moreira (University of Aveiro, Portugal)
Business Science Reference • © 2021 • 333pp • H/C (ISBN: 9781799843870) • US $185.00

Impact of Disruptive Technologies on the Sharing Economy
Ford Lumban Gaol (Bina Nusantara University, Jakarta, Indonesia) Natalia Filimonova (Vladimir State University, Russia) and Chandan Acharya (City University of New York, USA)
Business Science Reference • © 2021 • 350pp • H/C (ISBN: 9781799803614) • US $245.00

Innovation Management and Growth in Emerging Economies
Heather C. Webb (Higher Colleges of Technology, Dubai, UAE) Wendy Wu (Edinburgh Napier University, UK) and Hussain Al Numairy (Higher Colleges of Technology, Dubai, UAE)
Business Science Reference • © 2021 • 288pp • H/C (ISBN: 9781799841951) • US $195.00

IGI Global
PUBLISHER of TIMELY KNOWLEDGE

701 East Chocolate Avenue, Hershey, PA 17033, USA
Tel: 717-533-8845 x100 • Fax: 717-533-8661
E-Mail: cust@igi-global.com • www.igi-global.com

Table of Contents

Detailed Table of Contents

of military entrepreneurship. Through a critical review of literature, the presence of "extrepreneurship," which represents a crossbreed idea located between the concepts of entrepreneurship and intrapreneurship, is revealed. Extrepreneurs manage/operate for-profit spin-off organizations on behalf of their non-profit parent organizations to generate incomes/profits, among other requirements.

The chapter focuses on entrepreneurial training (ET) in the Nigerian armed forces and its significance for post-retirement era and discussed the opportunities and challenges for self-reliance. The chapter is qualitative and analytical in approach. It sourced data largely from secondary sources including reputable journals, books, book chapters, monographs, and records, and analysed through content analysis. Though it remains a much underemphasised area in most organisations, ET of the armed forces is the main fulcrum for their retirement preparation, if they are to achieve self-reliance as veterans. The chapter revealed that the retirement training provided for the armed forces differs from one country to the other.

This chapter aims to provide fresh insights into entrepreneurship innovation to the retirees of the Nigerian military from the perspective of an ex-serviceman (a retired military person). The chapter's methodology focused on the articulation of experiences and meanings, which is guided by the events in the author's life, recounting life circumstances and events located in a specific time and space. Consequently, the chapter examines the entrepreneurial opportunities for retired Nigerian military personnel vis-a-vis the challenges faced by veterans when engaging in entrepreneurship. The chapter also discusses the entrepreneurship issues to be considered before becoming an entrepreneur. The chapter further postulates on information and communication technology (ICT) skills as key requirements for those who want to become an entrepreneur in post-service life. Finally, it is suggested that prior knowledge on innovative entrepreneurship before the start of a business results in successful sustained retirement income.

The prior studies form a solid foundation for the emerging research on military entrepreneurship in China. This chapter is dedicated to providing a detailed review on the evolution of Chinese disarmament, with a focus on military-civilian transfer and settlement of demobilized military staffs. Such a review comprehensively lays backgrounds for Chinese military entrepreneurship and thus is expected to serve as a prelude to the emerging research in this area.

To have a thorough understanding of the current state of veteran entrepreneurship in China, a literature mapping was made on the basis of 235 related articles and research literature published in the past decade (from 2010 to 2019), which are open to the public and available on the China National Knowledge Infrastructure (CNKI). Via combing through the above findings, the authors tried to unlock a phase with prominent rise of corresponding research papers and its possible reason, reveal the leading research power and their correlation, and also explore a potential research trend in the future. On the basis of the overall context and generalization of the status quo and limitations of this field during the past 10 years, reference and guidance can be provided for future study and policy making.

The condition of survival within the Nigerian Armed Forces, in terms of post-retirement career options, has inadvertently produced a growing number of ex-service members (veterans) who turned to entrepreneurship to earn income and remain active. However, against the alleged failure of entrepreneurship in this group, this chapter sets out to investigate the nature and characteristics of veteran entrepreneurship.

Through the application of case study methodology, the study reveals that veteran entrepreneurship does not differ significantly to civilian entrepreneurship. Veteran entrepreneurs confront the same challenges as their civilian counterparts while veterans' military backgrounds and military training appear to have both facilitating and inhibiting effects on veteran entrepreneurships in Nigeria.

This chapter examines post-retirement career pathways of ex-service personnel in the Nigerian military via entrepreneurship activities. One of the measures taken to assist ex-service personnel get adjusted into the civil life is the establishment of vocational training, which helps to facilitate viable entrepreneurial events. However, there are psychological issues that must be tackled in order to effectively transit into entrepreneurship. The chapter, therefore, looks at these issues to address the concept of entrepreneurship and its tendencies in the Nigerian military. The findings suggest that objectives and components of entrepreneurship education being advocated should be given to personnel early enough and throughout their military career.

The franchise business model has proven particularly attractive to veterans. When former soldiers become franchisees, they sign up to follow the game plan of the franchisor, but they must apply their own personal aptitudes, skills, and training to ensure their entrepreneurial venture succeeds. This chapter explores the practitioner and academic literature to identify why franchising is attractive to veterans as well as how the franchise sector encourages those with prior military experience to enlist. The chapter also examines whether veterans are satisfied with their decision to become franchisees and identifies which franchise systems are rated "best" for veterans. Finally, the chapter offers thoughts about global research that is needed to help franchise systems be a gateway for veterans to pursue their dream of business ownership.

Many military-related innovation approaches can be followed, such as doctrinal, tactical changes, and innovations in the organizational structure of military units. These approaches examine innovation in its historical context and flow. Defense industries of the countries are an indicator of their power in the international arena and develop new war weapons, systems, and equipment with innovation. Innovations turn it into economic power. Militaries are the most important customers of the defense industries. From the design of the products to the feedback of the last user, the defense industry, and military are in mutual interaction. Military culture, which is shaped in the light of the experiences gained with blood on the battlefield and has its dynamics, is one of the main phenomena in the acceptance of innovations and shaping the culture of military innovation. In this chapter, the authors examine the contribution of the defense industry and military employees to innovation in these innovation processes and the organizational acceptance processes offered to the use of these innovations.

The chapter investigates military enterprise and entrepreneurship through the prism of the Nigerian Armed Forces Resettlement Centre, Lagos. Through a mixed methodology, the chapter unveils innovative schemes and entrepreneurship culture in the centre. However, some tension exists between the military culture and entrepreneurship culture at the centre. Suggestions are offered to improve on the centre's service delivery. Generally, there is a need for NAFRC to further enhance its dynamic collaborative efforts, involve more in skills mapping of both its trainers and trainees, boost its mentoring capacity, and provide employment support through rigorous articulation of the value of retired military personnel to potential employers or funders. It is also suggested that NAFRC should liaise with other relevant stakeholders to support projects that deliver long-term solutions to the challenges faced by the retired military personnel community. The combination of all these activities will enable NAFRC to realise its vision and mission.

and sometimes decrease of staff morale, with negative impact on development of organizational knowledge as well as values and culture. Innovation can also provide new forms of doing things, fuelling internal processes, either operational, logistical, or administrative ones. Highly innovative organizations usually make jobs more fulfilling, and ultimately contribute in making the world a better place. Therefore, driving innovation is crucial, and that needs an appropriate framework in order to promote the desirable involvement from the whole organization. By following a logical thinking process, one ends up at a pragmatic and more deployable model backed by cause and effect logics.

Foreword

It is crystal clear that the world currently operates in unprecedent era. The challenges are real and the threat to the global prosperity as linked to the global pandemic (COVID-19) that has affected every dimension of the business environment is consequential. To many, the phrase 'Things Fall Apart' applies to several parts of life vis-à-vis this experience. That unpleasant event is characterized by high unemployment in many business sectors, business closures, and significant changes to social-cultural systems which have witnessed a sustained strain for most part of the year 2020. At the macro level, Gross Domestic Output (GDP), Gross National Income (GNI), Inflation rates and other economic indicators are not as promising as they used to be due to various measures that are introduced as life-saving but are equally unfriendly to the economy. Evidently, drastic actions are needed to reboot the economy towards ensuring survival within the 'New Normal' business environment. Given its hallmark as a significant contributor to the overall health of the economy in many nations, entrepreneurship will be at the forefront of these global economic recovery efforts. Interestingly, over the years, it has being conceptualized in a number of ways to give researchers and practitioners the opportunity to have a closer scrutiny of its ecosystem as a phenomenon. Hence, we tend to hear nomenclatures like women entrepreneurship, ethnic entrepreneurship, diaspora entrepreneurship, entrepreneurship within the faith-based contexts, and military entrepreneurship to mention but few. The dire need of global recovery would necessitate exploring all applicable opportunities including military entrepreneurship.

Meanwhile, one of the contentions around military entrepreneurship is the question of whether military establishments are amenable to entrepreneurship. The premise of this stance is that the former is inherently bureaucratic with most decisions in that context following a top-down stratagem. This perspective then contends that entrepreneurship is characterized by creativity, opportunity recognition and independence. In fact, 'being one's own boss' is a recurring factor among what constitute the impetus for entrepreneurship. Notwithstanding, a critical and meticulous review of this shows that there is a point of convergence between the two phenomena. This is anchored on the fact that virtues such as discipline, versatility, and dedication which are notably associated with military culture are equally amenable to entrepreneurship towards succeeding in the marketplace. Consequently, military entrepreneurship is expected to be among the pivotal routes out of the current global economic quagmire.

Statutorily, the military establishments are geared towards playing its role of defense in the national system. At the macro level, all over the world, the military agents and agencies espouse entrepreneurship in various ways, in the fulfillment of this cardinal responsibility. At the individual level, the discourse touches on veteran entrepreneurship where the focus is not only on contributing to the national economic development but also on ensuring steady stream of income after retirement. It is meant to provide individual and family support system that lessens dependence on governmental assistance after retirement and facilitate job creation. Clearly, it is a worthwhile endeavour.

Although the notion of military entrepreneurship is projected to be relevant all over the world, its popularity is not supported by commensurate scholarship effort. It is pleasing to see that Dr Sanya Ojo has not only made this case robustly but also extended the literature through the publication of this compendium which comprises various thought-provoking themes on this important topic. I congratulate him and the team of scholars who have contributed to the treatise for this bold move to fill this palpable research gap. The wealth of experience, commitment, and rigour expended in this publication is commendable. They have unpacked the subterraneous issues in this important topic and provided a meticulous synthesis of the relevant themes including the divide of civilian entrepreneurship and military entrepreneurship, intrapreneurship, entrepreneurship innovation and knowledge economy, and franchising among others. The eclecticism of the book offers a plethora of benefits to readers; and positions it as a compelling companion for various stakeholders. Overall, it is a product of good effort in many ramifications and will continue to be relevant many years to come, far beyond the economic period characterized by the ravaging global pandemic.

Ayantunji Gbadamosi
University of East London, UK

Preface

Welcome to *Global Perspectives on Military Entrepreneurship and Innovation*. This book has been designed as an introduction to the subject of 'Military Entrepreneurship' and as an exploration of the essential knowledge needed to understand how the phenomenon of entrepreneurship is engaged by military agents and agencies. The book is also designed to examine the palpable contradiction in the concept's components; entrepreneurship and the military. Entrepreneurship is generally regarded as an event underpinned by spontaneity, creativity, independence, and possibly a bottom-up approach to ordering and information processing. The military, on the other hand, is a stratified group, concerned with top-down organizing, groupthink, authoritarian structuring, and bureaucratized system (Allen & Gerras, 2009; Vego, 2013). Hence, the term 'Military Entrepreneurship' appears to be a paradigm of incongruity. Whereas some scholars (e.g., Hope et al., 2011; Knox & Murray, 2001) see the military as conservative, inflexible, and lacking entrepreneurial spirit, which suggests that the military institutions and settings do not allow entrepreneurship to fester. Other scholars (e.g., Adrienne et al., 2017; Mares, 1998; Storlie, 2010) argue the opposite and view the military as conferring entrepreneurial attributes such as dedication, discipline, versatility, and innovativeness to its personnel. Thus, the military institutions are seen as providing a setting where entrepreneurship is facilitated to flourish. There is increasing evidence, including the chapters in this book, that military institutions are robust sources of entrepreneurial activities.

Nonetheless, there is a void in research on how the military institutions manage and exploit different, potentially contradictory entrepreneurial arrangements existing in their environments. Works of literature on the military and entrepreneurship generally remained distinct, with the connections made more implicit than explicit. Relatively little research has accounted for how the military institutions interact with the wider entrepreneurship events and logics with which they are implicitly bound up. Subsequently, this book seeks to highlight the manner different military agents and agencies employ different strategies to navigate and exploit multiple, potentially contradictory entrepreneurial logics of the different spheres in which they operate to facilitate business enterprise.

The book's approach indicates that a fertile course of inquiry in the emerging area of research at the interface of military entrepreneurship study comprises the mundane, everyday macro/micro-activities and strategies of entrepreneurship amidst multiple, potentially contradictory logics. This approach holds promise to bridge two diverging fields in the different, yet increasingly intersecting spheres of the military and entrepreneurship. Consequently, this book may enable cross-fertilization between studying entrepreneurship as an everyday practice of recombining resources (Tillmar, 2006; Sarasvathy, 2007) enfolded in the military contexts in the entrepreneurship literature. Nevertheless, what will be seen in the book is that military entrepreneurship does not offer universal solutions but respond to issues in innovative and creative ways in response to perceived local needs.

TARGET AUDIENCE

This book targets researchers, advanced-level students, practitioners, managers, and policy-makers, and anyone interested in the fields of military institutions and entrepreneurship. Other stakeholders, who are interested in entrepreneurship in unorthodox contexts will also find this book very useful in their research.

OBJECTIVE OF THE BOOK

This book's key objective is to interrogate the theme of 'Military Entrepreneurship' through the organization of theoretically- and empirically-based studies that highlight the tensions permeating the military entrepreneurship research space. The significance of the book resides in its capacity to enlarge our knowledge on how various military agents and institutions are engaging in entrepreneurship for personal and institutional survival, or as an expression of their agency. Consequently, the book's main goal is to provide an expansive and nuanced understanding that will deepen the ontology of the subject of 'Military Entrepreneurship'. There are 15 chapters in the book with each one focusing on topical issues of relevance to the concept of military entrepreneurship.

ORGANIZATION OF THE BOOK

The book is arranged into 14 chapters. The chapters are not organized in any particular themed format as each is projected to stand alone, advancing ample perspective on a particular subject. A brief description of each chapter is as follows:

Chapter 1 argues that the notion of military entrepreneurship (at least at the micro-level) is a fallacy given that a veteran's military background and training, if anything, could be rather inhibiting than facilitating entrepreneurship.

Chapter 2 appraises the idea of military entrepreneurship at the macro level to uncover the paradoxes underpinning the concept of military entrepreneurship. Ultimately, the chapter unveils the notion of "extrepreneurship", which represents a crossbreed idea located between the concepts of entrepreneurship and intrapreneurship.

Chapter 3 focuses on Entrepreneurial Training (ET) in the Nigerian armed forces and its significance for the post-retirement era and discussed the opportunities and challenges for self-reliance. The chapter then contends that the retirement training available to the armed forces differs from one country to the other.

Chapter 4 discusses important entrepreneurship matters to be considered before a retired military person goes into entrepreneurship. Some of the germane issues include the awareness of the value of Information and Communication Technology (ICT) skills and alertness to innovation.

Chapter 5 reviews the evolution of Chinese disarmament, with a focus on military-civilian transfer and settlement of demobilized military staffs. The review gives a background for interrogating military entrepreneurship in the Chinese context.

Chapter 6 undertakes a literature mapping of 235 related articles and research literature published in the past decade (from 2010 to 2019) to appreciate the current state of veteran entrepreneurship in China.

Chapter 7 investigates the utility of the entrepreneurship training and intervention arrangement for the veterans. The chapter shows that veteran entrepreneurship does not differ significantly from civilian entrepreneurship and that veteran entrepreneurs confront the same challenges as their civilian counterparts.

Chapter 8 examines post-retirement career pathway of ex-Service personnel in the Nigerian Military via entrepreneurship activities. The chapter then argues that there are psychological issues that must be tackled in order to effectively transit into entrepreneurship. Its findings suggest that objectives and components of entrepreneurship education should be given to personnel early enough and throughout their military career.

Chapter 9 explores the practitioner and academic literature to identify why franchising is attractive to veterans as well as how the franchise sector encourages those with prior military experience to enlist. The chapter then offers thoughts about global research that is needed to help franchise systems be a gateway for veterans to pursue their dream of business ownership.

Chapter 10 explores military innovation in its historical context and flow, thus considering the contribution of the defense industry and military employees to innovation in the Turkish military.

Chapter 11 investigates military enterprise and entrepreneurship through the prism of the Nigerian Armed Forces Resettlement Centre, Lagos. The chapter indicates the existence of tension between the military culture and entrepreneurship culture at the Centre and offers suggestions for improvement.

Chapter 12 focuses on military entrepreneurship to explore the entrepreneurial activities of Nigerian Defence Academy Consult Ltd to reveal problems and prospects of military institutions in Nigeria as spaces for entrepreneurial activities. The chapter concludes that military institutions are setting up various ventures through the incorporation of companies and this has broad implications for military professionalism.

Chapter 13 discusses the emergence of Russian private military enterprise and its use as non-state actors in state-sponsored actions. The chapter also introduces a diplomatic strategy for regulating the application of private contractors and security companies in warfare.

Chapter 14 appraises innovation as one of the main factors in driving organizations' effectiveness, and sustainable competitiveness.

REFERENCES

Adrienne, J., Heinz, A. J., Freeman, M. A., Harpaz-Rotem, I., & Pietrzak, R. H. (2017). American military veterans are nearly twice as likely to be self-employed compared to non-veterans, and are majority owners in nine percent of all businesses nationwide. *Military Psychology*, *29*(6), 513–523. PMID:29290645

Allen, C. D., & Gerras, S. J. (2009). Developing Creative and Critical Thinkers. *Military Review*, 80.

Hope, J. B., Oh, B., & Mackin, P. C. (2011). *Factors Affecting Entrepreneurship among Veterans Small Business Research Summary*. U.S. Small Business Administration, Office of Advocacy.

Knox, M., & Murray, W. (2001). *The Dynamics of Military Revolution, 1300-2050*. Cambridge University Press. doi:10.1017/CBO9780511817335

Mares, D. R. (1998). Civil-military relations, democracy, and the regional neighborhood. In D. R. Mares (Ed.), *Civil-Military Relations*. Westview Press.

Sarasvathy, S. D. (2007). *Effectuation: Elements of entrepreneurial expertise*. Edward Elgar.

Storlie, C. (2010). *Combat to corporate: Applying military Spec Ops principles to business success*. Praeger.

Tillmar, M. (2006). Swedish tribalism and Tanzanian entrepreneurship: Preconditions for trust formation. *Entrepreneurship & Regional Development: An International Journal, 18*(2), 91–107. doi:10.1080/08985620500531956

Vego, M. (2013). On Military Creativity. *Joint Forces Quarterly*, (70), 83-90.

Acknowledgment

The editor would like to acknowledge the help of all the people involved in this project and, more specifically, to the authors and reviewers that took part in the review process. Without their support, this book would not have become a reality.

First, the editor would like to thank each one of the authors for their contributions. My sincere gratitude goes to the chapter's authors who contributed their time and expertise to this book.

Second, the editor wishes to acknowledge the valuable contributions of the reviewers regarding the improvement of quality, coherence, and content presentation of chapters. Most of the authors also served as referees; I highly appreciate their double task.

Third, my gratitude also goes to my family and staff of IGI Global Publishers for their unflinching supports over the years; thanks a lot.

Sanya Ojo
Nigerian Defence Academy, Nigeria

Introduction

BACKGROUND

The military establishments all over the world, like any other organization, apply the concept of entrepreneurship in their day-to-day activities. This is not unexpected since the entrepreneurship concept has attracted interest from many interdisciplinary fields including psychology, sociology, economics, cultural, political, and historical studies (Brock & Evans, 1998) and is applied to numerous paradigms and settings (Bruyat & Julien, 2004). For instance, in business and commerce (Kaufmann & Dant, 1998), sports (Hall, 2006), accounting (Greenwood & Suddaby, 2006), law (Lee et al., 2007), medicine (Loscalzo, 2007), banking (Black & Strahan, 2002), governments (Link & Link, 2009), parastatals (Goyal, 2011), charities (Morris et al., 2001), Non-Governmental Organisations (NGO) (Auplat, 2006), politics (Younkins, 2000), etc.

Despite the pervasiveness of entrepreneurship in many professions in the academic literature, that of military entrepreneurship is thin. Admittedly, a few studies exist on the integration of military veterans (retirees) into a civilian-based entrepreneurship ecosystem (e.g., Vigoda-Gado et al., 2010; Hope et al., 2011; Kerrick et al., 2014; Hasik, 2016; Adrienne et al., 2017) however, other components of military involvement in entrepreneurship have received little or no mention in the literature. Elements such as intrapreneurship (i.e., serving personnel entrepreneurial agency) in the military and entrepreneurial agency of spouses (especially female) of serving military personnel are barely visible in mainstream academic literature. As far as entrepreneurship research is concerned, the military establishment exhibits the "Iceberg Phenomenon" – visible and hidden identity.

The book, 'Global perspectives on military entrepreneurship and innovation', is decidedly eclectic, designed to cover a broad range of topics and concepts in military entrepreneurship in order to promote entrepreneurship research within the military ecosystem. The book volume builds on existing theoretical and empirical studies in the areas of entrepreneurship and military business and enterprise to interrogate the concepts of military entrepreneurship, veteran entrepreneurship, and retirees' entrepreneurship. The book is a collection of studies on military entrepreneurship, treating the subject with emphasis on metacognition. The chapters are conceptual, review, empirical, from interdisciplinary perspectives to provide better outcomes in entrepreneurship cross-cultural learning between practitioners, investors, researchers, and policy-makers.

Key Areas of Focus in Military Entrepreneurship

Five strands of military entrepreneurship have received some mention in the literature. The first is the retired military personnel engagement in entrepreneurship (e.g., Smaliukienė, 2013), and the second relates to the practice of entrepreneurship within the military establishment by serving personnel (i.e., intrapreneurship) (e.g., Hasik, 2016). The third strand is the entrepreneurial activism of spouses (mostly female) of serving military personnel (e.g., Griswold, 2017), and the fourth strand relates to military institutions' direct involvement in commercial or business enterprises (e.g., Mani, 2011; Siddiqa, 2007). The fifth strand is the warfare aspect that relates to military entrepreneurship. In this strand, authors treat war as a profit-making venture, and entrepreneurs organize their men and materials (i.e., soldiers, weapons, armaments, etc.) to fight wars to earn incomes (e.g., Parrott, 2012; Redlich, 1964). Three of these strands, which received specific attention in this book, are briefly discussed below.

First, several ex-military officers turn to entrepreneurship to earn income when they retire, for example, in the US, more than one in ten businesses are owned by ex-military officers (Meadows, 2019). Many of the retired military personnel (RMP) gained highly specific competencies and resources (Smaliukienė, 2013) that they apply in their entrepreneurial engagements. These competencies and resources include risk management, performance under pressure, directness, speed, assertiveness, team decision-making, methodical approaches to problems, and leadership qualities (Storlie, 2010; Rockefeller, 2019). Nonetheless, Hope et al. (2013) argue that higher rates of self-employment among veterans are due to individual characteristics, rather than training, education, or other qualities imparted by the military service. All the same, the literature is not clear on the outcomes of retired military personnel's entrepreneurship. While some authors (e.g., Moran, 2012; Meadows, 2019) argue that several retired military persons achieve success in business (i.e., in the US), others (e.g., Madichie & Ayasi, 2018) contend that several retired military personnel's business ventures failed (i.e., in Nigeria). The reasons for failure are not unconnected with a lack of coordinated government assistance and lack of effective institutional support. The factors of failure (at least in Nigeria) may not be the same in other climes and the factors adduced to the success of many veteran entrepreneurs in the US may not be applicable in several other territories.

Second, the military tends to have individuals who are entrepreneurial-minded and whose practices internally generate innovation. These innovators are intrapreneurs who looked out for opportunities and make decisions under uncertainty (Hasik, 2016). However, the military hierarchy is reported to be bureaucratically minded, dislike risk, and detest uncertainty such that innovation (a component of entrepreneurship) is curtailed in many instances (Seifert, 2007; Ricks, 2014). For instance, the US military sector is said to incentivize unproductive entrepreneurship (Coyne et al., 2015). Furthermore, it has also been argued that military organizations struggle with innovation (Knox & Murray, 2001; Pierce, 2004) due to a lack of feedback on performance.

Third, there are many instances of military-run business ventures around the world as the military establishments are actively involved in commercial and profitmaking ventures. Military-run enterprises can be demarcated into two broad groups. The first group includes the military-controlled industries, which could consist of a wide range of businesses not all of which may be producing to satisfy military and security needs. The second group involves the military or defense industries, which develop and produce goods and services used largely by the military (Siddiqa, 2007). By and large, a military system has many of the characteristics of a business, and to be successful, the military formations must exhibit "world-class" business practices (Leipold, 2014).

Consequently, contributors to this volume interrogate these three areas of study comprising veteran entrepreneurship or military entrepreneurship, military-run enterprises, and the military-industrial complex (MIC). These areas of study cover different locational contexts for a clearer representation and understanding of military entrepreneurship in many of its forms.

It is worthy to note that different terminologies are used in this volume to describe retired military personnel. Some terms used include veteran, ex-Service personnel, ex-Military personnel, legionnaire, etc. The terms are not the same even though they are used interchangeably in many publications (including this volume). It seems the case those terms are employed interchangeably just to stay as much as possible close to their original use in the literature they are extracted from.

General Information on the Book

This book showcases informed treatises on the contemporary realities of military entrepreneurship and offers insightful perspectives on intrapreneurship within the military establishments in several locations. It also presents valuable assessments on what might become of the military institutions and military enterprises if apposite transformational strategies were to be embraced, sustained and institutionalized. The book delivers on the vision of providing a volume of compelling academic, managerial and policy significance, and an authoritative reference source that reflects and resonates with the current global socio-political and economic dynamics.

This book is structured into fifteen chapters to illuminate military entrepreneurship, military enterprise, and military institutions. The chapters also cover strategies, ideas and initiatives for innovation of military businesses and the underpinning institutions, environments and economies. Moreover, many articles in this volume highlight the interaction between the military and the social context in which the military institutions are embedded. Military entrepreneurs often play important roles in the economic development of their nations, according to Torres-Sánchez et al. (2017: 1): "Military investment provided an inexhaustible source of business opportunities, comparable only to consumer-driven trade expansion". Thus, an internationally acclaimed selection of authors was selected to push forward the discussion on the military entrepreneurship and enterprise in various parts of the world (i.e., Nigeria, China, Russia, Turkey, USA, Portugal, etc.). Topics covered include discussion on the nature and characteristics of military entrepreneurship, entrepreneurship training for military personnel, and entrepreneurship as a career option for retired military personnel. Other subjects of discussion include types of enterprise veteran engaged in (e.g., franchise), the historical context of military innovation, the business side of war (i.e., private military contractors), and psychological issues around military entrepreneurship. In addition, there is a contestation of entrepreneurship as a successful career-pathway for retired military personnel and a critical evaluation of the notion of military entrepreneurship that introduced the concept of 'extrepreneurship'.

Essentially, the chapters in this book have been carefully selected with an eye towards expanding the field of military entrepreneurship. The book aims to enhance current research on the nature, process, and outcomes of military entrepreneurship and military entrepreneurs' economic activities in different contexts, different backgrounds, and various ontological directions. The significance resides in its capacity to enlarge our knowledge of entrepreneurship in different military contexts.

REFERENCES

Adrienne, J., Heinz, A. J., Freeman, M. A., Harpaz-Rotem, I., & Pietrzak, R. H. (2017). American military veterans are nearly twice as likely to be self-employed compared to non-veterans, and are majority owners in nine percent of all businesses nationwide. *Military Psychology*, *29*(6), 513–523. PMID:29290645

Auplat, C. (2006). Do NGOs influence entrepreneurship? Insights from the developments of biotechnologies and nanotechnologies. *Society and Business Review*, *1*(3), 266–279. doi:10.1108/17465680610706337

Black, S. E., & Strahan, P. E. (2002). Entrepreneurship and Bank Credit Availability. *The Journal of Finance*, *57*(6), 2807–2833. doi:10.1111/1540-6261.00513

Brock, W. A., & Evans, D. S. (1989). Small Business Economics. *Small Business Economics*, *1*(1), 7–20. doi:10.1007/BF00389913

Bruyat, C., & Julien, P. A. (2001). Defining the field of Research in Entrepreneurship. *Journal of Business Venturing*, *16*(2), 165–180. doi:10.1016/S0883-9026(99)00043-9

Coyne, C. J., Michaluk, C., & Reese, R. (2015). *Unproductive Entrepreneurship in U.S. Military Contracting*. GMU Working Paper in Economics No. 15-50. Available at: doi:10.2139srn.2667905

Goyal, Y. (2011). Inefficient Parastatal Agencies and the Growing Modern Food Market in India: The need for Private Participation. *Asian Journal of Public Affairs*, *3*(2), 48–66.

Goyal, Y. (2011). Inefficient Parastatal Agencies and the Growing Modern Food Market in India: The need for Private Participation. *Asian Journal of Public Affairs*, *3*(2), 48–66.

Greenwood, R., & Suddaby, R. (2006). Institutional Entrepreneurship in Mature Fields: The big five accounting firms. *Academy of Management Journal*, *49*(1), 27–48. doi:10.5465/amj.2006.20785498

Griswold, J. (2017). *Mission Entrepreneur: Applying Lessons from Military Life to Create Success in Business Startups*. Mango Publishing Group.

Hall, M. C. (2006). Urban entrepreneurship, corporate interests and sports mega-events: The thin policies of competitiveness within the hard outcomes of neoliberalism. *The Sociological Review*, *54*(2_suppl), 59–70. doi:10.1111/j.1467-954X.2006.00653.x

Hasik, J. (2016). Defense Entrepreneurship: How to Build Institutions for Innovation Inside the Military. *Joint Force Quarterly*. Available at: https://ndupress.ndu.edu/JFQ/JointForce-Quarterly-81/Article/702056/defense-entrepreneurship-how-to-buildinstitutions-for-innovation-inside-the-mi/

Hope, J. B., Oh, B., & Mackin, P. C. (2011). *Factors affecting entrepreneurship among veterans*. SAG Corporation. Available at: https://www.sba.gov/sites/default/files/files/rs384tot.pdf

Kaufmann, P. J., & Dant, R. P. (1998). Franchising and the Domain of Entrepreneurship Research. *Journal of Business Venturing*, *14*(1), 5–16. doi:10.1016/S0883-9026(97)00095-5

Kerrick, S. A., Cumberland, D., Church-Nally, M., & Kemelgor, B. (2014). Military veterans marching towards entrepreneurship: An exploratory mixed methods study. *International Journal of Management Education, 12*(3), 469–478. doi:10.1016/j.ijme.2014.05.006

Knox, M., & Murray, W. (2001). *The Dynamics of Military Revolution, 1300-2050*. Cambridge University Press. doi:10.1017/CBO9780511817335

Lee, S., Peng, M., & Barney, J. (2007). Bankruptcy Law and Entrepreneurship Development: A Real Options Perspective. *Academy of Management Review*, *32*(1), 257–272. doi:10.5465/amr.2007.23464070

Leipold, J. D. (2014). *Is the Army a business?* Available at: https://www.army.mil/article/126882/is_the_army_a_business

Link, A. N., & Link, J. R. (2009). *Government as entrepreneur*. Oxford University Press. doi:10.1093/acprof:oso/9780195369458.001.0001

Loscalzo, J. (2007). Entrepreneurship in the Medical Academy: Possibilities and Challenges in Commercialization of Research Discoveries, Circulation. *Journal of the American Heart Association, 115*, 1504–1507. PMID:17389277

Madichie, N. O., & Ayasi, K. (2018). Entrepreneurial Opportunities and Challenges for Retired Senior Military Officers in Nigeria. In African Entrepreneurship. Palgrave Studies of Entrepreneurship in Africa. Palgrave Macmillan. doi:10.1007/978-3-319-73700-3_7

Mani, K. (2011). Military Entrepreneurship: Patterns in Latin America. *Latin American Politics and Society*, *53*(3), 25–55. doi:10.1111/j.1548-2456.2011.00124.x

Meadows, T. (2019). *Top Five Reasons Veterans Succeed as Entrepreneurs*. Available at: https://www.military.com/veteran-jobs/career-advice/military-transition/top-fivereasons-veterans-succeed-as-entrepreneurs.html

Moran, G. (2012). How military veterans are finding success in small business? *Entrepreneur*. Available at: https://www.entrepreneur.com/article/222649

Morris, M. H., Berthon, P. R., Pitt, L. F., Murgolo-poore, M. E., & Ramshaw, W. F. (2001). An Entrepreneurial Perspective on the Marketing of Charities. *Journal of Nonprofit & Public Sector Marketing*, *9*(3), 75–87. doi:10.1300/J054v09n03_05

Parrott, D. (2012). *The Business of War. Military Enterprise and Military Revolution in Early Modern Europe*. Cambridge University Press. doi:10.1017/CBO9781139023337

Pierce, T. C. (2004). *Warfighting and Disruptive Technologies: Disguising Innovation*. Taylor & Francis Ltd. doi:10.4324/9780203341551

Redlich, F. (1964). *The German Military Enterpriser and His Work Force: A Study in European Economic and Social History* (Vol. I). Franz Steiner Verlag GMBH.

Ricks, T. E. (2014). *A Pilot Speaks: The USAF Is Harder on Internal Ideas Than It Is on Evil Insurgents*. Available at: https://foreignpolicy.com/2014/12/04/a-pilot-speaks-theusaf-is-harder-on-internal-ideas-than-it-is-on-evil-insurgents/

Rockefeller, M. L. (2019). *Why the Military is the Best Entrepreneurship Training Program in America*. Available at: https://www.forbes.com/sites/marklrockefeller/2016/08/03/why-the-military-is-thebest-entrepreneurship-training-program-in-america/

Seifert, R.J. (2007). Iraq and the AC-130: Gunships Unleashed, *Joint Force Quarterly*, *45*, 78–83.

Siddiqa, A. (2007). *Military Inc.: Inside Pakistan's Military Economy*. Pluto Press.

Smaliukienė, R. (2014). Entrepreneurship Opportunities after Military Career: Practice in Central and Eastern versus Western Europe. *Entrepreneurial Business and Economics Review*, *1*(4), 97–108. doi:10.15678/EBER.2013.010408

Storlie, C. (2010). *Combat to Corporate: Applying Military Spec Ops Principles to Business Success*. Praeger.

Strzalkowski, B. (2015). *What Do Military Spouses REALLY Want?* Available at: https://www.militaryspouse.com/career/education/what-do-military-spouses-reallywant/

Torres-Sánchez, R., Brandon, P., & Hart, M. (2017). War and economy. Rediscovering the eighteenth-century military entrepreneur. *Business History*. Advance online publication. doi:10.1080/00076791.2017.1379507

Vigoda-Gadot, E., Baruch, Y., & Grimland, S. (2010). Career transitions: An empirical examination of second career of military retirees. *Public Personnel Management*, *39*(4), 379–404. doi:10.1177/009102601003900405

Younkins, E. (2000). Entrepreneurship Properly Understood. *Le Quebecois Libre*, (64).

Chapter 1
The Fallacy of the Idea of Military Entrepreneurship

Anthony Chukwu
Seneca College, Canada

ABSTRACT

In this chapter, the author argues that the mainstream Occam's razor narrative of military entrepreneurship as a successful income earning second career for veterans only rings true in intellectual circles. This is based on a presupposed reality that veterans lack challenges building a second career. He uses existing literature to show that contrary to the mainstream narrative, military entrepreneurship is not a smooth-sailing path to a veteran's second career. Entrepreneurs face the same challenges irrespective of whether they are veterans or civilians. Military training might equip someone with discipline, focus, tenacity, and calculated risk avowal approach or risk taking that a civilian may not have, yet it may not ensure entrepreneurial success. A veteran's military background and training, if anything, may be rather inhibiting than facilitating of entrepreneurship. It's a fallacy to stipulate otherwise.

INTRODUCTION

The discourse surrounding the possible career options of a soldier post-military is steeped in the discourse of post-modernity. Among other things, post-modernity brings new insights, concepts and contexts and operates discursively and subjectively to reorient the discussion around new insights, concepts and contexts. The term military entrepreneurship refers to the career paths of a retired soldier, and is an example of post-modern discourse to the extent that it disrupts the authorized understanding and entrenched meaning of entrepreneurship, i.e., the economic

DOI: 10.4018/978-1-7998-6655-8.ch001

Copyright © 2021, IGI Global. Copying or distributing in print or electronic forms without written permission of IGI Global is prohibited.

ventures of a civilian. This chapter argues that the idea of military entrepreneurship is a fallacy and questions the mainstream narrative that sees it as a path to a veteran's successful second career. Entrepreneurs are known to face the same challenges irrespective of whether they are veterans or civilians. And, as the chapter argues, in an attempt to present a counter-narrative of military entrepreneurship, a veteran's military background and training might not necessarily facilitate entrepreneurship.

Retirement exists in the military just as it does with other professions. But, because, military personnel retire on average 15-20 years earlier than their civilian counterparts (Smaliukiene, 2013), it does not carry the same meaning as its civilian counterpart. In the military, retirement does not mean the end of work, but instead means searching for another job. There are a number of reasons for retiring early from the military that include the hazards of going off to war and dying, injury, post traumatic stress disorder and fear of the unknown that lies ahead. Propelled by any or all of these reasons, a soldier may leave the service while still in the prime of life. The early retirement of a soldier and the possibility for a second career, may have led economists and Management scholars alike to see military entrepreneurship as a logical second career for veterans.

What is the basis for military entrepreneurship specifically? No existing or known study presents evidence that there is significant difference between entrepreneurial engagement by a civilian and that by a veteran. Moreover, veteran and civilian entrepreneurs face similar challenges. However, challenges that require spontaneous and flexible responses would be better handled by civilians than veterans as their military training means they are encumbered by rule following and adherence to a command structure that constrains spontaneity and flexibility. Because civilians are not used to obeying commands in a regimented setting like the military, they can more easily respond spontaneously and flexibly to situations. Veterans might easily shed their uniforms on retirement, but this does not mean that they can do the same with their regimented lifestyle, which has become second nature to them. Hence the saying: once a soldier, always one. In order words, veterans are largely set in their ways and like leopards lack the ability to change their spots. As such, veterans face challenges building a second career (e.g., Vigoda-Gadot et al., 2010). The challenges may be difficult, but they are not insurmountable.

It is this difficulty that is at the root of this chapter——a sceptical examination of the mainstream Occam's razor narrative of military entrepreneurship as a successful path to second career. This chapter is divided into five sections. Section one looks at entrepreneurship; section two views military entrepreneurship as a discourse with post-modern roots; section three describes the process of turning civilians into soldiers and soldiers back into civilians; section four shows the fallacious problem with the mainstream narrative of military entrepreneurship; and section five offers concluding remarks.

UNDERSTANDING ENTREPRENEURSHIP

Defining entrepreneurship and how the term should or ought to be understood has attracted scholarly inquiry. Ojo & Nwankwo (2017) note that scholarly interrogation of the concept differs according to discipline. For Knight (1961) entrepreneurship is a speculative endeavor. Schumpeter (1934) sees it as an innovative technical ability. Cole (1959) has developed the theory of enterprise creation. Kirzner (1973) posits that it is alertness to opportunity. Another view of entrepreneurship deems it as a means of enhancing growth and value creation (Sharma & Chrisman, 1999). Concepts often defy a single definition because there are so many diverse views. But, in the case of entrepreneurship, it has been approached from so many different perspectives, that there is no common understanding of just what it is. Thus, prompted by the immensely elastic and broad nature of the term, Ojo (2013) views entrepreneurship as nebulous, a term that can be ascribed to almost anything and everything. As an "anything goes"[1] term, entrepreneurship ends up having contradictory meanings. Consequently, it defies the Venn diagram which shows how things can be simultaneously the same and different. Instead, it only shows a diagram of how things are same without showing how different they are or seem. Dana (2006) observes that there is no consensus on the definition of entrepreneurship. Many scholars have offered different definitions of entrepreneurship that amount to stretching it over a wide range of theories and descriptions (Brock & Evans, 1989). Such definitions have merely served to portray it as a slogan for "anything goes." Accordingly, it has been a favorite concept copiously explored in interdisciplinary fields like military (Smaliukiene, 2013), psychology, sociology, economics, and cultural, political and historical studies (Brock & Evans, 1989). It has also been applied to numerous paradigms and settings (Bruyat & Julien, 2001). The term has also been taken up by nations seeking to improve their economic growth and play up their competitiveness on the global stage (Schaper & Volery, 2004; Venkatachalam & Waqif, 2005). Additionally, it has been construed as one of the best approaches to economic development. By extension, it has been used to explain the economic development of veterans forging a new career path. This is known as military entrepreneurship and the post-modern root of it is the focus of the next section.

The Post-Modern Roots of Military Entrepreneurship

In this section, I show that military entrepreneurship is a discourse with roots in post-modernism and has intellectual traction and utility, but lacks a practical grounding in reality. This will lay the groundwork for the subsequent section where I present a counter-narrative of the mainstream view of military entrepreneurship as a path to a veteran's second career and/or economic development.

The idea of military entrepreneurship reflects post-modernism's capacity to disrupt and dislodge any form of knowledge or ideology or concept that has gained authority, and has become entrenched; without any coherence, the concept fragments and leads to contingent and shifting perspectives. Unlike the modernist, the post-modernist lays no claim to truth-making. The humble quest of the post-modernist is to pry open spaces of possibility for troubling and challenging meanings that have gained currency. The emergence of the term military entrepreneurship is an effect of the post-modern tendency to open up the meaning of terms. In other words, the bid to expand the meaning of entrepreneurship allows for the emergence of military entrepreneurship as a way to describe the retired soldier's second career.

From its very first use in 1870 by J. W. Chapman, as a skeptical expression for departing from the status quo style of painting——"a Postmodern style of painting" (in Higgins 1978, 7)——, post-modernism has evolved over the years to now become an intellectual stance with an aversion to grand narratives, epistemic certainty and fixed meaning. Postmodern thinkers are also known to view claims to knowledge and value systems as idiosyncratic. This distinctive approach of post-modern discourse, which posits cultural contingencies or socially-conditioned realities unburdened by the difficulty of establishing universal criteria of rationality applicable in every culture, aided its ascendancy over modernism. The extension of this to entrepreneurship is the roots of military entrepreneurship. In the rest of this section, I will show the intellectual traction and utility of the discourse of military entrepreneurship.

Even though military entrepreneurship as an academic field of study is still in its infancy, the term has gained global currency in describing the potential economic value of military retirees. At the same time, there are few studies indicating successful transitions to full-fledged civilian entrepreneurship (e.g. Vigoda-Gado et al., 2010; Hope et al., 2011; Kerrick et al., 2014; Adrienne et al., 2017). Similarly, there is lack of academic literature on other components of military entrepreneurship such as intrapreneurship (i.e. when serving personnel undertake entrepreneurial activities) and entrepreneurial agency of spouses (especially wives) of serving military personnel.

The connection between the military and entrepreneurship can be seen in the 2018 Gallup Confidence Study showing that the military and small businesses are the two most trusted institutions in the US (SmallBusiness.com, 2020). Boldon et al. (2016) argue that this connection stems from a long and distinctive relationship between military and small business ownership. A veteran is actually more likely to own their own business than a non-veteran thereby likely to earn more than a non-veteran entrepreneur. Entrepreneurship is seen as a viable option because it will enable veterans, in theory, to use their military skills like resilience, ambition and leadership (Ross, 2015). Veterans are not only known to have engaged in different enterprises and business ventures ranging from farming, manufacturing, oil and gas, to baking, they have equally thrived based on the discipline gained during their time in military service (Smaliukiene, 2013). Veterans all over the world are involved in different kinds of businesses that directly or indirectly create jobs and contribute to national development (Chandra, 2014). In India, for example, about 75,000 people——the majority of whom are between the ages of 35 and 45——retire yearly from the military service, and take up entrepreneurship as a second career option (Kedia, 2019). Out of over 14,000 people that retire from the military in the UK every year, the majority take up employment in other sectors, while some become small business owners (Cook, 2019). The 2019 Federation of Small Businesses' Report captures this, showing that there are approximately 340,000 small businesses owned by veterans, which represent 6% of all small businesses in Britain (Cook, 2019).

Self-employment is increasingly a preferred post-retirement choice for retirees because of the opportunities and flexibility that are not offered in paid employment (Cahill et al., 2013). These advantages of self-employment make it an attractive, fall-back option for veterans seeking to transition back to civilian life and work (Blass & Ketchen, 2014). Kerrick et al. (2014) claim that as many as 45% of veterans engage in self-employment. Singh & DeNoble (2003) note the following factors that push veterans into post-retirement self-employment: financial hardship, labor market constrictions and discrimination.

Veteran entrepreneurs come from different backgrounds and have garnered distinctive experiences, yet they encounter challenges at every step of their journey to business ownership. Those who are successful do so by making quick, good and nimble decisions in chaotic environments, showing confidence, exercising independence, and high self-efficacy and achievement (Boldon et al. 2016). Notwithstanding, there are challenges to veteran entrepreneurship around financial capital, people and social capital, and decision making (Boldon et al., 2016). As Sankaran and Battisto (2018) contend, veteran entrepreneurs face more difficulty in accessing capital than non-veteran business owners as they usually apply for smaller loans of $100,000 or less, which big banks are less likely to grant. Also, most lack a strong credit history because of their military lifestyle, making it difficult to access bank loans.

Veterans face challenges in business. Military entrepreneurship is anything but a successful story of a veteran's second career. This is partly because they have a hard time overcoming their military lifestyle——daily routine, scheduled program, regimented events—and adjusting to life where no one is controlling their schedules. The only place where military entrepreneurship has traction and is deemed a success is among scholars who explore it for intellectual purposes.

To understand why military entrepreneurship is not as hopeful as some scholars make it out to be, I will turn to the making of a soldier.

From Civilian to Soldier and Back Again

This section looks at how civilians are made into soldiers and, when they retire, how they transition back to civilian life. Looking at the three stages of the life of a soldier enables us to understand why military entrepreneurship, in and of itself, may not be the second-career success it is claimed to be.

Soldiers are civilians at the beginning of their life, military professionals in the middle years, and civilians once again later in life. A soldier is born a civilian, becomes a professional soldier, and then eventually retires and transitions into a full-fledged civilian. Put differently, a soldier is one who stands on a highland in between two civilian lowlands. The initial lowland is the pre-soldier civilian life; the highland is the military career period, while the latter lowland is the post-soldier civilian life. A soldier has three stages of life: civilian (early life), soldier (middle stage), and civilian (later life). For Schlossberg et al. (1995: 27) these three stages are described as "moving in, moving through, and moving out phases." The peculiar aspect of these transitions is that the skill set of one stage is not wholly transferred to the next stage either because they are not needed or not useful (or both). At the core of transitioning from a civilian to a soldier is changing the civilian orientation. It is viewed as incompatible with what is needed to be a soldier and serve in the military. In the same manner, leaving the military needs a de-culturalization process to shed military norms and lifestyle that are at variance with civilian norms (Hale, 2017).

Why are soldiers needed at all? Every nation needs the military to defend sovereignty and territorial integrity of their nation or country——the power ceded to them by the Treaty of Westphalia (1648)——against foreign aggressors. The implication is that soldiers are needed to, when necessary; fight wars to defend their country and homeland. The peace that results from their gallantry gives their fellow citizens the freedom to produce wealth and prosperity and pursue happiness.

Given that soldiering is about fighting war, and fighting war for Sun Tzu (Giles 1910) is a matter of life and death, one gets an idea of what is entailed in becoming a soldier: turning civilians into soldiers by equipping them with military skills that prepare them for military service. More specifically, civilians are trained to endure suffering of all kinds and under any circumstance, to believe in a higher cause than self, to learn to be deferential, i.e. taking orders and giving them if and when need be, including the order to kill if given a lawful command to do so. Finally, in training, civilians are trained physically so they are ready and able to effectively carry out the above tasks.

When these points have been imparted into a civilian, he or she becomes a soldier. From here on in, they are active, professional soldiers until retirement or disengagement. And from this inception of active duty, soldiers are bound to conform to the codes of military conduct every time, whether on or off base, until the moment they leave the service (Arkin, 1978). Whether a civilian goes through enlistment or military school as a cadet, the goal is the same: making a civilian a soldier. The only difference is the duration of training. It takes a longer time to train cadets to become commissioned officers than it does training enlisted civilians to become soldiers, i.e. non-commissioned officers who serve at the lower rung of the military hierarchical structure.

Part of the training of soldiers includes schooling on other aspects, like inculcating an *esprit de corps*——i.e. culture of solidarity, instilling discipline and building confidence, imbuing a fighting spirit, creating trust in leadership, and transmitting institutional know-how. Everything in military service is regimented and controlled under a command structure. In other words, every professional circumstance routinely requires order that is not be defied except at the risk of court marshal or discharge (or both). The hallmark of a military career is about rule-following—taking and giving orders. Soldiers take orders to fight. They require an order to cease fire and stop fighting. And when they are not fighting, they take orders to train for the next fight (war). At the risk of hyperbole, it can be said that a good soldier is one who unquestioningly and uncritically marches happily to every instruction.

Leaving a military career and lifestyle steeped in the culture of solidarity, taking and giving orders, requires re-orientation——i.e. a de-culturalization away from military norms and lifestyle. It is a way to wean veterans away from the feeling of always being in the military, whether fighting or not. They require a civilian worldview to replace the lasting impact of military experience. Part of the reason for the de-culturalization of the military experience is to make sure that retirement dovetails with a second career for veterans, if possible. To embark on a second career, a veteran needs to become calmer and less deferential, conform to civilian life, and set and achieve goals. This is what de-culturalizing seeks to achieve. Military entrepreneurship has been deemed a good second career for veterans. It is exactly the type of role they need to try to fill for their organizational ability and leadership to show forth. But can a veteran ever get over their military experience to become a successful military entrepreneur? This brings me to the next section which looks at why the mainstream narrative of military entrepreneurship does not pan out as the critics describe it.

The Problem With Idea of Military Entrepreneurship

The post-modernist roots of military entrepreneurship as a means to help veterans close the "civil-military cultural gap" (Collins 1998, 216) has generated a mainstream narrative that this is a successful second career option for veterans. The idea is that, insofar as veterans can learn to shed their more extreme military characteristics, then military entrepreneurship is an assured path to a successful second career.

However, it is by no means a guaranteed success. This section looks at the fallacy of the military entrepreneurship idea. The thrust of this section is to present a counter-narrative of military entrepreneurship. Essentially, therefore, it is a critique of military entrepreneurship.

Any pursuit in life has practical value if it has clear metrics for measuring the effectivity and efficiency of its overall goal. If not, such a subject can share in the witty caricature of philosophy presented by Aristophanes, a contemporary of Socrates, famous for his satirical playwright. Having listened to Socrates many a times and yet unsure of what philosophy is, he wrote a play entitled *The Clouds*, and in it he depicted Socrates delivering his lofty philosophical lectures in a basket suspended from the clouds. The unmistakable rub of this joke, which has stuck with philosophers, is that that they do not have their feet on the ground in any way, shape or form. In other words, philosophy is a highfalutin erudite hobby with no subject matter of its own and therefore no practical value. Another implication of this caricature is that an idea or subject that falls short of the claim it makes for itself is a fallacy. Military entrepreneurship has not lived up to the narrative projecting it as a successful path to a veteran's second career, because it shares kinship with this caricature of philosophy.

Advancing the idea of military entrepreneurship hinges on minimizing or outrightly ignoring, the psychological problems that arise with the retirement of a soldier. Without this, it would be difficult to present a rosy picture of it (Osborne, 2012). No one leaves the military and jumps right into another career, including military entrepreneurship. Retiring or leaving the military comes with a host of anxieties——a mixture of known and unknown or anticipated or unanticipated outcomes. For retiring military personnel and their families, there are no guarantees when it comes to employment opportunities, handling finances, managing health care, pursuing education, family reintegration, and negotiating as well integrating into a new civilian community (Robertson & Brott, 2017; Vogt et al, 2018). The civilian life after military service is unclear for the retiree and so triggers unexpected feelings and problems, namely, loss of military identity, deprivation of military solidarity, discombobulation about the little-known civilian world, and adapting to family life (Pranger et al., 2009). The experience of grief and stress due to a loss of the military self and the corresponding sense of belonging (Mobbs & Bonanno, 2018) persists. This, as George's (1993) role theory explains, entails that a person's profession is at the core of their identity. And so any loss of professional identity and the familiar environment following retirement; not only reduces life satisfaction but increases the likelihood of depression. This is especially so when retirees perceive themselves as unproductive and non-contributing members of society (Ehsan, 2010). Some studies (e.g. Bergman et al., 2014; Interian et al., 2014) note that the difficulty and stress of retirement are the basis of mental and physical health problems that veterans face.

It is worse with female veterans according to Baechtold (2012). The treatment of females as inferior while in service becomes a complicating pre-existing factor for mental and physical struggles associated with veteran trauma.

Given that the transition experience is comparable to a "reverse culture shock" (Westwood, 1999), it is unclear how a veteran, even with military retirement training programs on entrepreneurship, can be in the right frame of mind to acquire the skill of entrepreneurship. And even if they were, do they have the right frame of mind to be successful? The problem is not the lack of a transition program, as several formal military retirement programs exist to help with planning and the general logistics of transitions (Wolpert, 2000). The problem lies with getting over the difficulties of leaving active service and entering civilian life, before one embarks on a second career in military entrepreneurship. And what research has shown in this regard is that veterans are emotionally unprepared to manage the transition to civilian employment (Baruch & Quick, 2009). In view of this, some researchers (Angrist, 1998; Smith-Osborne, 2013) argue that veterans may not be able to reach the end of a desired entrepreneurial career life path, the way civilians do. In general, people underestimate the difficulties involved in transitioning from a civilian to a soldier and then back again to a civilian life after years of military services (Higate, 2001). In Nigeria, for instance, a good number of veterans take to entrepreneurship as a second career post retirement, but, the rate of failure is high (Madichie and Ayasi (2018).

There are other reasons why many veterans fail in business even though they have received the type of training and skills needed to be successful. For Hope et al. (2011), there is a general inverse relationship between length of service and the chance of self-employment after retirement. Also, many American veterans' families live pay check to pay check thereby making it impossible for them to pursue any kind of entrepreneurial dreams (Nicholson 2019).

In Nigeria, ex-service men/women fail in entrepreneurship because there is no coordinated government support, effective institutional support is inoperative, and the agencies meant to help and promote military entrepreneurship are limited (Madichie & Ayasi, 2018). For Abubakar (2016), the problem is rooted in the historical inept career management of the Nigerian Armed Forces. Added to this, is the dual factor of lack of time due to preoccupation with military work and the lack of any kind of support system that officers can utilize to train themselves while in service.

Also, whilst military training may help veteran entrepreneurs in their business operations, it could also be counterproductive and may constitute a serious hindrance to veteran entrepreneurship, which demands flexibility and responsiveness in a volatile and market-driven business environment.

In Nigeria, veterans take advantage of the various initiatives that the Nigerian government has put in place to stimulate and support Small and Medium-scale Enterprises (SMEs)——which constitute about 80% of Small and Medium Enterprises

Development Agency - SMEDAN (SMEDAN, 2013). Other agencies created by governments to buoy up small- and medium-sized enterprises are the National Directorate of Employment (NDE), Peoples Bank of Nigeria (PBN), Microfinance Banks, National Economic Reconstruction Fund (NERFUND), Bank of Commerce, the Industry and Bank of Agriculture, among others (Kayode & Ilesanmi, 2014). But businesses encounter enormous challenges that leave them struggling to survive and when they are unsuccessful, they tend to fold up after only a short time (Kayode & Ilesanmi, 2014). Underscoring the extent of this, Adebisi and Gbegi (2013), say 80% of SMEs are unsuccessful and fail within the first five years of being set up.

Among the reasons for the failure of many SMEs are lack of access to finance (Ozioma-Elendinmuo, 2015; Gbandi & Amissah, 2014; Akinola & Iordoo, 2013), inadequate infrastructure, crime, regulations and corruption (Ekpo & Bassey, 2016; Bah & Fang, 2015; Alarape, 2014), incompetency, mismanagement, inadequate support mechanism and the general poor socio-economic situations (e.g. poverty) in Nigeria (Opara, 2011).

In view of all of these problems with military entrepreneurship, it is unclear why it is depicted as a successful second career path for veterans. This is not borne out by facts. Just as entrepreneurship does not guarantee automatic success for veterans, it is also not a warranty for failure. While some veterans can do it successfully, others cannot. Those who cannot should take other jobs or vocations they can thrive in. The main narrative of military entrepreneurship as a successful second career path for veterans is a fallacy championed by scholars whose work is a strain of reality. The military and entrepreneurship are worlds apart. There is nothing in the former that guarantees success in the latter. Success or failure is mitigated or provoked by different factors.

CONCLUSION

This chapter has examined entrepreneurship, considered military entrepreneurship as a post-modern discourse, described the process of turning civilians into soldiers and back to civilians again, and discussed the problem with the idea of military entrepreneurship. The chapter has argued that there is a wide gulf between military life and enterprising life that cannot be bridged in a non-fallacious way.

The chapter is not a denial of any connection between the military and entrepreneurship. Although a veteran's skill-set could be useful in the marketplace, it does not solely guarantee success nor should it. Rather than bring veteran entrepreneurs success, military skills will encumber them if they are unprepared and ill-equipped for entrepreneurship. The chapter plays down the optimistic narrative of military entrepreneurship as a business path for veterans. In its understanding of entrepreneurship, the chapter has shown that entrepreneurship is the same for veteran entrepreneurs and civilian entrepreneurs. Both operate in the same marketplace and face similar sets of institutional and infrastructural deficiencies. Military skills alone cannot lead to success. While section two showed that while military entrepreneurship has post-modernist roots with academic resonance and traction, section three demonstrated that the process of being and becoming a soldier does not prepare a veteran for a successful business life after service. Section four discussed the factors that attenuate the mainstream narrative of military entrepreneurship as a path to second career success. In sum, the Occam's razor position of military entrepreneurship as a kind of be all end all retirement success for veterans is fallacious. It does not check out.

REFERENCES

AbubakarU. (2016). Career management of officers in the Nigerian Army (1970-2014). https://ssrn.com/abstract=2722249 orhttp://dx.doi.org/10.2139/ssrn.2722249 doi:10.2139srn.2722249

Adebisi, J. F. & Gbegi, D. O. (2013). Effects of multiple taxations on the performance of small and medium scale business enterprises (A study of west Africa Ceramics Ajeokuta, Kogi State). *Mediterranean Journal of Social Sciences*, *4*(6), 324-334. doi:.2013.v4n6p323 doi:10.5901/mjss

Adrienne, J., Heinz, A. J., Freeman, M. A., Harpaz-Rotem, I., & Pietrzak, R. H. (2017). American military veterans are nearly twice as likely to be self-employed compared to non-veterans, and are majority owners in nine percent of all businesses nationwide. *Military Psychology*, *29*(6), 513–523. PMID:29290645

Akinola, A. O., & Iordoo, D. A. (2013). The effect of Nigerian capital market on the micro, small and medium scale enterprises (MSMEs) in Nigeria. *Journal of Finance and Accounting*, *4*(7), 1–14.

Alarape, A. A. (2014). Entrepreneurial orientation and the growth performance of small and medium enterprises in Southwestern Nigeria. *Journal of Small Business and Entrepreneurship*, *26*(6), 553–577. doi:10.1080/08276331.2014.892308

Angrist, J. D. (1998). Estimating the labor market impact of voluntary military service using social security data on military applicants. *Econometrica*, *66*(2), 249–288. doi:10.2307/2998558

Arkin, W., & Dobrofsky, L. R. (1978). Military socialization and masculinity. *The Journal of Social Issues*, *34*(1), 151–168. doi:10.1111/j.1540-4560.1978.tb02546.x

Baechtold, M. (2011). Women warriors: Supporting female student veterans. *ASHE Higher Education Report*, *37*(3), 69–80. doi:10.1002/aehe.3703

Bah, E., & Fang, L. (2015). Impact of the business environment on output and productivity in Africa. *Journal of Development Economics*, *114*(C), 159–171. doi:10.1016/j.jdeveco.2015.01.001

Baruch, Y., & Quick, J. C. (2009). Setting sail in a new direction: Career transitions of US Navy admirals to the civilian sector. *Personnel Review*, *38*(3), 270–285. doi:10.1108/00483480910943331

Bergman, B., Burdett, H., & Greenberg, N. (2014). Service life and beyond—Institution or culture? *RUSI Journal*, *159*(5), 60–68. doi:10.1080/03071847.2014.969946

Blass, F. R., & Ketchen, D. J. Jr. (2014). So, you want to be an entrepreneur? Lessons from the entrepreneurship bootcamp for veterans with disabilities. *Business Horizons*, *57*(1), 5–9. doi:10.1016/j.bushor.2013.09.006

Boldon, N. Y., Maury, R. V., Armstrong, N. A., & Van Slyke, R. (2016). *The State of Veteran Entrepreneurship Research: What We Know and Next Steps (Veteran Entrepreneurship Research, Paper No. 1)*. Institute for Veterans and Military Families, Syracuse University.

Brock, W. A., & Evans, D. S. (1989). Small Business Economics. *Small Business Economics*, *1*(1), 7–20. doi:10.1007/BF00389913

Bruyat, C., & Julien, P. A. (2001). Defining the field of Research in Entrepreneurship. *Journal of Business Venturing*, *16*(2), 165–180. doi:10.1016/S0883-9026(99)00043-9

Cahill, K. E., Giandrea, M. D., & Quinn, J. F. (2013). *New evidence on self-employment transitions among older Americans with career jobs*. Academic Press.

Chandra, S. (2014). Soldiers turn entrepreneurs. Small Business and Entrepreneurship Council.

Cole, A. H. (1959). *Business enterprise in a social setting*. Harvard University Press.

Collins, J. (1998). The complex context of American culture: A practitioner's view. *The Washington Quarterly*, *21*(4), 213–226. doi:10.1080/01636609809550359

Cook, S. (2019). *Ex-forces entrepreneurs: How veterans can start and grow businesses*. Available at: https://startups.co.uk/ex-forces-entrepreneurs/

Dana, L. P. (2006). *Handbook of research on international entrepreneurship*. Edward Edgar.

Ehsan, L. (2010). The impact of retirement on psychological well-being in Canada. *Journal of Socio-Economics*, *40*, 373–380.

Ekpo, U. N., & Bassey, G. E. (2016). An analysis of the economic consequences of infrastructural deficit in a developing economy: The case of electricity supply in Nigeria. *The International Journal of Social Sciences (Islamabad)*, *10*(1), 28–48.

Feyerabend, P. K. (1975). *Against Method*. New Left Books.

Gbandi, E. C., & Amissah, G. (2014). Financial options for small and medium enterprises (SMEs) in Nigeria. *European Scientific Journal*, *10*(1), 327–340.

George, L. T. (1993). Sociological perspective on life transitions. *Annual Review of Sociology*, *19*(1), 353–373. doi:10.1146/annurev.so.19.080193.002033

Giles, L. (1910). *Sun Tzu on the Art of War*. Luzac and Company.

Hale, J. (2017). *Military Culture and Translating it to the Civilian Workplace*. Available at: https://www.dvidshub.net/news/237637/military-culture-and-translating-civilian-workplace

Higate, P. (2001). Theorizing continuity: From military to civilian life. *Armed Forces and Society*, *27*(3), 433. doi:10.1177/0095327X0102700306

Higgins, D. (1978). *A Dialectic of Centuries: Notes Towards a Theory of The New Perspectives on the Humanities*. University of Wisconsin Press.

Hope, J. B., Oh, B., & Mackin, P. C. (2011). *Factors Affecting Entrepreneurship among Veterans Small Business Research Summary*. U.S. Small Business Administration, Office of Advocacy.

Interian, A., Kline, A., Janal, M., Glynn, S., & Losonczy, M. (2014). Multiple deployments and combat trauma: Do home front stressors increase the risk for posttraumatic stress symptoms? *Journal of Traumatic Stress*, *27*(1), 90–97. doi:10.1002/jts.21885 PMID:24464407

Kayode, K. B., & Ilesanmi, A. O. (2014). Determinants of factors influencing capacity of small and medium enterprises (SMEs) in employment creation in Lagos State, Nigeria. *International Journal of Financial Research*, *5*(2), 133–141. doi:10.5430/ijfr.v5n2p133

Kedia, S. (2019). *With this organisation's help, Indian army veterans are becoming entrepreneurs*. Available at: https://yourstory.com/socialstory/2019/03/indian-army-veterans-turn-entrepreneurs-8icuu43y47

Kerrick, S. A., Cumberland, D., Church-Nally, M., & Kemelgor, B. (2014). Military veterans marching towards entrepreneurship: An exploratory mixed methods study. *International Journal of Management Education, 12*(3), 469–478. doi:10.1016/j.ijme.2014.05.006

Kirzner, I. M. (1973). *Competition and Entrepreneurship*. University of Chicago Press.

Knight, F. H. (1961). *Risk uncertainty and profit* (2nd ed.). Kelley.

Madichie, N. O., & Ayasi, K. (2018). Entrepreneurial Opportunities and Challenges for Retired Senior Military Officers in Nigeria. In L. P. Dana, V. Ratten, & B. Honyenuga (Eds.), *African Entrepreneurship. Palgrave Studies of Entrepreneurship in Africa* (pp. 131–151). Palgrave Macmillan. doi:10.1007/978-3-319-73700-3_7

Mobbs, M. C., & Bonanno, G. A. (2018). Beyond war and PTSD: The crucial role of transition stress in the lives of military veterans. *Clinical Psychology Review, 59*, 137–144. doi:10.1016/j.cpr.2017.11.007 PMID:29180101

Nicholson, J. W. (2019). *Veterans Are the Future of America's Startups, And Nonprofit Leaders Can Help Them Succeed.* Available at: https://www.forbes.com/sites/forbesnonprofitcouncil/2019/11/05/veterans-are-the-future-of-americas-startups-and-nonprofit-leaders-can-help-them-succeed/#6f22065e61d4

Ojo, S. (2013). *Diaspora entrepreneurship: A study of Nigerian entrepreneurs in London* (PhD thesis). University of East London. Available at: http://hdl.handle.net/10552/3506

Ojo, S., & Nwankwo, S. (2017). Diaspora and Transnational Entrepreneurship: A Conceptual Exploration. In S. Ojo (Ed.), *Diaspora and Transnational Entrepreneurship in the Global Contexts* (pp. 1–23). IGI Global. doi:10.4018/978-1-5225-1991-1.ch001

Opara, J. O. (2011). Factors constraining the growth and survival of SME in Nigeria: Implications for poverty alleviation. *Management Research Review, 34*(2), 156–171. doi:10.1108/01409171111102786

Osborne, J. W. (2012). Psychological Effects of the Transition to Retirement. *Canadian Journal of Counselling and Psychotherapy, 46*(1), 45–58.

Ozioma-Eleodinmuo, P. (2015). Analysis of entrepreneurship policy for small and medium scale enterprise in Aba, Abia State Nigeria. *Journal of Economic Development, Management, IT, Finance and Marketing, 7*(1), 47–60.

Pranger, T., Murphy, K., & Thompson, J. (2009). Shaken World Coping with Transition to Civilian Life. *Canadian Family Physician Medecin de Famille Canadien, 55*, 159–161. PMID:19221074

Robertson, H. C., & Brott, P. E. (2017). *Military Veterans' Midlife Career Transition and Life Satisfaction*. Available at: https://tpcjournal.nbcc.org/military-veterans-midlife-career-transition-and-life-satisfaction/

Ross, E. (2015). *Life after war: veterans turned successful entrepreneurs*. Available at: https://www.theguardian.com/small-business-network/2015/mar/03/war-veterans-successful-entrepreneurs-military

Sankaran, S., & Battisto, J. (2018). *Financing Their Future: Veteran Entrepreneurs and Capital Access*. Available at: https://www.fedsmallbusiness.org/veteran-entrepreneurs-and-capital-access

Schaper, M., & Volery, T. (2004). *Entrepreneurship and small business: A Pacific Rim perspective*. John Wiley and Sons Australia Ltd.

Schlossberg, N., Waters, E., & Goodman, J. (1995). *Counseling adults in transition*. Springer.

Schumpeter, J. A. (1934). *The theory of economic development: An inquiry into profits, capital, credit, interest and business cycle*. Harvard University Press.

Sharma, P., & Chrisman, J. (1999). Toward a Reconciliation of the Definitional Issues in the Field of Corporate Entrepreneurship. *Entrepreneurship Theory and Practice*, *23*(3), 11–27. doi:10.1177/104225879902300302

Singh, G., & DeNoble, A. (2003). Early retirees as the next generation of entrepreneurs. *Entrepreneurship Theory and Practice*, *27*(3), 207–226. doi:10.1111/1540-8520.t01-1-00001

Smaliukienė, R. (2014). Entrepreneurship Opportunities after Military Career: Practice in Central and Eastern versus Western Europe. *Entrepreneurial Business and Economics Review*, *1*(4), 97–108. doi:10.15678/EBER.2013.010408

SmallBusiness.com. (2018). *Americans Rank Military and Small Business as Nation's Two Most Trusted Institutions*. Available at: https://smallbusiness.com/about-small-businesses/americans-trust-in-small-business/

SMEDAN. (2013). *SMEDAN and national bureau of statistics collaborative survey: Selected findings 2013*. Abuja: SMEDAN. Retrieved from Small and Medium Enterprises Development Agency of Nigeria: http://nigerianstat.gov.ng

Smith-Osborne, A. (2013). Veterans Administration health care policies as a protective mechanism supporting an expected life trajectory after military service. *Social Work in Public Health*, *28*(2), 81–96. doi:10.1080/19371918.2011.552038 PMID:23461344

Vigoda-Gadot, E., Baruch, Y., & Grimland, S. (2010). Career transitions: An empirical examination of second career of military retirees. *Public Personnel Management, 39*(4), 379–404. doi:10.1177/009102601003900405

Vogt, D., Perkins, D. F., Copeland, L. A., Finley, E. P., Jamieson, C. S., Booth, B., Lederer, S., & Gilman, C. L. (2018). The Veterans Metric Initiative study of US veterans' experiences during their transition from military service. *BMJ Open, 2018*(8), e020734. doi:10.1136/bmjopen-2017-020734 PMID:29895650

Westwood, M. (1999). *Career transition program for Canadian peacekeeping veterans*. Veterans Affairs Canada.

Wolpert, D. S. (2000). Military retirement and the transition to civilian life. In J. A. Martin, L. N. Rosen, & L. R. Sparacino (Eds.), *The military family: A practice guide for human service providers* (pp. 103–119). Praeger.

ENDNOTE

1 This term is associated with Feyerabend, P. K., a philosopher of science who did two things in his *tour de force* book; *Against Method* (London: New Left Books, 1975). One, he vehemently objected to a single scientific method as a way to not stunt scientific progress. Two, instead of a single scientific method, he recommended theoretical anarchism, i.e. "anything goes" as more a desirable means to promote human welfare. In a similar fashion, the definition of entrepreneurship in a nebulous way gives it a similar anarchical——"anything goes"——quality.

Chapter 2
Military Enterprises and Entrepreneurship:
A Critical Perspective

Sanya Ojo
https://orcid.org/0000-0002-2585-9052
Nigerian Defence Academy, Nigeria

ABSTRACT

The main aim of this chapter is to advance a structure for understanding the notion of military-run enterprise/entrepreneurship. The chapter appraises the macro-level of military entrepreneurship rather than the micro-level (e.g., veteran, military families, or military intrapreneurs) to uncover the paradoxes underpinning this genre of military entrepreneurship. Through a critical review of literature, the presence of "extrepreneurship," which represents a crossbreed idea located between the concepts of entrepreneurship and intrapreneurship, is revealed. Extrepreneurs manage/operate for-profit spin-off organizations on behalf of their non-profit parent organizations to generate incomes/profits, among other requirements.

INTRODUCTION

Several studies on entrepreneurship focus on the micro-level, i.e., the characteristics of individuals or the networks of associations those individuals are engaged in. Progressively, researchers have paid attention to the macro-level, i.e., group or institutional activities that support entrepreneurial behavior, and the broader ecosystem that serves to reinforce or hinder risk-taking behavior. This chapter follows this line of research in its review of studies on institutional aspects of entrepreneurship

DOI: 10.4018/978-1-7998-6655-8.ch002

Copyright © 2021, IGI Global. Copying or distributing in print or electronic forms without written permission of IGI Global is prohibited.

through the prism of the military institution. The chapter aims to appraise the role of the military, as an institutional actor, in the processes of nurturing entrepreneurship and entrepreneurial behavior. A broad view of entrepreneurship is adopted in this chapter. This view focuses on the creation of new business organizations and the generation of new organizational paradigms and procedures that change the direction and flow of the entrepreneurial organizational endeavor. In other words, the chapter focuses on how entrepreneurial activity is shaped and reshaped in existing institutions to create entrepreneurial entities that may, in turn, foster new entrepreneurship patterns. The chapter discusses how shifts in the institutional environment create opportunities for organizations to reconstruct existing behaviors and bring about new forms of organizing. In a similar fashion to Hwang and Powell (2006: 180), it is expedient to reiterate that an institutional perspective on entrepreneurship is more "constructivist" than "agentic". With this distinction, this chapter assumes that while much entrepreneurial activity is purposive, it is not necessarily directly intentional. According to Hwang and Powell (2006: 180) "As organizational goals and missions are contested and reshaped, organizational participants often discover their interests "on the fly," so to speak, as strategies and goals co-evolve".

Against this backdrop, the chapter argues that entrepreneurship culture is well and alive in the military institution even though the design of military culture and traditions (e.g. firm hierarchy and strict bureaucracy) seem not to conform to popular tenets of entrepreneurship practice. In the military, entrepreneurship is demonstrated but its character and implications for the military system remain contradictory. The heterogeneity of activities and groups that make up the military - serving personnel, veterans, military families, and military-run enterprises - threatens to make the notion of military entrepreneurship a representation of incongruity. Hence, in the spirit of the tradition of critical entrepreneurship scholarship, (e.g. Steyaert & Hjorth, 2003; Steyaert & Hjorth, 2006; Hjorth & Steyaert, 2009), this chapter interrogates the notion of military entrepreneurship. The chapter sets to find out, through a review of literature, the nature, and organization of entrepreneurship in the military. In addition, the chapter will interrogate whether military entrepreneurship does indeed align or largely adhere to most forms of entrepreneurship in the civil society in its rules and norms of conduct. The overarching question at the heart of the paper is: To what extent does military entrepreneurship replicates entrepreneurship in the civil society? Other subordinate questions include: (a) What are the characteristics of military entrepreneurship? (b) What are the processes and procedures of military entrepreneurship? (c) What are the benefits and drawbacks of military entrepreneurship to the military in particular and the society in general? (d) How does the military establishment reconfigure entrepreneurial activity in its institution to create different entrepreneurial entities?

To make sense of these questions, a comprehensive review of academic literature, practitioners' bumf, internet sources, newspapers' reports, and other relevant corpora on military enterprise and entrepreneurship literature is carried out. It is necessary to notify that, in this paper, some terms and expressions that are contiguous were used interchangeably largely to keep in line with the literature from where they are extracted. Such terms include military-run enterprise, military entrepreneurship, military commercial enterprise, and military for-profit business. A caveat is added though, the intention is not to equate "entrepreneurship" with "enterprise" since it is understood that not every business enterprise is (or remains) entrepreneurial; this point has been clarified by several authors (e.g., Bhattacharyya, 2006; Drucker, 1985; Lumpkin & Dess, 1996). For instance, Ahmad and Seymour (2008: 13) declared: "Clearly not all businesses are entrepreneurial despite the fact that they take risks, create products, employment, revenue and taxes".

The paper is arranged over five main sections including (1) entrepreneurship and the nature of military enterprise/entrepreneurship (2) contextual analysis of military enterprise (3) consequences of military entrepreneurship (4) critical evaluation – the concept of "extrepreneurship" (5) summary and conclusion.

ENTREPRENEURSHIP AND THE NATURE OF MILITARY ENTERPRISE/ENTREPRENEURSHIP

Generally, the term entrepreneurship has been subjected to assorted meanings and approaches such that the term has been arrogated by a broad range of activities including creating, founding, adapting, discovering opportunities, generating values, and managing an enterprise (Cunningham & Lischeron, 1991; Kanter, 1983; Kao, 1989). According to Cunningham and Lischeron (1991: 46), these activities are delineated in six schools of thought: (a) The "Great Person" School of Entrepreneurship - assessing personal qualities (b) The Psychological Characteristics School of Entrepreneurship - assessing personal qualities (c) The Classical School of Entrepreneurship – recognizing opportunities (d) The Management School of Entrepreneurship - acting and managing (e) The Leadership School of Entrepreneurship - acting and managing (f) The Intrapreneurship School of Entrepreneurship - reassessing and adapting. The schools (and their facets) provide different perspectives on entrepreneurship (Woo et al. 1988), for instance, some approaches concentrate on personality characteristics and some on entrepreneurship as starting a small enterprise. Yet, one perspective cannot be said to be more important than the other. The usage and appropriateness of any perspective in explaining certain aspects of the entrepreneurial process depend on the researcher's judgment concerning the information he/she wishes to emphasize (Cunningham & Lischeron, 1991).

Nevertheless, the perspectives that focus on the creation of value using a unique variety of resources to exploit an opportunity (Kao 1989; Stevenson et al., 1985) are more valuable in terms of wider applicability. According to Anderson (1998), the essence of entrepreneurship is the generation and extraction of value from a situation by entrepreneurs. The foregoing sets the background and the wider prism from which military enterprise and entrepreneurship are interrogated in this chapter. To effectively capture the concept of military entrepreneurship as a product of the military institution, this paper adopts Mani's (2011: 29) definition of military entrepreneurship "as the innovative creation of resources and new means of production by commissioned military officers acting in an institutional capacity as formal owners, managers, and stakeholders of enterprises that generate financial resources or goods directly benefiting the military".

A paradoxical situation seems to exist within the notion of military entrepreneurship. On the one hand, the military with its culture and tradition has several practices (e.g. top-down command structure) that do not align with entrepreneurship's precepts (e.g. independence judgment). On the other hand, there are conceptual and contextual pieces of evidence of entrepreneurship within the military establishments. It is easy to assume the incompatibility of entrepreneurship with the military given its rigid hierarchical and highly bureaucratic structure (Vego, 2013). Yet, there are many instances of military-run enterprises and examples of creativity/innovation exhibited by several military organizations around the world. A military system has many of the characteristics of a business, and to be successful, the military formations must exhibit "world-class" business practices (Leipold, 2014). This contradiction sets the tone for an exploration of entrepreneurship, which is an ambiguous and multifaceted contested concept, within the context of the military. Moreover, commercial or profitmaking ventures operated by the military, with the involvement of armed forces personnel or using the personal economic stakes of members of the defense establishment constitute a major part of the political economy that has not received deserved attention (Siddiqa, 2007).

In many countries of the world, the military establishments are actively involved in commercial and profitmaking ventures, which may seem to deviate from their main statutory function – 'defense of the realm'. Military-run enterprise can be delineated into two broad categories. The first category includes the military-controlled industries, which could be involved in a wide range of businesses not all of which may be producing to satisfy military and security needs. The second category involves the military or defense industries, which develop and produce goods and services used largely by the military (Siddiqa, 2007).

Military-Controlled Industries (MCI)

A review of Siddiqa's (2007) work on military business enterprises indicates that military-run enterprises exist in most militaries around the world, and the extent to which they prevail in a military depends upon the civil-military relations and the strength of political institutions in the country. Siddiqa (2007) uses the term "Milbus" to denote military-run business enterprises, which exploit military capital for the personal benefit of military fraternity. Accordingly, military participation in commercial activities comes in two formats. The first often practiced in developed economies, is through the privatization of security, which involves privileged members of the military offering services such as training or weapons production to generate profit that is shared with the investors who provide capital for the venture. The other format, often prevalent in developing economies, is the military engagement in business ventures (e.g. farming, hotelling, airlines, banks, or real estate agencies). These are neither non-conventional roles nor related traditional functions (e.g. security), which the military is set up to perform. These two types of military commercial venturing are differentiated, not just by the volume of financial dividends earned, but also to the extent of penetration of the military in its society and economy. Furthermore, the first type is conducted abroad, but the second type takes place in the military homeland (Siddiqa, 2007).

Military business enterprise structures and manifestations differ from country to country. In some countries (e.g. USA, UK, France, Israel, and South Africa), it operates in partnership with the civilian corporate sector and the government. In other places (e.g. Iran, Cuba, and China), it is manifested through a partnership with the dominant ruling party or individual leader, and in countries such as Turkey, Indonesia, Pakistan, Myanmar, and Thailand, the military is the sole driver of military business enterprise. In this last category, military entrepreneurial activity is caused by the military's involvement in politics (Siddiqa, 2007). Some examples of military-run enterprises around the world are narrated in section two.

The Military-Industrial Complex (MIC)

The second category of military-run enterprise can be found in the military-industrial complex (MIC). MIC has been described as an informal alliance between a country's military and the defense industry that equips it, perceived together as a vested interest that influences public policy (Dunne & Sköns, 2010; Roland, 2009). The term is often used in reference to the system behind the military of the USA, where it is most prevalent due to close links between defense contractors, the Pentagon (Department of Defense), and politicians (SIPRI, 2008).

In the context of the USA, the appellation is sometimes extended to military–industrial–congressional complex (MICC), adding the United States' Congress to form a three-sided relationship termed an iron triangle (Higgs, 2006). These relationships include political contributions, political approval for military spending, lobbying to support bureaucracies, and oversight of the industry. It could also broadly include the entire network of contracts and flows of money and resources among individuals as well as corporations and institutions of the defense contractors, private military contractors, the Pentagon, the Congress, and the executive branch (Pursell, 1972). The vast influence wielded by the MIC is reinforced in the USA's Pentagon, which has grown to become enormously powerful over the years, and even though its components may have changed but the dynamic and impact of vested interests remain (Dunne & Sköns, 2010). The American MIC is deemed the largest and most generously financed organization ever created by man (Avlon, 2017), for instance, the USA expenditure on the military/defense outstripped that of any country in the world. The military-industrial complex has grown beyond been a loose collaboration, mainly through market relations, of senior military officers, industrial managers, and congressmen to become a system of 'state-management' (Avlon, 2017; Melman, 1970; History.com Editors, 2018). In the MIC system, the free market has been replaced and a new management group, which by the measure of the scope and scale of its decision-power, is the most important single management in the USA (Avlon, 2017; Melman, 1970, 1985; Walia, 2013). For instance, Walia (2013) argues that the MIC is used to "push elitist agendas and conceal information". The MIC has, thus, become a self-generating structure (agency) that embodies the interests of various groups in society. The strength of the vested interests and their competition for resources leads to internal pressures for military spending, where external threats are often exaggerated to provide necessary justification (Melman,1985; Dunne & Sköns, 2010).

Another facet of the MIC is revealed in vast military/defense corporations that conduct international business and invested in international military ventures. These huge corporations are not governed by anyone nation as they transcend nations. Among these leading military contractors are Lockheed Martin, Boeing, Raytheon, General Dynamics, Northrop Grumman, Leidos Holdings, Inc., Huntington Ingalls Industries, L-3 Communications Holdings Inc., United Technologies, BAE Systems, SAIC, McKesson Corporation, Bechtel Group Inc., Veritas Capital Fund, Booz Allen Hamilton Holding, etc. (The Millennium Report, 2016). Military-industrial complexes have a role in the global market via international arms sales and other forms of military contracting, often involving sale for the private profit of goods and sometimes services funded publicly (Avlon, 2017; Melman,1985; Rosen, 1973). Generally, the MIC narrative broadly depicts the use of the military to promote and protect certain economic enterprises abroad (Kimball, 2015). MIC ultimately enhances the influence of the military in politics, economics, and policymaking.

CONTEXTUAL ANALYSIS - MILITARY ENTERPRISES AROUND THE WORLD

This section gives insights into business enterprises run by military establishments in some countries around the world. The list is not exhaustive and the selected countries are chosen due largely to the availability of data in different sources on them. Some of the countries known to have their military establishments involved in economic enterprises include Argentina, China, Cuba, Ecuador, Egypt, Ethiopia, Indonesia, Iran, Myanmar, Nigeria, Pakistan, Sri Lanka, Turkey, Venezuela, Vietnam. Each of these countries' military-run enterprises is listed below.

Argentina: The Argentina military has long been involved in entrepreneurship, for instance, defense-related industries in aviation and petroleum were formed after World War 1 to transformed Argentina's armaments production capability. Through the military-run holding company, Dirección General de Fabricaciones Militares (DGFM), Argentina's military was able to participate in sectors like steel, chemicals, mining, shipyards, aviation and aerospace, transport (Mani, 2011). However, the military-run enterprises were virtually dismantled in the 1990s due to factors of chronic inefficiencies that bled the state coffers and turn the military-run sector into a state liability (Mani, 2011).

China: Defense firms in China fall under two hierarchies: Those belonging to the military, or the People's Liberation Army (PLA), and those in the defense industries under the State Council. The PLA operates, factories, mines, hotels, brothels, paging, and telephone companies, and airlines, as well as major trading firms, many of which have become firmly enmeshed in the global economy. For instance, the purported red chips firms listed on the Hong Kong Exchange but which are in fact mainland Chinese firms, are the hottest stocks in the market (Busch, 2008). Besides, conglomerates such as the China Poly Group, China Carrie, NORINCO (Defense), Viettel (the military-run telecom group) continued to take the lead among defense businesses with a huge turnover. It is the case that Military-run firms' sustainable growth over time has considerably contributed to the national economic growth and the State budget (Busch, 2008).

Cuba: The Armed Forces Business Enterprises Group (GAESA) is a conglomerate participating in all sectors of the Cuban economy and is led by General Luis Alberto Rodriguez, reportedly President Raul Castro's son-in-law. GAESA was initiated in the 1980s as an attempt to modernize the Cuban economic management, which was mired in the ways of Soviet-style administration. Currently, GAESA has dozens of companies that control 40 percent to 60 percent of Cuban's foreign exchange earnings. The conglomerate also has two banks and engages in credit card and money transfer transactions through Fincimex. RAFIN, the conglomerate's mini-hedge fund, owns shares in the telecommunications monopoly ETECSA (VOA, 2017). Likewise, the military-run Tecnotex company is one of the most important trading firms in the country. The firm purchases equipment, technology, construction materials, and other goods for many military-owned firms in the civilian sector of the economy (VOA, 2017).

Ecuador: The Ecuadorian military owns and controls a group of industries, which have firms producing explosives, munitions, uniforms, shoes and boots, tents, packs, and miscellaneous military gear. For instance, the Army, through Dirección de Industrias de Ejército (DINE), operates more than two dozen enterprises, producing everything from explosives and steel to bananas and real estate. The navy and the Air Force operate commercial fleet and commercial airlines respectively (Mani, 2011). The military enterprises in Ecuador are said to actively support the development of the country's economy as they create employment, investment in research, development, and innovation (RDI), and generally contribute to the growth of the Ecuadorian economy (GlobalSecurity.org, 2019). However, the military-run enterprises are devoid of transparency and legislative oversight (Gallegos, 2004).

Egypt: The country's military-run firms hold strong positions in a wide range of key industries, including food (olive oil, milk, bread and water, cement and gasoline; vehicle production, and construction (Naguib, 2012). The Egyptian's military commercial ventures fall under one of three main bodies - the Ministry of Military Production, which manages 20 businesses, the Ministry of Defense, which operates dozens of ventures, and the Egyptian government-owned Arab Organization for Industrialisation, which runs at least 12 enterprises (makes mechanical and electronic products) (Reuters, 2018). It is estimated that the Egyptian military controls 25 to 40 percent of Egypt's economy. Military-run firms gain competitive advantages from having a ready supply of free labor (in the form of conscripts) and having other exceptional rights granted to them by law - most importantly the right to acquire public land. Moreover, some military-military cooperation agreements enable the military to sell its products to foreign armies. Yet, military production is non-competitive because they forcibly sell their products to government agencies. For instance, some public universities are compelled to buy food products from the army. The particular reliance of military business on compulsory drafting causes many youths in their prime to be deployed to military firms to work as forced labor for free. This also has a knock-on damaging effects on the Egyptian economy. Workers in military-run factories, farms, and service enterprises are also deprived of basic rights (Naguib, 2012). Military-owned firms in Egypt also enjoy tax and other advantages granted to military-owned firms. For instance, the military and other security institutions were given exemptions in a new value-added tax (VAT) law enacted as part of IMF-inspired reforms in 2016 (Reuters, 2018). In 2017, the International Monetary Fund expressed a concern that private sector development and job creation "might be hindered by involvement of entities under the Ministry of Defense" (Reuters, 2018).

Ethiopia: The Ethiopian military engages in commercial activities, for instance, Metals & Engineering Corp, (METEC) is a military-run corporation. Ethiopian's military-run enterprises are used to develop the country's economy that grew an average of 8.7 over the past five years, according to the International Monetary Fund (Davison, 2013).

Indonesia: The country's military has a longstanding practice of raising independent income outside the approved budget process, and earns funds from businesses it owns, services it provides for hire, and the protection rackets it operates. In 2007, the Indonesian military-owned 23 foundations and over 1,000 cooperatives, including ownership of 55 companies, as well as leases on thousands of government properties and buildings. It is commonly accepted that Indonesian military involvement in the economic enterprise is harmful as it undermines civilian control over the armed forces, encourages human rights abuses, and promotes corruption. To curb these excesses, Indonesia's parliament passed a law in September 2004 to reform the military such that military commercialism was banned and the Indonesian government asked to take over all military businesses by 2009 (Human Rights Watch, 2007; Mercier, 2010).

Iran: The Iranian Revolutionary Guards' (military) involvement in the economy is traced back to the end of the Iran-Iraq war in the 1980s when senior officers were rewarded with contracts to build roads, dams, and bridges to help rebuild the country. Some of these firms are involved in oil and gas projects (e.g. Sadra Iran Maritime Industrial Company), construction (e.g. Shahid Rajaee Professional Group), telecom (e.g. Etemad Mobin Development Company), banking (e.g. Ansar Bank), etc. Other areas covered by the military enterprises stretch across many other sectors, such as health, agriculture, and petrochemicals. Yet, like in other countries, the Guards' entrepreneurship is marred by corruption and its stranglehold on the Iranian economy (Bozorgmehr, 2017).

Myanmar: The country's military establishment is involved in a commercial enterprise through an entity known as Tatmadaw, which is run by senior military officers. Aside from doing legitimate business (e.g., hold a substantial stake in Myanmar's lucrative jade trade), the military enterprises are reported to be involved in illegitimate enterprises such as using mining areas as staging grounds for abductions, forced labor, sexual violence, and murder. These illegal activities generate additional income to the tune of around $31 billion a year, which is close to half of the country's GDP (Heijmans, 2019).

Nigeria: Defense Industries Corporation of Nigeria (DICON) is the state-run defense corporation of Nigeria and operated by the Nigerian Armed Forces. Formed in 1964, DICON is responsible for the production of defense equipment and civilian products. DICON began with a focus on producing small arms and ammunition, and its entire technological base was imported from West Germany, and an initial team of West German technologists was brought in to develop the company's technical competence at inception (IMANI, 2011). Presently, the organization's production capability is constrained due to funding and other institutional challenges (International Crisis Group, 2016).

Pakistan: The military business in Pakistan is pervasive and is tightly intertwined with Pakistan's economy. For instance, the military owns 12 percent of Pakistan's fertile land with two-thirds of that land in the hands of senior serving and retired officers (Siddiqa, 2007). Pakistani's military business is conducted in three areas of agriculture, manufacturing, and services with its subsidiaries including the Fauji Foundation, Army Welfare Trust, Shaheen Foundation, and Bahria Foundation. These subsidiaries are headed by top serving military officers, they are positioned to enjoy an unfair economic advantage over non-military firms and used to generate perks and favors for individual members of the military echelon (Siddiqa, 2007). Many of Pakistan's largest corporations are controlled by the military, and through their proxies (the Foundations) control over 100 separate commercial entities involved in several industries from cement to cereal production (Wilson, 2008).

Sri Lanka: Sri Lanka's military is also involved in commercial enterprises ranging from landscaping projects and the military is steadily increasing its grip on the economy and business activities. Sri Lanka's military incursion into commercial enterprises has been said to stifle competition in certain ways. First, the military business enterprises have access to cheap labor offered by service personnel and second, local competition is intimidated and warned against competing with the businesses run by the Defense Ministry (*Colombo Telegraph*, 2014).

Turkey: Turkey's military has considerable economic interests through its conglomerate known as OYAK. OYAK has more than 60 firms operating in very diverse industries from bed frames to mining, from car companies to cement and construction firms to the food sector. The organization controls over TL 28 billion of capital and has investments in countries like Romania, Cyprus, Spain, and the Netherlands. OYAK has been accused of enjoying tax privileges and other advantages over ordinary commercial companies in Turkey (Seibert, 2010).

Venezuela: Military enterprises abound in Venezuela and are run in total secrecy. The Venezuelan military, also known as National Bolivarian Armed Forces (NBAF), owns companies in industries such as oil extraction, construction, agriculture, insurance, banking, and the manufacture of vehicles, tires, and clothes (Lugo-Galicia, 2018). The management of military-run enterprises is shrouded in mystery as they do not publish their accounts even though they receive state funds. The NBAF also refuses to regularly provide the legislature with a list of all armed forces enterprises. It has been suggested that the government allows the military a free rein to quell discontent and possible coup d'état (Lugo-Galicia, 2018).

Vietnamese: The Vietnamese military-run enterprises involve large-scale corporations and groups operating in fields where the military have a great advantage. The Vietnamese military businesses are integrated into domestic and foreign markets, creating employment and contributing to the country's income. For example, in the first half of 2017, military-run enterprises contributed over VND 21 trillion to the State coffers (Thang, 2017). However, despite reformations, the Vietnamese military-run businesses remain cumbersome as their structure is inept. Some of the firms within the business establishment are sluggishly responsive to the market mechanism, have low competitiveness, and produced a poor business performance that belies their resources (Thang, 2017).

Characteristics of Military Entrepreneurship

Military entrepreneurship as seen in the examples of enterprises seems to replicate main-stream (civilian) entrepreneurship in many aspects in which entrepreneurship is defined, e.g. creating, finding opportunities, managing, controlling, and changing (Cunningham & Lischeron, 1991). All the military establishments in the different listed countries spawn off new business enterprises (e.g. farming, construction firms, banking, factories, etc.) that are run and managed like other civilian-run commercial enterprises. The various military-run enterprises have motives for profit, value stakeholders, growth, etc. like the mainstream enterprises. This is in alignment with Ahmad and Seymour's (2008) perspective on entrepreneurship. The authors contend that entrepreneurship is associated with entrepreneurial activity, which, is the enterprising human action in pursuit of the generation of value, through the creation or expansion of economic activity, by identifying and exploiting new products, processes or markets.

Furthermore, several military entrepreneurial activities as listed appear to generate what Baumol (1990) refers to as unproductive and destructive entrepreneurship such as encouraging rent-seeking, illegal and shadow activities, and different forms of corruption. Hence, as it is in conventional entrepreneurship, military entrepreneurship promotes social ills such as forced labor in Egypt, human rights abuses and corruption in Indonesia, intimidation in Sri Lanka, illegitimate enterprises in Myanmar, etc.

CONSEQUENCES OF MILITARY ENTREPRENEURSHIP

Military entrepreneurship seems to have both positive and negative effects as could be deduced from the reviews in the last section. These positive and negatives effects are crystallized as below.

Benefits of Military Entrepreneurship

On the positive side, many military-run factories and plants directly produce and manufacture national defense products such as weaponry and defense equipment, which strengthening the capability of the defense industry as well as providing employment. For example, the Pakistanis' military entrepreneurship diversifies into new markets and industries and steadily consolidates power in the key sectors of agriculture, energy, natural resources, logistics, and construction (Wilson, 2008). Military entrepreneurship creates an avenue for a bilateral and multilateral relationships among countries such that military-military cooperation agreements allow one military to sell its products to another foreign army. Military-run factories do not produce defense products en masse and then put them back in the warehouse to prepare for warfare; instead, they need to maintain production and innovate to meet the rising internal and external demand of military organizations. Moreover, aside from the production of military/defense materials, many military factories use their machinery and facilities to produce dual-purpose products usable for both defense and civil needs (*Tuoi Tre,* 2017). In developed economies, the sale of military equipment and services generates profits primarily for the private sector that invests the capital; though the military is one of the secondary beneficiaries of those investments (Siddiqa, 2007).

Military entrepreneurial engagements also serve as an avenue for creating a system of welfare or a social security net for retired and serving military personnel. It is deemed important to provide for the welfare of armed forces personnel whose typical remuneration is generally less than the private sector norm (Smith, 2020); though Maynard and Blalock (1977) argued that the USA military welfare entitlements are significantly more benevolent and equitable than that provided to civilians. According to Siddiqa (2007), retired military personnel, especially senior officers, benefitted well from military business venturing since the military, more than any other group or organization, spreads its patronage to its former members. Retired officers, thus, are an essential part of the military business formation. This serves the military business well as the loyalty of the retired officers to their organization is relatively greater than could be found in any other organized group, particularly in the civilian sector. The camaraderie established in military academies and service postings engendered a well-knit 'old-boys' network between retired and serving officers and they tend to stick together and support each other even after retirement from active duty. In essence, military entrepreneurship could be justified for its provision of welfare package for military personnel even though, the military alone defines the parameters of this welfare (Siddiqa, 2007).

One important benefit of military entrepreneurship is its spill-over effects on the informal sector. Authors (e.g. Moser, 1994; Slavnic, 2010; Taiwo, 2013) contend that formal and informal activities are not separate and independent, but in the general capitalist system the informal activities are integrated or subordinated to, and dependent on, the formal sector in a sort of informal-formal continuum. Viewed from this structuralist perspective (Davis, 2006; Hudson, 2005) of cost reduction, military entrepreneurship generates business ventures in the informal sector when hordes of informal entrepreneurs deliver or undertake some functions for military enterprises. Invariably, military entrepreneurship can then be said to impart entrepreneurial skills and training, not only for its workers but also to others who partnered (e.g. private contractors and/or informal entrepreneurs) in its activities. Thus, military entrepreneurship facilitates military-civilian interface that could be assumed, not only to generate good working relationship but also provides a channel for creativity and innovation in its ecosystem. Given this background, the claim that military entrepreneurship inspires efficiency and disciplined enterprise, organizing and structuring, especially in developing countries (Halpern, 1963; Huntington, 1996; Mares, 1998; Stepan, 1971), is understandable. Although, it was the sensitivity around the development of inventions such as stealth technology, missile systems, radar, etc. that most vindicated military involvement in business enterprise, and not some idea of military discipline, efficiency or uprightness (IMANI, 2011).

Perhaps, the most auspicious benefit of military entrepreneurship is the generation of extra-budgetary income to fill in gaps in military finances. In most cases, military-run enterprises help to provide financial autonomy to meet military organizations' needs, especially personnel costs. This has historical precedence in the Middle Ages when militaries acted as 'war entrepreneurs' to garner resources for waging wars (Redlich, 1964). Likewise, in medieval periods, military formations exploited, looted, and plundered to finance campaigns and meet their financial needs (Brömmelhörster & Paes, 2004; Crefeld, 1977). In the modern epoch, some military formations (e.g. Russia, Indonesia, and China) have depended on their internal economies to meet their personnel and operational costs (e.g. Mulvenon, 2001). In countries like the USA, UK, and South Africa, retired officers start businesses that offered military training and equipment for sale to their national and foreign governments (Siddiqa, 2007). Thus, the internal economy is one of the sources of off-budget funding of military obligations.

Downsides of Military Entrepreneurship

Many observers (e.g., Bozorgmehr, 2017; Siddiqa, 2007; Thang, 2017) believe that military-run commercial enterprises do more harm than good in many areas. Taken the economic angle, it is argued that military entrepreneurship promotes the production of "public bads", for example, prostitution and gangsterism (e.g. in Indonesia and Myanmar) just as easily as "public goods". Military entrepreneurship is mostly unaccountable and non-competitive, can also damage civilian entrepreneurial activities, which are crowded out of lucrative economic space. That is, it turns investment away from the private sector (Goel & Saunoris, 2018; Mani, 2011; Siddiqa, 2007). Military entrepreneurship also initiates resource capable of producing profits and a potential source of monopoly by individuals in the military fraternity, and in this sense, military entrepreneurship mostly promotes the personal economic stakes of military personnel and their partners (Siddiqa, 2007). Siddiqa (2007) also argued that military business is predatory as it involves the informal transfer of funds from the public to the private sector and operates on the principle of limited transparency, and hence, could be deemed illegitimate. Largely, military commercial enterprises facilitate the transfer of resources and opportunities from the public and private sectors to a group or an individual within the military informally solely for personal gratification (Siddiqa, 2007). Consequently, military entrepreneurship perpetuates patronage practices to preserve the privileged positions in a country (e.g. Mani, 2011).

From the political perspective, military entrepreneurship encourages the officer cadre to perpetuate their organizational influence to reap financial benefits (Siddiqa, 2007; Wilson, 2008), which gives them considerable power to shape the political discourse in some countries (e.g. Pakistan, Egypt). This political power is employed to appropriate national resources and monopolize opportunities. For example, the Turkish military entrepreneurship confers financial autonomy, which enhances the military's political power to the detriment of other groups in the country (Seibert, 2010; Siddiqa, 2007). In some countries, engagement in business enterprise intensifies the interest of the military to remain in power or in direct/indirect control of governance, which has direct consequences for the growth of democracy or rule of law in the long-run (Siddiqa, 2007). Mani (2011) argued that military entrepreneurship reduces the authority of elected officials to oversee the military through budgetary allocation – "power of the purse" (Brömmelhörster & Paes, 2004). In addition, military entrepreneurship encumbers the military in the performance of its traditional roles. Engaging in entrepreneurship can divert the attention of the military from its statutory responsibilities (Siddiqa, 2007).

Based on sociocultural standpoint, military entrepreneurship encourages cronyism, corruption, and discrimination (e.g. Mani, 2011; Seibert, 2010), which can be in the form of exclusion of outsiders in the sharing of the economic dividends. Military enterprises often enjoy privileges (e.g. subsidies and tax exemptions) that are not available to other firms in the public or private sectors, and those military enterprises are not accountable to any government body. Furthermore, military-run firms benefit not only from having a ready supply of free labor, which comes in the form of conscripts but also from other exceptional rights granted to them by law, e.g. the right to acquire public land in Myanmar (Tang, 2015). Furthermore, military business encourages collusion between civilian and military personnel to tacitly cooperate in accommodating each other's interests for mutual benefit. This could be related to a case of collective plundering, which Olson's (2000) theoretical framework of kleptocratic distribution of resources (which is based on the negotiation of mutual interests) succinctly explained. Taken together, military entrepreneurship provides an avenue for corruption and malfeasance.

On ethical grounds, military entrepreneurship heightens involvement in illegal practices as well as a range of activities in the 'black economy'. Moreover, it is the case that the Military-Industrial Complex (MIC), another form of military entrepreneurship, is a faceless cadre of profit-seeking warmongers that seeks to perpetuate war rather than peace (Sottile, 2017). For instance, because of the enormous financial benefits the USA MIC, in cahoots with Israel, are heavily vested in seeing that the military aid continues (Green, 2016). Making it harder, to nearly impossible to get a peaceful settlement with Palestine.

Altogether, there are inherent benefits and detriments of military entrepreneurship, and Table 1 gives an overview of these.

Table 1. Consequences of Military Entrepreneurship

Advantages	Disadvantages
Contributes to the national economy through employment and R&D	Compromises military professionalism
Stimulates spill-over effects in the informal sector	Encourages 'black economy' and loss of tax revenue
Provides entrepreneurial skills and training for members	Incites corruption and official malfeasance
Delivers welfare package for veterans and serving members	Crowding out civil commercial enterprises
Inspires efficiency and disciplined enterprise organizing and structuring	Exploitation of labor and promotion of "public bads" (e.g. prostitution, racketeering)
Facilitates military-civilian interface/relationship	Stifles competition in the economy
Provides an avenue for creativity and innovation in the military	Subverts democratic process in some countries
Provides extra-budgetary income to fill in gaps in the military finances	Reduces the "power of the purse" – compromising the authority of elected officials to oversee the military through budgetary allocation
Boosts inter-governmental cooperation through arms sales and joint-venture in arms production	Disturbs world peace through arms sales to warring parties around the globe

Source: Literature Review

CRITICAL APPRAISAL: INTRODUCING THE THEORY OF EXTREPRENEURSHIP

A critical assessment of the nature and characteristics of military entrepreneurship reveals a form of enterprising that is positioned between entrepreneurship and intrapreneurship. For easy identification, the term 'extrepreneurship' is formulated to describe this phenomenon. Extrepreneurship illustrates the emergence of military-run business enterprises that are controlled by military top echelon or its proxy. These business enterprises are usually managed by 'extrepreneurs' who behave like entrepreneurs but are similar to intrapreneurs in format. Consequently, an extrepreneur, like an intrapreneur, is nothing but an entrepreneur within the boundaries of an organization, and he/she also integrates risk-taking within his/her corporate management approach.

A key objective of extrepreneurship is to provide extra income (through commercial spin-offs) for supposedly non-profit organizations (e.g. charities, public sector hospitals, civil service, etc.) to fill in revenue gaps or meet their expenditure requirements, which their statutory budget allocation is unable to fulfill. Another objective may be to launch or commercialize inventions (like in the case of universities). Most of these spin-offs are often led and managed by staff of the parent organization, and these individuals are the extrepreneurs. Extrepreneurs are quite distinct from intrapreneurs in several ways. First, extrepreneurs operate outside the parent organization in a business outfit, unlike intrapreneurs who can be found both in the parent organization or its spin-offs. Second, whilst intrapreneurs may have some 'freedom' to operate and introduce the necessary innovation to the organization, the extrepreneurs have greater authority and autonomy in their domains. Third, extrepreneurs work for organizations that are a spin-off from supposedly not-for-profit organizations such as the military, university, civil service, and third sector organizations (e.g. charity establishments). Whereas intrapreneurs work in any sort of organization but they have less control over their respective environments and therefore assume less financial risk (Luchsinger & Bagby, 1987). Fourth, the level of remuneration for extrepreneurs is far higher than that of intrapreneurs who may only be rewarded nominally above their regular salary. Fifth, any employee can become intrapreneur (if he/she exhibits entrepreneurial traits), but not anyone can be extrepreneur. Extrepreneurs operate at the top echelon of their organization, that is, they are in the management cadre whilst intrapreneurs can be found at all levels in an organization. Putting it differently, any extrepreneur can become intrapreneur but not all intrapreneurs can be extrepreneurs.

Likewise, the differences between entrepreneurs and extrepreneurs mirror the differences between entrepreneurs and intrapreneurs. For instance, Shrader and Simon (1997) showed that while intrapreneurs emphasized internal capital sources, proprietary knowledge, and marketing expertise in strategic decision making, entrepreneurs emphasized external capital sources, technical expertise, and development of the brand. Unlike entrepreneurs, both extrepreneurs and intrapreneurs do not have to worry about getting resources (e.g. capital, staff, equipment, etc.) for their ventures as those are provided by their organizations. In addition, the entrepreneurs bear all the risks and appropriate all the profits derived from their business. Extrepreneurs and intrapreneurs do not bear any risk associated with the business but share in the profit. Extrepreneurship/extrepreneur is, thus, a form of hybrid idea situated between entrepreneurship/entrepreneur and intrapreneurship/ intrapreneur. However, there are differences between the three concepts as listed in Table 2.

Table 2. Distinguishing between Entrepreneur, Intrapreneur, & Extrepreneur

Classification	Entrepreneur	Intrapreneur	Extrepreneur
Enterprise Structure	Sets up own business	Works inside an organization	Works inside an organization
Ownership Structure	Full ownership of the organization	Does not own the organization	Does not own the organization
Management Structure	Full control	No control	Management control is devolved to the extrepreneur by the parent organization
Income Structure	Appropriate profit	Mainly receives salary only	Receives salary and share of profit
Liability Structure	Appropriate losses	Does not suffer income losses	Does not suffer income loss
Innovation Structure	Active	Active	Passive
Attachment Structure	Emotional attachment	Emotional detachment	Emotional detachment

Source: Literature Review & Author's Analysis

Interrogating Extrepreneurship

The idea of extrepreneurship is not new as it is noticeable in various institution-led commercialization projects in many countries. According to Hwang and Powell (2006), public service institutions (e.g. hospitals, schools, and universities), community agencies and volunteer organizations (e.g. Red Cross, professional and trade associations), and many others are particularly well-positioned to be successful entrepreneurs and innovators provided they organize themselves for entrepreneurial management. Institutions in the public sector such as universities, civil service, armed forces, hospitals, and third sector organizations such as religious bodies, NGOs, etc., which are ordinarily non-profit by charter, often establish spin-off organizations to raise fund. For instance, a related term is academic entrepreneurship (Mowery et al., 1999), which refers to efforts undertaken by universities to promote commercialization within and outside the university environment (Shane, 2004). Entrepreneurial activities involving informal knowledge transfer activities such as consultancy, contract research, joint/collaborative research, shared facilities, secondments, training, and continued professional development, student placements and student projects are all within the remits of intellectual/academic entrepreneurship. Abreu and Grinevich (2013) contended that these activities can generate significant economic and social value for both academics and external partners. Academic entrepreneurship has been variously described by appellations such as 'entrepreneurial universities' (Etzkowitz, 1983), 'academic capitalism' (Slaughter & Leslie, 1997), and 'entrepreneurial academics' (Gintaras, 2012). Entrepreneurial academics and/or academic entrepreneurs are best known as intellectual entrepreneurs, and cognizance of the ethical obligation to contribute to society, they exemplify academic engagement to discover and put to work knowledge that makes a difference. This group usually adopts a hybrid role identity that comprises a focal academic self and a secondary commercial persona (Jain et al., 2009).

Another form of extrepreneurship is discernible in the civil service. For instance, the UK's civil service established Government Commercial Organization (GCO) whose mandates include improving the effectiveness and delivery of commercial activities across government and enhancing senior commercial capability and leadership to enable the successful delivery of commercial activities across government. The GCO is managed by experienced civil servants (serving or retired) and it employs staff on terms and conditions that are more aligned to the pay and bonus arrangements used in the private sector (GCF, 2018). Such civil service spin-off organizations are regulated by the market in contrast to the civil service system which is typically complex, formalized, and risk-averse.

Similarly, extrepreneurship occurs in the UK's National Health Service (NHS). For example, Essentia Trading Limited (ETL, 2020) is a wholly-owned subsidiary of Guy's and St Thomas' NHS Foundation Trust in London and is involved in commercial enterprise such as property consultancy, estate, and capital development, etc. Another NHS example in the UK is King's Commercial - a wholly-owned subsidiary of King's College Hospital NHS Foundation Trust, which provides expertise in consulting, healthcare management, education and training, recruitment, and clinical unit commissioning. The income generated is reinvested in the Trust's NHS (KCH, 2017).

Furthermore, extrepreneurship could be inferred in the commercial activities of the Third Sector (e.g. charity organizations). Creating a for-profit spin-off allows charity organizations to diversify their revenue base (Foster & Meinhard, 2000) and many third sector organizations are following this route. For instance, Meinhard et al. (2004) highlighted some cases of Canadian charity organizations that created spin-off commercial ventures. Likewise, Cherry (2012: 346) discussed the trend of charitable organizations becoming involved in commercial activities as they created "commercial" type ventures as part of their non-profits spin-off or subsidiary organizations in the USA.

Similarities Between Concepts

Despite their contextual differences, it is expected that entrepreneurs, intrapreneurs, and extrepreneurs will share certain traits. For instance, Carrier (1996) reviewed the literature and concluded that most studies have implied no significant difference between entrepreneurs and intrapreneurs. Such studies portray intrapreneurs and entrepreneurs as possessing or employing similar cognitive and behavioral characteristics, thus, the troika of entrepreneurs, intrapreneurs, and extrepreneurs will have certain traits in common. First is the presence of strong leadership skills, which give them the creative management competencies to galvanize others towards achieving set goals. Second is the possession of intelligence and vision that enable them to spot and grasp emergent opportunities such that assist them to balance passion and innovation with business shrewdness. The third is the flexibility and the ability to adapt to the dynamism of the business environment, i.e., the ability to respond effectively to emerging situations in the marketplace. Fourth is the passion for innovation, which entrepreneurs, intrapreneurs, and extrepreneurs shared.

SUMMARY AND CONCLUSION

The chapter appraised the military enterprising/entrepreneurship at the institutional level. The appraisal revealed the characteristics of military entrepreneurship and enabled a critical reflection on how practices are altered through the formation of new organizations (e.g. for-profit organizations) by existing institutions (e.g. not-for-profit establishments). Even though in some instances, military entrepreneurship has positive effects on the economy and society (e.g. job creation, R&D, welfare package for veterans, etc.), yet, its negative effects on the economy, society, politics and military professionalism are overwhelming in the literature. The negatives effects stretch from financial costs deriving from the formation of monopolies that causes market distortions, to unfair advantages over civilian enterprises, and to the creation of a system of patronage that results in praetorian political systems (Siddiqa, 2007). There is a general realization that mixing the military and business is not a good idea, and some countries (e.g. Israel, Chile, Argentina, Brazil, etc.) have taken steps to divest many enterprises once controlled by their military organizations to the civilian-state or private sectors. Mixing business enterprises with soldiering could breed corruption, which harms the military's defense capabilities and compromises national security such as in the examples of Egypt and Thailand (IMANI, 2011). In Pakistan, military entrepreneurship has, according to Siddiqa (2007), affected the growth and sustenance of democracy.

Nevertheless, beyond the merits and demerits of military entrepreneurship, a critical evaluation of military entrepreneurship draws attention to the notion of extrepreneurship. Extrepreneurship signposts the formation of for-profit business outfits by public or not-for-profit organizations such as the military, civil service, charity organizations, universities, etc. These spin-off ventures are ostensibly created to generate funds for their parent organizations and they are managed by extrepreneurs who are seconded from the parent organizations. Undoubtedly, the notion of extrepreneurship is still an evolving, open-ended enterprise engagement whose importance will depend on the ability of scholars and researchers to further interrogate and illuminate the characteristics of the idea.

CONTRIBUTIONS

The paper contributes to re-energize and intensify entrepreneurship research, and also to broaden the space for reflexivity and experimentation in the field. This is in line with Bill et al.'s (2010) view that both the spectacular and mundane aspects of entrepreneurship can be equally emphasized in order to generate a balanced socially productive narrative. In addition, there is a substantial body of theoretical insight and empirical evidence on entrepreneurs/entrepreneurship (e.g. Honig, 2001) and on intrapreneurs/intrapreneurship (e.g. Carrier, 1996), yet, there is no codify work on extrepreneur/extrepreneurship. Thus, this paper brought to view the notion of 'extrepreneurship', an obscure but easily detectable concept straddling both concepts of 'entrepreneurship' and 'intrapreneurship'.

LIMITATION AND FURTHER STUDIES

This study is not without its limitations. The study could be accused of over-stressing the notion of entrepreneurship by its application to military enterprise activities. But the entrepreneurship field has grown tremendously such that all manner of activities is reframed and redefined as entrepreneurial (Hwang & Powell, 2006). Another weakness is the superficial treatment of espoused concepts (e.g. military entrepreneurship, extrepreneurship, extrepreneur). Although this paper joins others in highlighting the processes and nature of military entrepreneurship concept, but it is conceptual and does not deeply interrogate the concept. Thus, empirical studies that robustly appraise the concept of military entrepreneurship are imperative to deepen knowledge on this phenomenon. Military entrepreneurship as a concept needs more studies to enhance its credibility as a veritable field of study within the larger entrepreneurship domain.

Moreover, given that there is a potential for interpretive ambiguity on the concept of extrepreneurship/extrepreneurs raised in this paper, more studies will be needed to further interrogate the concept. Extrepreneurship in different contextual applications, as mentioned in this study, will required in-depth analysis to discover its manifested characteristics and/or its embedded contradictions.

REFERENCES

Abreu, M., & Grinevich, V. (2013). The nature of academic entrepreneurship in the UK: Widening the focus on entrepreneurial activities. *Research Policy*, *42*(2), 408–422. doi:10.1016/j.respol.2012.10.005

Ahmad, N., & Seymour, R. G. (2008). *Defining Entrepreneurial Activity: Definitions Supporting Frameworks for Data Collection*. OECD Statistics Working Paper. doi:10.2139srn.1090372

Anderson, A. R. (1998). Cultivating the Garden of Eden: Environmental entrepreneuring. *Journal of Organizational Change Management*, *11*(2), 135–144.

Avlon, J. (2017). *The Military Industrial Complex is Real and it's Bigger than Ever*. Available at: https://www.thedailybeast.com/the-military-industrial-complex-is-real-and-its-bigger-than-ever

Bash, B. L. (1999). Leadership and Parochialism: An Enduring Reality. *Joint Force Quarterly*, *22*, 64.

Baumol, W. J. (1990). Entrepreneurship: Productive, unproductive and destructive. *Journal of Political Economy*, *98*(5), 893–921.

Bhattacharyya, S. (2006). Entrepreneurship and Innovation: How Leadership Style Makes the Difference? *Vikalpa*, *31*(1), 107–115.

Bozorgmehr, N. (2017). *Iran cracks down on Revolutionary Guards business network*. Available at: https://www.ft.com/content/43de1388-9857-11e7-a652-cde3f882dd7b

Brömmelhörster, J., & Paes, W.-C. (2004). *The Military as an Economic Actor: Soldiers in Business*. Palgrave Macmillan.

Busch, G. K. (2008). *The Chinese Military-Commercial Complex*. Available at: http://www.ocnus.net/artman2/publish/Editorial_10/The_Chinese_Military-Commercial_Complex.shtml

Carrier, C. (1996). Intrapreneurship in small businesses: An exploratory study. *Entrepreneurship Theory and Practice*, *21*(1), 5–20.

Cherry, J. B. (2012). Charitable Organizations and Commercial Activity: A New Era - Will the Social Entrepreneurship Movement Force Change? *Journal of Business. Entrepreneurship & the Law*, *5*(2), 346–371.

Colombo Telegraph. (2014). *Increasing Military Involvement in Sri Lankan Business Ventures*. Available at: https://www.colombotelegraph.com/index.php/increasing-military-involvement-in-sri-lankan-business-ventures/

Cunningham, J. B., & Lischeron, J. (1991). Defining Entrepreneurship. *Journal of Small Business Management*, 45–61.

Davis, M. (2006). *Planet of Slums*. Verso.

Davison, W. (2013). *Ethiopian Military-Run Corporation Seeks More Foreign Partners*. Available at: http://nazret.com/blog/index.php/2013/02/18/ethiopian-military-run-corporation-seeks-more-foreign-partners

Drucker, P. F. (1985). *Innovation and Entrepreneurship*. Elsevier.

Dunne, J. P., & Sköns, E. (2010). *The Changing Military Industrial Complex*. Available at: https://www.researchgate.net/publication/46450061_The_Military_Industrial_Complex

ETL. (2020). *ETL is a Great Place to Work*. Available at: https://www.etl.co.uk/

Etzkowitz, H. (1983). Entrepreneurial scientists and entrepreneurial universities in American academic science. *Minerva*, *21*, 1–21.

Foster, M., & Meinhard, A. (2000). *Revenue diversification among Canadian voluntary organizations: A response to the external environment*. Centre for Voluntary Sector Studies Working Paper Series, Working Paper No. 16, Toronto: Ryerson University.

Gallegos, G. B. (2004). *Transparencia del presupuesto de defensa en Ecuador*. Working Paper. Buenos Aires: RESDAL Proyecto Transparencia. www.resdal.org/presupuestos/caso-ecuador.pdf

GCF. (2018). *Becoming the Best: The Government Commercial Function will be the best commercial function in the UK*. Available at: https://jobs.jobvite.com/gcf/

Gintaras, B. (2012). Academic entrepreneurship: Barriers and fears versus wishes and opportunities. *International Journal of Technology Management & Sustainable Development, 11*(3), 231–244.

GlobalSecurity.org. (2019). *Ecuador - Defense Industry*. Available at: https://www.globalsecurity.org/military/world/ecuador/industry.htm

Goel, R. K., & Saunoris, J. W. (2018). Military spending and entrepreneurship: Spatial effects of cross-country spillovers. *Managerial and Decision Economics, 39*(3), 363–373.

Green, E. (2016). *Why Does the United States Give So Much Money to Israel?* Retrieved from: https://www.theatlantic.com/international/archive/2016/09/united-states-israel-memorandum-of-understanding-military-aid/500192/

Halpern, M. (1963). *The Politics of Social Change in the Middle East and North Africa*. Princeton University Press.

Heijmans, P. (2019). *UN Calls for Sanctions Against Firms Owned by Myanmar Military*. Available at: https://www.bloomberg.com/news/articles/2019-08-05/un-calls-for-sanctions-against-firms-owned-by-myanmar-military

Higgs, R. (2006). Depression, War, and Cold War: Studies in Political Economy: Studies in Political Economy. Oxford University Press.

History.com Editors. (2018). *Military-Industrial Complex*. Available at: https://www.history.com/topics/21st-century/military-industrial-complex

Hjorth, D., & Steyaert, C. (Eds.). (2009). *The Politics and Aesthetics of Entrepreneurship*. Edward Elgar.

Hudson, R. (2005). *Economic Geographies: Circuits, Flows and Spaces*. Sage.

Human Rights Watch. (2007). *Indonesia: Reform of Military Business: A Human Rights Watch Background Briefing*. Retrieved from https://www.hrw.org/news/2007/02/16/indonesia-reform-military-business

Huntington, S. P. (1996). *Political Order in Changing Societies*. Yale University Press.

Hwang, H., & Powell, W. W. (2006). Institutions and entrepreneurship. In H. Hwang & W. W. Powell (Eds.), *The handbook of entrepreneurship* (1st ed., pp. 179–210). Springer Publishing.

IMANI. (2011). *IMANI Report: The Dangers of Military Commercialisation in Ghana*. Available at: https://www.modernghana.com/news/344019/imani-report-the-dangers-of-military-commercialis.html

International Crisis Group. (2016). *Nigeria: The Challenge of Military Reform*. Crisis Group Africa Report N°237. Available at: https://www.refworld.org/pdfid/5756664c4.pdf

Jain, S., George, G., & Maltarich, M. (2009). Academics or entrepreneurs? Investigating role identity modification of university scientists involved in commercialization activity. *Research Policy*, *38*, 922–935.

Kanter, R. (1983). *The Change Masters: Innovation and Entrepreneurship in the American Corporation*. Simon and Shuster.

Kao, J. (1989). *Entrepreneurship, Creativity and Organization*. Prentice-Hall.

KCH. (2017). *About Us*. Available at: https://www.kchcommercial.com/about-us/

Kimball, A. (2015). *Long-term Historical Reflection on the Rise of Military-Industrial, Managerial Statism or "Military-Industrial Complexes"*. Available at: https://pages.uoregon.edu/kimball/MIC.htm

Leipold, J. D. (2014). *Is the Army a business?* Available at: https://www.army.mil/article/126882/is_the_army_a_business

Lugo-Galicia, H. (2018). *Maduro turns Venezuela military officers into businessmen to quell discontent*. Available at: https://www.miamiherald.com/news/nation-world/world/americas/venezuela/article210233099.html#storylink=cpy

Lumpkin, G. T., & Dess, G. G. (1996). Clarifying the Entrepreneurial Orientation Construct and Linking it to Performance. *Academy of Management Review*, *21*(1), 135–172.

Mani, K. (2011). Military Entrepreneurship: Patterns in Latin America. *Latin American Politics and Society*, *53*(3), 25–55.

Mares, D. R. (1998). Civil-military relations, democracy, and the regional neighborhood. In D. R. Mares (Ed.), *Civil-Military Relations*. Westview Press.

Maynard, C., & Blalock, A. (1977). The Welfare State within the Military. *Journal of Sociology and Social Welfare*, *4*(8), 494–521.

Meinhard, A., Moher, L., & Fitzrandolph, S. (2004). *Case Studies of Commercial Ventures in Nonprofit Organizations: Determining Probability for Success.* Centre for Voluntary Sector Studies Working Paper Series, Working Paper No. 27, Toronto: Ryerson University.

Melman, S. (1970). *Pentagon Capitalism: The Political Economy of War*. McGraw Hill.

Melman, S. (1985). *The Permanent War Economy*. Simon and Schuster.

Mercier, G. (2010). *Indonesia: The Dangerous Business Empire of The Military*. Available at: http://newsjunkiepost.com/2010/01/12/indonesia-the-dangerous-business-empire-of-the-military/

Moser, C. (1994). The Informal Sector Debate, Part 1: 1970-1983. In C. A. Rakowski (Ed.), *Contrapunto: The Informal Sector Debate in Latin America* (pp. 11–29). State University of New York Press.

Mowery, D., Nelson, R., Sampat, B., & Ziedonis, A. (1999). The effects of the Bayh-Dole Act on U.S. university research and technology transfer. In L. Branscomb, F. Kodama, & R. Florida (Eds.), *Industrializing knowledge* (pp. 269–306). MIT Press.

Mulvenon, J. (2001). *Soldiers of Fortune*. M.E. Sharpe.

Naguib, R. (2012). *Boycott them: Activists raise awareness about military's economic empire*. Retrieved from https://www.egyptindependent.com/boycott-them-activists-raise-awareness-about-militarys-economic-empire/

Olson, M. (2000). *Power and Prosperity*. Basic Books.

Pursell, C. (1972). *The military-industrial complex*. Harper & Row Publishers.

Redlich, F. (1964). The German Military Enterpriser and His Work Force': A Study in European Social and Economic History (2 Vols.). Wiesbaden.

Reuters. (2018). *From war room to boardroom. Military firms flourish in Sisi's Egypt*. Available at: https://www.reuters.com/investigates/special-report/egypt-economy-military/

Roland, A. (2009). The Military-Industrial Complex: lobby and trope. In A. J. Bacevich (Ed.), *The Long War: A New History of U.S. National Security Policy Since World War II* (pp. 335–370). Columbia University Press.

Rosen, S. J. (1973). *Testing the theory of the military-industrial complex*. Lexington Books.

Seibert, T. (2010). *Turkey's military has a stake in 60 companies*. Available at: https://www.thenational.ae/world/europe/turkey-s-military-has-a-stake-in-60-companies-1.557015

Shane, S. (2004). *Academic Entrepreneurship: University Spinoffs and Wealth Creation*. Edward Elgar Publishing Limited.

Siddiqa, A. (2007). *Military Inc.: Inside Pakistan's Military Economy*. Pluto Press.

Slaughter, S., & Leslie, L. (1997). *Academic Capitalism: Politics, Policies and the Entrepreneurial University*. Johns Hopkins University Press.

Slavnic, Z. (2010). Political economy of informalization. *European Societies, 12*(1), 3–23.

Smith, S. (2020). *Most Military and Government Jobs Pay Less Than the Private Sector*. Available at: https://www.thebalancecareers.com/historic-military-pay-raises-3354557

Sottile, J. (2017). *America's Military-Industrial Addiction*. Retrieved from: https://consortiumnews.com/2017/12/01/americas-military-industrial-addiction/

Stepan, A. (1971). *The Military in Politics: Changing patterns in Brazil*. Princeton University Press.

Stevenson, H., Roberts, M., & Grousback, H. (1985). *New Business Ventures and the Entrepreneur*. Richard D. Irwin.

Steyaert, C., & Hjorth, D. (Eds.). (2003). *New Movements in Entrepreneurship*. Edward Elgar.

Steyaert, C., & Hjorth, D. (Eds.). (2006). *Entrepreneurship as Social Change*. Edward Elgar.

Taiwo, O. (2013). Employment choice and mobility in multi-sector labor markets: Theoretical model and evidence from Ghana. *International Labour Review, 152*(3–4), 469–492.

Tang, A. (2015). *Business, military, government seize land for rubber in Myanmar: rights group*. Retrieved from: https://www.reuters.com/article/us-myanmar-rights-land/business-military-government-seize-land-for-rubber-in-myanmar-rights-group-idUSKBN0MM1N120150326

Thang, V. H. (2017). The restructuring and improved performance of military-run enterprises. *National Defense Journal*. Available at: http://tapchiqptd.vn/en/theory-and-practice/the-restructuring-and-improved-performance-of-militaryrun-enterprises/10726.html

The Millennium Report (2016). *Who Owns and Controls the Military-Industrial Complex?* Available at: http://themillenniumreport.com/2016/03/who-owns-and-controls-the-military-industrial-complex/

Tuoi tre. (2017). *Vietnam's deputy defense minister on why military must engage in business activities*. Available at: https://tuoitrenews.vn/business/41955/vietnam-deputy-defense-minister-on-why-military-must-engage-in-business-activities

van Crefeld, M. (1977). *Supplying War: Logistics from Wallenstein to Patton*. Cambridge University Press.

Vego, M. (2013). On Military Creativity. *Joint Forces Quarterly*, (70), 83-90.

VOA. (2017). *Military-linked Business Enterprises Dominate in Cuba*. Available at: https://www.voanews.com/americas/military-linked-business-enterprises-dominate-cuba

Walia, A. (2013). *Eisenhower and Kennedy Blow: The Whistle: The Military Industrial Complex*. Available at: https://www.collective-evolution.com/2013/02/15/eisenhower-and-kennedy-blow-the-whistle-the-military-industrial-complex/

Wilson, E. (2008). *The military millionaires who control Pakistan Inc*. Available at: https://www.spectator.co.uk/2008/01/the-military-millionaires-who-control-pakistan-inc/

Woo, C. Y., Cooper, A. C., & Dunkelberg, W. C. (1988). Entrepreneurial Typologies: Definitions and Implications. In Frontiers of Entrepreneurship Research. Babson College.

Year Book, S. I. P. R. I. (2008). *Armaments, Disarmaments and International Security*. Oxford University Press.

KEY TERMS AND DEFINITIONS

Extrepreneurs: Individuals who are selected/appointed to operate/manage commercial spin-off of a public or not-for-profit organization.

Extrepreneurship: A process in which a not-for-profit organization creates a separate for-profit organization in order to realize its commercial objectives.

Military Capital: A form of financial and non-financial resources available to military entrepreneurs to compete in the marketplace.

Military Controlled Industry: A representation of military-run business enterprises that exploit military capital for personal benefit of the military fraternity.

Military Entrepreneurship: A process of commercial enterprise engagement by the military establishment outside its statutory obligations. It can also involve business enterprise engaged by members of the military group (i.e., personnel serving, veterans, and families of military personnel).

Military Industrial Complex (MIC): An informal alliance between a country's military and the defense industry that equips it, and both are perceived as vested interest that has strong influence on the country's public policy formulation.

Chapter 3
Entrepreneurial Training for the Nigerian Armed Forces and Its Significance in Post-Retirement Era:
Opportunities and Challenges for Self Reliance

Usman Tar
https://orcid.org/0000-0002-2585-9052
Nigerian Defence Academy, Nigeria

Sharkdam Wapmuk
https://orcid.org/0000-0002-7553-8716
Nigerian Defence Academy, Nigeria

ABSTRACT

The chapter focuses on entrepreneurial training (ET) in the Nigerian armed forces and its significance for post-retirement era and discussed the opportunities and challenges for self-reliance. The chapter is qualitative and analytical in approach. It sourced data largely from secondary sources including reputable journals, books, book chapters, monographs, and records, and analysed through content analysis. Though it remains a much underemphasised area in most organisations, ET of the armed forces is the main fulcrum for their retirement preparation, if they are to achieve self-reliance as veterans. The chapter revealed that the retirement training provided for the armed forces differs from one country to the other.

DOI: 10.4018/978-1-7998-6655-8.ch003

Copyright © 2021, IGI Global. Copying or distributing in print or electronic forms without written permission of IGI Global is prohibited.

INTRODUCTION

The major argument put forward in this chapter is that Entrepreneurial Training (hereafter, ET) plays an instrumental role in preparing the armed forces for self-reliance in the post-retirement era. Globally, with increased emphasis being placed on ET for post-service life, the Nigerian armed forces cannot afford to be left out. The world over, retirees face the challenge of finding alternative means of livelihood, especially given the fact that pensions tend to be less than the previous remuneration while in active service. For instance, Hope, Oh and Mackin (2011) have argued that retired servicemen are more likely than other employed individuals to be self-employed because the retirement pension is lower than previous salary. Given this reality, the option for retiring members of the armed forces is to seek alternative employment or become self-employed. At the time of exit from service, retirees that have not zeroed down to any specific business venture they can undertake may find themselves confronted with the challenge of not knowing how to invest part of their gratuity or pension. Even when they identify a business of interest, lack of ET may hamper development of the businesses leading to its failure.

Veterans acquire vast experience in discipline, courage as well as tactical skills necessary for the post-retirement life. These skills acquired during active service could be useful in the post retirement era. Fallon (2020) who examined some businesses established by former members of the United States armed forces concluded that military veterans are well-suited to undertake entrepreneurship. He further stated that during their time in the Armed Forces, military service members gain a variety of skills that are essential to entrepreneurship. They learn to build and lead a team, solve problems quickly and execute under immense pressure. Many current and former military personnel choose to start their own businesses. In February 2017, the number of veterans in the USA stood at 20.7 million (Sobota, 2017). Veterans had majority ownership interests in 2.52 million businesses in 2012. Overall, it was estimated that 9.1 percent of all U.S. businesses were veteran-owned. These were in the areas of mining, quarrying, oil and gas group, accommodation and food services industry, finance and insurance, transportation and warehousing, construction, agriculture, forestry and fishing, utilities, professional, scientific, and technical services and manufacturing (Sobota, 2017). In a study on entrepreneurial aspirations and expectations of Sri Lanka military veterans, Perera, Premarathna and Welamedage (2017) found that returning to civilian life presents new opportunities and challenges for veterans. Many veterans look forward to life after the military but wonder what they are going to do with this new phase of their lives or whether they will be able to find suitable jobs. With respect to the Indian army, Vombatkere (2015) and Sofat (2016) argued that the continued neglect of veterans over the years is actually cost a country doubly. On one hand, valuable trained manpower is being lost and on the other, unengaged veterans are joining the ranks of the unemployed or under-employed, exacerbating the levels of economic challenges and discontent.

The Nigerian army, like other employers of labour, owe soldiers the duty to ensure that they are adequately prepared and equipped for post-retirement life by exposing them to new skills through ET long before they finally take their exit from the service. Unfortunately, ET programmes for employees are not given due attention not only within the army, but many employers, including the government. Given the opportunities and needed support by the Nigerian army, army personnel and veterans can develop into successful entrepreneurs. The Nigerian army has retired many of its veterans over the years, many of whom have also been trained. For example, it was reported that in preparation for their retirement, the Nigerian military provided ET for 41,000 veterans between 1945 and 2016 (Ango, 2017; Thisday, December 11, 2016). Given the number of army personnel that most have retired within the period of 71 years (1945-2016) vis-à-vis the number trained, it is evident that many must have retired without receiving the necessary ET and exposure to opportunities and challenges for self-reliance in post-retirement era.

Our major task in this chapter is to examine ET in the Nigerian armed forces and its significance for post-retirement era and to discuss the opportunities and challenges for self-reliance. The chapter is divided into sections beginning with the introduction and followed by conceptual understanding of entrepreneurship and entrepreneurship training. The third and fourth sections examine the retirement and entrepreneurship theories and transition from active military service to entrepreneurship, respectively. The fifth section discusses the opportunities for entrepreneurship training in Nigeria. The sixth section focuses on the challenges of entrepreneurship training and implications for self-reliance and concludes.

UNDERSTANDING THE CONCEPTS OF ENTREPRENEUR, ENTREPRENEURSHIP AND ENTREPRENEURSHIP TRAINING

In the 16th century, people who organized and managed military and exploration expeditions in France were called "entreprendre". The word entrepreneur originated from the French word "entreprendre" and the German word "unternehmen" and both terms mean to undertake (Vaziri, Hosseini & Jafari, 2014). The French Economist, Richard Cantillon, is said to have introduced the term entrepreneurship in the early 18th century. In his writings, Cantillon defines the entrepreneur as the agent who buys means of production at certain prices in order to combine them into a new product. He also defines entrepreneurship as self-employment of any sort where the entrepreneur is the bearer of uncertainty and risk (Vaziri, Hosseini & Jafari, 2014). Another the French economist, Jean Baptiste Say (1824) defined the entrepreneur as someone who shifts economic resources out of an area of lower to an area of higher productivity and greater yield. He added to Cantillon's definition by including the idea that an entrepreneur is one who brings other people together in order to build a single productive organization. However, since coining the terms entrepreneur and entrepreneurship, almost two hundred years ago, there has been lack of consensus over the definition of entrepreneur and entrepreneurship.

Scholars have provided diverse definitions of an entrepreneur and entrepreneurship. Meredith (1983) stated that an entrepreneur is a person who possesses the ability to recognize and evaluate business opportunities, assemble the necessary resources to take advantage of them and take appropriate action to succeed. In the opinion of Hisrich, Peters and Shepherd (2017) an entrepreneur is a person who acts on what he/she believes is an opportunity by initiating a business, organizes, controls, and combines other factors of production and directing the processes of production. While formal education such as in areas of finance, strategic planning, marketing and distribution, and management. remains important for an entrepreneur, experiences have shown that they are not the dominant criteria. School dropouts such as Andrew Carnegie, William Durant, Henry Ford, and William Lear have demonstrated that success in entrepreneurship goes beyond formal education (Hisrich, Peters & Shepherd, 2017). The ability to communicate clearly with both the written and the spoken word is also important in any entrepreneurial activity.

Steinfioff and Burgers (1993) defines entrepreneurship as "the ability to develop a new venture or apply a new approach to an old business". The new approach can be in terms of marketing, packaging or production by way of using resources in a new way. Suleiman (2006, p.6) is of the view that entrepreneurship is "the willingness and ability of an individual to seek for investment opportunities to establish and run an enterprise successfully". These points have also been reflected in the definitions provided by some other scholars. According to Stevenson and Gumpets (2002) entrepreneurship is a process in which individuals pursue opportunities, fulfilling needs and wants through innovation together with the attendant risk. Also, as noted by Salami (2011), entrepreneurship is a process of carefully determined and analysing unmet needs through creatively satisfying those needs by bearing the related risks. Another perspective presented by Alarape (2008) is that entrepreneurship is the process of being self-employed by owning a small business, and its management for growth. We can deduce from these definitions that entrepreneurship is a valuable strategy for creating jobs and improving livelihood and economic self-reliance for not only retirees, but most especially young people. We can deduce from these definitions that certain features of entrepreneurship, which are necessary for a successful self-reliant business. These features include: identification of unmet needs and wants, idea conceptualisation, creativity and innovation, risk-taking, strategic thinking, ability to organise and coordinate resources, team spirit, funding and leadership

(Akinnawo, 2013). Another important ingredient for successful entrepreneurship is the willingness to take responsibility and sensing opportunities, which must be reconceptualised by starting in a new form.

Njorge and Guthunga (2013) defined training as an intended and ordered effort to develop knowledge or modify existing knowledge and skills, through learning experience to accomplish performance in specific activities or series of activities. According to Isaac, Visser, Fredrick and Brijlal (2000), entrepreneurship training is the purposeful intervention by a trainer in the life of the trainee to learn to survive in the world of business. Putta (2014) views ET as a practical process where employees could receive knowledge through experiencing entrepreneurial process, reflecting on the lesson learned, thinking through the learning process, and acting upon the lesson learned. The essential set of 21st century entrepreneurship skills may include capabilities for analytical problem solving, innovation and creativity, self-direction and initiative, flexibility and adaptability, critical thinking, and communication and collaboration skills. The European Union (2002) notes that the purpose of entrepreneurship training is to raise awareness for self-employment as a career option, promoting the development of personal qualities that are relevant to entrepreneurship; and providing the technical and business skills that are needed to start a new venture.

The purpose of ET is to make employees attain information on entrepreneurship, recognize and encourage entrepreneurship skills (Putta, 2014). The aim is also to attain entrepreneurship information on the use of techniques, analyse business situations and to develop action plans for business, develop empathy and maintaining of entrepreneurship, mature in attitude for the uncertainty and change, and encourage new enterprises that could lead to job creation for future entrepreneurs (Putta, 2014). It is expected to lead to the acquisition of skills, creativity, innovation, competencies, confidence, drive, courage in order to create employment for self and others. It empowers individuals to create real wealth through the establishment of small or micro business thereby advancing the cause of development in the country. In essence, the objective of entrepreneurship training is to empower the individuals to start their own business or to be self-reliant thereby becoming a job or wealth creator and consequently advancing the cause of economic growth of the country. The major challenges that the provision of ET poses for the employees is the non-utilisation of the entrepreneurial skills acquired on the job. Over the years, employees attend several entrepreneurial skills courses during employment some of the knowledge acquired a lost before retirement. Secondly, employees are not able to differentiate between a general business idea and opportunity (Reeuwijk, de Wind, Westerman, Ybema, van der Beek, & Geuskens, 2013). Effective entrepreneurship training would ensure that the employees' interest is represented; identify employees' passion toward learning needs, design training to suit the learning needs, delivers training according to design, and evaluate training through feedback and ability to transfer such training to other employees (Nyambura, 2014).

The Resource-Based Dynamic Theory and its Relevance for Post-Retirement Entrepreneurial Engagements of the Military

The chapter adopts the resource-based dynamic theory on retirement and entrepreneurship proposed by Hobfoll (2002) and adjusted by Wang and colleagues (2011). Hobfoll (2002) defined resources as a person's total capability to accomplish his/her valued needs and goals. He further noted that the conditions of life after retirement greatly depend upon an individual's access to resources valued by him/her. The central premise of the resource-based dynamic theory is that levels and changes in well-being in the retirement transition are directly influenced by the individual's access to resources. Inspired by Hobfoll's conservation of resources theory, Wang et al. (2011) classified various forms of personal resources into six types. These include: physical (illness, physical strength), financial (savings, pension), social (social support, social network), emotional (mood, affectivity), cognitive (perceived control, memory ability, processing speed), and motivational resources (adaptability and flexibility in goal pursuit).

According to the resource-based dynamic theory, the quality of retirement adjustment varies by the amount of retirement resources and overall changes in total resources during the retirement transition. In particular, three possible patterns of adjustment outcomes exist: (1) Retirees will maintain their well-being if their total resources do not change significantly after retirement. This implies that if retirees encounter a decline in their resources, they will experience poor adjustment and psychological distress. Secondly, if retirees gain more resources after retirement, especially if they are engaged in some form of productive venture, they will demonstrate positive adjustment to retirement (Wang et al. 2011). Wang and colleagues (2011) argue that retirement is a longitudinal dynamic process in which individual well-being is influenced by available resources and changes in these resources over time. The theory is proposed as an integrative theoretical framework suitable for the study of retirement and venture into entrepreneurship as well as the underlying mechanisms through which training impacts on retirement.

Factors on various levels, including individual, household, job, organizational, and macro level variables are expected to influence the availability of and changes in individual resources, which are described as the driving mechanism behind changes in well-being. Emotional, motivational, social, physical, cognitive, and financial resources are suggested to be of particular importance in this process. Resources are described as means or assets that can be used to cope with challenges associated with the transition. Resources are assumed to be key elements because they define the conditions of retirement and influence what people are able to do physically and what they can afford financially in retirement. For instance, individuals with limited financial resources and poor health may be constrained in the maintenance of their pre-retirement lifestyle and the possibilities to take up new activities in retirement. More resources are expected to lead to fewer adjustment problems and greater well-being (Wang et al., 2011). The applicability of the resource-based dynamic theory for studying the retirement adjustment process and entrepreneurship has received considerable support in scholarly studies (Barbosa, Monteiro, & Murta, 2016, Earl, Gerrans, & Halim, 2015; Muratore & Earl, 2015; Muratore, Earl, & Collins, 2014; Wang et al., 2011).

In terms of relevance and applicability of the theory for the study on post-retirement entrepreneurial engagements of the military it can be deduced from the works of Hobfoll (2002) and Wang and colleagues (2011) that the presence of resources will create opportunities; while the absence can restrict the intentions of an individual to opt for the path of entrepreneurship. The resources include one's access to financial, health, knowledge, and household resources. Salaries often constitute the main financial resource during the pre-retirement life. In post-retirement life, this is substituted by income from savings, pension or earning from post-retirement job. A retiree with good health condition, and good family condition, is likely to make use of his/her time and energy in a career after retirement (Wang et al., 2008). Resources held by an individual can be viewed as the knowledge derive from entrepreneurship training during service, which is a key factor in determining his/her choices for entrepreneurship in after retirement. In general, individuals with greater access to training have higher chance/opportunities in post-retirement era (Lytle, Foley, & Cotter, 2015). The resource theory of retirement provides valuable insights on resources that can be availed and deployed for post-retirement entrepreneurship. On a whole, the theory is deployed to explain the nexus between entrepreneurship training for the armed forces and post-retirement engagements, including the realities of opportunities and challenges for the retiring military personnel in Nigeria.

Transition From Active Military Service to Entrepreneurship

Retirement is like any transition that must be seen in the context of individual life's journey. It is a natural process of self-renewal and a process of disorientation and reorientation that marks the individual turning point in the path of growth. The life of military personnel during the service and after the service is not the same. While some continue to accept life as it is with meager income from pension allowance, some search for new jobs and others tend to engage in entrepreneurial businesses to generate more income for themselves and for their families. According to Ango (2017) old workers are influenced by both pull and push factors to engage in post-career entrepreneurship. The push factors include the prospects of collecting lower wages, where jobs are available, as well as financial necessity. On the other hand, the pull factors are considerations that self-employment provides opportunity for flexible working hours; provide job autonomy and independence as well as greater opportunities for learning and development.

It has been argued by Smaliukiene (2013) that military personnel retire as much as twenty years earlier that other civilian counterparts in Europe and the United States of America (USA). Henning (2011) argued that military personnel are likely to retire 15-20 years earlier in the US, one in seven veterans is self-employed or a small business owner. This is different from the perspective of Europe that encourages the reintegration of ex-military personnel into civil life through employment in public sector or big businesses rather than starting self-owned business. Comparative practices in transition to retirement for the military reveal two best practices globally. They are either prepared towards seeking to bridge employment or in the alternative, to train them to learn how to start a new business - entrepreneurship training. Brown and Gross (2011) were of the opinion that there is a need to understand the peculiar requirement of individuals and category of people before preparing them either for bridging employment or entrepreneurship. This is necessary to avoid failure that may result in a fruitless entrepreneurship experience, accompanied with loss of self-confidence and life's savings that may have been ploughed into the venture.

The reality is that there is no one size fit all yardstick to determine who should go for bridging employment or become an entrepreneur. Even so, De la Porte and Jacobsson (2012) have noted that there is he need to assess the interests and special skills in order to equip people with necessary skills to accommodate the change in their circumstances and provide supportive services to develop their entrepreneurial activities. This is necessary because every service man is unique and his life might have been shaped by institutional factors such as previous work experiences, the rank attained, communicability, and temperament, differences in individual personality and characteristics and flexibility. A study carried out by Smaliuekiene (2013) on *Entrepreneurship Opportunities after Military Career; Practice in Central and Eastern Versus Western Europe*, revealed the varied practices on transition from military service to retirement in the different European countries examined. Smaliuekiene (2013) divided European countries into four groups. Group one consisted of Lithuania, Great Britain, Croatia, France, Ireland, Romania, Poland and Germany. The common characteristics of these countries are that servicemen go into early retirement and are subjected to measures of reintegration into labour market or entrepreneurship and coordinated by an institution of the National Defence. For instance, in both Britain and France, the process of reintegration into civilian life is mainly focused on making the veteran employable or guiding them to pursue a self-reliant employment option. The training is usually provided by a contractor – a private company that would have won a public tender. Before this, each serviceman is first expected to have a talk with his/her supervisor who provides general guidance on the process of the training for reintegration into society in the post retirement era. The second group consist of Belgium, and Germany. In Belgium, the difference between retirement age for servicemen and the full retirement age is 5 years and difference between the pension and previous salary is 15 per cent. Integration programme is available for only those who leave the service voluntarily at an early age of 40 to 45 and pension is usually not paid until a particular age such as 60. The third group of countries include Estonia, Slovakia, Latvia and Finland, all of which have no special reintegration plans for service men going into retirement. According to Smaliuekiene (2013), the servicemen are expected to key into the national or local entrepreneurship development programmes like other citizens of the countries. The fourth categories of countries examined by Smaliuekiene (2013) are Denmark, Luxemburg and the Netherlands. These countries do not subject servicemen to early retirement or reintegration programmes. Persons who retire earlier voluntarily can apply for support to national programmes for entrepreneurial skills development like other citizens.

On a whole, our examination of the transition from active military service to entrepreneurship shows that in every part of the world, military retirees tend to look for economic activities to support their pensions. The comparative experience of countries in Europe and USA also shows that while some countries have designed transition programmes including entrepreneurship trainings for servicemen for retirement, others expect them to key into the local, national or regional programmes like other citizens. It is against this backdrop that we proceed to examine entrepreneurship training for the military and opportunities for self-reliance in Nigeria

Entrepreneurship Training for the Nigerian Military

Generally, post-retirement engagements of the military in Nigeria reveals varied experiences. Yusuf and Minai (2016) are of the opinion that over the years, retired military personnel in Nigeria have charted various career paths and the successful ones are often being publicised by the media. For instance, many retired top ranking military personnel are involved in various businesses, spreading across oil and gas, manufacturing, constructions, quarries, mechanized agriculture, poultry, educational services, and small-scale businesses among others. However, some have gone through psychological, sociological and economic challenges upon retirement from service as a result of joblessness, rejection and social stigmatization from the society (Yusuf & Minai, 2016). Adjusting to a new life upon retirement presents huge challenges, particularly with regard to the individual's financial and economic condition. The situation that some veterans find themselves is not because of lack of plan for training for retirement in the Nigerian military, but also resource based. Ango (2017) rightly noted that the Nigerian Armed forces have a plan for training of retiring soldiers. It was reported in Thisday newspapers (2016), that the first training for retiring soldiers was done as far back as 1945 and by 2016, the army had trained 41,000 personnel in various vocational training courses. The vocational and ET are in areas such as mechanized farming, soap making, shoe and leather works, foundry, welding, poultry, furniture making among other skills. In addition, years of serving in the Nigeria military affords the individual military personnel, valuable opportunities to acquire professional and trade qualifications, that are provided for them. It would be noted that while the Nigerian army has plans for the training of its personnel for retirement, it would appear that not many have benefited from opportunity between 1945 and 2016. The original intention was to have the beneficiaries seamlessly adjust to post-retirement life and to have them adapt to changes of retirement. Most of the post-retirement programmes were anchored by the Nigerian Armed Forces Resettlement Centre (NAFRC).

The NAFRC was established as a world class training institution capable of repositioning ex-service men and women to cope with challenges of service in their post service life. The institution has been providing quality training, geared towards preparing Nigerian Armed Forces personnel to face the challenges of re-integrating into civil life. The history of ET for the military dates back to the post-World War II period. Following the end of World War II, the British colonial government under the auspices of the West African Frontier Force, (WAFF) established 2 Vocational Resettlement Centres in Nigeria and Ghana. The Centres were charged with the responsibility of imparting skills relevant to the resettlement needs of the colonial West African Ex-Servicemen. Subsequently the school was later renamed Nigerian Armed Forces Resettlement Centre aimed at giving vocational skills to retirees. Ango (2017) further notes that while the training was limited to soldiers, not all were involved. He specifically noted that commissioned officers may not have been involved. Recently, attempts have been made to expand the scope of the entrepreneurship training to including retiring commissioned officers. This is to be achieved through partnership with some Non-Governmental Organisations (NGOs) and some universities, polytechnics and training institutions in the country.

As noted in the case of Europe and America, ET of the military is not only done by the military institutions alone. Local, national and regional entrepreneurship training intuitions, private institutions and contractors are involved to ensure wide coverage of such trainings. Odia and Odia (2013) submitted that the Federal Government of Nigeria issued a directive through the National University Commission (NUC) in 2000 that all universities in Nigeria should develop a course on entrepreneurship development. This was to ensure that graduates improve on their capacity to develop innovative thought and develop entrepreneurial mind-sets for self-reliant employment. The reality is that this objective is far from being realised as most universities in Nigeria are far behind in the area of development of entrepreneurship education (Odia & Odia, 2013). That notwithstanding, the Federal government of Nigeria began establishing government agencies and departments for promotion of entrepreneurship activities since the 1960 (Odia & Odia, 2013). According to Aikhuomogbe (2016), examples include Entrepreneurship Development Center (EDC), Center for Management Development (CMD), and National Directorate of Employment (NDC). Other similar organization established for entrepreneurship promotion in Nigeria are the Nigeria Industrial Development Bank (NIDB), Nigerian University Commission (NUC), Nigeria Youth Service Corps (NYSC), National Economic Empowerment and Development Strategy (NEEDS), National Open Apprenticeship Scheme (NOAS), Small and Medium Enterprise Development Association of Nigeria (SMEDAN), and the Small and Medium Enterprises Equity Investment Scheme (SMEEIS). The establishment of SMEDAN is the promotion of Micro, Small and Medium Enterprises (MSMEs) sector in Nigeria toward the creation of employment and national development (Odia & Odia, 2013). The Federal Government of Nigeria in 2012, initiated programs that are aimed at developing and promoting entrepreneurship activities such as the Subsidy Reinvestment and Empowerment Program (SURE-P), the Youth Entrepreneur (YE), the Youth Enterprise with Innovation in Nigeria (YouWIN), and the Graduate Internship Scheme (GIS) programs (Aikhuomogbe, 2016; Odia & Odia, 2013). Despite the efforts committed to promoting entrepreneurship in Nigeria by the government, several underlying factors such as lack of an enabling environment, poor funding and resource base, corruption, poor infrastructure and others continue to undermine the success of these initiatives aimed at promoting entrepreneurship development in Nigeria.

Business Opportunities for Training the Nigerian Military for Self-Reliance in Post Retirement

One of the major problems that would be retired military entrepreneurs face in the course of developing a self-reliant business is to identify and select business which he is able to operate successfully. Once this is done, a major hurdle has been scaled. While this may appear to be simple, it is often not, however, doable. Given the focus of this chapter on ET of the Nigerian military for post-retirement era, our attention here shall be on small and micro businesses that can be undertaken by emerging military entrepreneurs. The opportunities for small and medium businesses are legion especially in today's globalised world. However, in the context of Nigeria, and for analytical purposes, we have classified the wide range of small and medium scale businesses into four sectors namely, agricultural and agro-allied, manufacturing, services/commercial ventures and private security outfits.

Agriculture and Agro-Allied Businesses

The agricultural sector remains the backbone of all countries of the world. It ensures the supply of food and raw materials to the industries. Agro-Allied industries or Agro-based industries are industries whose primary raw materials are agricultural products. Given the importance of the agricultural and agro-allied sector, it has huge opportunity for self-reliant work for retired soldiers (Yusuf & Minai, 2016). Opportunities in these areas include crop production, fish farming, dairy farming, poultry, piggery, sheep fattening, goat fattening, cow fattening, grass-cutter farming, yam flour, plantain flour, cassava flour, gari processing, ginger powder, condiments and spices, cassava chips, plantain chips, and many others (Akinnawo, 2013). Beyond requiring modest capital to startup, most of the identified SME opportunities have huge markets at various levels in the country. Yam flour, gari, and cassava flour are in high demand as is chicken, which until recently was still being smuggled into the country through the porous borders.

Small-Scale Manufacturing Businesses

Retired military entrepreneurs also have huge opportunities to tap from setting up businesses in small manufacturing operations. Because small manufacturers are able to offer more than their larger counterparts, they are in high demand globally. This is largely because of their flexibility and availability. A smaller manufacturer tends to be personally involved in the production process, and tailor production to meet customers' needs and specifications. These manufacturers use their size to their advantage to offer their customers what big manufacturers may not be able to provide on time. Some of the opportunities in this area that fit the Nigerian context include: soap and detergent production, cosmetics production, clothes and garment production, school chalk, raincoat, shower curtains and caps, envelops, umbrellas, baking, ice cream, plastic production, bottled and sachet water production, blocks and brick production, carpentry and woodwork productions (Crampton, 2020). Others include recycling waste materials to wealth, jewelry production, towel manufacturing, toothpick, charcoal, insecticides, ice blocks, leather works (shoes, bags, wallets etc), bed linen, label manufacturing, amongst others (Akinnawo, 2013).

Small-scale manufacturing businesses provide opportunities for entrepreneurs with limited capital. Setting up these businesses identified above require not only less resource base, but also less investment in technology and machines when compared to large scale enterprises. Therefore, retired military intended entrepreneurs can start small-scale manufacturing businesses easily and succeed. Japan, which was devastated by the World War II, became a major economic power because of many small entrepreneurs, who contributed greatly to the nation's development. Countries like India, China, India, Singapore, Malaysia and other countries have taken advantages of small manufacturing to boost domestic production and exports, which have generated huge economic benefits for these countries.

Services/Commercial Business Ventures

Another area with huge opportunities for retired military entrepreneurs requiring modest resource base is that of services/ commercial ventures. These are enterprise that provides work performed in an expert manner by an individual or team for the benefit of its customers. The typical service business provides intangible products, such as, consulting, cleaning, landscaping, education, treatment, and transportation services, amongst others. The major advantage for retired soldiers in the service-based businesses is that it will allow them the freedom to leverage their previous skills and earn a profit (Smaliukiene, 2013). Examples of areas for establishing service business in Nigeria include laundry services, cleaning services, fumigation and pest control services, electrical and electronics business, information and communication technology related services (web designing and development services, computer schools, sale computer and accessories) sale of phones and accessories. Others include extra-mural classes, horticulture and landscaping services, car wash services, modern restaurants, plumbing, day care and old people's homes, and so many others.

Beyond the challenges of pricing, steep competition and marketing of the service business, they offer several advantages. A military retiree is likely to be confronted with the reality that developing a physical business and selling a physical product takes time, money and energy (Caramela, November 27, 2017). Even though running a service business also requires packaging, marketing and time, the main product to market in a service-based business is the business owner and his skills. Hence, there are little to no startup, overhead or production costs. The business owner has to devote much time to marketing himself and the services he/she can render.

Private Security Outfits, Guards Companies and Security Consultancy Services

Retired military entrepreneurs also have opportunities for establishing businesses in the areas of private security, guards companies and security consultancy services. The U.S. Bureau of Labour viewed Private Security Outfits (PSO) as private security companies primarily engaged in providing private guards and patrol services (Sobota, 2017). In Nigeria, the Private Security Act defined private security outfits as a private guard company which provides a wide range of guard-ship responsible for private and corporate entities. According Esuong (2013) private security outfits are "business corporations, which provide unarmed security services and expertise to private and public clients whose objective is profit oriented. Private security outfits, guard companies and security consultancy firms provide security related services on demand.

It has been argued that the increasing complexity of security threats in Nigeria makes it difficult for the security forces to effectively address the security challenges in Nigeria at this time. Against this backdrop, by establishing security outfits as businesses, the experiences of the retired military could be brought to bear in containing the vast security threats confronting Nigeria. The practice of establishing private security companies, guard companies, and security consultancies is neither new nor peculiar to Nigeria. Phillips (2019) observed that several countries including the United States, Britain, France, and South Africa, amongst others operating private security companies engage the services of veterans in these countries. The private security and guard companies in Nigeria provide services in several areas such as personal protection, special investigations, escort service, maritime security service, arrest of culprits, giving of information to state security actors, prevention of crime through oral strategies and the prevention of unauthorized activities or entry to restricted areas, traffic regulations, access control, fire and prevention and detection of theft (Dambazau, 2011; Esuong, 2013; Phillips, 2019). Major companies such as banks, insurance companies, manufacturing companies, hospitals, shops, universities, oil firms, private schools, churches and other cooperate bodies and private individuals engage the services of the private security, guard companies and security consultancy outfits.

Challenges of Entrepreneurship for Retired Military Personnel and Assistance Towards Self-Reliance

Being members of a society, retired military personnel are not immune to challenges of entrepreneurship. Starting a small business may appear simple in theory, but in practice this may be a challenging task. It is, therefore, not surprising that many businesses that start up on a very promising note fail within a very limited time due to number of reasons. These include, but not limited to poor conceptualisation of the business, lack of business plan to guide operations of the business; lack of separation between personal and business account, poor records and accounts keeping; poor management; inadequate funding including working capital; lack of staff commitment and loyalty; lack of knowledge about the market and inability to deal with competitors; and poor customer services (Akinnawo, 2013). Veterans who may locate their businesses in rural areas are likely to be confronted with even broader challenges such as distance from markets and services, capital availability, absence of basic infrastructure, such as electricity, water supply, and absence of other entrepreneurs (Sobota, 2017). The lack of an enabling environment for the smooth take-off for the budding veteran entrepreneur may result in early business collapse.

Every country has its own peculiar challenges in its business environment. The Nigerian business environment is faced with numerous challenges which budding veteran entrepreneurs, particularly those with interest in micro and small-scale enterprises must adapt to if they have to start and sustain a successful business in the country. According to the 2011 World Bank Investment Climate Assessment report, the major challenges include electricity, taxation, funding. Others include transportation, collapse infrastructure, corruption, crime and insecurity, problem of access to land and frequent changes of business laws and regulations. In order to ensure that budding veteran entrepreneurs are able to establish and run successful business in the post retirement period and achieve self-reliance, ET should also be accompanied with support for entrepreneurs even in the post retirement period (Sobota, 2017).

Assistance for emerging entrepreneurs from the crop of retired military personnel could be in forms of stimulatory assistance, support assistance, and sustaining assistance (Akinnawo, 2013). Stimulatory assistance motivates retired military personnel to take self-employment as a career option. They include entrepreneurship education, publicity on entrepreneurial activities, creating entrepreneurial forum, and demonstration of self-reliant projects. Support assistance helps retired military personnel to set up and run their businesses successfully. Such assistance includes directing them to areas of finance, access to land, provision of electricity, getting licences, permits, tax relief and subsidies for machines for all military retirees setting up business ventures. Support assistance require the military getting the assistance of government in this regard. The sustaining assistance includes help to ensure that retired military entrepreneurs sustain their businesses against challenges of actual business operation. This requires training on expanding marketing, getting additional funding, negotiating and deferring loans payments and strategies for navigating the changes in policy regimes as they concern the business. While challenges of entrepreneurship cannot be wished away, it is necessary to train retiring military personnel, not only to identify and take advantage of opportunities for establishing businesses for self-reliance, but also to navigate challenges that could affect the sustainability the business.

CONCLUDING REMARKS

There is no denying the fact that ET is necessary in preparing the armed forces for self-reliance in the post-retirement era. We have noted in the chapter that the retirement training provided for the armed forces differs from one country to the other. They are either prepared towards seeking to bridge employment or in the alternative, to train them to learn how to start a new business. The chapter also sought to clarify the concepts of entrepreneur, entrepreneurship and entrepreneurship training. The resource-based dynamic theory was adopted in analyzing the ET and post retirement engagement of the military. On a whole, a major lesson to be derived from juxtaposing the theory and realities discern from literature is that while major factors such as resources various forms of resources - physical, financial, social, emotional, and motivational, amongst others are critical for intended entrepreneurs in among retired military personnel especially if they are to be self-reliant. Other critical factors include infrastructure, investment opportunities, marketing opportunities, availability of market and technology. Furthermore, for retried military personnel to succeed as entrepreneurs, training of the armed forces is the main fulcrum for their retirement preparation. Our analysis reveals that there is a need to understand the peculiar requirement of each individual and category of people before preparing them either for bridging employment or entrepreneurship.

The Nigerian Armed forces have been training retiring soldiers since 1945 and several personnel have been trained over the years. The entrepreneurship trainings afford the individual military personnel valuable opportunities to acquire business skills and beneficiaries to adjust to post-retirement life. Despite the challenges that characterise the business environment in Nigeria, there are vast business opportunities, which ET can focus on for the Nigerian military for self-reliance in post-retirement. The opportunities examined in this chapter in the areas of agricultural and agro-allied businesses, small-scale manufacturing businesses, services/commercial businesses ventures, and, private security outfits and guards companies and security consultancy services, are in no way exhaustive. There is a plethora of entrepreneurship opportunities for the veterans, which entrepreneurship training will go a long way in preparing them to take advantage of. As demonstrated in the case of the US, where many former military personnel choose to start their own businesses, and had majority ownership interests in 2.52 million businesses in 2012, it is evident that military veterans are well-suited to undertake entrepreneurship. It is evident that given the size of the armed forces, the military establishment alone, may not be able to cover the entrepreneurship training of a large number of personnel before their retirement. Our comparative examination of countries comparative revealed that some countries use private contractors that would have won a public tender for the training programmes. Also, the scope of the entrepreneurship training could be expanded through partnership with some Non-Governmental Organisations (NGOs) and universities, polytechnics, and reputable training institutions in the country.

REFERENCES

Adams, G. A., & Beehr, T. A. (Eds.), *Retirement: Reasons, processes, and results.* Springer.

Aikhuomogbe, S. O. (2016). *Preparing employees for entrepreneurship in retirement: A case study* (Doctoral Dissertation submitted to Walden University). Retrieved on 18 May, 2020 from https://scholarworks.waldenu.edu/cgi/viewcontent.cgi?article =4017&context=dissertations

Ajzen, I. (1991). The theory of planned behavior. *Organizational Behavior and Human Decision Processes, 50*(2), 179–211. doi:10.1016/0749-5978(91)90020-T

Akinnawo, T. (2013). *Framework and guidelines for entrepreneurship development as a sustainable employment generation strategy in Nigeria.* African Consulting Professionals Ltd.

Alarabe, A. (2008). On the road to institutionalising entrepreneurship education in Nigerian universities. *International Journal of Management Education, 7*(2), 23-45.

Ango, Y. I. (2017). Entrepreneurship as an option for Nigerian retiring soldiers: A global review and lessons. In A. M. Ashafa & H. Jibrin (Eds.), *The Nigerian army in a democracy since 1999: A professional demonstration of military subordination to civil authority: Essays in honour of Lt. Gen. T.Y. Burutai* (pp. 615–625). Pyla-Mak Services Ltd.

Ashforth, B. E., Kreiner, G. E., & Fugate, M. (2000). All in a day's work: Boundaries and micro role transitions. *Academy of Management Review, 25*(3), 472–491. doi:10.5465/amr.2000.3363315

Atchley, R. C. (1989). A continuity theory of normal aging. *The Gerontologist, 29*(2), 183–190. doi:10.1093/geront/29.2.183 PMID:2519525

Barbosa, L. M., Monteiro, B., & Murta, S. G. (2016). Retirement adjustment predictors – a systematic review. *Work, Aging and Retirement, 2*(2), 1–19. doi:10.1093/workar/waw008

Barnes-Farrell, J. L. (2003). Beyond health and wealth: attitudinal and other influences on retirement decision-making. In G. Adams & T. Beehr (Eds.), *Retirement: Reasons, processes, and results* (pp. 159–187). Springer.

Beach, L. R., & Frederickson, J. R. (1989). Image theory: An alternative description of audit decision. *Accounting, Organizations and Society*, *14*(1-2), 101–112. doi:10.1016/0361-3682(89)90036-6

Becker, K., Fleming, J., & Keijsers, W. (2012). E-learning: Ageing workforce versus technology-savvy generation. *Education + Training*, *54*(5), 385–400. doi:10.1108/00400911211244687

Beehr, T. A. (1986). The process of retirement: A review and recommendations for future investigation. *Personnel Psychology*, *39*(1), 31–55. doi:10.1111/j.1744-6570.1986.tb00573.x

Caplan, R. D. (1987, December). Person-environment fit theory and organizations: Commensurate dimensions, time perspectives, and mechanisms. *Journal of Vocational Behavior*, *31*(3), 248–267. doi:10.1016/0001-8791(87)90042-X

Caramela, S. (2017, November 27). *How to start a service-based business*. Retrieved on 18th May, 2020 from https://www.businessnewsdaily.com/8180-start-service-based-business.html

Cooper, A. D., & Beehr, T. A. (2015). Retirement and continuity theory. In N. Pachana (Ed.), *Encyclopedia of Geropsychology*. Springer. doi:10.1007/978-981-287-080-3_48-1

Crampton, N. (2019, August 1). *300 examples of business ideas to help you start a successful business*. Retrieved on 18 May, 2020 from https://www.entrepreneur.com/article/337316

Crampton, N. (2020). *Examples of manufacturing business ideas*. Retrieved on 18 May, 2020 from https://www.entrepreneur.com/article/335090

Cumming, E., Dean, L. R., Newell, D. S., & McCaffrey, I. (1960). Disengagement: A tentative theory of aging. *Sociometry*, *23*(1), 23–35. doi:10.2307/2786135

Dambazau, A. B. (2011). *Criminology and criminal justice*. Spectrum Books Ltd.

David, C., & McClelland, D. C. (1961). *The achieving society*. Van Nostrand Company.

Drucker, P. F. (1985). *Innovation and entrepreneurship*. Harper & Row Publishers.

Earl, J. K., Gerrans, P., & Halim, V. A. (2015). Active and adjusted: Investigating the contribution of leisure, health and psychosocial factors to retirement adjustment. *Leisure Sciences*, *37*, 354–372.

Elder, G. H. Jr. (1995). The life course paradigm: Social change and individual development. In P. Moen, G. H. Elder Jr, & K. Lüscher (Eds.), *Examining lives in context: Perspectives on the ecology of human development* (pp. 101–139). Springer.

Esuong, P. J. (2013). *Intelligent investigation*. Willing Rose and Appleseed Publishing Company.

European Union. (2002). *Final report of the expert group "best procedure" project on education and training for entrepreneurship*. Brussels: European Commission.

Fallon, N. (2020). *12 veteran-owned businesses making it big*. Retrieved on 18 May, 2020 from https://www.uschamber.com/co/good-company/growth-studio/veteran-owned-small-businesses

Feldman, D. C. (1994). The decision to retire early: A review and conceptualization. *Academy of Management Review*, *19*, 285–311.

Greller, M. M., & Stroh, L. K. (2003). Extending work lives: are current approaches tools or talismans? In G. A. Adams & T. A. Beehr (Eds.), *Retirement: Reasons, processes, and results* (pp. 115–135). Springer.

Gustman, A. L., & Steinmeier, T. L. (1986). A Structural Retirement Model. *Econometrica*, *54*(3), 555–584.

Hagen, E. E. (1956). *The process of economic development (A revision of elements in a theory of economic development)*. Center for International Studies.

Hisrich, R. D., Peters, M. P., & Shepherd, D. A. (2017). *Entrepreneurship* (10th ed.). McGraw-Hill Education.

Hobfoll, S. E. (2002). Social and psychological resources and adaptation. *Review of General Psychology*, *6*(4), 307–324.

Hope, J. B., Oh, B., & Mackin, P. C. (2011). *Factors affecting entrepreneurship among veterans*. SAG Corporation.

Isaac, E., Visser, K. J., Frederick, C., & Brijlal, P. (2007). Entrepreneurship education and training at the further education and training (FET) level in South Africa. *South African Journal of Education*, *27*, 613–629.

Kim, J. E., & Moen, P. (2002). Retirement transitions, gender, and psychological well-being a life-course: Ecological model. *The Journals of Gerontology. Series B, Psychological Sciences and Social Sciences*, *57*(3), 212–222. PMID:11983732

Landstrom, H. (1998). The roots of entrepreneurship research. *Conference Proceedings*.

Lytle, M. C., Foley, P. F., & Cotter, E. W. (2015). Career and retirement theories: Relevance for older workers across cultures. *Journal of Career Development*, *42*(3), 185–198. PMID:26101455

Meredith, O. (1983). *The practice of entrepreneurship*. International Labour Office.

Muratore, A. M., & Earl, J. K. (2015). Improving retirement outcomes: The role of resources, pre-retirement planning and transition characteristics. *Ageing and Society*, *35*, 2100–2140.

Muratore, A. M., Earl, J. K., & Collins, C. G. (2014). Understanding heterogeneity in adaptation to retirement: A growth mixture modeling approach. *International Journal of Aging & Human Development*, *79*, 131–156. PMID:25536703

Nigerian Finder. (2020, May 18). *100 small scale businesses ideas in Nigeria*. Retrieved from https://nigerianfinder.com/small-scale-business-ideas-in-nigeria/

Njorge, C. W., & Guthunga, J. M. (2013). The effect of entrepreneurial education and training of small and medium size enterprises in Githungari District-Kenya. *International Journal of Education and Research*, *1*(8), 1–22.

Nyambura, J. N. (2014). An analysis of entrepreneurship aspects of current training programs conducted on practicing micro and small enterprises (MSEs): A case study of Roysambu. *International Journal of Academic Research in Business & Social Sciences*, *4*(10), 1–15. doi:10.6007/IJARBSS/v4-i10/1224

Odia, J., & Odia, A. A. (2013). Developing entrepreneurial skills and transforming challenges into opportunities in Nigeria. *Journal of Educational and Social Research*, *3*, 289–299. doi:10.5901/jesr.2013.v4n3p289

Parker, S. C. (2018). Entrepreneurship and economic theory. *Oxford Review of Economic Policy*, *34*(4), 540–564. doi:10.1093/oxrep/gry013

Perera, M. H. S. B., Premarathna, W., & Welamedage, I. (2017). *Entrepreneurial aspirations and expectations of Sri Lanka military veterans*. Retrieved on 18 May, 2020 from http://ir.kdu.ac.lk/handle/345/1726

Phillips, U. U. (2019). Security management and private security outfits in Nigeria. *International Journal of Social Sciences and Management Research*, *5*(1).

Pilon, A. (2017, February 2). *50 Small business manufacturing ideas*. Retrieved on 18 May, 2020 from https://smallbiztrends.com/2017/02/manufacturing-business-ideas.html

Putta, S. S. (2014). Improving entrepreneur's management skills through entrepreneurship training. *Journal of Commerce & Management Thought*, *5*(3), 459–474. doi:10.5958/0976-478X.2014.00334.6

Reeuwijk, K. G., de Wind, A., Westerman, M. J., Ybema, J. F., van der Beek, A. J., & Geuskens, G. A. (2013). All those things together made me retire: Qualitative study on early retirement among Dutch employees. *BMC Public Health*, *13*(1), 516–524. doi:10.1186/1471-2458-13-516 PMID:23714371

Salami, C. G. E. (2011). Entrepreneurial interventionism and challenges of youth unemployment in Nigeria. *Global Journal of Management and Business Research*, *II*(7), 4–25.

Smaliukiene, R. (2013). Entrepreneurship opportunities after military career: Practice in Central and Eastern Versus Western Europe. *Entrepreneurial Business and Economics Review*, *1*(4), 97–108. doi:10.15678/EBER.2013.010408

Sobota, J. (2017). *Veteran-owned businesses and their owners: Data from the U.S. Census Bureau's Survey of Business Owners*. U.S. Small Business Administration Office of Advocacy.

Sofat, P. (2016). Human resource management in the armed forces: Transition of a soldier to a second career. IDSA Monograph Series No. 54.

Steinfioff, D., & Burgers, J. (1993). *Small business fundamentals*. McGraw Hill International.

Steven, H., & Gumpert, D. E. (2002). The heart of entrepreneurship. *Harvard Business Review*, (June-July), 77–85.

Suleiman, A. S. (2006). *The business entrepreneur: Entrepreneurial development and small enterprises*. Entrepreneurship Academy Publishing.

Thisday. (2016, December 11). *Armed forces retire: 507 trained military retirees for post service life*. Retrieved on 18 May, 2020 from https://www.thisdaylive.com/index.php/2016/12/11/armed-forces-retire-507-train-military-retirees-for-post-service-life/

Van Solinge, H., & Henkens, K. (2000). Adjustment to and satisfaction with retirement: Two of a kind? *Psychology and Aging*, *23*(2), 422–434. doi:10.1037/0882-7974.23.2.422 PMID:18573015

Vaziri, S. A., Hosseini, S. E., & Jafari, A. (2014). The Impact of entrepreneurship education on entrepreneurial skills of university graduates. *International Conference on Arts, Economics and Management (ICAEM'14)*. Retrieved on 25 December, 2020 from http://icehm.org/upload/9718ED0314050.pdf

Vombatkere, S. G. (2015). Is the 'babu' scared of veterans' skills? *Indian Defence Review*, 31. Retrieved on 25 December, 2020 from http://www.indiandefencereview.com/isthe- bab-scared-of-veterans-skills/

Vroom, V. H. (1964). *Work and motivation*. Jossey-Bass.

Wang, M., Henkens, K., & van Solinge, H. (2011). Retirement adjustment: A review of theoretical and empirical advancements. *The American Psychologist*, *66*(3), 204–213. doi:10.1037/a0022414 PMID:21341882

Wang, M., & Shultz, K. S. (2010). Employee retirement: A review and recommendations for future investigation. *Journal of Management*, *36*(1), 172–206. doi:10.1177/0149206309347957

Yusuf, L., & Minai, M. S. (2016). Entrepreneurial training and career path of retired military personnel as entrepreneurs in Nigeria. *International Journal of Sciences, Basic and Applied Research*, *28*(3), 217–230.

Chapter 4
Entrepreneurship Innovations and Knowledge Economy:
Veterans in Perspective

Sagir Lawan
Nigerian Defence Academy, Nigeria

ABSTRACT

This chapter aims to provide fresh insights into entrepreneurship innovation to the retirees of the Nigerian military from the perspective of an ex-serviceman (a retired military person). The chapter's methodology focused on the articulation of experiences and meanings, which is guided by the events in the author's life, recounting life circumstances and events located in a specific time and space. Consequently, the chapter examines the entrepreneurial opportunities for retired Nigerian military personnel vis-a-vis the challenges faced by veterans when engaging in entrepreneurship. The chapter also discusses the entrepreneurship issues to be considered before becoming an entrepreneur. The chapter further postulates on information and communication technology (ICT) skills as key requirements for those who want to become an entrepreneur in post-service life. Finally, it is suggested that prior knowledge on innovative entrepreneurship before the start of a business results in successful sustained retirement income.

INTRODUCTION

According to Merriam-Webster Dictionary, a military veteran is defined as "a person who has served and is no longer serving in a military". A cursory appraisal of the post-service life of veterans in Nigeria indicates the need to prepare veterans

DOI: 10.4018/978-1-7998-6655-8.ch004

Copyright © 2021, IGI Global. Copying or distributing in print or electronic forms without written permission of IGI Global is prohibited.

towards innovative entrepreneurship for economically useful life after service. This is because veterans found themselves in a society where many criminally-minded people are bent on defrauding veterans and relieve them of their gratuity payments. From a personal experience, criminals often picked on veterans who are looking to go into business (i.e. Entrepreneurial self-employment), as a result, many veterans get duped and lose hard-earned retirement benefits.

In some cases, retiring military personnel plan and look forward to their retirement, and when it finally comes, either through redundancy due to statutory age limit or time served (i.e. 35 years), they want to engage in entrepreneurship in post-service life. So, starting a business in retirement helps the veterans to put the knowledge, skills, and experience gained during service to work. The chapter provides an avenue for veterans to carefully appraise business opportunities in order to ensure that they spend the period of their post-retirement life wisely. There is a need for veterans to carefully invest in business ventures and be careful with who they relate with because a lot of fair-weather friends will want to come around them to try to take the little money they have. Moreover, in this information and digital era – an era underpin by repositioning and inventing of new approaches in the knowledge economy, there is the need for every entrepreneur in the veteran community to be conversant with networks, tools, and resources they need to start their own business.

In the digital society, an innovative veteran entrepreneur would prosper through the employment of the instrument of entrepreneurship, innovation, knowledge economy, and digital enterprise. Consequently, as a veteran, I want to share my views and experience on the germane issues such as challenges and prospects relating to post-service entrepreneurship. The author's articulation of personal experience is based on an intuitive understanding of rooted actions, which leads to identifying relationships that are established between those actions and the contextual and socio-cultural aspects in which they develop (Cornejo, 2008). Personal experience seeks to study phenomena through a person's perspective, paying attention to the context where they emerge (Denzin & Lincoln, 2005).

The chapter is segmented into five sections. Section one focuses on the theoretical framework, section two highlights pre-retirement entrepreneurial issues, and section three discusses post-service occupational engagement. Section four considers what motivates military entrepreneurs; section five examines the application of ICT in veteran entrepreneurship, and section six concludes.

THEORETICAL FRAMEWORK

Various theories could be employed to interrogate the relationship between veteran entrepreneurship and the knowledge economy. These include structural functionalism theory, modernization theory, system theory, Max Weber's (1905) theory of social change (emphasis on the impact of religion), and Schumpeter's (1949) theory of innovation. Schumpeter believed that entrepreneurs disturb the stationary circular flow of the economy by introducing innovation and takes the economy to a new level of development.

Schumpeter's theory is relevant to this chapter because it highlights the interconnectivity of various processes involved in innovative veteran entrepreneurship. The theory pointed out that innovations of entrepreneurs are responsible for the rapid economic development of any country. Consequently, innovation could involve innovation of new products, innovation in novel methods or processes of production, and the opening up of a new market.

Schumpeter's theory was criticized for overemphasizing the innovative functions of the entrepreneur. It ignored the organizing aspects of entrepreneurship. It also completely ignored the risk-taking function of the entrepreneur, which cannot be ignored. Whenever an entrepreneur develops a new combination of factors of production, there is enough risk involved. Despite all the criticisms, Schumpeter's theory is considered a landmark in the expansion of entrepreneurship theories. The theoretical lens of Schumpeter's theory is employed in this paper because of its value in interrogating innovation in veteran entrepreneurship.

ENTREPRENEURIAL ISSUES TO BE CONSIDERED BEFORE RETIREMENT

From my personal experience, the entrepreneurial issues a serving military person needs to consider before retirement and becoming a veteran includes policy framework, funding of SME, entrepreneurial training, technological advancement (Internet base knowledge economy), and power supply. These issues are discussed in the following paragraphs.

Policy Framework

Veterans need to know the existing government entrepreneur policies before venturing into entrepreneurship. Policy framework is defined as long-term principles and goals that form the basis of making rules for developing military entrepreneurship Murtala (2005). According to Anyadike (2012), there is no doubt that a robust policy framework could be useful for military entrepreneurship.). The policy framework would be a means of guiding veterans' enhanced post-service life. While a robust policy framework plays a significant role in military entrepreneurship, knowledge of all the policies that influence Small and Medium Enterprises (SMEs) would be of great benefit to veterans.

Some of those policies include the Central Bank of Nigeria (CBN) monetary policies, Family Economic Advancement Programme (FEAP), the Fiscal Dispute Resolution Mechanisms (FDRM), etc. should have some impacts on innovative veteran entrepreneurship. Invariably, veterans need to understand that the policy framework is positioned towards a successful business life.

Funding for Enterprises

Finance is the bedrock of any enterprise and meaningful development. Adequate funding is an essential requirement for the veteran entrepreneurship events. From my veteran experience, many veteran entrepreneurs go through funding issues and problems. The limited funding for veterans could therefore be attributed to the paucity of funds and high-interest rates (Baliamoune, 2015). According to Babangida (2005), most of the veterans are new entrants or start-ups in entrepreneurship, they find it difficult to access funds from banks due largely to unauthorized high-interest rates and a dearth of acceptable collateral. Funding is thus a factor in the growth of veteran entrepreneurs. Therefore, there is a need for veterans to have financial counsellors on the ground to counsel them on sourcing and funding innovative entrepreneurship.

Entrepreneurial Education/Training

Victor (2018), observed that the logic behind entrepreneurship education is that it can stimulate entrepreneurial intention which potentially leads to innovative entrepreneurship. To equip its veteran is requisite entrepreneurial education, the Armed Forces of Nigerian (AFN) adopted training strategies at various levels to strengthen veteran entrepreneurship capabilities during post-service life. According to AVM Kingsley Lar, one-time Commandant, Nigerian Armed Forces Resettlement Centre (NAFRC): "the AFN have provided personnel with entrepreneurship skill, management skills, some vocational training to be able to cope, if they want additional income". At NAFRC, various courses for would-be veteran include Agriculture which comprises of Rabbitry, Fisheries, etc, Engineering, Technical, Management, Security, etc. Military personnel that benefited from the courses judiciously utilize the knowledge acquired into entrepreneur skills practice during post-service life. Murtala (2005) pointed out that entrepreneur training in business enterprises is indubitable means of revenue generation. Thus, there is the need for veterans to enroll in any organized training process that would translate ideas for invention into a good or service that can create value. Consequently, entrepreneurial training is necessary for generating viable enterprises towards the reduction of poverty.

Adequate entrepreneurial training is critical to providing direction in the day to day running and development of an enterprise. To this end, serving military personnel need to utilize the training at Nigerian Armed Forces Resettlement Centre (NAFRC) Oshodi, in order to acquire the desired entrepreneurship and management skills.

Internet Base Entrepreneurship as Technological Advancement

Internet Technology has dramatically changed people's way of life all over the world and the world today has become a true manifestation of the global village. Communication across the globe has been enhanced exponentially leading to an increase in cross-border trading of goods and services. Internet-based military entrepreneurship is an important source of job creation and opening career opportunities for both women and men. The Internet is regarded as the mainstream of the knowledge economy. In view of this, the veteran need to embrace the employment of internet and the use of social media for data transmission and exchange of information of their entrepreneurial activities. For example, Oyinlola (2013) maintains that email is now the backbone services required for banking, medical, industrial supply, and entertainment. Accordingly, the supply of online serves and innovations shows reorganization and reconciliation of the position of the enterprise in the industry by building a monopoly-like control or dismantling the existing monopoly of others in the industry. The veteran needs to imbibe and cultivate in totality entrepreneurial innovation through data-driven Internet of Things (IoT). The IoT is now a key ingredient to a phenomenon that describes the modern knowledge economy Okoro, (2017). Innovative knowledge economy transforms traditional enterprise into a smarter business venture by turning each machine into an information system that enables intelligent decision making based on data. An efficient smart business would positively affect the productivity and success of an entrepreneur. Thus, to facilitate universal, ubiquitous and cost-effective business, access to communications infrastructure is paramount. The veteran needs to promote the utilization of ICT in all spheres of life. ICT assists in digital content creation, domestic software applications, and the delivery of private and public services over the internet. ICT is a deciding factor for making the best use of limited resources in the pursuit of achieving military entrepreneurship.

Power Supply

The availability of adequate and reliable power supply is a crucial factor in veteran entrepreneurship. For example, Chibundu (2006), stated that the Aluminum Casting Enterprise set up by veteran El Hussain at Chikokwabo needs a lot of power for its operation. Power supply connotes the provision of sufficient electrical energy to effectively run Small and Medium Enterprises (SMEs) as a means of generating revenue for enhanced post-service life. From the statistical records on power supply, Nigeria produced an average of 4,600 Mega Watts (MW) of electricity with an improved generating capacity of 7,008 MW (Ajibade, 2017). Several power plants, including the Mambila and Zungeru projects amongst others, are currently under construction to provide an additional 7,840 MW of electricity (Nigerian Electricity Regulatory Commission, 2015)). These projects would increase electricity supply to SMEs thereby business enterprises. It is important for veterans to note that the provision of adequate power and sustainable power supply is one of the major challenges in Nigeria.

POST-SERVICE OCCUPATIONAL ENGAGEMENT

Egbe-Okpenge (2012) stated that it is a recognized fact that the monthly pensions for veterans are inadequate, notwithstanding, veterans should be a source of pride and be engaged in post-service occupational engagement. To succeed in post-service occupational engagement veterans, need to choose new friends who can add positive values to you and network with them. Also, ensure that you downsize your large monthly expenses so that your income is greater than or equal to such expenses, then, you shall have happiness in retirement.

One major problem and challenge veterans experience is the mere thought that the lifestyles of veterans must be consistent and continues as it were. Veterans should not forget that the only constant thing is change. Therefore, in moving from service-life to retirement, changes in all aspects will come, this is the irony of life and nature. In this circumstance comes the need for post-service occupational engagement. Veterans challenges become more complex and pitiable when he is prematurely retired or even when retired at the mandatory count of 35 years of service without adequate entrepreneurial planning and preparation. To venture into contractual business, veterans need to be well tutored in the art of business marketing process due to forces of competition within the business environment (Michael 2008). In our age, qualitative growth of stokes is not enough, but it has to be sustained. By sustainably growth we mean a rate of output that meets the needs of the present society by compromising the ability of future generations to meet their own needs.

Another challenge facing veteran entrepreneurship is the lack of time to monitor the progress and sustainability of the enterprise. The comforts of the life of service personnel could not allow officers to come to terms with the realities of their actual worth within the wider society. Soldiers are carried away by the largesse of the Army which portrays cosmetic assumption or egocentrism of self-actualization to build capacity for sustaining their enterprise in post-service life. It must be submitted at this stage that the travails of a military entrepreneurship lack of time to monitor internal stakeholders. These internal stakeholders have been kept in the dark over-time on the likely happenings in the course of the active career of their subject. Secondly, they become ill-prepared for sudden 'death'. Thirdly, they may perceive their relocation from the present abode in the city to new terrain as obscure, unsecured, remote to civilization and business, etc. Finally, they could become resistant to the sudden change and as such may whip up sentiments and support from those within the external stakeholders such as family/relations, friends, religious clerics, etc. Should this occur, the retiree became weighed-down rather than enlivened and motivated by those around him.

Today's world is being dominated by knowledge industries. The emphasis in such knowledge is not on physical or tangible assets, but on intangible knowledge assert. Therefore, increasing the traditional factors of production through labor, land, and capital have become less important when compared to the technology brought by ICT. This set-in the fear of the unknown that always frightens retirees and leads to ripples of mistakes in the decision-making processes because of all his appreciations of knowledge. Hence, the military entrepreneur put his or her career and financial security on the line and take risks in the name of an idea, spending time as well as capital on an uncertain venture.

WHAT MOTIVATES MILITARY ENTREPRENEURS?

The factors that are identified to motivate veteran entrepreneurs are not different from those that motivate other entrepreneurs (Safiya, 2013). Accordingly, Nzelibe (2006) identified factors such as the need for achievement; the need for independence; risk-taking ability; desire for responsibility, and provision for job opportunities for self. Others are pressure from family members; economic power to control business and employees and retirement plan. Notwithstanding these factors, and despite the abundance of natural resources and opportunities prevailing in the Nigerian entrepreneurial environment, the veteran entrepreneurship has remained under-developed, especially in the sphere of innovative entrepreneurship (Bankole, 2011). According to the World Bank (2014), innovative entrepreneurship in a form of social security has not been the pre-occupation of many military authorities. Invariably, pre-retirement entrepreneurship training to promote the overall well-being of the serving personnel within the context of a growing economy is vital. In this context, the Nigerian Armed Forces Resettlement Centre (NAFRC) Oshodi, was established to equip military retires on entrepreneurship and management. Although, some Nigerian military retirees had knowledge, training, and experience in enterprise and small-scale business operations.

Since its inception, NAFRC trained veterans in Small and Medium Scale Enterprise (SME) such as farms, artisans' trade, and petty trading schemes amongst others. NAFRC has transformed and revolutionized several aspects of retirees' life (Babangida, 2005). This assertion is attested to by many veteran officers and soldiers. For example, Sgt M Dauda member of NAFRC Course 3 confirmed in a conversation (with me) his achievements in livestock animal husbandry. He was a product of NAFRC and was able to manage and care for Sokoto species of goats, sheep, and cows for profits and livelihood. In addition to supplying milk, meat, and hides, his bullocks, are his major source of power. Sgt Dauda's sheep and goats are major sources of meat, skin and farmyard manure for more than 40% of the indigenous population of his Jareri village of Jigawa State. The productivity of these ventures for over ten years is, however, hampered by several factors amongst which is the lack of application of Information Communication Technology (ICT) in promoting the business Olomola, (2015).

Babangida (2005), posits that transiting from military life after a prescribed period of years' national service is not always smooth-sealing. It is even more devastating in the case of premature retirement as a result of age in rank, failure of promotion examination, and promotion board. When any of these happens and with insufficient preparation for entrepreneurship, those victims live below the World Bank Poverty Level benchmark of $1.9 a day (Paul, 2019). Pursuing a program of modernizing and equipping retirees with a creative enterprise program will enable the identification of potentials, skills, and sources of funds. Thus, it is important to determine the factors that motivate the veteran to start their own businesses. This knowledge regarding the profile of the military entrepreneur might enable policy-makers to create an encouraging environment for military entrepreneurs to start their own businesses.

THE APPLICATION OF ICT IN VETERAN ENTREPRENEURSHIP

In terms of the application of technology, it is necessary for the veteran entrepreneurs to take advantage of ICT capabilities and use them to boost their business ventures. Veteran entrepreneurs could engage the knowledge economy by utilizing, for instance, social media and emerging technology to add more value to their enterprise and business life. The knowledge economy approach to entrepreneurship demands the transportation of a large quantity of information to the customer worldwide promptly and presented properly. Asides from the lack of planning and making adequate preparation for retirement, suffice to state that most of the challenges confronting retirees in post-service life centered around the lack of adequate knowledge in entrepreneurial skills (Akintoye, 2010). The internet could help create new socially inclusive forms of entrepreneurship that fall more on data usage in communication (Ace et al, 2007; World Economic Forum, 2012) for a veteran entrepreneur. The Internet allows everyone to run a business from his or her home at a lower cost than before wowing to global connectivity. Thus, has given rise to new forms of economic activity. Nowadays, customers tend to enjoy personalized service and attention because of the keen competition, focus, and innovation, which characterize the operations of business using ICT. Consequently, military entrepreneurs are motivated or compelled by the competition to learn and broaden their knowledge and skills in order to meet up with the challenges of maintaining a good relationship with their customers, suppliers, financiers (banks and other financial institutions), auditors, regulators, and even their competitors.

Gunelie (2011), stated that prospective entrepreneurs are to understand that business can be a simple system as well as complex. At the simple stage of the enterprise, ownership of the business is not always distinct from the management; this means that supervision of the business is in the hand of the owner. When the scope of business organization increases, it becomes very difficult for one person to coordinate, direct, and control. It will be easier here for a military entrepreneur to pursue goals that are different from the objectives set by the owner; which brings about conflicting objectives that can result in business failure. Failure to manage a small-scale business enterprise that is owned and managed by the owner can collapse within a twinkle of an eye. There is nothing a retiree and his family will cherish most than a peaceful life in all ramifications, this means peace within one's heart peace at home with others, etc. Notwithstanding that, ICT can now suddenly turn a man into a successfull trader or merchant/major distributor. Although, without income generation from the entrepreneurial sector, a monthly pension alone could not make positive impacts on the life of a retiree (Babangida, 2005).

CONCLUSION

Veteran entrepreneurial activities are important factors in creating and increasing employment opportunities and fueling the economic growth of the veterans. Entrepreneurship is an important source of job creation and opening career opportunities for both serving and retired military personnel. Veterans are less likely to have successful enterprises or businesses due to a lack of innovation in their business venture. This chapter provided insights into veteran entrepreneurship by focuses on entrepreneurial issues to be considered before retirement. Then, post-service occupational engagement was discussed. Afterward, what motivates military entrepreneurs were considered. Subsequently, the application of ICT in veteran entrepreneurship was examined. Finally, analyses on theoretical framework reviewed. The chapter shows that veteran entrepreneurs participate more in the micro-business (informal sector). Consequently, poor performance and contribution are a result of the constraints they face.

REFERENCES

Abdulkareem, A. (2016). *Evaluation and Mitigation of Technical Losses on Power Lines: A Case Study of Nigeria 330-Kv NetworK*. Covenant University.

Academy. (2019). *Whole-life Costing of Asset: Compact Course on Principles of Asset Management*. London: Asset Management Academy.

Ajibade, A. (2017). *Nigeria Imports 70M Generators*. The Nation. Asset Management.

Akintoye, S. A. (2011). The Economic Foundations of Ibadan in the Nineteenth Century. In Topics on Nigerian Economic and Social History. Ife: University of Ife Press Ltd.

Aliyu, S. M. (2013). An Assessment Of Women Entrepreneurship Performance In Nigeria. *Malaysian Management Journal*, *17*, 1–12.

Anyadike, N., Emeh, I., & Ukah, F. O. (2012). Entrepreneurship development and employment generation in Nigeria: Problems and prospects. *Journal of Education and General Studies*, *1*(4).

AutoSmart. (2014). *Learn the Facts: Horsepower's Effect on Fuel Consumption*. Natural Resources Canada.

Babangida, I. (2005). Quotes of a General: Selected Quotes of Major General Ibrahim Babangida. Lagos: Terry Publishers.

Babatunde, O. M., Adedoja, O. S., Babatunde, D. E., & Denwigwe, I. H. (2019). Off-grid hybrid renewable energy system for rural healthcare centers: A case study in Nigeria. *Energy Science & Engineering*, *7*(3), 676–693. doi:10.1002/ese3.314

Baliamoune-Lutz, M. (2007). *Entrepreneurship, reforms and development: Empirical evidence* (Working paper no. 38/2007). ICER.

Bankole, P. (2011). *The Entrepreneurship Challenge in Nigeria*. Retrieved August 27, 2011 from https://knowledge.wharton.upenn.edu/article.cfm?articleid=1675

Bawuah, K., Buame, S., & Hinson, R. (2006). Reflections on Entrepreneurship Education in African Tertiary Institutions. *Acts Commercial,* 1-8.

Burger, L., O'Neil, C., & Mahadea, P. (2005). The Impact of Previous Knowledge and Experience on the Entrepreneurial Attitude of Grade Learners. *South African Journal of Education, 25*(2), 29–94.

Chappel, R., & Read, W. L. (1990). Definitions of Communications. In Introduction to Communication for Business and organizations. Ibadan: Spectrum Books Limited.

Chibundu, E. (2006, September 29). How Nigerian SMEs can grow the economy. *Vanguard Newspaper*, p. 46.

Cornejo, C. (2008). Intersubjectivity as co-phenomenology: From the holism of meaning to the being-in-the-world-with-others. *Integrative Psychological & Behavioral Science, 42*(2), 171–178. doi:10.100712124-007-9043-6 PMID:18196357

DeNoble, G. S. (2003). Early retirees as the next generation of entrepreneurs. *Entrepreneurship Theory and Practice, 27*(3), 207–226. doi:10.1111/1540-8520.t01-1-00001

Denzin, N., & Lincoln, Y. (2005). Introduction: The discipline and practice of qualitative research. In N. Denzin & Y. Lincoln (Eds.), *The SAGE handbook of qualitative research* (pp. 1–32). Sage.

Drucker, P. F. (1985). *Innovation and Entrepreneurship*. Pan Books Ltd.

Egbe-Okpenge, E. G., & Orhungur, M. M. (2012). Gender issues in entrepreneurial development in Benue state (Nigeria) and counselling implications. *Bulgarian Journal of Science and Education Policy, 6*(2).

Fakehinde, O. B., Fayomi, O. S., Efemwenkieki, U. K., Babaremu, K. O., Kolawole, D. O., & Oyedepo, S. O. (2019). Viability of hydroelectricity in Nigeria and the future prospect. *Energy Procedia, 157*, 871–878. doi:10.1016/j.egypro.2018.11.253

Force A.P.T. (2010). *A Primer for Emergency Physicians in Pre-Retirement Years*. Author.

Gunelius, S. (2011). *30-minute social media marketing: Step-by-step techniques to spread the word about your business*. McGraw-Hill.

Igwe, Madichie, & Newbery. (2019). Determinants of livelihood choices and artisanal entrepreneurship in Nigeria. *International Journal of Entrepreneurial Behavior & Research*.

Knight, F. H. (1961). *Risk uncertainty and profit* (2nd ed.). Kelley.

Murtala, S. S. (2005), Entrepreneurship development policy: A renewed perspective for achieving economic development in Nigeria. A paper presented at the Inaugural National conference organised by the Academy of Management Nigeria.

Muto, M., & Yamano, T. (2009). Impact of mobile phone coverage expansion on market participation: Panel data evidence from Uganda. *World Development*, *37*(12), 1887–1896. doi:10.1016/j.worlddev.2009.05.004

Nigerian Electricity Regulatory Commission. (2015). *Multi-Year Tariff Order (MYTO): 1st February 2016 to 2024 (Ikeja DISCO)*. Nigerian Electricity Regulatory Commission.

Nigerian Electricity Regulatory Commission. (2019). *Power Generation in Nigeria*. Nigerian Electricity Regulatory Commission.

Nzelibe, G. C. (2006). *Entrepreneurship and management of small scale business*. Optimal Publishers.

Oghojafor, E. A., Kuye, O. L., Sulaimon, A. A., & Okonji, P. S. (2009). Empowering Nigerian Youths For National Economic Development: The Role of Entrepreneurship Education. *Journal Of Research In National Development*, *7*(2). Advance online publication. doi:10.4314/jorind.v7i2.50945

Olomola, A. S. (2015). *Driving agricultural transformation with the power of information and communication technology: the performance of Nigeria's growth enhancement support scheme*. NSSP Working Paper 30. Washington, DC: International Food Policy Research Institute (IFPRI).

Owuala, E. I., & Obokoh, L. O. (2008). Tackling Youth Restiveness in the Niger Delta Region of Nigeria through Entrepreneurship. *Journal of Enterprising Communities, People and Places in Global Economy*, *2*(2), 168–179.

Oyinlola, O. T., Ajiboshin, I. O., Raimi, L., Raheem, S., & Igwe, C. N. (2013). Entrepreneurship for sustainable economic growth in Nigeria. *Journal of Sustainable Development Studies*, *2*(2).

Schumpeter, J. A. (1949). Economic Theory and Entrepreneurial History, Change and the Entrepreneur. Harvard University Press.

Udeozor, V. (2016). *Evaluating Compulsory Entrepreneurship Education Across Private And Public Higher Education Institutions in Nigeria*. Available at: http://irep.ntu.ac.uk/id/eprint/38446/1/1239809_udeozor.pdf

Usman, E. (2016, June 23). DHQ retires 464 Military personnel. *Vanguard Nigeria Newspaper*.

van Solinge, H. (2014). Who opts for self-employment after retirement? A longitudinal study in the Netherlands. *European Journal of Ageing, 11*(3), 261–272. doi:10.100710433-013-0303-7 PMID:28804332

Van Vuuren, J. J., & Groenewald, D. (2007). A critical analysis of the influence of start-up factors in small businesses and entrepreneurial ventures in South Africa. *Acta Commercii, 7*(1), 269–280. doi:10.4102/ac.v7i1.39

Weber, M. (1905). The Protestant Ethic and the Spirit of Capitalism. London: Unwin Paperbacks.

KEY TERMS AND DEFINITIONS

Knowledge Economy: This is an economic system in which the production of goods and services is predominantly established on knowledge-intensive activities. It also defines the process of consumption and production events that are discharged from the application of peoples' expertise (intellectual capital).

Military Veteran: People who have served in the military and are retired voluntarily or involuntarily from the Armed Forces.

Veteran Entrepreneurship: Retired military personnel who elected to go into self-employment or business ventures after retirement from the military service.

Chapter 5
Prelude to Military Entrepreneurship in China:
A Retrospective View

Hongjun Yu
Charhar Institute, China

Yang Gao
China Center for Contemporary World Studies, China

Jiancheng Liu
Guangdong University of Finance and Economics, China

Qingan Huang
University of East London, UK & Guangdong University of Finance and Economics, China

ABSTRACT

The prior studies form a solid foundation for the emerging research on military entrepreneurship in China. This chapter is dedicated to providing a detailed review on the evolution of Chinese disarmament, with a focus on military-civilian transfer and settlement of demobilized military staffs. Such a review comprehensively lays backgrounds for Chinese military entrepreneurship and thus is expected to serve as a prelude to the emerging research in this area.

DOI: 10.4018/978-1-7998-6655-8.ch005

Copyright © 2021, IGI Global. Copying or distributing in print or electronic forms without written permission of IGI Global is prohibited.

INTRODUCTION

"Teaching leadership, strategic planning, creative problem-solving, task execution, and resiliency—all traits are essential to business ownership. It is not a fancy MBA or university program" (Rockefeller, 2016). This statement fully manifests the business community's perception of how military serving experience efficiently cultivates strong entrepreneurs. More specifically, veterans are believed to excel at key attributes including top-notch teamwork, rich leadership experience (particularly for the retired officers), high sense of discipline, robust performance under pressure, and willingness to sacrifice, etc. Given these business-desirable characteristics, military veterans have become a fast-growing force in the civilian business world. For instance, according to a study by Syracuse University, among World War II veterans in the US, around 49% chose to own or operate their own business. The likelihood of US military veterans being self-employed doubles that of non-veterans. As a result, the group has become majority owners in 9% of all businesses in the US, which proves to be a shocking number compared with other communities (United States Census Bureau, 2007).

Heinz et al. (2017) and Hope et al. (2011) indicate that the success of military veterans as entrepreneurs has been associated with demographic (e.g., age, education), military service history (e.g., serving location, serving length, level of combat exposure, military branch served), and psychosocial characteristics (mental or behavioral disorder, perceived quality of life, level of openness, extraversion, optimism, achievement-orientation, need for autonomy). In addition, preparation for demobilization, social capital, perception of organizational politics, and work-family conflict are also related to military veterans achieving success in starting their own businesses (Vigoda-Gadot et al., 2010).

With the above-mentioned attributes, military veteran entrepreneurs, or "vetrepreneurs" approach the business problems differently by applying lessons from military to business (Moutray, 2007). For example, veteran entrepreneurs could be more prone to taking more risks, seeking support from a closed network of their fellow veterans, and showing unique perseverance when confronted with economic downturns. Overall, the international research has generally reached the consensus that military veterans' extraordinary potential for being successful entrepreneurs is rooted in their training and exposure to pressured/competitive environment when serving in the army, which can be complemented by their unique characteristics at individual levels (Waldman Associates & REDA International, 2004; Mid-Atlantic Research, 1984).

The interesting findings from developed countries (US, Israel, etc.) naturally raise curiosity about the military veteran entrepreneurship in emerging markets among which China has been playing an increasingly important role. Considering the institutional differences between China and more developed countries, the research findings based on more developed countries' institutional backgrounds may not be fully generalized to China. Although the research on military entrepreneurship is just at the starting stage, there has been a prolific stream of literature on how military veterans perform as top managers (owner managers in some cases). Consistent with Bertrand and Schoar's (2003) view on heterogeneous managers being the main driving factor of management decisions, the literature on military CEOs in China documents evidence of military experience significantly affecting CEOs' business decision-makings.

Specifically, it finds that the CEOs with military experience is associated with better corporate governance (Liao, Han & Chen, 2018), lower audit risk (Quan, Xu & Cai, 2018), lower earnings management (Zhang, Lin & Sun, 2019; Wang & Xu, 2020), lower compensation stickiness (Cai & Ou, 2019). More importantly, CEOs' military experience also explains their risk-averseness (Wang & Xu, 2019), innovative activities (Luo, Li & Xiang, 2017; Quan, Cu & Yin, 2019), acquisition decisions (Lai et al., 2017), financing preference, and firm performance (Lai, Gong & Ma, 2016). Moreover, military CEOs are more likely to engage in philanthropic activities and attain more governmental subsidies (Shao & Wu, 2018).

The above studies form a solid foundation for emerging research on military entrepreneurship in China. The remaining part of this chapter is dedicated to providing a detailed review of the evolution of Chinese disarmament, with a focus on military-civilian transfer and settlement of demobilized military staffs. Such a review comprehensively lays backgrounds for Chinese military entrepreneurship and thus is expected to serve as a prelude to the emerging research in this area.

The following review proceeds as follows. Section I introduces the background and results of disarmaments in New China. Section II discusses the significance and influence of disarmament in the new era of China's modernization. Section III focuses on the settlement of demobilized troops, while Section IV reviews the history and current status of military-civilian transfer. Section V finishes to emphasize military-civilian integration as a new strategy of balanced development of economy and defense.

Disarmament, Military-Civilian Transfer and Integration in Contemporary China

The Chinese nation cherishes peace and the People's Republic of China pursues an independent foreign policy of peace. It has been an important position in China's domestic and foreign policies to promote world peace, oppose the threat of war, stop the arms race, and advocate appropriate disarmament. Disarmament has been a major issue to the grave concern of the entire international community yet difficult to solve. It is related to cutting down a country's armed forces and military equipment, lowering military spending, demobilizing troops, and transferring military technologies, etc. However, in different countries and during different times, the specific policies and measures of disarmament differ, leading to different results. In this regard, what China has done in both policy and practice might offer some reference to others.

BACKGROUND AND RESULTS OF DISARMAMENTS IN NEW CHINA

The PRC was founded in October 1949, when the People's Liberation Army (PLA), a revolutionary force developed during war times, had a total number of over 5.5 million. In the following seven decades, China has gone through large-scale disarmament more than ten times, resulting in the revocation of dozens of military areas, corps, services and commands, and merging, transfer and downsizing of over 1000 hospitals, institutes, cultural and art groups, and farms affiliated to the military. The total number of troops has decreased from its peak of 6.27 million during the Korean War to in the 1950s to 2.3 million now.

China conducted large-scale disarmament for the first time in 1950. At that time, the Chinese military was mainly about the army, and there were basically no air force, navy or other services, let alone Special Forces, but the military spending accounted for 41.1% of the total fiscal expenditure. In order to meet the urgent need of economic recovery, peaceful development, and military modernization in China, Chairman Mao Zedong set forth the goal of restructuring the military to a number of 4 million. After repeated research and discussions, the size of the military has been set including 3.8186 million for the army, 126,400 for the air force and 55,000 for the navy. However, the Korean War broke out in October of the year, when the Chinese troops went to the battlefield again, making it impossible to continue disarmament but necessary to enlarge the military. At the end of 1951, the total number of the military reached 6.279 million.

In January, 1952, with the Korean War still going on but the Chinese troops able to gain the initiative in the battlefield, China restarted disarmament for the sake of regional and world peace and domestic economic development. According to the military restructuring plan approved by Chairman Mao Zedong at that time, the Chinese troops would be cut down to 3 million within three years, for which the army would be reduced from 1.34 million from 2.74 million, and other troops including the navy, air force, artillery, armored force, engineering corps, and air defense force increased to 843,000. The local troops were all handed over to the jurisdiction of the public security authorities, and some troops were transferred to agricultural reclamation personnel. After that disarmament, the Chinese military was downsized by 19 armies and 78 divisions, totaling 2 million troops. The number of the entire military was reduced to about 4.2 million and the ratio of military spending to the entire fiscal expenditure dropped to 32.9%.

After cease-fire in Korea in July, 1953, China immediately began its third disarmament. By the end of 1955, the whole military was cut down by 23%. After that disarmament, military headquarters, various military zones, and administrative bodies of services were adjusted. The navy, air force and new services were further strengthened, and the military effectiveness was greatly improved.

The fourth disarmament in China took place in 1957 and 1958. The overall objective of the disarmament was to cut down one third of the size of the military on the basis of strengthening its quality, which meant that the size of the military would be reduced from 3.8 million to about 2.5 million. At the same time, the five major services of army, navy, air force, air defense force and the police force would be streamlined into three major services of army, navy and air force. At the end of 1958, the fourth disarmament was completed. After that, China did not conduct disarmament for many years due to various reasons, and the size of the military kept growing, increasing by 600,000 by the end of 1974.

In June, 1975, China began its fifth disarmament, with the objective of reducing its military by 1.6 million within three years. The focus was on downsizing administrative organs of the military, streamlining redundant institutions, and phasing out excess personnel. Efforts were also made to phase out old equipment and strengthen Special Forces. By the end of the disarmament in 1976, the military was cut by 13.6%. The downsized engineering corps, railway corps and others accounted for over 90% of the total of the downsized army.

In August, 1980, China began its sixth disarmament. At that time, China already started its reform and opening-up and the central task has been shifted to modernization. In order to adapt to the new situation to minimize military spending, the focus of disarmament this time was to downsize and merge various overlapping institutions, and at the same time revoke independent divisions of all provincial military areas. Part of field operation divisions was also downsized from full division into streamlined division. It was in that year that China began to participate in the United Nations Conference on Disarmament and related activities and assigned an ambassador in charge of disarmament affairs.

China began its seventh disarmament in 1982. The basic principle of disarmament was “streamlining the military, optimizing the troops, increasing preparedness in both peacetime and wartime, and raising efficiency”. The overall objective was to reduce the size of the military to about 4 million. The major measures adopted included changing the administrative organs of the artillery, armored force and engineering corps subordinate to the Central Military Commission into artillery department, armored force department and engineering corps department subordinate to the General Staff Department, transferring the railway corps to the Ministry of Railways, relocating the infrastructure engineering corps to organs affiliated to the State Council or local authorities, and handing over the jurisdiction of most frontier forces to the police. However, due to long-term complex historical problems, the military was seriously oversized and that disarmament didn't achieve full success. At that time, Deng Xiaoping who was in charge of military affairs wrote that "this is not a satisfactory scheme. It can only be implemented as the first step now and further efforts have to be made in the future". In that year, the Chinese representative presented six basic principles and four major measures on disarmament at the Second UN Special Conference on Disarmament, solemnly stating China's constructive and highly responsible stand on disarmament.

The year 1984 was the 35th anniversary of the founding of New China. After a military parade on the National Day, Deng Xiaoping chaired a meeting to discuss China's eighth disarmament. Given the serious problems of excessive military administrative organs, fewer soldiers yet more officers and a total number of 4 million, Deng Xiaoping gave the instruction of "streamlining the military with the focus of downsizing personnel, cadres and institutions above the army level. In other words, a drastic measure would be taken to reduce the military by one million. That disarmament was basically completed at the end of 1986, reducing the military by 1.04 million.

That disarmament did not impact the modernization drive or combat effectiveness of the Chinese military, but instead strengthened its ability. Because when reorganizing several group armies, China set up the new army aviation corps and electronic warfare troops. Achievements were also made in building special forces and promoting integrated development of the navy, air force and other services. In December of that year, based on its own needs and experience, China put forward two proposals on nuclear disarmament and conventional disarmament at the UN General Assembly, winning the Assembly's approval. China's policy and practice on disarmament won the growing recognition of the international community increasingly. By 1990, the total number of Chinese troops was fewer than 3.2 million.

After the end of the Cold War, profound changes took place in the world, resulting in a big change in China's external environment. Peace and development have become the calling of the times. In 1995, Chinese leaders put forward the strategy of building a strong military through science and technology, and in September, 1997, made a major decision of downsizing the military by 500,000 within three years. This was the ninth disarmament in the history of New China conducted based on the principle of "streamlining the military, optimizing the troops, and raising efficiency". During this disarmament process, the military management and command system was adjusted, and most local garrison forces were dissolved. Some Type-B divisions were incorporated into armed police forces, and more than 200,000 military officers were transferred to the local governments and institutions. The military was downsized to 2.3 million and the weaponry's high-tech feature was strengthened.

Since the beginning of the 21st century, the world scientific revolution has been developing by leaps and bounds, bring about profound changes in new military revolution. In the process of accelerated rejuvenation, China faces the major task of defense modernization, and the military has somewhat increased. Against such a backdrop, the Chinese government put forward the new objective of downsizing the military by 200,000 by the year 2005, dropping to 2.3 million. In this process, 20,000 troops were transferred to the armed police mobile forces, and another nearly 180,000 non-combatant troops and administrative personnel also left the military.

SIGNIFICANCE AND INFLUENCE OF DISARMAMENT IN THE NEW ERA OF CHINA'S MODERNIZATION

In 2012, China entered a new historical stage in building socialism with Chinese characteristics and national defense modernization. In the spring of 2013, President Xi Jinping visited Russia and gave a speech on the global situation and the future of mankind, in which he made the scientific judgment that peace, development, and win-win cooperation are the calling of the times and that human society is a community with shared destiny living in the same global village in the same historical time and space. The building of a community with a shared destiny for all mankind has thereafter become the core concept and basic proposition of the major-country diplomacy with Chinese characteristics. At the 70th Anniversary of the Victory of the Chinese People's War of Resistance against Japanese Aggression and The World Anti-Fascist War held in September, 2015, President Xi Jinping announced to the international community China's major decision of cutting its troops by 300,000. This means the acceleration in China's efforts to upgrade its military from emphasis on quantity to quality, and from high population-density to high-tech development.

As mentioned before, the Chinese government attaches great importance to the issue of disarmament, both in China and in the world. China has not only sent representatives to attend the special session of the First Committee of the UN General Assembly on disarmament and security issues every year, but also sent delegations to attend Special Sessions on Disarmament held by the UN in 1978, 1982 and 1987. China has also donated to the UN World Disarmament Campaign and Institute for Disarmament Research. In 1987 and 1992, China and the UN jointly held the International Disarmament Seminar in Beijing and Shanghai respectively. China's support to the world armament control and disarmament efforts is genuine and evident.

The Chinese leaders made such a decision on large-scale disarmament for two reasons. First, peace and development remain the calling of our times, and there is a growing need for win-win cooperation. Second, there has been new development in the global military and security situation. Being the world's top military power, the US military has a number of just 1.4 million. In 2014, the US announced to cut its troops by 100,000 in three years, for which the number of its army would be cut down to the level of 1940, and its marine troops would also be cut significantly. Russia, another world military power, was also disarming continuously, and the size of its military would be controlled to one million.

The size of the Chinese military was much larger than that of the US and Russia. In particular, it has an excessive army. Its military command system remains to be improved. The logistics support departments were still very complicated. And there were many military academies and other non-combatant units. Moreover, the military also undertook many tasks that should be done by the public security and armed police. In order to keep pace with the trend of world military revolution, it is imperative to streamline the military, improve the military's quality, and focus more on services such as the air force and navy, special forces, technical arms, space force, and cyber force.

As China's top leader and commander-in-chief, Xi Jinping made the announcement of cutting China's troops by 300,000 at the historic moment of the 70th Anniversary of the Victory of the Chinese People's War of Resistance against Japanese Aggression and The World Anti-Fascist War, which demonstrated the Chinese people's love of peace and the nation's strong will for a peaceful rise. It also worked to counter the so-called "China threat theory" promoted by those with ulterior motives. The international community generally spoke positively of this move by China, believing that China's disarmament effort had far-reaching significance. Of course, some experts emphasized that China's disarmament this time was closely related to its military reform, readjustment of its military strategy, and its overall plan for military modernization.

China's current disarmament is indeed closely related to its military reform, readjustment of its military strategy, and its overall plan for military modernization, which the Chinese government has never denied. Under whatever circumstances and at whatever time, China's disarmament is based on the efforts to enhance its overall military strength and combat capability. Because the world is far from being peaceful, with the cold war mentality still lingering and noises of hot war still persisting. Expansionism, hegemonism, new interventionism and some countries' military adventurism are still on the rise. The Sword of Damocles of war is still hanging above the human society. In order to faithfully fulfill the dual obligations of safeguarding the country's safety and maintaining world peace, the Chinese troops must keep up with the world's pace of new military revolution, gain strength in developing remote, precise, intelligent, invisible, and unmanned weaponry, and win the initiative in space, cyber, space and other new strategic fields.

Based on the trend of the world and its own needs, China combines economic and social development with its overall plan of military reform, and safeguards its own safety while promotes world peace. China's efforts of appropriate disarmament and readjustment are reasonable and understandable. The current disarmament embodies the will and determination of the Chinese government and people to maintain and promote world peace, and manifests the objective and direction of modernization of the Chinese military. The international community agrees that through this round of disarmament, the Chinese military will have higher efficiency and morale, and be able to safeguard China's endeavor to of national rejuvenation. The political influence and historic significance of that disarmament will be shown with the passage of time.

SETTLEMENT OF DEMOBILIZED TROOPS

For all countries at all times, it has always been a tough issue to settle a large number of demobilized troops, especially officers. This issue, if not handled well, will result in apparent social and livelihood issues that may influence the country's political image and stability, but also damage the military's reputation and enthusiasm of its citizens to serve in the army according to law. This is indeed a very challenging issue. The Chinese government is fully aware of this and has put in place feasible policy measures accordingly.

At ordinary times or during disarmament, the Chinese government has always taken seriously the issue of troops' placement and re-employment. However, at different times and places, there have been different policies and practices. In the 1950s and 1960s, the reorganized military personnel, apart from returning to their home village for farm work, moving to work according to the government arrangement, were often collectively transferred into workers at state-run reclamation farms or into soldiers in production and construction corps. So it was common that they later worked as employees of State-Owned Enterprises (SOEs). In the 1970s to 1980s, demobilized military personnel were resettled according to government policies at that time. Some returned home to do farm work. Some went to work in industry and mining enterprises. Some worked in schools affiliated with government agencies or engaged in professional management in government agencies. Some military personnel such as railway troops became employees of the agencies affiliated to the Ministry of Railways after collective transfer. Generally speaking, demobilized soldiers mostly went back home to do farm work or were sent to factories as workers, while officers were sent to local government agencies according to their different ranks, with some even assuming leadership positions. There were also exceptions.

For example, in 1955, during China's fourth disarmament, in order to reduce the burden on the government, Major General Gan Zuchang, then head of logistics department of Xinjiang military area, applied for being demobilized and returning home to do farm work twice, and was finally approved. Over 29 years after he returned to his home village, he turned down the housing and vehicles given to him by the government, raised pigs and planted vegetables to lead a simple life, and participated in local economic construction together with fellow villagers and invested much of his retired salaries into road works, bridges and other infrastructures. He became a leading model of veterans with highest ranking and played an exemplary role in encouraging demobilized troops to go back home to do farm work. The huge number of demobilized troops has always been an important force for China's economic, cultural and social development at all times.

Since the introduction of the reform and opening-up in the late 1970s and early 1980s, especially after the beginning of the new century, China has adjusted many times the policies and measures for resettling demobilized troops at ordinary times and demobilized officers during disarmament times, and the specific resettlements differed greatly at different times and in different places. Resettlement offices for demobilized troops were set up at county-level and higher administrative bodies, which were responsible for reception, resettlement, care, management and other work related to demobilized military personnel. At that time, the main way for the government to settle demobilized troops was to arrange work with fixed income for demobilized personnel accordingly, which was also the most popular institutional arrangement among demobilized troops and the society.

In the new century, the government continues its traditional approach of sending demobilized troops coming from rural areas back to their home villages and of arranging work for demobilized troops coming from urban areas, and at the same time, independent job seeking has been widely implemented as a national policy. The so-called independent job seeking means that demobilized officers with the rankings at division, regiment and battalion head levels and with no fewer than 20 years of military services can seek jobs by themselves or start their own businesses, apart from taking monthly demobilization wages exempt from individual income tax monthly according to government regulations. However, if the demobilized troops were recruited as employees of government agencies, their demobilization wages will no longer be paid. The demobilized troops seeking jobs independently no longer receive demobilization wages after their death. If their spouses lead a hard life, the local government of resettlement shall provide allowances according to relevant national and local regulations.

According to the policy effect, the policy of independent job seeking by demobilized troops is very successful. The policy of independent job seeking meets China's needs for economic and social development in contemporary times, and is in line with the general trend of increasingly diversified employment orientations by demobilized troops, thus becoming increasingly popular. Many demobilized officers work hard and achieve great success in their jobs, making outstanding contribution to the society. Chen Xieying, a demobilized serviceman as reported by Chinese official website people.com.cn on May 15, 2020, is an outstanding representative of veterans. When leaving the troops as a battalion commander in 2004, Chen Xieying didn't rely on the government arrangement but started a business on his own. His company has worked with large SOEs and private enterprises to develop the African market across more than 30 countries, and has signed contracts worth nearly US$1 billion on infrastructure, energy and high technology, creating nearly 10 million direct and indirect profits and taxes. Of course, there are many people like Chen, who seek or start businesses on their own. For contemporary China, the policies and systems for independent job seeking and startup for demobilized troops have become increasingly mature with increasingly bright prospects.

In April, 2018, the Ministry of Veterans Affairs of the PRC, as a department of the Chinese government, was officially established, and the national safeguard policies and systems for demobilized troops have become better. One typical policy was that since August, 2019, the periodical allowances provided by the government to demobilized veterans in rural areas, military personnel with disabilities, elder children of martyrs was raised by 10%. Given the different financial strengths of various localities and the possibility of some local governments having difficulty in implementing the policy, the central government shall be responsible for the budget. The discharge bonus paid to the government, including settlement, living, medical treatment and other expenses such as retired wages, military severance fee, demobilization payment, discharge fee, local-transfer resettlement fee, etc. has also been adjusted in time according to increasingly improved economic development in the whole country.

HISTORY AND CURRENT STATUS OF MILITARY ENTERPRISES TRANSFERRED INTO CIVILIAN PRODUCTION

Generally speaking, "military-to-civilian transformation (converting military-oriented enterprises to civilian production)" involves two major parts: transformation of scientific research units and production enterprises for military purposes into ones focusing on R & D and manufacturing of products for civilian use, and transfer of related people from the former to the latter. This transformation or transfer can be both complete or partial, absolute or relative, conditional or unconditional, permanent or temporary. In the process of modernization of national defense, adjustment of the industrial structure and development of the military industries, China has been attaching high importance to military-to-civilian transformation, and has made many constructive explorations and trials and accumulated rich experiences and lessons as well.

The transformation of Chinese military enterprises into civilian production started soon after the founding of the PRC, and continued along with continuous adjustment of China's economic structure and national defense modernization. It presented different patterns and yielded different results in different periods of time. After the introduction of comprehensive reform and opening-up in late 1970s and early 1980s, "adjustment, reform, rectification and improvement" became the most important guideline for economic development. Since then, the enormous military industry started being transformed from purely serving national defense and the needs of the military into focusing on serving economic development and the improvement of people's livelihood, or into meeting both military and civilian needs. Due to substantial adjustment of product mix, the proportion of civilian products in the military industry was greatly raised, and transferred military enterprises started playing a more and more important role in meeting the ever-growing needs of the people for material products, and thus became an important force in boosting comprehensive economic development, enriching people's lives and participating in opening up and international cooperation. The following are a few examples in this regard.

Changhong Electric Co., Ltd, located in Sichuan Province, used to be a state-run company called Changhong Machinery Factory. It was a major national defense engineering project developed in late 1950s, and also the then only production base producing onboard fire control radar in China. At the end of the 1970s, this enterprise started being transformed from the production of just military products into the production of diversified civilian products, and now has grown into a comprehensive multinational company integrating production of various civilian products and provision of services including television, air conditioner, refrigerator, communication, network, digital products, chip, energy, E-commerce and intelligent manufacturing, and life services. It became one of the Top 500 businesses with global competitiveness and influence in 2005.

Chongqing Jialing Industry Co., Ltd used to be an arsenal mainly producing military products like artilleries after the founding of PRC. It was later restructured into state-run Jialing Machinery Factory. In 1979, Jialing Machinery Factory started implementing "military-to-civilian" development strategy and soon became a leading enterprise specialized in R & D and production of motorbikes. In 1980, the company adopted the development guideline of "internal improvement and external connection", and established the Jialing motorbike economic complex, becoming one of the first Chinese enterprises to engage in economic integration. It carried out cooperation with Japanese Honda Motor Co., Ltd in 1982. Later in 1987, it was restructured into China Jialing Group, owning two core enterprises: China Jialing Industry Co., Ltd and Chongqing Jialing Special Equipment Co., Ltd. China Jialing Industry Co., Ltd is a state-owned listed company affiliated to China South Industries Group Co.,. It has developed a comprehensive R & D, manufacturing and marketing system, mainly producing motorbikes and their engines, special vehicles, general machines and related downstream products, which are exported to several hundred countries and regions in the world. Founded in 2004, Chongqing Jialing Special Equipment Co., Ltd mainly produces special equipment such as sporting shotgun cartridges, and motorbike parts and components as well. It is a major large-scale military-civilian combined state-owned enterprise affiliated to China South Industries Group Co., Ltd.

Harbin Aircraft Factory, which was established in Harbin, Heilongjiang Province, in 1952, was called "122 Factory" at that time. Since its establishment, it had a feature of military-civilian dual use. It was not only an important R & D center on large-scale bomber aircrafts and military helicopters, but also R & D and production base for multiple types of business jets. In 1957, this factory was renamed "State-run Weijian Machinery Factory". To adapt to the requirements of the reform and opening-up, this factory was externally renamed "Harbin Aircraft Factory" in 1979, and thus the military-to-civilian transformation was accelerated. In order to exploit domestic and foreign civilian markets, the factory took the lead in using international airworthiness standard in 1980, and then successfully designed and produced a civil aircraft—Yun 12 Aircraft. In October of the same year, the factory introduced French patented technologies to produce a "Dolphin" helicopter. In 1986, its products were exported abroad, becoming the first Chinese aircraft to enter the international market. With its growing cooperation with business partners in France and Singapore, the factory was renamed Harbin Aircraft Manufacturing Company. In 1998, the company was upgraded and restructured into Harbin Aircraft Manufacturing Co., Ltd.

Entering the new century, the company has developed more diversified products with higher quality, improved its independent research ability, and considerably expanded external cooperation. It set up the Harbin Embraer Aircraft Industry Co., Ltd together with Empresa Brasileira de Aerona, successfully producing feeder liners in China, cooperated with Boeing of the U.S. and formally joined in Boeing's supplier system, and then smoothly completed Bell helicopter subcontract production task in cooperation with Bell Corporation. In 2006, this company became a shareholder of Tianjin Zhongtian Airlines to draw world advanced aerospace manufacturing technology. As a result, its ability of independent R & D of large aircraft, production management ability and product marketing means have all been improved markedly. It soon started participating in Final Assembly Line of China (FALC) construction of Airbus A320. In this year, it was restructured into four relatively independent companies respectively on aircraft industry, aircraft engine, automobile industry and automobile engine according to its professional development direction. On the whole, the company continuously expanded research and development of civilian products and forged ahead on the road of marketization and internalization while maintaining its original military production ability.

MILITARY-CIVILIAN INTEGRATION: NEW STRATEGY OF BALANCED DEVELOPMENT OF ECONOMY AND DEFENSE

On March 12, 2015, President Xi Jinping put forward the idea of elevating military-civilian integration as a national strategy for the first time. On January 22, 2017, the Central Commission for Integrated Military and Civilian Development led by Xi Jinping was formally established in order to strengthen the unified leadership of in-depth military-civilian integration and conduct decision-making, deployment and coordination on major issues related to military-civilian integration at the national level. At the 19th National Congress of the Communist Party of China (CPC) held in October of the same year, Xi Jinping stated that we should ensure that efforts to make our country prosperous and efforts to make our military strong go hand in hand. We will strengthen unified leadership, top-level design, reform, and innovation. We will speed up the implementation of major projects, deepen reform of defense-related science, technology, and industry, achieve greater military-civilian integration, and build integrated national strategies and strategic capabilities. The CPC Central Committee, the State Council and the Central Military Commission issued *Opinions on Integrated Development of Economy and National Defense*. The State Council and the Central Military Commission released *The 13th Five-Year Plan for Integrated Development of Economy and National Defense*. These marked the transformation of the military-civilian integration strategy from an idea and policy design into reality.

According to the proposition of President Xi Jinping, by promoting in-depth military and civilian integration, China needs to proceed from its own reality, find a path of military and civilian integration with its own features, implement the idea and policy of military and civilian integration throughout the entire process of economic and national defense development. We need to earnestly implement Opinions on Strengthening Law-based Military and Civilian Integration of the Chinese government, promote legislation in this field, accelerate the transformation of government functions, and advance scientific and technological innovation through strategic major projects. During this process, the government needs to make overall arrangements for major projects, plans and schemes, and unify, coordinate, mobilize various resources.

The leading and coordinating role played by the Chinese government in military and civilian integrated development is mainly manifested in two aspects: directly intervening in mergers and acquisitions (M & A) of military enterprises and participating in their major reform and M & A decisions; and influencing military enterprises indirectly through legal and economic means as social managers. Of course, military and civilian integration also needs a complete system of laws and regulations to regulate behaviors of participants in the cooperation process and guarantee comprehensive promotion and smooth implementation of various "military-to-civilian transformation" tasks. In this process, particular importance should be attached to continuously improving the organization and management system, operation system, policies and institutions. From legal and institutional perspectives, military-civilian integration has just started in China, and efforts to build related laws and standards have just started.

Apart from continuously strengthening governmental leadership, policy support, legal and institutional guarantee, we must vigorously develop advanced technologies for both military and civil use and accelerate their integration and unification, which is the key issue determining whether military-civilian integration can achieve success and sustainable development. China has mainly done two things in this regard. First, we have drawn advanced experience overseas to restructure our existing national defense institutions, or expand the scope of scientific research project application, so that civilian scientific research institutions can participate in defense project application. Second, we work to develop a scientific and technological innovation system of military and civilian integration to promote two-way exchange between military production and civilian production and realize technology and standard integration and compatibility.

At present, the industrial pattern of military-civilian integration in China includes two types: "military-to-civilian transformation" and "participation of civilian enterprises in military production". "Military-to-civilian transformation" means that military enterprises produce civilian products and military technologies are shifted to serve people's livelihood, which is not difficult to understand and not something new. However, it is a new phenomenon in China for civilian enterprises including both private ones and SOEs on civilian product production to participate in military production.

Although it has not been long for the civilian sector to participate ins in military production, it has developed initial features like flexible mechanism, high efficiency and extensive implementation, thus attracting wide attention. First, the civilian sector has entered the market of military products to participate deeply or partially in research, production and supporting services of military products. Second, the civilian sector has entered the military capital market to participate in shareholding reform of state-owned military enterprises or establish a new shareholding corporation in the form of joint venture. Third, the civilian sector has entered the military talent market. While more and more military industry professionals are joining private businesses, private scientific and technical personnel and management have also been recruited by military enterprises. Statistics show that against the backdrop of "military-to-civilian transformation" and "participation of civilian enterprises in military production", by March, 2016, first anniversary of the introduction of the strategy of "military-to-civilian transformation", over 1,000 private enterprises have been granted scientific research and production licenses for military equipment in China.

In today's world where technological revolution, IT revolution, in particular, is advancing fast, accelerated matching of military and civilian technologies through military-civilian integration can fully promote military modernization, thus making the military industry and civilian sector an interdependent and mutually reinforcing community. This is the choice of the times and history. Continuous deepening of military-civilian integration in China can help to eliminate institutional and structural barriers hindering mechanization and information based integrated development of the Chinese military, and thus greatly improve the independent innovation capability of China's defense. On the other hand, it will fully leverage the great potential of private high-tech enterprises in China, and thus ensure traditional military industry and modern private science and technology can draw on each other's strength, so as to accelerate collaborative military and civilian scientific and technological innovation.

All Chinese civilian product R & D and production enterprises, no matter whether they are state-owned or private, warmly welcome and highly support the strategy of military-civilian integration. For example, China Aerospace Science and Industry Corporation, an important military enterprise, decided immediately to elevate operation revenue of the military and civilian integration industry to 147 billion yuan in 2017 after this development strategy was put forward. The company put in place R&D system for military-civilian integration industry, and developed a new business format combining manufacturing and service, online and offline operations, and innovation and entrepreneurship. Nanjing Horizon Base Communication Technology Inc. strived to realize "5G + space-based internet + space calculation" integration through technological innovation by building a low-earth-orbit millimeter-wave satellite constellation communication on its own, and has become the first licensed private space broadband operator in China.

Under unified leadership and planning of the central government, local governments in China have successively formulated their own programs and plans for local military-civilian integration. They have set up leadership institutions and working bodies and integrated national defense and local economic development, thus continuously deepening military- civilian exchange in scientific and technological information and the sharing of scientific research resources. Efforts have also been made to establish national demonstration areas for military-civilian integration and innovation.

Facts have shown that China's practice of defining military-civilian integration as a national strategy, conducting restructuring and readjustment on military industries, and providing strong policy support and guidance for "military-to-civilian transformation" has not only enabled military enterprises to be able to better adapt to the ever-changing environment of the market economy, but also win more development opportunities and gain broader prospects. At the same time, this can fully unleash the scientific and technological strength, innovation potential and human resources of private enterprises, thus realizing the best possible allocation of military capital and private capital in economic development and international exploration, equal participation of military and private enterprises in national defense and areas related to wellbeing, and balanced development between economic modernization and modernization of national defense.

CONCLUDING REMARKS

As discussed above, the continuous evolution of disarmaments in China warrants more diversified approaches to settling the demobilized military staff, which thus calls for more research on military entrepreneurship in China. Drawing on the evidence from prior literature, military entrepreneurship can be facilitated through effective entrepreneurship development policies for military veterans (Smaliukienė, 2013), the involvement of relevant NGOs (Non-Governmental Organizations) (Auplat, 2006), supportive law settings (Lee, Peng, and Barney, 2007), and provision of entrepreneurship education (Kerrick et al., 2014).

Among these factors, the provision of entrepreneurship education is believed to significantly enhance military veterans' entrepreneurship passion and their business awareness, which more likely leads to success in starting their own businesses (Kerrick et al., 2014; US Small Business Administration, 2013). Taking the examples in the US, there are currently several military veteran entrepreneurship programs in academia, including Syracuse University's Entrepreneurship Bootcamp for Veterans with Disabilities which provides both online and one-week in-person trainings. This program has extended to involve 7 additional universities to provide entrepreneurship training to military veterans. Efforts have also been made by government agencies at the city level, where several cities work with the Small Business Administration to provide military veteran entrepreneurship training programs. Likewise, the US

Department of Veterans Affairs established Veteran Entrepreneur Portal to provide training and support to military veterans looking for business opportunities.

In October 2018, the Ministry of Veterans Affairs of the People's Republic of China officially issues the document "Opinions on Facilitating the Employment and Entrepreneurship for Demobilized Troops in the New Era". This document sets forth the basic rules for better settling the demobilized military staff and introduces a wide variety of specific policies supporting the Chinese military veterans' employment and entrepreneurship. The supporting policies range from entrepreneurship training, financing and tax preference policy, to building entrepreneurship information platforms and establishing veteran-focused venture capital funds. With these supports from the government, military entrepreneurship is set to see a prosperous development. Such a development will fuel increasingly more empirical and theoretical studies on military entrepreneurship in China. And these forthcoming studies are expected to enrich the international literature on entrepreneurship as a whole. We hope this chapter could serve the entrepreneurship research community by providing a detailed review of the evolution of disarmaments in China, the second-largest economy increasingly embracing entrepreneurship in the new era. And we look forward to seeing more academic research, either empirical or theoretical, inspired by the ideas lined up here.

REFERENCES

Auplat, C. (2006). *Do NGOs influence entrepreneurship?* Society and Business Review. doi:10.1108/17465680610706337

Bertrand, M., & Schoar, A. (2003). Managing with style: The effect of managers on firm policies. *The Quarterly Journal of Economics, 118*(4), 1169–1208. doi:10.1162/003355303322552775

Cai, S., & Ou, J. (2019). Does Managers' Military Experience Reduce Executive Compensation Stickiness? *Communication of Finance and Accounting*, (30), 16–21.

Heinz, A. J., Freeman, M. A., Harpaz-Rotem, I., & Pietrzak, R. H. (2017). American military veteran entrepreneurs: A comprehensive profile of demographic, service history, and psychosocial characteristics. *Military Psychology*, *29*(6), 513–523. doi:10.1037/mil0000195 PMID:29290645

Hope, J. B., & Mackin, P. C. (2011). *Factors affecting entrepreneurship among veterans*. SAG Corporation.

Kerrick, S. A., Cumberland, D., Church-Nally, M., & Kemelgor, B. (2014). Military veterans marching towards entrepreneurship: An exploratory mixed methods study. *International Journal of Management Education, 12*(3), 469–478. doi:10.1016/j.ijme.2014.05.006

Lai, L., Gong, Y., & Ma, Y. (2016). Managers' Military Experience, Financing Preference and Business Performance. *Management World*, (8), 126–136.

Lai, L., Gong, Y., Xia, X., & Ma, Y. (2017). Managers' Military Experience and Company M&A. *Japan and the World Economy*, (12), 141–164.

Lee, S. H., Peng, M. W., & Barney, J. B. (2007). Bankruptcy law and entrepreneurship development: A real options perspective. *Academy of Management Review, 32*(1), 257–272. doi:10.5465/amr.2007.23464070

Liao, F., Han, H., & Chen, L. (2018). Does Executives' Military Experience Improve Internal Control Quality? Empirical Evidence from Listed Companies in China. *Auditing Research*, (6), 121–128.

Mid-Atlantic Research, Inc. (1984). *Profiling Entrepreneurial Veterans*. U.S. Small Business Administration, Office of Advocacy.

Moutray, C. M. (2007). *Educational attainment and other characteristics of the self-employed: an examination using data from the panel study of income dynamics.* Hudson Institute Research Paper, (07-06).

Padilla, A., Coyne, C.J., Michaluk, C., & Reese, R. (2016). Unproductive entrepreneurship in US military contracting. *Journal of Entrepreneurship and Public Policy*.

Quan, X., Cu, W., & Xu, X. (2019). Executives' Military Experience and Corporate Earnings Management: A New Perspective on the Military-Civilian Integration Strategy. *Finance & Trade Economics, 40*(1), 98–113.

Quan, X., Cu, W., & Yin, H. (2019). Military Service Experiences of Top Management, Management Style and Corporate Innovation. *Nankai Business Review*, (6), 140–151.

Quan, X., Xu, X., & Cai, W. (2018). Does Executives' Military Experience Affect Audit Fees: A New Perspective Based on Organizational Culture. *Auditing Research*, (2), 80–86.

Rockefeller, M. L. (2016). Why The Military Is The Best Entrepreneurship Training Program In America. *Forbes*.

Shao, J., & Wu, S. (2018). Military Experience of Managers and Government Subsidies: From Dual Perspectives of Corporate Philanthropy and Redundant Employees. *Journal of Shanghai University of Finance and Economics*, *20*(3), 63–78.

Smaliukienė, R. (2013). Entrepreneurship opportunities after military career: Practice in Central and Eastern versus Western Europe. *Entrepreneurial Business and Economics Review*, *1*(4), 97–108. doi:10.15678/EBER.2013.010408

United States Census Bureau. (2007). *Veteran-owned businesses and their owners*. Data from the Census Bureau's Survey of Business Owners. Retrieved from https://www.sba.gov/sites/default/files/393tot.pdf

U.S. Small Business Administration. (2013). *Small business development centers (SBDCs)*. Retrieved from https://www.sba.gov/content/small-businessdevelopment-centers-sbdcs

Vigoda-Gadot, E., Baruch, Y., & Grimland, S. (2010). Career transitions: An empirical examination of second career of military retirees. *Public Personnel Management*, *39*(4), 379–404. doi:10.1177/009102601003900405

Waldman Associates & REDA International. (2004). *Entrepreneurship and Business Ownership in the Service-Disabled Veteran Community*. U.S. Small Business Administration, Office of Advocacy.

Wang, Y., & Xu, K. (2019). Conservative or Radical: The Influence of Managers' Military Experience on the Company's Risk-Taking. *Foreign Economics & Management*, *41*(9), 17–30.

Wang, Y., & Xu, Ye. (2020). Does Military Experience of Managers Affect Corporate Governance? Evidence from China's Listed Companies. *Management Review*, *32*(1), 153–165.

Chapter 6
The Studies on Veteran Entrepreneurship in the Past Decade in China:
A Literature Mapping

Hua Geng
Xi'an University of Architecture and Technology, China

Benzhao Yang
Northwestern Polytechnical University, China

Qingan Huang
Guangdong University of Finance and Economics, China & University of East London, UK

ABSTRACT

To have a thorough understanding of the current state of veteran entrepreneurship in China, a literature mapping was made on the basis of 235 related articles and research literature published in the past decade (from 2010 to 2019), which are open to the public and available on the China National Knowledge Infrastructure (CNKI). Via combing through the above findings, the authors tried to unlock a phase with prominent rise of corresponding research papers and its possible reason, reveal the leading research power and their correlation, and also explore a potential research trend in the future. On the basis of the overall context and generalization of the status quo and limitations of this field during the past 10 years, reference and guidance can be provided for future study and policy making.

DOI: 10.4018/978-1-7998-6655-8.ch006

Copyright © 2021, IGI Global. Copying or distributing in print or electronic forms without written permission of IGI Global is prohibited.

RESEARCH BACKGROUND

Definite verification can be seen that a high level of the overall entrepreneurial activity is related to high rates of economic growth (Urbano & Aparicio, 2016) and necessary economic sustainability (Henry et al., 2003). Therefore, the notion of entrepreneurship has appeared in numerous literature and become an important research field of management and academic literature. There has been a recent, burgeoning interest in the factors behind entrepreneurial dynamics and firm performance (Toth, 2012). Although most firms are small compared with the companies that economists usually study in the long run, these small firms are playing an increasingly important role in the economy (Brock & Evans, 1989). Studies were carried out from diversified perspectives, such as the relationship between entrepreneurial orientation (EO) and firm performance, environmental dynamism (Lee & Chu, 2013), positive influences of human capital and management quality on entrepreneurial firms (He & Li, 2016), understanding the effects and importance of entrepreneurship training (Fairlie et al., 2015), personal characteristics of entrepreneurial spirit, creativity, and innovativeness (Puffer et al., 2018) and entrepreneurship within university research labs (Roach, 2017) etc. According to Black S. E. and Strahan P. E. (2002), no matter what the focus is, entrepreneurial activity is measured by the log of new business incorporations per capita in a state during the year. Wherein, the same subject, entrepreneurs, who get unavoidably involved in entrepreneurial activities, thread throughout the researching process and cannot be ignored as elites sharing responsibility for any of the individuals and institutional perspectives (Greenwood & Suddaby, 2006).

Because entrepreneurs are critically important, they are considered as individuals responsible for the process of watching for opportunities (Kirzner, 1973), without whom no new value would be created (Bruyat & Julien, 2001). The idea of a public entrepreneur originates with the noted economist Joseph Schumpeter in the 1940s, but was brought to fuller understanding by Robert Dahl in the 1960s (Sheingate, 2003). Since the 1980s, small business owners and entrepreneurs have been receiving greater recognition as drivers of economic growth (Soriano, 2017), because the private players have shown strong possibility of "colluding and speculating behavior" (Goyal, 2011). Self-employed individuals are considered to be more likely to experience more autonomy, exercise more judgement, have more creative and entrepreneurial tasks, and experience more task diversity (Bjørnskov & Foss, 2020). The relations between the institutional environment and entrepreneurship are an area which is largely understudied, and the entrepreneurship literature tends to assume a positive approach by focusing on the individual-opportunity nexus in entrepreneurship (Auplat, 2006). By further exploration of the relationship, a special group, military veterans, is gradually drawing more attention, whose military values of hard work and being a part of something bigger than themselves have permeated everything they do (Griswold, 2017). Former military servers in U.S. and U.K have lead the direction of entrepreneurship and already achieved noticeable results. American military veterans are nearly twice as likely to be self-employed compared to non-veterans, and are majority owners of nine percent of all business nationwide (Heinz et al., 2017). A recent Small Business Administration (SBA) (n.d.) study found that military service exhibits one of the largest marginal effects on self-employment, and veterans are 45% more likely to be self-employed than non-veterans. Moreover, the U.S. military sector is characterized by an entangled network of government bureaus and private firms whose existence is largely dependent on continued government funding and spending (Coyne et al, 2015), which may also offer business opportunities for companies owned by ex-servicemen. In the UK, according to the Federation of Small Businesses' (FSB) 2019 A Force for Business report, there are approximately 340,000 small businesses run by ex-military personnel, representing 6% of all small businesses in Britain (Cook, 2019) . The Centre for Entrepreneurs suggests that the UK can do far more to capitalize on the unique skills and experience our ex-forces possess (Centre for Entrepreneurs, n.d.). In China, attention has also been paid to veterans recently. For instance, The Ministry of Veterans Affairs was unveiled in April 2018 with the country vowing to provide better services to veterans and protect their legal rights and interests (Xinhua Press, 2019), yet literature on this topic in China seems to be rather limited. Since army veterans' entrepreneurship has become a trend worldwide and we have witnessed some different cross-country researches on firms (Bloom et al, 2010), this study will have a macroscopic inspection of the articles and research papers published during the last ten years with the help of Citespace, so as to have a better understanding of the contemporary veteran entrepreneurial condition in China. Such a timely awareness of recent trends in scientific domains is proved to be necessary to support information intensive activities in academic research (SanJuan, 2011).

This chapter is divided into four main sections. A brief and general introduction of the research background is presented first, then the second section is an overall description of data resources CNKI and research tool CiteSpace. The following section, also the core of this study, includes visualization of the research field from different angles and corresponding interpretation and discussion to present an overall image of army veteran entrepreneurship in China. The last section works as the conclusion, emphasizing the significance of this research and pointing out the drawbacks that need further exploration in the future.

DATA SOURCES AND RESEARCH METHOD

Knowledge domain are the categorization of different types of knowledge. Byosiere and Inham (2002) has identified 40 types of knowledge and classify them into four specific content areas: basic knowledge, experiential knowledge, creative/emotional knowledge and innovative knowledge. No matter which area it belongs to, a knowledge domain is typically represented by a set of bibliographic records of relevant publications (Chen, 2014). Although there are lots of electronic literature available on line, the data of scientific study must be presented in a comprehensive and systematic way. This research takes the comprehensive searchable Chinese journal full-text database (Tucker et al., 2011), the China National Knowledge Infrastructure (CNKI), as the basic literature database to have an overview of the knowledge domain and research condition of military veteran entrepreneurship in China, for it is the largest and continuously updated Chinese journals database and the most comprehensive gateway of knowledge of China (CNKI, n.d.). What's more, the number of Chinese core periodicals in CNKI is far more than other databases at present (Jiang, 2015).

With aims for providing insight into Chinese researchers' output on army veteran, CNKI was chosen as a preferable database in this study. On the basis, a sub-database named "Army veteran Entrepreneurship & Soldier Entrepreneurship" is set up. The reason why the entry "Soldier Entrepreneurship" is also included in the searching process is because the actual national conditions in China, i.e., China's Regulations on the Discipline of the People's Liberation Army, in which one provision interprets that a serviceman is not permitted to be involved in business or profitable commercial activities (Ministry of National Defense of the People's Republic of China (MOD, 2018), Ministry of Veterans Affairs of the People's Republic of China (MVA, 2019). Thus researches papers which mention "soldier entrepreneurship" actually refer to their entrepreneurial activities after they are discharged from the active service.

Like in sciences and other fields of social sciences, there is a tradition among entrepreneurship scholars to pause to take stock of what has been done in the past and reflect on the future (Chandra, 2018) through bibliometric method. CiteSpace is used worldwide, whose central idea is that focal points of research change over time, either incrementally or significantly. It is designed to answer questions about a knowledge domain, a broadly defined concept that covers a scientific field, a research area, or a scientific discipline (Chen, 2014). By studying the footprints uncovered by scholarly publications, we can trace science's development over time (Chen, 2016). CiteSpace is conceived to provide an alternative way to keep abreast of the scientific literature as the knowledge domain continuously matches on, so that our own datasets can be used to answer questions about an ever-changing knowledge domain (Chen, 2006). As a methodology for generating systematic scientometric reviews of a knowledge domain, it bridges the formally mutual exclusive globalism and localism by providing a scalable transition mechanism between them (Chen & Song, 2019). Those visual images generated by CiteSpace are of higher clarity and readability compared with previous software. In this chapter, the latest version of CiteSpace 5.6. R5 is used, whose functions are recently updated and can visualize the data in a better way. Since CiteSpace cannot directly identify and analyze the downloaded data from CNKI, the format of documents should be further adjusted to match the requirements of CiteSpace.

Besides because the later software often requires a relatively large amount of data, Microsoft Excel is used as supplement of the mapping of CiteSpace to further analyze the condition, which will be presented in the format of either tables or figures, due to Excel's extensive range of Statistical Functions, performing calculations from basic mean, median & mode to the more complex statistical distribution and probability tests. (ExcelFunctions.net., n.d.)

MAPPING KNOWLEDGE DOMAIN OF DYNAMIC VETERAN ENTREPRENEURSHIP

Research Literature on Military Veteran Entrepreneurship as the Database

With two pieces of input entries "veteran * entrepreneurship" or "solider * entrepreneurship" by subject in CNKI database, a total of 288 papers in Chinese are found through an automatic search during the period from 1st Jan. 2010 to 31st Dec. 2019, which are recently updated on 2 Jun. 2020. A search for information by subject can be really inclusive, ranging from papers with the two entries in titles, abstract to those with entries in key words, in this way any missing detection can be avoided. After manual elimination of 8 papers included in the search results because of mismatched words such as "leader" which share two same characters with "soldier" in Chinese, and another 45 irrelevant papers do not accord with the subject like news in pictures, advertisements, or papers only covering segments of the search entries such as "entrepreneurship in US", there are a total of 235 available papers left. Among these papers, 208 research papers are extracted as the foundation of mapping knowledge domain, which will be further analyzed and visualized in the following procedure through CiteSpace. These research papers can be further divided into two types: 172 journal papers, 36 master's theses and 2 doctor's dissertations. The rest 27 are newspaper reports, which show the degree of social attention paid on veteran group from the media perspective in the past ten years. However, since they are not genuine research papers, these reports are separately listed and analyzed as a social perspective.

The detailed information of the data can be seen in Figure 2. The literature appropriate for this study is downloaded and saved in a plain text format for further analysis.

Figure 1. Literature search flow

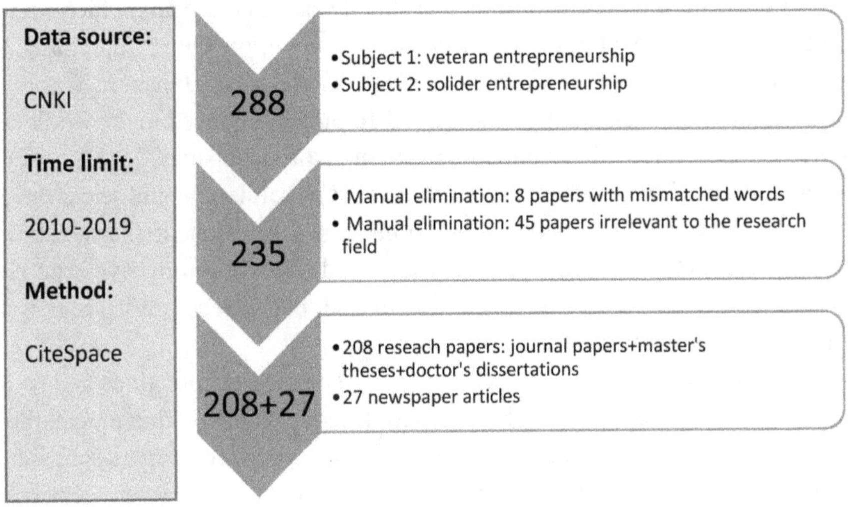

Figure 2. Composition of database for this study

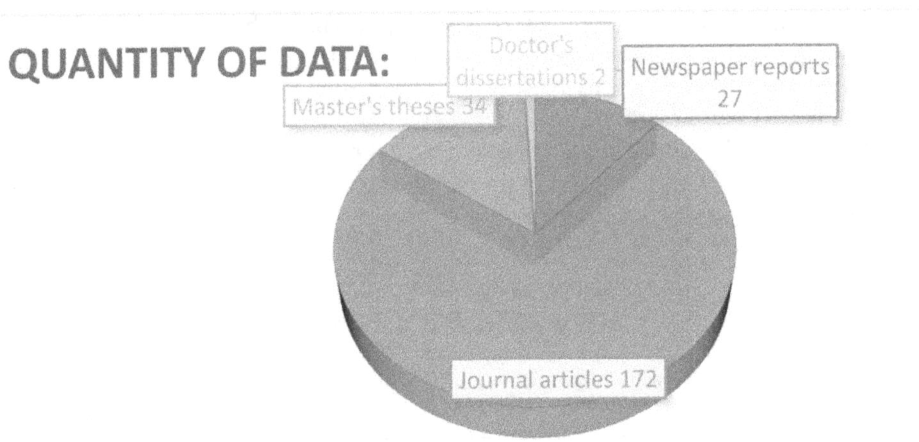

DYNAMIC TREND OF VETERAN ENTREPRENEURSHIP IN RESEARCH FIELD

With raw data, 172 of the 208 research paper are journal articles, which is around five times more than the total of master's theses and doctor's dissertations. In Figure 3, we can discover literature data extracted from CNKI were mainly taking an upward trend, different types of literature have experienced an unsteady development with some ups and downs during these years, especially during the period between 2014 and 2017. The period 2017 to 2019 has witnessed a dramatic increase in amount of research papers from the lowest point of this decade to the peak, which might be the immediate consequence of the previous demobilization. On 3rd September 2015, the 70th anniversary of the victory in Chinese people's Anti-Japanese War and the world anti-fascist war, Chinese President Xi Jinping announced to the whole world that China would have substantial disarmament involving up to 300,000 servicemen (China. com.cn., 2015), which signified that more soldiers would leave the army and the placement of these veterans might become a milestone in the society in the coming years. Yet the changes that references and cited literature have experienced were not as obvious. There were short-term rise, but in recent 3 years they were both on a downward trend.

By tracing the academic papers, we can fix the research directions and research areas on veteran entrepreneurship in the past decade. When looking into all the data involved (Figure 4), we found that there were only 2 research papers sponsored by scientific research foundations, which are Chinese Postdoctoral Science Foundation and National Social Science Foundation respectively. The quantity of papers sponsored by foundations was quite limited compared with other research direction in management field. It could also been understood as that there wasn't sufficient support from the government or management level. To improve the efficiency and influence in this research field, more policy support should be given and academic management measures should be taken to address this issue.

Figure 3. General dynamic trend of research papers

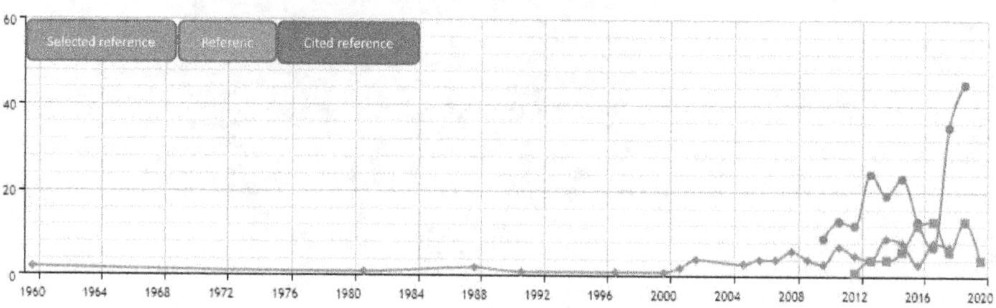

Figure 4. Foundation support

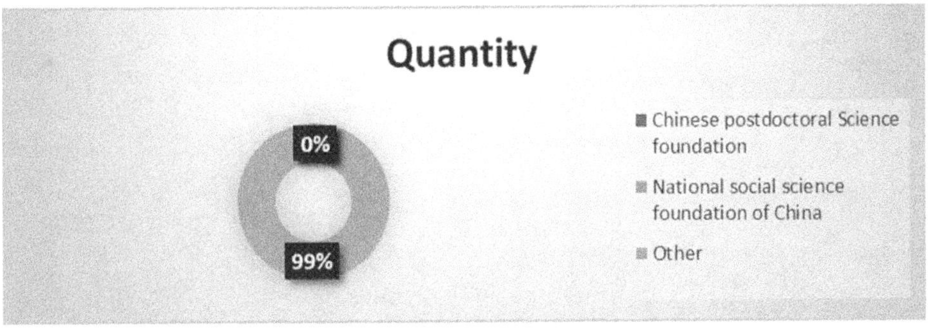

Figure 5 obviously shows that authors who were doing researches on veteran entrepreneurship scattered without forming a research mainstream and were not so closely related to each other. Besides Guogeng Liao, who contributed two papers, other researchers only have one paper published each during this period. What's more, their co-citation remained at a low level because we can only see very weak and small clusters here in the figure. On one hand, this phenomenon shows that a large number of researchers get involved in this field; on the other hand, it means that the researchers are still in lack of a relatively systematic and ripe theoretical system in this field. Therefore, research topics in the past decade are lack of a scientific and in-depth understanding and long-term research atmosphere from a chronological view.

Figure 5. Author cooperation network

Figure 6. Knowledge domain of institutions

The distribution of institutions in Figure 6 has shown a similar status as the factor of authors. Among all the institutions, only three of them have 3 papers published each in the last ten years, which are respectively: Daqing Technician College, Nanjing University of Science and Technology, and Tsinghua University. Not only that, there are few connections or cooperation among these institutions on the study of veteran entrepreneurship. Lacking of inter-school or inter-institution cooperation may result in a situation that related researches cannot be based on effective cooperation network among different universities. Even so, Table 1 helps to indicate that colleges and universities are still pioneers in opening up novel research areas, and also the powerful driving force in carrying out scientific research. Therefore, financial and policy support should be increased in the future if more academic achievements are expected.

Table 1. Top 5 institutions with most published articles on veteran entrepreneurship

Institutions	Amount of published articles
Daqing Technician College	3
Nanjing University of Science and Technology	3
Tsinghua University	3
Hunan Normal University	2
Shandong University	2

Figure 7. Mapping of key words co-occurrence

Figure 8. Word cloud of buzzword in research of veteran entrepreneurship

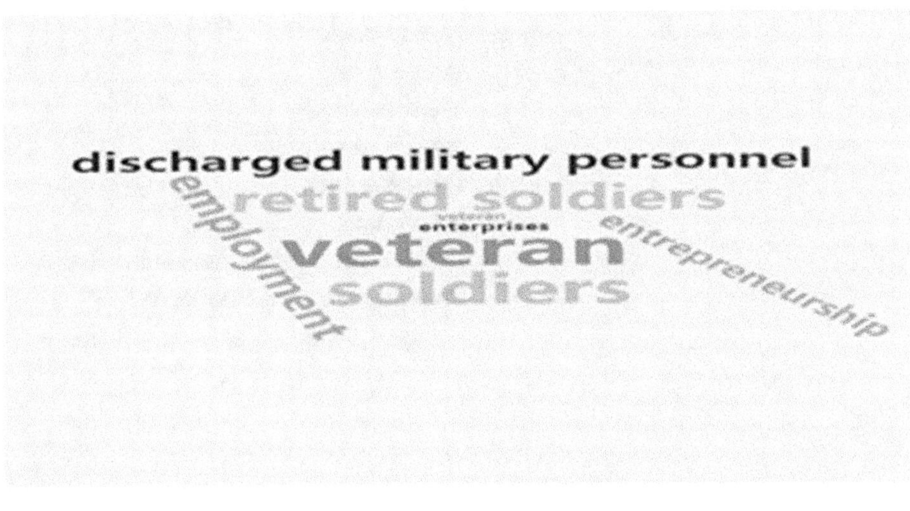

In the analyzing process above, although we have found little connections among different authors and institutions, mapping of key words has shown us there are obvious clusters among them (Figure 7). Key words are specific words that we can query with to allow users to easily find the needed information quickly (Niwattanakul et al., 2013). After observing the co-occurrence of key words, we can easily unfold the fact that researchers from different institutions share similar research interests when exploring the topic of army veteran entrepreneurship. However, no obvious burst was observed in the process of running CiteSpace for data analysis, which means that within the period of ten years, there was no sharp rise in citation of a certain term, and the research focus on veteran entrepreneurship in China has remained almost unchanged. In Figure 8, top key words are highlighted to present the general concern of the study during this period. Among them, "veteran" is the term appeared with the highest frequency of 28 times. The terms at the top of the list all focused the identification of the research subject. Whereafter, terms reflecting their main activities came into our sight, such as "independent choosing profession", "obtain employment", "entrepreneurship" and "entrepreneurship training". Thus, researchers focusing on veteran training took these words as the core of their starting point as well as the foothold. In this data processing procedure, enterprise, as an unavoidable concept, worked as a key medium.

Figure 9. Top 10 sources of literature related to veteran entrepreneurship

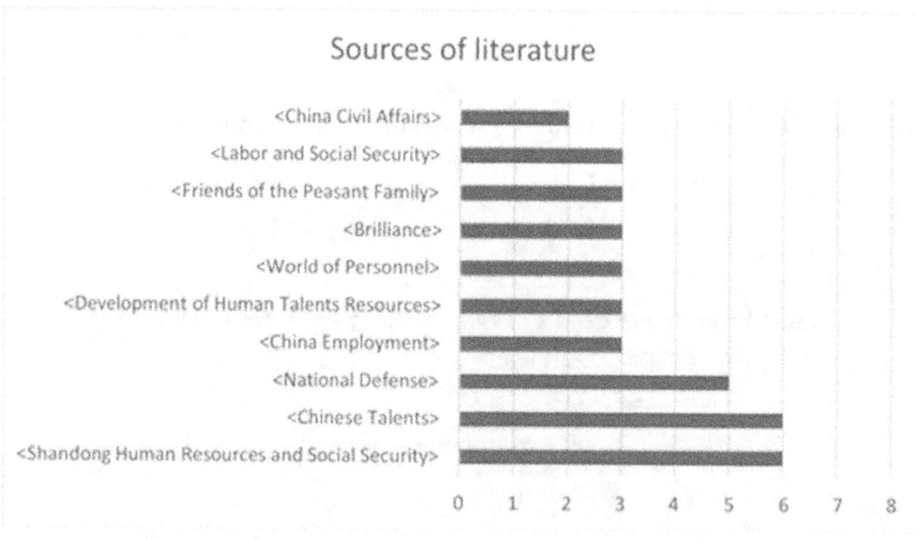

When it comes to the main sources of literature related to veteran entrepreneurship, only two of them are military magazines among all the top ten magazines. In contrast, magazines focusing on human resource occupy the vast majority of the top 10, i.e. 7 in 10, which has verified the publication diversity in this field during past decade. According to the data, a conclusion can be drawn that there are insufficient attention paid on veteran entrepreneurship from the armed forces during the last ten years. Yet much emphasis comes from magazines attaching importance to manpower, which means the employment and entrepreneurship of those ex-military personnel are brought into focal point of the society and need to be settled within the society.

DEVELOPING TREND OF MILITARY VETERAN ENTREPRENEURSHIP IN NEWSPAPER ARTICLES

There are a total of 27 newspaper articles which are related to veteran entrepreneurship in CNKI during the past ten years. Since the size is too small, it is not suitable to be processed by CiteSpace. Thus, these data will be analyzed and visualized through Excel to have an overview of veteran entrepreneurship from the media perspective.

Figure 10. General developing tendency of newspaper reports on veteran entrepreneurship in the past decade

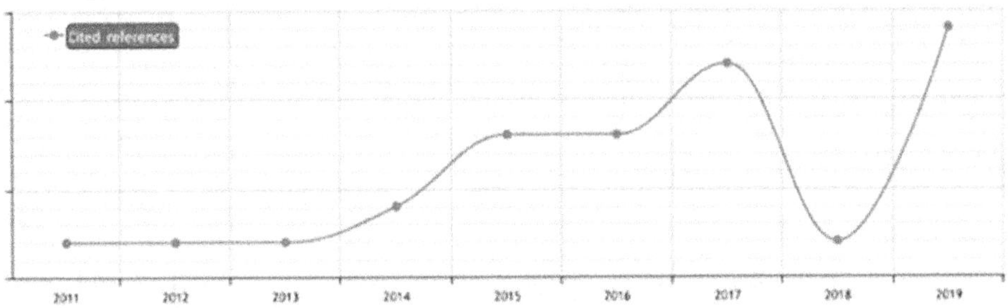

From the developing tendency above in Figure 10, we can have a clear impression of the attention paid on veteran entrepreneurship during the past ten years from the perspective of newspapers. During the first three years ranging from 2011 to 2013, newspaper articles almost kept a steady flow. Starting from 2014, more newspapers articles were published, which presented a steady rising trend in the coming four years. 2018 was a quite special year witnessing a sharp drop in amount of newspaper articles, the bottom of the curve was almost the same as what it was like in the three years ranging from 2011. A rebound brought the figure to a higher level, and we observed a peak of this decade in 2019. Yet, although the curve kept a fluctuating trend during this period, the total amount could not be quite influential or representative because of the relatively small data size.

Table 2 listed the top 5 newspapers publishing articles related to military veteran entrepreneurship. China Military which published 8 articles was listed as the first, taking 29.6% of the total articles; China National Defense News and China' Armed Police, ranking at 3rd and 4th in the list published 2 articles respectively. These three different newspapers, which were all founded by different branches of People's Liberation Army, have published nearly half of the 27 articles in these ten years. It means that the armed force in China paid the most attention on the external publicity of retirees from the army and their future career, which is quite different from the analytical results of the academic sources of literature. In doing so, the newspaper articles promote the entrepreneurial condition to the general public and make people be aware of its significance. China Society News, listed at the second position, published 3 articles taking 11.1% of the total amount. The focus from the social media reveals veteran entrepreneurship has already come into the sight of the society, which might further develop into a social phenomenon.

Table 2. Top 5 sources of newspaper articles

Newspapers	Amount of articles	Percentage
China Military	8	29.6%
China Society News	3	11.1%
China National Defense News	2	7.4%
China's Armed Police	2	7.4%
Tongliao Daily	1	3.7%

Fostering entrepreneurship is not just about finding the smartest and most motivated entrepreneurs; it requires crafting the right rules of the game for those entrepreneurs to succeed (Hasik, 2016). To have an in-depth exploration, another typical situation was detected. Since the national economic development level is an objective restriction to the scale of military manpower, the military establishment reform must develop in tune with economic construction (Xue, 2011). When a new entry "develop*" is added to the original search, a total of 61 articles are presented, among which 3 newspaper articles are ignored first. Then following the same deleting principle, irrelevant papers deviated from the subject such as papers only involving segments of the search entries such as "entrepreneurship in US", "development" or "entrepreneurship" are ignored. Only 42 research papers are left for further contrast in Figure 10. It is obvious that although the research papers involving the entry “develop*” is only around 1/5 of the total research papers, their performance in download frequency, number of citation and references is quite impressive, each item of which has at least doubled the general data. Through contrast, the general case of the bar graph in Figure 11 might be interpreted as a future trend in veteran entrepreneurship study, in which long-term development shows enormous potential, thus great attention should be paid to chase the developing process.

Figure 11. Contrast of papers with and without “develop”

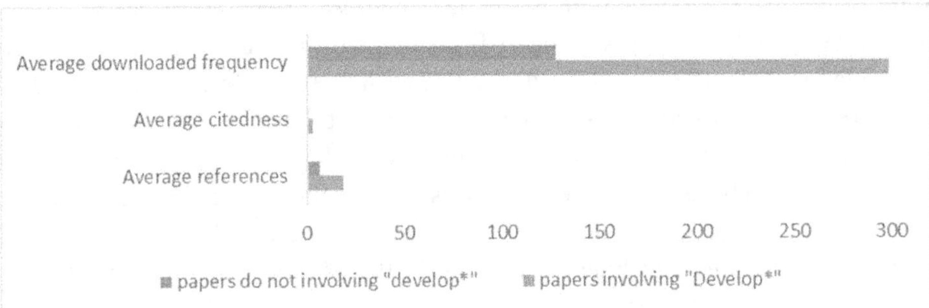

CONCLUSION

The globally implemented scientometric software, CiteSpace, is adopted in this study for the analysis and interpretation of data on veteran entrepreneurship in CNKI in last decade, which offers an opportunity for synthesizing the public opinions as well as the research achievements. Through mapping the chronological evolution military veteran entrepreneurship during this period from perspectives of authors, institutions, key words and sources of literature, an overall profile of 235 publications on CNKI was presented, which is subdivided into two main types: journal articles and research papers. The results of different knowledge domains of veteran entrepreneurship showing a general trend of veteran entrepreneurship from 2010 to 2019 are mapped out into figures and tables, which can be easily and directly perceived by readers. There aren’t distinct features from the perspectives of authors or institutions, the co-operation and interaction among them are also proved to be so weak and need to be further strengthened. However, the analysis on keywords shows us the of hot research areas of entrepreneurship in the period, which are diversified although there is not burst then. Sources of literature reveals the main journals focusing on veteran entrepreneurship, and the classification of them has highlighted the social power and influence. By contrasting the results of data sources from research articles and newspapers, we find that the two territory varies with each other and show different trend. Military still takes a crucial position in publicizing veteran entrepreneurship through the channel of media so as to draw attention from the whole society. In addition, a further insertion of papers concerning "development" indicates that research on "veteran entrepreneurship" might become a potential and sustainable research trend in the long run from a progressing point of view. After combing through the general evolution in this field from 2010 to 2019 in China, a better understanding of the research condition can be achieved. Thus, the chapter can provide better outcomes in veteran entrepreneurship in China over the span of ten years, which is not only a trustworthy reference for future researchers who want to continue the exploration in this field, but also offers the chance of cross-cultural learning between practitioners from a global view, investors, researchers, and policy-makers. Besides, this study also contributes to filling the gap between literature of chronological analysis and visualization on veteran entrepreneurship.

Nevertheless, some limitations are dug out in the analyzing process. First, CiteSpace cannot be used to make an analysis of the collected data from CNKI from the angle of reference, cited authors or cited journal because the original version of data are presented in Chinese. As a result, the general condition can still be perfected or improved if the software might be updated or upgraded in dealing with Chinese documents in the future. Then, the research results have shown the research condition of domestic researchers in China through CNKI, future studies could use another database, Web of Science, to further expand the vision of research from China to other countries all over the world to reveal the similarities and differences in the form of a comparative study. Finally, the data only cover a period of ten years ranging from 2010 to 2019, which still leaves space to deepen and extend the range to verify the accuracy of this study as well as explore the possibility of adopting other database or software in this research area. In general, although this research has some deficiencies, it provides valuable and promising prospect for the upcoming intensive study in both software updating and profession exploration.

REFERENCES

AuplatC. A. (2006). Do NGOs influence Entrepreneurship?: Insights from the developments of Biotechnologies and Nanotechnologies. *Society and Business Review*. https://www.researchgate.net/publication/228263059 doi:10.2139srn.1263584

Bjørnskov, C., & Foss, N. J. (2020). Well-being and entrepreneurship: Using establishment size to identify treatment effects and transmission mechanisms. *PLoS One*, *15*(1), e0226008. doi:10.1371/journal.pone.0226008 PMID:31940306

Black, S. E., & Strahan, P. E. (2002). Entrepreneurship and bank credit availability. *The Journal of Finance*, *57*(6), 2807–2833. doi:10.1111/1540-6261.00513

Bloom, N., Nahajan, A., Mckenzie, D., & Roberts, J. (2010). Why do firms in developing countries have low productivity. *The American Economic Review*, *2*(2), 619–623. doi:10.1257/aer.100.2.619

Brock, W. A., & Evans, D. S. (1989). Small Business Economics. *Small Business Economics*, *1*(1), 7–20. doi:10.1007/BF00389913

Bruyat, C., & Julien, P. A. (2001). Defining the field of Research in Entrepreneurship. *Journal ofBusiness Venturing*, *16*(2), 165–180. doi:10.1016/S0883-9026(99)00043-9

Byosiere, P., & Ingham, M. (2002). *Knowledge domains as driving force for competitive advantages: empirical evidence in a telecommunications MNC*. Strategic Management Society Conference. Paris Centre for Entrepreneurs. https://centreforentrepreneurs.org/cfe-research/the-military-entrepreneurship-manifesto/

Chandra, Y. (2018). Mapping the evolution of entrepreneurship as a field of research (1990–2013): A scientometric analysis. *PLoS One*, *13*(1), e0190228. doi:10.1371/journal.pone.0190228 PMID:29300735

Chen, C. (2006). CiteSpace II: Detecting and visualizing emerging trends and transient patterns in scientific literature. *Journal of the American Society for Information Science and Technology*, *57*(3), 359–377. doi:10.1002/asi.20317

Chen, C. (2014). *The CiteSpace Manual*. http://cluster.ischool.drexel.edu/~cchen/citespace/CiteSpaceManual.pdf

Chen, C. (2016). *CiteSpace: Apractical guide for mapping scientific literature*. Nova Science Publishers, Inc.

Chen, C., & Song, M. (2019). Visualizing a field of research: A methodology of systematic scientometric reviews. *PLoS One*, *14*(10), e0223994. doi:10.1371/journal.pone.0223994 PMID:31671124

China. com.cn. (2015). http://t.m.china.com.cn/convert/c_uPQQeDGz.html

CNKI. (n.d.). http://www.oversea.cnki.net/rkns55/support/en/company.aspx

Cook, S. (2019). Ex-forces entrepreneurs: how veterans can start and grow businesses. *Startups*. https://startups.co.uk/ex-forces-entrepreneurs/

Coyne, C. J., Michaluk, C., & Reese, R. (2015). *Unproductive Entrepreneurship in U.S. Military Contracting*. GMU Working Paper in Economics No. 15-50. doi:10.2139srn.2667905

ExcelFunctions.net. (n.d.). https://www.excelfunctions.net/excel-statistical-functions.html#:~:text=Excel%20Statistical%20Functions.%20Excel%20provides%20an%20extensive%20range,into%20categories%2C%20to%20help%20you%20to%20easily%20find

Fairlie, R. W., Karlan, D., & Zinman, J. (2015). Behind the gate experiment: Evidence on effects of and rationales for subsidized entrepreneurship training. *American Economic Journal. Economic Policy*, *7*(2), 125–161. doi:10.1257/pol.20120337

Goyal, Y. (2011). Inefficient Parastatal Agencies and the Growing Modern Food Market in India: The need for Private Participation. *Asian Journal of Public Affairs*, *3*(2), 48–66.

Greenwood, R., & Suddaby, R. (2006). Institutional Entrepreneurship in Mature Fields: The big five accounting firms. *Academy of Management Journal*, *49*(1), 27–48. doi:10.5465/amj.2006.20785498

Griswold, J. (2017). *Mission Entrepreneur: Applying Lessons from Military Life to Create Success in Business Startups*. Mango Publishing Group.

Hasik, J. (2016). Defense Entrepreneurship: How to Build Institutions for Innovation Inside the Military. *Joint Force Quarterly*, *81*(2), 112–117.

He, S., & Li, C. W. (2016). Human capital, management quality and the exit decisions of entrepreneurial firms. *Journal of Financial and Quantitative Analysis*, *51*(4), 1269–1295. doi:10.1017/S0022109016000363

Heinz, A. J., Freeman, M. A., Harpaz-Rotem, I., & Pietrzak, R. H. (2017). American Military Veteran Entrepreneurs: A Comprehensive Profile of Demographic, Service History, and Psychosocial Characteristics. *Military Psychology*, *29*(6), 513–523. doi:10.1037/mil0000195 PMID:29290645

Henry, C., Hill, F., & Leitch, C. M. (2003). Education and Training for Aspiring Entrepreneurs: The Issue of Effectiveness. Ashgate Publishing.

Jiang, H. B. (2015). A review of the quality of full-text databases of three major Chinese periodicals. *Modern Intelligence*, *35*(9), 84-88. doi:10.3969/j.issn.1008-0821.2015.09.016

Kirzner, I. M. (1973). *Competition and Entrepreneurship*. University of Chicago Press.

Lee, T. K., & Chu, W. Y. (2013). How entrepreneurial orientation, environmental dynamism, and resource rareness influence firm performance. *Journal of Management & Organization*, *19*(2), 167–187. doi:10.1017/jmo.2013.33

Ministry of National Defense of the People's Republic of China (MOD). (2018). *China's Regulations on the Discipline of the People's Liberation Army*. http://www.mod.gov.cn/topnews/2018-04/18/content_4809753.htm

Ministry of Veterans Affairs of the People's Republic of China (MVA). (2019). http://www.mva.gov.cn/gongkai/zfxxzdgkml/fgzc/gfxwj/201903/t2019321_23376.html

Niwattanakul, S., Singthongchai, J., Naenudorn, E., & Wanapu, S. (2013). Using of Jaccard Coefficient for keywords similarity. *Proceedings of the International MultiConference of Engineers and Computer Scientists (IMECS).*

Puffer, M. S., Mccarthy, D., & Satinsky, M. D. (2018). *Hammer and Silicon*. Cambridge University Press. doi:10.1017/9781108120302

Roach, M. (2017). Encouraging entrepreneurship in university labs: Research activities, research outputs, and early doctorate careers. *PLoS One*, *12*(2), e0170444. doi:10.1371/journal.pone.0170444 PMID:28178270

SanJuan, E. (2011). Mapping knowledge domains combing symbolic relations with graph theory. *Processing of the International Conference on Knowledge Discovery and Information Retrieval (SSTM-2011)*, 519-528. DOI: 10.5220/0003721105190528

Sheingate, A. D. (2003). Political entrepreneurship, institutional change, and American economic development. *Studies in American Political Development*, *17*(2), 185–203. doi:10.1017/S0898588X03000129

Soriano, D. R. (2017). Small business and entrepreneurship: their role in economic and social development. *Entrepreneurship & Regional Development*, *29*(1-2), 1-3. doi:10.1080/08985626.2016.1255438

Toth, R. (2012). Entrepreneurial human capital and entrepreneurial dynamics: evidence from natural experiment. *Economics*. https://www.semanticscholar.org/paper/Entrepreneurial-Human-Capital-and-Entrepreneurial-a-Toth/10d60012b1eebd6730070778fdbd4bbdc325dac0

Tucker, J. D., Chang, H., Brandt, A., Gao, X., Lin, M., Luo, J., Song, P., Sun, K., & Zhang, X. (2011). An Empirical Analysis of Overlap Publication in Chinese Language and English Research Manuscripts. *PLoS One*, *6*(7), e22149. doi:10.1371/journal.pone.0022149 PMID:21765946

U. S. Small Business Administration. (n.d.). https://www.sba.gov/content/facts-veterans-and-entrepreneurship

Urbano, D., & Aparicio, S. (2016). Entrepreneurship capital types and economic growth: International evidence. *Technological Forecasting and Social Change*, *102*, 34–44. doi:10.1016/j.techfore.2015.02.018

Xinhua Press. (2019). *Most beautiful veterans' urge ex-service personnel to contribute more to China's development.* http://www.chinadaily.com.cn/a/201901/23/WS5c47d7f5a3106c65c34e6072.html

Xue, J.F. (2011). Structural reform of military establishment should coordinate with the level of social and economic development. *Military Economic Research*, 2.

KEY TERMS AND DEFINITIONS

Army Veteran Entrepreneurship: Refers to the act and ability of ex-military servers to seize business opportunities and then create, run a business enterprise esp. small businesses, and manage multiple aspects of a business operation, involving risks and uncertainties, in order to make a profit through overcoming the challenges based on their previous unique skills and experience.

Citespace: Is a worldwide popular software and methodology designed to generate systematic and scientometric reviews of a knowledge domain covering a scientific field, a research area, or a scientific discipline; or to trace the footprints uncovered by scholarly publications with focal points of research change over time.

Mapping Knowledge Domain: Aims at visualizing and displaying knowledge and making the structure of knowledge and dynamic development of a discipline evident through ways of charting, mining, analyzing, sorting a set of bibliographic records of relevant publications, etc.

Chapter 7
Investigating Entrepreneurship Among Nigerian Retired Military Veterans

Sanya Ojo
https://orcid.org/0000-0002-2585-9052
Nigerian Defence Academy, Nigeria

ABSTRACT

The condition of survival within the Nigerian Armed Forces, in terms of post-retirement career options, has inadvertently produced a growing number of ex-service members (veterans) who turned to entrepreneurship to earn income and remain active. However, against the alleged failure of entrepreneurship in this group, this chapter sets out to investigate the nature and characteristics of veteran entrepreneurship. Through the application of case study methodology, the study reveals that veteran entrepreneurship does not differ significantly to civilian entrepreneurship. Veteran entrepreneurs confront the same challenges as their civilian counterparts while veterans' military backgrounds and military training appear to have both facilitating and inhibiting effects on veteran entrepreneurships in Nigeria.

INTRODUCTION

Background

Retirement from the military is not "retirement" in the real sense of retirement. Most retired military personnel (veterans) go on to work a second career following their military service Others may leave the military before they are eligible for

DOI: 10.4018/978-1-7998-6655-8.ch007

Copyright © 2021, IGI Global. Copying or distributing in print or electronic forms without written permission of IGI Global is prohibited.

retirement from service as many are abruptly retired (i.e., for any possible reason such as victimisation or misconduct) at a youthful age bracket. Military personnel in Nigeria retire at the age of 52 (proposal to raise it to 62 is ongoing) or after 35 years of service. On average, military personnel retire 15-20 years earlier than their civilian counterparts (Smaliukiene, 2013). Veterans can be overwhelmed by the number of adjustments and choices they have to make in retirement. They can suffer "choice dilemma" because they are new to their current situation. Depending on individual's idiosyncratic disposition, and the effect of age on self-confidence, some veterans may distrust their ability to make suitable decisions because there is so much at stake. Others may feel they can no longer marshal the required energy to take decisive actions and slip into procrastination and decision paralysis. Thus, following retirement from the military, veterans are often faced with the challenge of building a second career (e.g., Vigoda-Gadot et al., 2010).

Nevertheless, many veterans in Nigeria are turning to entrepreneurship as a career option in retirement. This could be due to the euphoria of autonomy of self-employment or the pre-retirement training programs (e.g., at the Nigerian Armed Forces Resettlement Centre, Oshodi) they undertook. In a way, while in service, they keep the country safe. Once retired, they are choosing to serve the economy - by turning veteran entrepreneurs. However, circumstantial evidence suggests that many of the veteran entrepreneurs' ventures are not doing well (Madichie & Ayasi, 2018). This anecdotal signal serves as prompt for this study, which is positioned to bring fresh insights into veteran entrepreneurship.

Essentially, this study seeks to understand the characteristics of veteran entrepreneurship and its qualities by seeking to answer two questions: (1) What is the nature of veteran entrepreneurship in Nigeria? (2) What are the factors facilitating or inhibiting veteran entrepreneurship in Nigeria?

Statement of the Problem

The transition from military to civilian life continues to be a particularly difficult process and given the state of the Nigerian economy and the reported hardship people are in, veterans are exposed to great challenges. Many individuals of the rank and file in the Nigerian military establishment are retired when they were not ready to be demobilized. Many of these individuals are often on lower remuneration structure and their post-retirement benefits usually amount to nothing (Adekanye, 1999). Several veterans (especially the junior ranks) are individuals who, according to Ntiwunka (2012) wallow in abject poverty and generally finding it difficult to make ends meet because the little income (pension) they depend on is meagre and not regular. The task of constructing a new lifeworld whose center-point is retirement rather than a work-life is challenging and as many veterans reflect on their career, they may struggle with feelings of isolation and grief for a career that has passed its "expiry date". Moreover, money problem and/or unemployment could become serious issues for the retirees (Bergman et al., 2014). Research has shown that military service members transitioning from active duty back into a civilian lifestyle are confronted with a 21% overall unemployment rate (Bressler et al., 2013).

The paper is structured into five sections; section one is the conceptual analysis, section two describes the contextual background, section three explains the methodology, section four illustrates the findings and analysis, and section five presents the discussion, recommendations, limitations, and conclusion.

CONCEPTUAL BACKGROUND

The Concept of Entrepreneurship

The concept of entrepreneurship has for long been interrogated along several dimensions by various authors depending on their orientations (Ojo & Nwankwo, 2017). Entrepreneurship as a *speculative endeavor* has been championed by Knight (1961), Schumpeter (1934) advocated entrepreneurship as an *innovative technical ability,* Cole (1959) formulated the theory of *enterprise creation*, whilst Kirzner (1973) positioned entrepreneurship as *alertness to opportunity*. Other orientations of entrepreneurship include growth and value creation (Sharma & Chrisman, 1999), etc. According to Ojo (2013), the term "entrepreneurship" has become nebulous such that everything is ascribed to it. Thus, the term is quite elastic and has a broad range of different and, sometimes, contradictory meanings. As a result of these multitude positioning, there is hardly any consensus on the definition of entrepreneurship (Dana, 2006). Numerous scholars have presented varied definitions of entrepreneurship such that the bases and elements of entrepreneurship spread over a broad range of theories and descriptions (Brock & Evans, 1989). Consequently, the concept of entrepreneurship is explored in many interdisciplinary fields including military (Smaliukiene, 2013), psychology, sociology, economics, cultural, political, historical studies (Brock & Evans, 1989), and it is applied to numerous paradigms and settings (Bruyat & Julien, 2001). Today, entrepreneurship is considered one of the best economic development approaches for promoting nations' economic growth and sustaining a nation's competitiveness in an increasingly globalized world (Schaper & Volery, 2004; Venkatachalam & Waqif, 2005).

Military Entrepreneurship

The military establishments all over the world, like any other organization, apply the concept of entrepreneurship in their day-to-day activities. Military entrepreneurship is a growing field that is yet to be developed in the mainstream academic research domain. Admittedly, a few studies exist on the integration of military veterans (retirees) into a civilian-based entrepreneurship ecosystem (e.g. Vigoda-Gado et al., 2010; Hope et al., 2011; Kerrick et al., 2014; Adrienne et al., 2017). However, other components of military involvement in entrepreneurship have received little or no mention in the literature. Elements such as intrapreneurship (i.e. serving personnel entrepreneurial agency) in the military and entrepreneurial agency of spouses (especially female) of serving military personnel are barely visible in mainstream academic literature. Noticeably, the military establishment exhibits the "Iceberg Phenomenon" – visible and hidden identity in entrepreneurship research.

The connection between the military and entrepreneurship is strikingly highlighted in the USA's Gallup Confidence Study, which indicated that the military and small business are the two most trusted institutions in 2018 (SmallBusiness.com, 2020). According to Boldon et al. (2016), the military and small business ownership share a long and distinctive relationship. Veterans are more likely to own a business than non-veterans and often tend to out-earn non-veteran entrepreneurs. As far as military veterans are concerned, entrepreneurship is a viable option that offers the opportunity to apply the skills developed in the army such as resilience, ambition and leadership (Ross, 2015). Veterans, like any other group, have been reported to be involved in several enterprises and business ventures including farming, manufacturing, oil and gas, bakery, etc. Their business enterprises are said to flourish owing to the discipline acquired during their time in the military (Smaliukiene, 2013). Previous studies suggest that veterans do have a positive impact on self-employment (Kerrick et al., 2014) as they are involved in different businesses and, directly or indirectly, generating employment and contributing to national development (Chandra, 2014). There are recorded cases of veterans engaging in entrepreneurship. For instance, 75,000 people (many of them between the ages of 35 and 45) are retired from the India military service every year, and many of them, "adopt entrepreneurship for their life's second innings" (Kedia, 2019). Every year, according to Cook (2019), more than 14,000 people leave the Armed Forces in the UK and while some may look into re-entering employment in another sector, a small number become start-up founders. The Federation of Small Businesses' 2019 Report shows that there are approximately 340,000 small businesses run by ex-military personnel, representing 6% of all small businesses in Britain (Cook, 2019).

Research has indicated that self-employment increases considerably after retirement, partly because self-employment provides retirees with opportunities and flexibility not found in paid employments (Cahill et al., 2013). As veteran populations increase due to military downsizing, veterans transitioning to the civilian life may focus on self-employment as a viable option in seeking work (Blass & Ketchen, 2014). This fact was supported by Kerrick et al.'s (2014) projection that 45% of veterans do become self-employed. Furthermore, financial hardship, labor market constrictions and discrimination may push retirees into entrepreneurship (Singh & DeNoble, 2003).

Essentially, veteran entrepreneurs derive from a diverse population with unique experiences but they also encounter challenges at all stages of their business ownership journey. Successful entrepreneurs tend to demonstrate good decision-making in chaotic environments, confidence, independence, and high self-efficacy and achievement - all traits commonly found in service members and veterans Boldon et al. (2016). Nevertheless, there are challenges with veteran entrepreneurship. Three central barriers/themes facing veteran entrepreneurs include access to financial capital, people and social capital, and decision making (Boldon et al., 2016). For example, Sankaran and Battisto (2018) contended that veteran entrepreneurs face more difficulty in accessing capital than non-veteran business owners. Some of the reasons adduced include the fact that veterans often apply for smaller loans of $100,000 or less, which can be harder to get from big banks. In addition, the military lifestyle can make it difficult to build a good credit history, which frustrates easy access to bank loans.

CONTEXTUAL FRAMING

Retiring/Retired Military Personnel

The transition to retirement is often a combination of the anticipated and the unanticipated. It is capable of generating major psychological issues that are sometimes ignored by those who paint a radiant picture of retirement (Osborne, 2012). The Military service is a unique form of employment and way of life that creates a strong culture and solidarity among members, and which for some may have a lasting impact even after they have returned to civilian life. Due to the pervasiveness and uniqueness of these experiences there exist a tension between military identity and post-discharge resettlement within the civilian setting (Jolly, 1996). The military is a closed social system where individual experiences of work, living, and emotional expression are controlled. Whilst on active duty, soldiers dutifully obey codes of military conduct at all times, on and off base, from the moment they enter the military until the moment they leave (Arkin, 1978). This acculturation process into the military culture, which is profoundly and unceasingly imposed, does not decline easily even after retirement (Demers, 2011). Unfortunately, when returning to civilian life, veterans continue to conform to this military culture, which in many cases are incongruent with civilian norms (Hale, 2017). It was Collins (1998: 216) who argued that the differences in values between civilian society and military society create a "civil-military cultural gap". Apparently, the civilian-military-civilian transition sequence, which Schlossberg et al. (1995: 27) described as "moving in, moving through, and moving out phases" has an arduous impact on many veterans.

Consequently, many retiring military individuals and their families are challenged by the transition to civilian life - particularly in securing employment, managing finances and health care, pursuing education, family reintegration, and negotiating their new community (Robertson & Brott, 2017; Vogt et al, 2018). Transition to civilian life can bring unexpected feelings and problems including loss of the military self and the military camaraderie, disorientation in an unfamiliar civilian world, and a period of re-adjusting to being with family full-time (Pranger et al., 2009). Veterans may also experience symptoms of grief and stress in response to the perceived "loss of the military self" (Mobbs & Bonanno, 2018). According to George's (1993) role theory, a person's profession is central to his/her identity and the loss of this critically important work role, and or the environmental loss accompanying the retirement, produces a concomitant decline in life satisfaction and increases depressive symptoms. Hence, retirement brings to an end work role and the retired individual suffers psychologically since she/he no longer views herself/himself as productive and contributing member of the society (Ehsan, 2010). Invariably, some studies (e.g. Bergman et al., 2014; Interian et al., 2014) found that transition difficulty and stress are predictive of mental and physical health problems among veterans. Female veteran could also be more disadvantaged, for instance, Baechtold (2012) argued that female veteran inferiority issues compounded pre-existing mental and physical struggles associated with veteran trauma.

The transition experience can be compared to a "reverse culture shock" as personnel unexpectedly face difficulties with adjustment after retiring from active service (Westwood, 1999). This shock is experienced not only by the veterans themselves but by other key persons in their lives (Westwood et al., 2002), that is, the effect of retirement is also felt by other members of the family, particularly the spouse. For instance, when a veteran encounters difficulty in finding a new job, the burden of economic support of the family shifts to the spouse and older children (Bradburn, 1969). Military spouses are at the frontlines domestically, maintaining the home and keeping the family together while their partners are deployed. Due to the continuous and repeated separation of the military family as a result of deployment (Strange, 1984), retirement may be the first time the husband and wife live together for a prolonged period. This new lifestyle often requires restructuring of the marital relationship (Yanos, 2004) as families may have created new routines during absence, thus, both the veteran and family members will have to adjust to changes. The long and continuous absence due to military duties and regular deployment makes adjusting to the full-time spouse at home very difficult especially during the transitioning period (Ray & Heaslip, 2011).

While formal military retirement programs are organized to provide support with planning and general logistics of transitions (Wolpert, 2000), research suggests that veterans feel emotionally underprepared to manage the transition to civilian employment (Baruch & Quick, 2009). Some researchers (e.g. Angrist, 1998; Smith-Osborne, 2013) have argued that veterans may not be able to achieve the desired life trajectory, compared to civilians of similar background and age. It is the case that the shift from a civilian to a recruit then back to civilian life after years of serving in the military is usually underestimated (Higate, 2001).

Nevertheless, many military retirement programs prominently feature "entrepreneurship training" as part of their packages to empower retirees to grow as skilled entrepreneurs. For instance, the Nigerian Armed Forces Resettlement Centre (NAFRC), Oshodi, Lagos, mandated to provide necessary training geared towards preparing retiring servicemen/women for reintegration into civil life, has trained over 41,000 since its inception (Chinyem, 2018). NAFRC was formally constituted in 1982. The NAFRC trains retiring service personnel (non-commissioned officers) in vocational courses such as tailoring, plumbing, music, refrigeration and air-conditioning, barbing and hairdressing, electrical and electronics, electroplating and hydrographic as well as bakery and many others. Ideally, service in the military often provides highly specific competencies that can be adapted as transferable expertise and knowledge for entrepreneurship (Smaliukienė, 2013). Military personnel are equipped with skills and know-how inherent in military training, which include risk management, performance under pressure and leadership - qualities that can be moderated and exploited as potent entrepreneurship skills and essential to effective venture management. According to Storlie (2010), ex-service people acquired adapting skills such as directness, speed, assertiveness, team decision-making, methodical approaches to problems through military training.

Consequently, several veterans in Nigeria turn to entrepreneurship to earn income when they retire, however, according to Madichie and Ayasi (2018), the attrition rate in terms of failure is disquieting even though no official figure is available. The question is: Why do many veterans fail in business despite the type of training, skills, and resources at their disposal? Within the veteran entrepreneurship literature, there is a major gap in analyzing the factors that affect entrepreneurship among veterans. Hope et al. (2011) analyze some general trends, including the general inverse relationship between the length of service and likelihood of self-employment post-transition. According to Nicholson (2019), many American veterans are single-income households, many are living paycheck to paycheck, and finances are usually the biggest stressor for veterans after the stressor of war. Many veterans have financial worries that keep them from pursuing their entrepreneurial dreams.

In Nigeria, however, reasons ex-servicemen/women (veterans) fail in entrepreneurship include lack of coordinated government assistance, lack of effective institutional support, and very few agencies exist to assist and promote military entrepreneurship (Madichie & Ayasi, 2018). In addition, Abubakar (2016) argues that entrepreneurship education for retired/retiring officers that could enhance their reintegration into civilian life is grossly lacking or inadequate. Abubakar (2016) also contends that the problem was not unconnected with the historical ineffective career management practice/administration of the Nigerian Armed Forces. Another problem is the lack of time and allowance for the officers to develop themselves individually while in service due to the nature of the military job. For example, the erratic work-life associated with a military career led to military personnel, on average, to spend less time with their families, have spouses who are less likely to work, and experience higher divorce rates (Angrist & Johnson, 2000). This unsettled work-life could be a factor for inadequate preparedness for 'Civvies Street' and/or entrepreneurship.

Military Training

It is necessary to disaggregate and contextualized the term 'military training' as employed in this paper. First, military training means different things to different people. According to Fletcher and Chatelier (2000), military commanders see training to mean exercising troops in the field so that they operate as an integrated, coordinated unit. But military personnel managers perceive training to mean organizing and certifying individuals across a full spectrum of occupational specialities e.g., cooks, carpentry, mechanics, technicians, and fighter pilots. Yet, developers and providers of major military systems consider training to mean exercises performed in simulators or on the systems themselves. To others, training could refer to preparing individuals from a civilian society to perform as professional military personnel, this last interpretation will be applied in this paper.

RESEARCH METHODOLOGY

Method

The research method and design used for this study consisted of a qualitative methodology using a multiple case study design. A multiple case study design enables the consolidation of research data from numerous sources and uses varying data collection options (Yin, 2012) to explore, illustrate, and analyze (Hanson et al., 2011) veteran-owned enterprises. This multiple case study design is useful in investigating the factors affecting work practices, management, and leadership experiences of veteran entrepreneurs. Case study involves empirical and experiential exploration of specific processes within its real-world setting, and thus, advances first-hand information that facilitates understanding of context (Harness, 2009). Case study approach also enables in-depth evaluation of the whole context with more attention paid to detail (Bell, 2005). This focused attention allows researchers to analyze the relationship between procedures and processes enacted as well as the participants (Zikmund et al., 2010). The application of the qualitative methodology is informed by the study's objectives of identifying and uncovering the specific characteristics of veteran entrepreneurship.

A semi-structured interview is used for data collection as it allows the investigation of attitudes, perceptions, prejudices, experiences, opinions, feelings, and representations of participants, freely and at depth (Dunbar et al., 2001; Kincheloe & McLaren, 2005; Kvale, 1996). The method is suitable because it allows the realization of clarifying questions to reach the necessary depth. The research was conducted over a total period of six months in Kaduna, Nigeria. Kaduna is a suitable location for the fieldwork for several reasons. First, it is the capital city of the old Nigeria's Northern Region and home to several military institutions such as the Nigerian Defence Academy (NDA), the Nigerian Army 1st Division, Nigerian Air Force Base, etc. Second, as a garrison city, the city is home to several retired veterans. Third, several of the veterans established business enterprises in Kaduna and environ.

Nigerian Business Environment

To give a background knowledge; the awareness of the importance of entrepreneurship and enterprise in generating employment has caused successive Nigerian governments to initiate many schemes to stimulate and support Small and Medium-scale Enterprises (SMEs). SMEs in Nigeria employed about 80% of the Nigerian workforce (SMEDAN, 2013). Several agencies were created by governments to encourage the development of the small business sector including Small and Medium Enterprises Development

Agency (SMEDAN), National Directorate of Employment (NDE), Peoples Bank of Nigeria (PBN), Microfinance Banks, National Economic Reconstruction Fund (NERFUND), Bank of Commerce and Industry and Bank of Agriculture among others (Kayode & Ilesanmi, 2014). However, SMEs continue to encounter challenges such that many of them struggle to survive or cease trading after a short while (Kayode & Ilesanmi, 2014). According to Adebisi and Gbegi (2013), 80% of SMEs fail within the first five years of establishment.

Some of the reasons many SMEs failed include lack of access to finance (Ozioma-Elendinmuo, 2015; Gbandi & Amissah, 2014; Akinola & Iordoo, 2013), crime, inadequate infrastructure, corruption, regulations (Ekpo & Bassey, 2016; Bah & Fang, 2015; Alarape, 2014). Other key factors involve mismanagement, incompetency, corruption, inadequate support mechanism and the general poor socio-economic situations (e.g. poverty) in Nigeria (Opara, 2011).

Data Collection Process

Respondents were identified and selected through initial referral and snowball sampling (Goodman, 1961) method. In-depth interviews were conducted with 6 individuals who were retired military personnel and are presently engaged in businesses that fall within the SMEs categorization (see Table 1). The six individuals were men and commissioned officer's cadre (i.e. from Second Lieutenant). This is deliberate in order to maintain homogeneity that eliminates variations (e.g. gender/ rank) that might affect results. Data was collected through interviews. Interviews help to reveal the views of respondents, which is unprejudiced by the researcher's evaluative responses. Questions were carefully structured (Fodd, 1993), to minimize the possibility of responses reflecting social desirability (Zerbe & Paulhus, 1987). The questions were open-ended, which allowed room for explanations as Rezaei et al. (2014) acknowledged that open-ended questions are more valid and reliable and therefore, more desirable than non-structured questions. Non-structured question could degenerate into conversations. The open-ended style questions enabled both interviewer and interviewees to reflect on some topics in more detail. The interviewer used cues or prompts to persuade the interviewees to reflect more on questions or to elaborate on an initial response, and to follow a line of inquiry initiated by the interviewees (Hancork & Algozzine, 2006). Questions around themes such as business plan, business funding, support system, future plans and strategy, and evaluation of business performance were asked. Moreover, replicating Rezaei et al.'s (2014) approach, past entrepreneurial experience/training questions (e.g., do you have any formal or informal training/experience of business?) complemented situational questions (e.g., how does your past experience/training assist in the formation and growth of your enterprise?). The interviews were then transcribed for further analysis, which led to the sorting out of different issues that developed from the narratives. Subsequently, the collected data were subjected to content analysis, which assists the analysis of transcribed material and the reduction of the data (Krippendorff, 2004), and key themes well-identified and collated.

Table 1. Summary of characteristics and basic profiles of the cases

Case studies Case 1 Case 2 Case 3 Case 4 Case 5 Case 6
Profile (gender/age) Male, 45
Male, 65
Male, 48
Male, 55 Male, 67
Male, 51
Rank at retirement Major Group Captain Colonel Major Commodore Lt. Colonel
Service Army Air Force Army Army Navy Army
Funding Source Personal Savings Personal Savings & Bank Loan Friends & Family Personal Savings Bank Loans & Personal Savings Personal Savings & Friends
Years in Business 5 3 3 4 7 6
Business Type Farming (fishery) Hoteling Taxi Service Property developer Security Outfit Farming (poultry) Service Duty Transport/Logistics
Number of Employees 6 15 4 10 50 5
Source: Fieldwork, 2020

FINDINGS AND ANALYSIS

The mass of data yielded three core themes that encapsulate the thrust of this study. These are the military training attributes of veteran entrepreneurs, military background attributes of veteran entrepreneurs, and business environmental factors. Although these reflect the convergence of observations of the respondents, verbatim quotations are liberally applied to strengthen and support thematic areas as a means of providing a deep description of the veteran entrepreneurship event.

Military Training Attributes of Veteran Entrepreneurship

The effects of the military training received by the respondents when in service were discernible in their narratives. All the respondents alluded to their military training as helping them in their enterprise vocations after leaving service. The respondents insisted that military training help them in ways enumerated as follows:

Perseverance and Resilience: Respondents agreed that the military taught them perseverance and resilience, for instance, respondent 1 said: "Once enlisted in the military, you cannot quit just because you had some dreadful moments". He further reiterated:

Soldiers are expected to ram through any barrier to become strong, and this ethos had seen me through difficult times in business. For example, my business is still struggling after three years of existence, yet I believe my perseverance will be rewarded in the long run

Discipline and Determination: The respondents infer they were trained to be mentally and physically strong through surmounting weaknesses and the temptation to give up when things get difficult. Respondent 4 buttressed this point by saying:

Although it is hugely rewarding to work for oneself and to create work for others, being an entrepreneur is tough and it requires determination and heavy lifting (hard work). When things get tough, it is one's passion and determination that keep one going. There are several occasions my military induced self-discipline was a great asset in my business enterprise armory. For instance, I resisted wasting money on non-essentials (e.g. air-conditioned office) when growing my business.

Confidence: The respondents also concurred that military training infused them with confidence, which proved to be beneficial in their entrepreneurship. According to respondent 5:

As an ex-serviceman, I am expected to carry out my duties under some of the most stressful situations possible. Thus, I am able to develop the confidence to deal with everyday challenges I encounter in the course of doing business and in other spheres of life.

Competitiveness: Respondents consented that the military encourages competition, particularly if one is to achieve rapid promotions. The spirit of competition they garnered in the military became useful in their ventures. Respondent 2 testimony summarized: "*I brought this competitive spirit into my ventures.... though some people think I am too aggressive......but I pursue my goals relentlessly and made sure I maintain a competitive edge in pricing and customer service*".

Directness and Speed: The respondents acknowledged that the military instils in them the quality of directness, speed, and methodical approaches to issues, according to respondent 4:

The military invests more time and resources into training its personnel than most organizations I know in Nigeria". I applied my military training in my business everyday...... I realized the importance of giving a clear and unambiguous message to my staff, and I am also aware of the benefits of acting with speed to get things done in business as in the military.

Assertiveness: All the respondents acceded that military taught them to be assertive. In buttressing this point, respondent 6 stated: "In the Army, I learnt the quality of being self-assured and confident as I was able to skillfully communicate with my staff and customers without being aggressive".

Leadership and Teamwork: Respondents acquiesced that they gained leadership and teamwork qualities during their time in the military. Respondent 3 affirmed: "The military inculcates leadership trait in people, the notion of 'serving to lead' is nurtured and encouraged. This commitment to leadership equipped me with the confidence and motivation in my entrepreneurial pursuits". Similarly, respondent 5 declared:

My time in the military instilled in me the power of teamwork and how to build and manage a strong network of people. Since becoming self-employed after retirement, I have a great opportunity to put all of my leadership and management into practice in a different environment.

Taken together, it seems the training received whilst in the military helps the veteran entrepreneurs in their business operations. However, this is not always the case as respondents' narratives indicate that military training could also constitute a serious hindrance to veteran entrepreneurship. Some of the military qualities the respondents find helpful in their business ventures seem to have a counter effect on their enterprises. According to some respondents, sometimes the attributes of directness and speed obtained in the military could be counter-productive when dealing with civilians (e.g. workers and suppliers). For instance, respondent 1 claimed: "The speed, precision, and directness with which I work are not matched by my staff and suppliers.... this was a constant friction point between us and it is affecting me and the business". Majority of the respondents recounted damaging outcomes when they expected their workers to be as 'discipline' as themselves. For instance, respondent 3 confirmed:

The essence of time-keeping is lost to many of my civilian staff. In the military, keeping to time or tight schedule is sacrosanct.... I frequently sacked recalcitrant workers, but now I have retired veterans in my employ....... we understand each other since we have the same background!

Unsurprisingly, all the respondents admitted that given the choice they will employ ex-servicemen/women over civilians anytime. Their reasons include compatibility of ethos due to similar background, compassionate ground (i.e., helping out a fellow veteran), and their skill-set lends itself well to smooth running of business operations compared to others (i.e. civilian workers). In essence, employing ex-servicemen helped some veteran entrepreneurs as they have people who share similar values and united for a common purpose like in the military.

Military Background Attributes of Veteran Entrepreneurship

From the data analysis, the researcher was able to recognize the key roles a military background (i.e., culture and identity) plays in the respondents' entrepreneurial undertakings. The military culture and identity create "disciplined bodies" capable of carrying out military labor and fighting a war. According to Woodward and Jenkings (2011), military identities are rooted in the process of training and everyday practices that personnel carry out in military settings (e.g. capabilities in weapon handling and operating technical equipment), which serve as markers of identity for military personnel. This process of training, whereby personnel acquire such skills, is described by Woodward and Jenkings (2011) as a transformative act in which personnel take on new identities grounded in their military capabilities.

Thus, veterans had become assimilated into the military body and had absorbed military cultural values such as loyalty, integrity, courage, determination, and a commitment to duty (Bergman et al., 2014; Cooper et al., 2016). The respondents' narratives were interspersed with terminologies that underpin these cultural values. Statements such as: "I attacked my business ventures with steely determination and a 'never say die' commitment of a rugged soldier" (respondent 6); "business is like war, and must be fought with courage and strong commitment" (respondent 2); "I demand loyalty from my staff… a disloyal worker is useless and cannot be relied on" (respondent 3). These cultural attributes appear to help strengthen their resolve in entrepreneurship and help them forge ahead even in the face of business adversities. For instance, respondent 1 disclosed: "My orientation and state of mind as ex-serviceman greatly help to sustain my business…. The popular mantra: 'old soldier never dies' is firmly etched into my sub-consciousness and is guiding my attitude to business enterprise".

Furthermore, the military ethos, which is decidedly masculine (e.g. Cooper et al., 2016) seems to underscore respondents' approach to business. For instance, male workers dominate most of the respondents' workforce, even respondent 2, whose hospitality business should be assumed to generate higher female positions (e.g. catering, house-keeping, cleaners, etc.), has more men (12) than women (3) in his hotel's payroll. The dominance of male in the respondents' workforce could be seen as a typical example of hegemonic masculinity, which refers to a "culturally idealized form of masculine character" (Connell, 1990: 83). It has been said that the military culture fosters hegemonic masculinity (Connell, 1995), highlighting the dominance of masculine attributes (e.g. emotional toughness, stoicism, self-reliance, aggressiveness), practices, and identities, which are privileged over femininity qualities

(Bulmer, 2013; Higate, 2003). Respondent 4, for instance, justifies the dominance of male workers in his establishment saying: "men are better focused and can do more heavy-lifting than women". This view encapsulates other respondents' perspective and could be attributed to their military background. As already canvassed, the tenacity of military masculinities, linked with the formation of a military identity could have strong implications for soldiers' self-concept, which then act both for and on them when they retired into civilian life (Cooper et al., 2016).

All the respondents admitted to experiencing some level of disorientation immediately after their demobilization as they tried to adjust and re-order their lives to fit into civilians' routine. Respondent 5 claimed: "Initially, I find it difficult to comprehend some of civilians' conducts as I find it hard to communicate effectively with non-military people". The respondents' disorientation could partly be due to the loss of cultural capital. Cooper et al. (2016) argued that some forms of cultural capital that are highly valued in the military may not be recognized in civil society. For example, rank, which has great weight in the military, is usually misunderstood or ignored outside the military circle, thus, making an erstwhile respected officer undergo "culture shock" when they are out of service (Bergman et al., 2014).

However, the respondents' military background does confer certain benefits occasionally. For example, respondent 3 asserted:

I occasionally benefit from the esprit de corps shown by security and law enforcement operatives (Military, Police, Vehicle Inspectors, Traffic Wardens, etc.) at check-points/ roadblocks when driving on the road doing my business....it is a kind of advantage over fellow competitors who are not ex-servicemen.

It appears some of the respondents' choice of business venture is informed by their vocations in the military. Respondents 3 and 5 confirmed that their experiences in the military dictate the type of ventures they started when they retired from active service. Respondent 5 said: "I knew that by the time I left the army I will be self-employed and will use the skills I had learnt in the military to earn income". According to respondent 3:

Based on my experiences in the military (I worked in Logistics while in service) I decided to operate a transport business. Starting a Taxi service (started with two cars) as an entrepreneur is an extension of that interest and experience.

Moreover, the respondents' military background also appears to have detrimental effects on their entrepreneurship as they sometimes find it difficult to shake-off their deep-rooted acquired military culture. Respondent 6 put this into perspective:

The regimented life I lived while in service has some negative impact on me. Serving in the military has 'institutionalized' us because we were instructed where to be when to eat and what to wear. I believe in structure as I tend to unconsciously ordered people around, and many of my staff considered it as bullying.

It is then assumed that veterans tend to have a regimented way of thinking and working that they carry with them into other vocations.

Business Environmental Factors

Data interrogation reveals operational issues in the business environment the entrepreneurs have to contend with in their day-to-day activities. Issues such as infrastructural deficiency, access to finance, labour relations, safety and security dominate discussions.

On infrastructural deficiency, it is clear from the data that the conditions of infrastructure in Nigeria are critical factors in processing and initiating productive ventures. One of the main infrastructural problems cited by the respondents is the inadequate supply of power to operate their ventures optimally. According to respondent 2: "No serious business can work in the absence of regular power supply……I spend enormous expenses on electric generators to keep the hotel running every day". The poor conditions of other infrastructural facilities such as road, water supply, internet connectivity, etc. were decried by all the respondents. The respondents' frustration at inadequate facilities is not new knowledge as several authors have highlighted these issues, for instance, Ekpo and Bassey (2016) raised the issue of inadequate power supply as barriers to business venturing in Nigeria. Other barriers to enterprise success in Nigeria are inadequate social infrastructure, multiple taxations, and lack of managerial skills of owners and managers (Agwu & Emeti, 2014).

Lack of access to mainstream finance (e.g. bank loans) was raised by most of the respondents. Respondent 6 declared:

Getting the banks to give you a loan is very difficult…. I struggled to keep my business afloat, particularly at the initial stage when new ventures usually undergo some teething problems. Thanks to my savings and goodwill of a few friends/acquaintances I managed to weather the storm so to speak.

Restricted access to funding is not peculiar to veteran entrepreneurs as according to Cole and Sokolyk (2016), most of the small businesses do not access loans from financial institutions because of the bureaucracies involved in loan application procedures. Moreover, Kanayo et al. (2013) found SMEs avoid loans from microfinance institutions because they charge high-interest rates which make it difficult for them to make profits. Generally, the inability to access long-term finance has been found to contribute to business failure in Nigeria (Gbandi & Amissah, 2014; Oliyide, 2012) such that inadequate financial institutions funding contributed to the massive failure of small businesses in Nigeria (Obokoh & Asaolu, 2012).

Other structural issues that most of the respondents identify as constraining in their entrepreneurship concern labour relations, safety and security. Aside from respondent 3, who hired ex-servicemen, other respondents confirmed they have issues such as discipline and lack of commitment with most of their employers. Respondent 5 said: “It takes ages to develop my staff to my acceptable standard.... I kept hiring and firing repeatedly ......”

The concerns around safety and security received unanimous opinion among the respondents as they all complained about how the general insecurity situation in Nigeria is affecting their business operations. The impact of safety and security problem on businesses in Nigeria has been variously discussed in several media – academic (e.g., Achumba et al., 2013) and non-academic (e.g., Nigeria - South Africa Chamber of Commerce, 2016). By and large, the Nigerian business environment has variously been said to be hostile to business as a multitude of barriers existed to frustrate entrepreneurs and enterprise (Ojo, 2017).

Nevertheless, the respondents also accepted that the Nigerian business environment, despite its numerous problems, has certain munificence in terms of the sheer size of the market. With a population of over 200 million (Worldometer, 2020), the Nigerian marketplace is huge and provides opportunities for hardworking entrepreneurs. Respondent 4 viewpoint coalesced the other respondents’ position: “The Nigeria market is so huge that there will always market for whatever product or service you choose to vend”.

DISCUSSION

Veterans are usually highly skilled, qualified, and adaptable people, making them effective entrepreneurs who are reliable, ambitious, and adapting military resources to solve problems (e.g., job creation) in a civilian setting. Veteran entrepreneurs, aside from providing jobs for themselves, create employment for others, thus giving back to the society they once served as military personnel and serving again as civilians. Veteran entrepreneurship has certain peculiarities that underpin its characteristics, which differentiate it from ‘civilian’ entrepreneurship. The three themes that form the core of the data analysis have both advantages and disadvantages to veteran entrepreneurship in Nigeria. It is clear veteran entrepreneurs bring some of the acquired military skills and experiences into their business enterprises, and these have both positive and negative impacts. Military training supports veteran entrepreneurs in their enterprises, but the difference between the highly structured military environment and the less structured civilian environment created challenges in organizing veteran entrepreneurship in some occasions. Though the skill-sets veteran acquired in the military promote veteran entrepreneurship, yet the same skill-set could also create an impediment for the unwary veteran entrepreneur.

The military culture/identity can be argued to be largely an albatross to veteran entrepreneurship, particularly in term of difficulties around the ability to adapt seamlessly into civil life. Furthermore, the Nigerian business environment could be very problematic for veteran entrepreneurship (like any other enterprise) to flourish due to factors including infrastructural deficit, unsupportive institutions, dis-alignment between military and civilian structures. Yet, the business environment has its redeeming features (e.g. large market space). Ojo (2017: 601) claimed that "…. opportunities and challenges of entrepreneurship are often a function of the environment".

Contribution

The paper makes three important contributions. First, it contributes to the literature on veteran entrepreneurship in Nigeria, which has received less attention in academia. Periodic retirement of highly trained military personnel into the overcrowded Nigerian labour market can only exacerbate the security pressure in the country if the ex-service personnel are not gainfully employed. The link has been made between unemployment and worsening insecurity in Nigeria (Achumba et al., 2013). Second, the paper enables researchers to shape the narrative around veteran entrepreneurship and open up the discourse on veteran resilience. Given the prevalence of entrepreneurship concept in the global arena, the central task facing the discipline is to reemphasize the entrepreneurship voice in discussions of sustainable livelihood at every level of Nigerian society. One of the most important arenas for making this voice heard is veteran entrepreneurship research, which is still at the infancy stage in Nigeria. Lastly, the problem of business success or failure among retired military personnel (veterans) in Nigeria is not just an academic curiosity; it is a matter of substantial differences in economic survival and penury. By adding new knowledge to our understanding of veteran entrepreneurship, this paper contributes to the discussion at policy and technical levels on rejuvenating the entrepreneurship programs among veterans. Furthermore, successful veteran entrepreneurship can promote positive social values, stakeholder satisfaction, and employment opportunities for other veterans. For example, veteran enterprises are shown to be valuable as they have a positive ripple effect on unemployment among veterans in the USA where veteran-owned businesses are 30% more likely to employ other veterans (Franchise Business Review, 2014).

LIMITATIONS AND FURTHER STUDIES

Even though the paper shine lights on a group that is less discussed in academic studies, it has certain limitations. First, the study does not allow for generalization due to its adopted methodological approach (i.e. qualitative) and its few numbers of respondents. This calls for quantitative studies into other aspects of veteran entrepreneurship. Second, aspects such as women veterans' entrepreneurs and non-commission officers (NCO) who form the bulk of retired military personnel anywhere in the world (on account of their numerical numbers) are not interrogated in the study. In addition, the paper did not interrogate the distinctions between pre-NDA (Nigerian Defence Academy) and NDA trained officers. The NDA, though formed in 1964 did not begin degree programs for its cadets until 1985. In essence, the pre-NDA officers' training emphasis development of character only compared to NDA cadets whose training incorporates character and learning (Nigerian Defence Academy, 2018). The latter group are said to be better informed and presumed to do things a bit different from the formal group when engaged in entrepreneurship.

Hence, further studies are needed to bridge these identified gaps. It will be worthwhile to appraise the nature and character of distinctive types of entrepreneurship events by different groups around the military establishment. Such distinctive entrepreneurial events involve groups like spouses of serving military personnel, widows of military personnel, and military intrapreneurship.

Furthermore, studies that seek answers to the questions listed below are necessary:

1. What interventions promote veteran entrepreneurship and how can they be best operationalised?
2. How can various interest groups (e.g. mentors, corporate bodies, NGOs, etc.) be incentivised to engage with veterans to participate in an enterprise as post-retirement income earner?
3. To what extent do dynamics of gender, pre-retirement business experience, education, service type (i.e. military branches), rank, and appointments facilitate veteran entrepreneurship?

RECOMMENDATIONS

After the analyses and observations derived from this study, the following recommendations are made. First, veterans need to attack retirement just as they would any other activity through planning, preparing, rehearsing and finally executing. With the right support (e.g. mentoring and follow-ups), their acquired skills would be harness for a successful entrepreneurial career. Mentorship, business and financial training, and financial assistance can be made available to expand entrepreneurial opportunities for Nigeria's retired and retiring veterans. Mentorship by skilled professionals in finance, marketing, public relations, operations and technology can help veterans gain valuable business skills and resources they need to succeed. Business training and financial education will help veteran entrepreneurs to write business plans, connect with mentors, partners, and legal advisors. Financial assistance in the form of a funding mechanism (specific to military veterans) could be instituted and dedicated to veteran entrepreneurs.

CONCLUSION

While entrepreneurship and the military may seem worlds apart at first, a closer look will reveal the connection between the two concepts along with the skill-set that could take veterans from the garrisons to the marketplace. On the one hand, the skills acquired in the military could be a valuable asset that can be applied in entrepreneurship, but on the other hand, those skills could also become incumbrances for the unprepared veteran entrepreneurs. In general, it could be said that, on many parameters, there are not many differences between veteran entrepreneurs/ entrepreneurship and civilian entrepreneurs/entrepreneurship. Both categories encounter the same set of institutional and infrastructural deficiencies that affect businesses in Nigeria. It is expected that the recommendations of the study will help to improve the success rate of veterans' entrepreneurship within the context of the high failure rate alluded to in the literature.

REFERENCES

AbubakarU. (2016). Career management of officers in the Nigerian Army (1970-2014). https://ssrn.com/abstract=2722249orhttp://dx.doi.org/10.2139/ssrn.2722249 doi:10.2139srn.2722249

Achumba, I. C., Ighomereho, O. S., & Akpor-Robaro, M. O. M. (2013). Security Challenges in Nigeria and the Implications for Business Activities and Sustainable Development. *Journal of Economics and Sustainable Development*, *4*(2), 79–99.

Adebisi, J.F. & Gbegi, D.O. (2013). Effects of multiple taxations on the performance of small and medium scale business enterprises (A study of west Africa Ceramics Ajeokuta, Kogi State). *Mediterranean Journal of Social Sciences*, *4*(6), 324-334. doi:.2013.v4n6p323 doi:10.5901/mjss

Adekanye, J'B. (1999). *The Retired Military Emergent Power Factor in Nigeria*. Ibadan: Heinemann Educational Book.

Adrienne, J., Heinz, A. J., Freeman, M. A., Harpaz-Rotem, I., & Pietrzak, R. H. (2017). American military veterans are nearly twice as likely to be self-employed compared to non-veterans, and are majority owners in nine percent of all businesses nationwide. *Military Psychology*, *29*(6), 513–523. PMID:29290645

Agwu, M. O., & Emeti, C. I. (2014). Issues, challenges, and prospects of small and medium scale enterprises (SMEs) in Port Harcourt city, Nigeria. *European Journal of Sustainable Development*, *3*(1), 101–114. doi:10.14207/ejsd.2014.v3n1p101

Akinola, A. O., & Iordoo, D. A. (2013). The effect of Nigerian capital market on the micro, small and medium scale enterprises (MSMEs) in Nigeria. *Journal of Finance and Accounting*, *4*(7), 1–14.

Alarape, A. A. (2014). Entrepreneurial orientation and the growth performance of small and medium enterprises in Southwestern Nigeria. *Journal of Small Business and Entrepreneurship*, *26*(6), 553–577. doi:10.1080/08276331.2014.892308

Angrist, J. D. (1998). Estimating the labor market impact of voluntary military service using social security data on military applicants. *Econometrica*, *66*(2), 249–288. doi:10.2307/2998558

Angrist, J. D., & Johnson, J. H. IV. (2000). Effects of work-related absences on families: Evidence from the Gulf War. *Industrial & Labor Relations Review*, *54*(1), 41–58. doi:10.1177/001979390005400103

Arkin, W., & Dobrofsky, L. R. (1978). Military socialization and masculinity. *The Journal of Social Issues*, *34*(1), 151–168. doi:10.1111/j.1540-4560.1978.tb02546.x

Baechtold, M. (2011). Women warriors: Supporting female student veterans. *ASHE Higher Education Report*, *37*(3), 69–80. doi:10.1002/aehe.3703

Bah, E., & Fang, L. (2015). Impact of the business environment on output and productivity in Africa. *Journal of Development Economics*, *114*(C), 159–171. doi:10.1016/j.jdeveco.2015.01.001

Baruch, Y., & Quick, J. C. (2009). Setting sail in a new direction: Career transitions of US Navy admirals to the civilian sector. *Personnel Review*, *38*(3), 270–285. doi:10.1108/00483480910943331

Bell, J. (2005). *Doing your Research Project: A guide for first-time researchers in Education, Health and Social Science* (4th ed.). McGraw.

Bergman, B., Burdett, H., & Greenberg, N. (2014). Service life and beyond—Institution or culture? *RUSI Journal*, *159*(5), 60–68. doi:10.1080/03071847.2014.969946

Blass, F. R., & Ketchen, D. J. Jr. (2014). So, you want to be an entrepreneur? Lessons from the entrepreneurship bootcamp for veterans with disabilities. *Business Horizons*, *57*(1), 5–9. doi:10.1016/j.bushor.2013.09.006

Boldon, N. Y., Maury, R. V., Armstrong, N. A., & Van Slyke, R. (2016). *The State of Veteran Entrepreneurship Research: What We Know and Next Steps (Veteran Entrepreneurship Research, Paper No. 1)*. Institute for Veterans and Military Families, Syracuse University.

Bradburn, N. M. (1969). *The structure of psychological well-being*. Aldine.

Bressler, M. S., Bressler, L., & Bressler, M. (2013). A study of veteran-owned small businesses and the impact of military reserve call-ups since 9/11. *Academy of Entrepreneurship Journal*, *19*(2), 1–22.

Brock, W. A., & Evans, D. S. (1989). Small Business Economics. *Small Business Economics*, *1*(1), 7–20. doi:10.1007/BF00389913

Bruyat, C., & Julien, P. A. (2001). Defining the field of Research in Entrepreneurship. *Journal of Business Venturing*, *16*(2), 165–180. doi:10.1016/S0883-9026(99)00043-9

Bulmer, S. (2013). Patriarchal confusion? *International Feminist Journal of Politics*, *15*(2), 137–156. doi:10.1080/14616742.2012.746565

Cahill, K.E., Giandrea, M.D., & Quinn, J.F. (2013). *New evidence on self-employment transitions among older Americans with career jobs*. Academic Press.

Chandra, S. (2014). Soldiers turn entrepreneurs. Small Business and Entrepreneurship Council.

Chinyem, V. (2018). *FG to retire 320 military personnel*. Available at: https://newsofnigeria.com/fg-to-retire-320-military-personnel/

Cole, A. H. (1959). *Business enterprise in a social setting*. Harvard University Press.

Cole, R., & Sokolyk, T. (2016). Who needs credit and who gets credit? Evidence from the surveys of small business finances. *Journal of Financial Stability*, *24*(691), 40–60. doi:10.1016/j.jfs.2016.04.002

Collins, J. (1998). The complex context of American culture: A practitioner's view. *The Washington Quarterly*, *21*(4), 213–226. doi:10.1080/01636609809550359

Connell, R. W. (1990). An iron man: The body and some contradictions of hegemonic masculinity. Sport, men, and the gender order: Critical feminist perspectives, 83-114.

Connell, R. W. (1995). *Masculinities*. Polity Press.

Cook, S. (2019). *Ex-forces entrepreneurs: How veterans can start and grow businesses*. Available at: https://startups.co.uk/ex-forces-entrepreneurs/

Cooper, L., Caddick, N., Godier, L., Cooper, A., & Fossey, M. (2016). Transition from the Military into Civilian Life: An Exploration of Cultural Competence. *Armed Forces and Society*. Advance online publication. doi:10.1177/0095327X16675965

Dana, L. P. (2006). *Handbook of research on international entrepreneurship*. Edward Edgar.

Demers, A. (2011). When Veterans Return: The Role of Community in Reintegration. *Journal of Loss and Trauma*, *16*(2), 160–179. doi:10.1080/15325024.2010.519281

Dunbar, C., Rodrigues, D., & Parker, L. (2001). Race, subjectivity, and the interview process. In J. Gubrium & J. Holstein (Eds.), *Handbook of interview research* (pp. 279–298). Sage Publications.

Ehsan, L. (2010). The impact of retirement on psychological well-being in Canada. *Journal of Socio-Economics*, *40*, 373–380.

Ekpo, U. N., & Bassey, G. E. (2016). An analysis of the economic consequences of infrastructural deficit in a developing economy: The case of electricity supply in Nigeria. *The International Journal of Social Sciences (Islamabad)*, *10*(1), 28–48.

Fletcher, J. D., & Chatelier, P. R. (2000). *An Overview of Military Training. Institute for Defense Analyses*. Available at: https://apps.dtic.mil/dtic/tr/fulltext/u2/a408439.pdf

Fodd, W. (1993). *Constructing Questions for Interviews and Questionnaires: Theory and Practice in Social Research.* Cambridge University Press. doi:10.1017/CBO9780511518201

Franchise Business Review. (2014). *Veterans in Franchising*. Available at: https://www.franchise.org/sites/default/files/201906/VetFran%20Progress%20Report%20 2014.pdf

Gbandi, E. C., & Amissah, G. (2014). Financial options for small and medium enterprises (SMEs) in Nigeria. *European Scientific Journal, 10*(1), 327–340.

George, L. T. (1993). Sociological perspective on life transitions. *Annual Review of Sociology, 19*(1), 353–373. doi:10.1146/annurev.so.19.080193.002033

Goodman, L. A. (1961). Snowball sampling. *Annals of Mathematical Statistics, 32*(1), 148–170. doi:10.1214/aoms/1177705148

Hale, J. (2017). *Military Culture and Translating it to the Civilian Workplace*. Available at: https://www.dvidshub.net/news/237637/military-culture-and-translating-civilian-workplace

Hancock, D. R., & Algozzine, B. (2006). *Doing case study research: A practical guide for beginning researchers*. Teachers College Press.

Hanson, J. L., Balmer, D. F., & Giardino, A. P. (2011). Qualitative research methods for medical educators. *Academic Pediatrics, 11*(5), 375–386. doi:10.1016/j.acap.2011.05.001 PMID:21783450

Harness, T. (2009). Research Methods for the Empirical Study of Strategic Human Research Management. *Qualitative Market Research, 12*(3), 321–336. doi:10.1108/13522750910963836

Higate, P. (2001). Theorizing continuity: From military to civilian life. *Armed Forces and Society, 27*(3), 433. doi:10.1177/0095327X0102700306

Higate, P. (2003). 'Soft clerks' and 'hard civvies': Pluralizing military masculinities. In P. Higate (Ed.), *Military masculinities: Identity and the state* (pp. 27–43). Praeger.

Hope, J. B., Oh, B., & Mackin, P. C. (2011). *Factors Affecting Entrepreneurship among Veterans Small Business Research Summary*. U.S. Small Business Administration, Office of Advocacy.

Interian, A., Kline, A., Janal, M., Glynn, S., & Losonczy, M. (2014). Multiple deployments and combat trauma: Do home front stressors increase the risk for posttraumatic stress symptoms? *Journal of Traumatic Stress*, *27*(1), 90–97. doi:10.1002/jts.21885 PMID:24464407

Jolly, R. (1996). *Changing step; From military to civilian life: People in transition.* Brassey.

Kanayo, O., Jumare, F., & Nancy, S. (2013). Challenges of micro finance access in Nigeria: Implication for entrepreneurship development. *Mediterranean Journal of Social Sciences*, *4*(6), 611–618. doi:10.5901/mjss.2013.v4n6p611

Kayode, K. B., & Ilesanmi, A. O. (2014). Determinants of factors influencing capacity of small and medium enterprises (SMEs) in employment creation in Lagos State, Nigeria. *International Journal of Financial Research*, *5*(2), 133–141. doi:10.5430/ijfr.v5n2p133

Kedia, S. (2019). *With this organisation's help, Indian army veterans are becoming entrepreneurs*. Available at: https://yourstory.com/socialstory/2019/03/indian-army-veterans-turn-entrepreneurs-8icuu43y47

Kerrick, S. A., Cumberland, D., Church-Nally, M., & Kemelgor, B. (2014). Military veterans marching towards entrepreneurship: An exploratory mixed methods study. *International Journal of Management Education*, *12*(3), 469–478. doi:10.1016/j.ijme.2014.05.006

Kincheloe, J. L., & McLaren, P. (2005). Rethinking critical theory and qualitative research. In N. Denzin & Y. Lincoln (Eds.), *The Sage Handbook of Qualitative Research* (3rd ed., pp. 303–342). Sage Publication.

Kirzner, I. M. (1973). *Competition and Entrepreneurship*. University of Chicago Press.

Knight, F. H. (1961). *Risk uncertainty and profit* (2nd ed.). Kelley.

Krippendorff, Ȁ. (2004). *Content analysis: An introduction to its methodology* (2nd ed.). Sage Publications.

Kvale, S. (1996). *Interviews: An introduction to qualitative research interviews.* Sage Publications.

Madichie, N. O., & Ayasi, K. (2018). Entrepreneurial Opportunities and Challenges for Retired Senior Military Officers in Nigeria. In African Entrepreneurship. Palgrave Studies of Entrepreneurship in Africa. Palgrave Macmillan. doi:10.1007/978-3-319-73700-3_7

Mobbs, M. C., & Bonanno, G. A. (2018). Beyond war and PTSD: The crucial role of transition stress in the lives of military veterans. *Clinical Psychology Review, 59*, 137–144. doi:10.1016/j.cpr.2017.11.007 PMID:29180101

Nicholson, J. W. (2019). *Veterans Are the Future of America's Startups, And Nonprofit Leaders Can Help Them Succeed*. Available at: https://www.forbes.com/sites/forbesnonprofitcouncil/2019/11/05/veterans-are-the-future-of-americas-startups-and-nonprofit-leaders-can-help-them-succeed/#6f22065e61d4

Nigeria - South Africa Chamber of Commerce. (2016). *Security Challenges in Nigeria and the Implications for Business Activities and Sustainable Development*. Available at: http://nsacc.org.ng/security-challenges-in-nigeria-and-the-implications-for-business-activities-and-sustainable-development/

Nigerian Defence Academy. (2018). *Our History*. Available at: https://www.nda.edu.ng/#news/item/277

Ntiwunka, G. (2012). An Assessment of the Relevance of Adekanye's The Retired Military as Emergent Power Factor in Nigeria to Contemporary Nigeria. *Canadian Social Science, 8*(2), 117–126.

Obokoh, L. O., & Asaolu, T. O. (2012). Examination of relationship between financial market liberalization and the failures of small and medium sized enterprises in Nigeria. *International Business Research, 5*(1), 182–193. doi:10.5539/ibr.v5n1p182

Ojo, S. (2013). *Diaspora entrepreneurship: A study of Nigerian entrepreneurs in London* (PhD thesis). University of East London. Available at: http://hdl.handle.net/10552/3506

Ojo, S. (2017). Interrogating returnee entrepreneurship in the Nigerian context. *Journal of Enterprising Communities: People and Places in the Global Economy, 11*(5), 590–608. doi:10.1108/JEC-07-2016-0025

Ojo, S., & Nwankwo, S. (2017). Diaspora and Transnational Entrepreneurship: A Conceptual Exploration. In S. Ojo (Ed.), *Diaspora and Transnational Entrepreneurship in the Global Contexts* (pp. 1–23). IGI Global. doi:10.4018/978-1-5225-1991-1.ch001

Oliyide, O. (2012). Law, credit risk management and bank lending to SMEs in Nigeria. *Commonwealth Law Bulletin, 38*(4), 673–695. doi:10.1080/03050718.2012.707350

Opara, J. O. (2011). Factors constraining the growth and survival of SME in Nigeria: Implications for poverty alleviation. *Management Research Review, 34*(2), 156–171. doi:10.1108/01409171111102786

Osborne, J. W. (2012). Psychological Effects of the Transition to Retirement. *Canadian Journal of Counselling and Psychotherapy*, *46*(1), 45–58.

Ozioma-Eleodinmuo, P. (2015). Analysis of entrepreneurship policy for small and medium scale enterprise in Aba, Abia State Nigeria. *Journal of Economic Development, Management, IT, Finance and Marketing*, *7*(1), 47–60.

Pranger, T., Murphy, K., & Thompson, J. (2009). Shaken World Coping with Transition to Civilian Life. *Canadian Family Physician Medecin de Famille Canadien*, *55*, 159–161. PMID:19221074

Ray, S., & Heaslip, K. (2011). Canadian military transitioning to civilian life: A discussion paper. *Journal of Psychiatric and Mental Health Nursing*, *18*(3), 18. doi:10.1111/j.1365-2850.2010.01652.x PMID:21395911

Rezaei, S., Goli, M., & Dana, L.-P. (2014). Beyond legal entrepreneurship: The case of Austria. *International Journal of Entrepreneurship and Small Business*, *21*(2), 202–215. doi:10.1504/IJESB.2014.059473

Robertson, H. C., & Brott, P. E. (2017). *Military Veterans' Midlife Career Transition and Life Satisfaction*. Available at: https://tpcjournal.nbcc.org/military-veterans-midlife-career-transition-and-life-satisfaction/

Ross, E. (2015). *Life after war: veterans turned successful entrepreneurs*. Available at: https://www.theguardian.com/small-business-network/2015/mar/03/war-veterans-successful-entrepreneurs-military

Sankaran, S., & Battisto, J. (2018). *Financing Their Future: Veteran Entrepreneurs and Capital Access*. Available at: https://www.fedsmallbusiness.org/veteran-entrepreneurs-and-capital-access

Schaper, M., & Volery, T. (2004). *Entrepreneurship and small business: A Pacific Rim perspective*. John Wiley and Sons Australia Ltd.

Schlossberg, N., Waters, E., & Goodman, J. (1995). *Counseling adults in transition*. Springer.

Schumpeter, J. A. (1934). *The theory of economic development: An inquiry into profits, capital, credit, interest and business cycle*. Harvard University Press.

Sharma, P., & Chrisman, J. (1999). Toward a Reconciliation of the Definitional Issues in the Field of Corporate Entrepreneurship. *Entrepreneurship Theory and Practice*, *23*(3), 11–27. doi:10.1177/104225879902300302

Singh, G., & DeNoble, A. (2003). Early retirees as the next generation of entrepreneurs. *Entrepreneurship Theory and Practice*, *27*(3), 207–226. doi:10.1111/1540-8520.t01-1-00001

Smaliukienė, R. (2014). Entrepreneurship Opportunities after Military Career: Practice in Central and Eastern versus Western Europe. *Entrepreneurial Business and Economics Review*, *1*(4), 97–108. doi:10.15678/EBER.2013.010408

SmallBusiness.com. (2018). *Americans Rank Military and Small Business as Nation's Two Most Trusted Institutions*. Available at: https://smallbusiness.com/about-small-businesses/americans-trust-in-small-business/

SMEDAN. (2013). *SMEDAN and national bureau of statistics collaborative survey: Selected findings 2013*. Abuja: SMEDAN. Retrieved from Small and Medium Enterprises Development Agency of Nigeria: http://nigerianstat.gov.ng

Smith-Osborne, A. (2013). Veterans Administration health care policies as a protective mechanism supporting an expected life trajectory after military service. *Social Work in Public Health*, *28*(2), 81–96. doi:10.1080/19371918.2011.552038 PMID:23461344

Storlie, C. (2010). *Combat to Corporate: Applying Military Spec Ops Principles to Business Success*. Praeger.

Strange, R. E. (1984). Retirement from the service: The individual and his family. In F. W. Van Praag, M. (2003). Business survival and success of young small business owners. *Small Business Economics*, *21*(1), 1–17.

Venkatachalam, V. B., & Waqif, A. A. (2005). Outlook on integrating entrepreneurship in management education in India. *Decision (Washington, D.C.)*, *32*(2), 57–71.

Vigoda-Gadot, E., Baruch, Y., & Grimland, S. (2010). Career transitions: An empirical examination of second career of military retirees. *Public Personnel Management*, *39*(4), 379–404. doi:10.1177/009102601003900405

Vogt, D., Perkins, D. F., Copeland, L. A., Finley, E. P., Jamieson, C. S., Booth, B., Lederer, S., & Gilman, C. L. (2018). The Veterans Metric Initiative study of US veterans' experiences during their transition from military service. *BMJ Open*, *2018*(8), e020734. doi:10.1136/bmjopen-2017-020734 PMID:29895650

Westwood, M. (1999). *Career transition program for Canadian peacekeeping veterans*. Veterans Affairs Canada.

Westwood, M., Black, T., & McLean, H. (2002). A Re-entry Program for Peacekeeping Soldiers: Promoting Personal and Career Transition. *Canadian Journal of Counselling*, *36*, 221–232.

Wolpert, D. S. (2000). Military retirement and the transition to civilian life. In J. A. Martin, L. N. Rosen, & L. R. Sparacino (Eds.), *The military family: A practice guide for human service providers* (pp. 103–119). Praeger.

Woodward, R., & Jenkings, N. (2011). Military identities in the situated accounts of British military personnel. *Sociology*, *45*(2), 252–268. doi:10.1177/0038038510394016

Worldometer. (2020). *Nigeria Population (Live)*. Available at: https://www.worldometers.info/world-population/nigeria-population/

Yanos, R. (2004). *Perception of adjustment to civilian life among recently retired airforce officers*. Available from: https://drum.lib.umd.edu/bitstream/1903/2321/1/umi-umd-2126.pdf

Yin, R. K. (2012). *Applications of case study research*. Sage.

Zerbe, W. J., & Paulhus, D. L. (1987). Socially desirable responding in organizational behavior: A recognition. *Academy of Management Review*, *12*(2), 250–264. doi:10.5465/amr.1987.4307820

Zikmund, W. G., Babin, B. J., Carr, J. C., & Griffin, M. (2010). *Business research methods*. Wadsworth.

KEY TERMS AND DEFINITIONS

Military Entrepreneurship: Involvement of military, either as institution or individual components (e.g. serving personnel, retired personnel, family members of service personnel), in business ventures to generate income, employment, and contributing to development agendas.

Military Training: Act of preparing and shaping individuals from the civilian society to perform as professional military personnel.

Veteran: An individual who has been discharged (or retired) from the military service, also often referred to as ex-service personnel.

Veteran Entrepreneurship: Engagement of retired military personnel in business enterprises as avenue for generating income and employment.

Chapter 8
Counselling and Psychological Strategies for Improved Entrepreneurial Tendencies in the Nigerian Military

Mogbekeloluwa Oluyinka Fakokunde
https://orcid.org/0000-0002-2585-9052
Nigerian Defence Academy, Nigeria

ABSTRACT

This chapter examines post-retirement career pathways of ex-service personnel in the Nigerian military via entrepreneurship activities. One of the measures taken to assist ex-service personnel get adjusted into the civil life is the establishment of vocational training, which helps to facilitate viable entrepreneurial events. However, there are psychological issues that must be tackled in order to effectively transit into entrepreneurship. The chapter, therefore, looks at these issues to address the concept of entrepreneurship and its tendencies in the Nigerian military. The findings suggest that objectives and components of entrepreneurship education being advocated should be given to personnel early enough and throughout their military career.

INTRODUCTION

Career is a term that has been variously defined by different authors as a result of different orientations of the authors. Hence the terms is variously understood. In many instances, the terms career, vocation and occupation are used synonymously. Such a narrow view of career is problematic in that it is aligned only with paid

DOI: 10.4018/978-1-7998-6655-8.ch008

Copyright © 2021, IGI Global. Copying or distributing in print or electronic forms without written permission of IGI Global is prohibited.

employment. Rather, a career encapsulates the variety of occupational roles which individuals will undertake throughout life. It includes paid and self – employment, the different occupations which person may have over the years and periods of unemployment and unpaid occupations such as that of student, voluntary worker or parent. Arthur, Lawrence and Hall (1989) suggested that a career is the evolving sequence of a person's work experience over time. The concept of career has broadened to include pre-vocational, vocational and post vocational activities and other life roles and contexts. The above is a slight illumination into an individual's lifetime engagement. Meanwhile, career roles could manifest in different forms and dimensions to include entrepreneurial activities. The Nigerian military recognized the potential of its personnel and the need for them to have a lifelong fulfilling career (including post retirement) coupled with the fact that most of the personnel, upon retirement are still at the productive age and able to contribute significantly to the economy and development of the nation. Hence the Nigerian military made adequate provision for vocational and entrepreneurial training of its retiring personnel. The aim of this pre-retirement entrepreneurial training is to build, sustain, enhance small business development and create jobs through the retired military personnel as well as to prepare the individuals for resettlement into civil life (Yusuf & Minai, 2016). This training could be said to have positive impact on self-employment and significant growth of small and medium scale enterprises (SMEs) in Nigeria. However, most of these ventures are often short-lived. This is because entrepreneurship is developmental and involves a lot of intricacies in terms of processes, decision making, competencies and skills which in most situations require professional assistance and making interventions from experts. Therefore, this paper tries to identify some of these challenges. In addition, it highlights counselling as an intervention strategy by professionals to improve entrepreneurial tendencies in the Nigerian military.

Concept of Entrepreneurship

The term "entrepreneurship" is derived from the French verb "entrepren ire" and the German word" unternehmen both of which means to undertake. Entrepreneurship has many definitions by various theorists in the enterpreunship field, from the classical period of Irishman Richard Cantilton, who in 1437 first defined enterpreunship as "self-employment of some sort". It has been observed that there are no single definitions of enterpreunship, this is partly due to differentiated traditions within the field of enterpreunship research including anthropology (De montoya, 2000) social science (Swedbury 1993), economics (Casson 2003; Shane, 2003) and management (Drucker, 1999). Consequently, Hisrich, Peters and Shepherd (2007) define enterpreunship as the process of creating something new with value by devoting the necessary time and effort assuming the accompanying financial, psychic and social risks and receiving the resulting rewards of monetary, personal satisfaction and independence .Oni and Adekola (2002) also define enterpreunship as the willingness and ability of an individual to seek out investment opportunities, establish and run an enterprise successfully. Hisrich (1990) gave what could be considered as perhaps the most expensive definition of enterpreunship as "the process of creating something different with value by devoting the necessary time and effort, assuming the accompanying financial psychic and social risks and receiving the resulting records of monetary and personal satisfaction".

The Importance of enterpreunship cannot be underestimated. Olu-Young (2019) observed that entrepreneurship is fast becoming a tried and tested vehicles towards economic growth, and one that will certainly inspire the African continent to a greater future. In addition, studies have established a positive relationship between entrepreneurship and employment generation, alleviation and economic development (Olu- Young 2019). In Nigeria, successive governments have realized the importance of entrepreneurship to the overall growth of the country. Olu-Young (2019) and Akinade (2016) enumerated various measures/schemes aimed at promoting entrepreneurship and alleviating poverty in Nigeria as:

1. Small and Medium Industries Equity Investment Scheme (SMIEI'S) 2003.
2. Small Scale Industries Scheme (1970s)
3. Nigerian Bank of Commerce and Industry Loan Scheme (2001)
4. Small and Medium Enterprise Development Agency of Nigeria (SMEDAN) 2003.
5. Subsidy Reinvestment and Empowerment Programme (SURE-P).
6. N-Power programme of the Federal Government
7. Youth Initiative for Sustainable Agriculture (YISA)
8. Tony Elumelu Foundation Entrepreneurship programme (2015).
9. National Economic Reconstruction Fund (2001)

In addition, Olu-young (2019), identified some characteristics of entrepreneurship in Nigeria as:

1. Entrepreneurship activity in Nigeria is primarily based on necessity.
2. The majority of entrepreneurs in the country are operating in Lagos, former capital of the country.
3. Nigerian's economic decline since 1980's has created a hostile environment that is unfavourable to entrepreneurial success.
4. The Nigerian infrastructure limits entrepreneurial effectiveness and is a barrier to success.

5. The high cost of doing business in Nigeria, such as the lack of adequate electricity and basic needs by a large amount of the population stifle entrepreneurial activity.
6. Getting venture capital to finance entrepreneurial endeavour in Nigeria is very difficult because of political and economic instability.
7. The lack of enforcement of Nigerian patent laws discourages entrepreneurs from commercializing their ideas and inventions.
8. The constant political turmoil in the country greatly limits foreign investors who will be willing to provide resources for entrepreneurship in the country, which is very rich in natural resources.
9. Political and social movements strongly affect the level of entrepreneurial activity in Nigeria. Religious intolerance and ethnic warfare limit country progress in some areas of the country.
10. Female entrepreneurs in Nigeria are often underestimated and overlooked.
11. Female entrepreneurs in Nigeria are often hindered because of cultural barriers such as male/female role definitions that label women inherently inferior to men.
12. Nigeria has the largest GDP in Africa and South Africa has the second largest.
13. The Igbo ethnic group in Nigeria is recognized internationally for its culture of entrepreneurship. According to Robert Neuwirth, the Igbo apprenticeship system is the largest business incubator platform in the world because when an apprentice serves, his master is expected to set him up in business.
14. The majority of the entrepreneurs in the country are operating in Lagos.
15. Control own life, to be my own boss, freedom to adopt personal approach to work and attain family security are some of the reasons Nigerians engage in entrepreneurial activity.
16. The Nigerian government has a programme in place that promotes exports from Nigeria to other countries, which can be helpful for entrepreneurs looking to do business in Europe or the United State.
17. Lower taxes and increased price ceiling have increased the incentives to entrepreneurs in the country.
18. Nigeria is progressively trying to incorporate modern technology into its country.
19. Nigeria is trying to actively promote technology in its educational system with the use of the internet.
20. Although there are a lot of barriers, entrepreneurship in Nigeria is necessary for the country to become a developed nation.

Entrepreneurship Tendencies in Nigerian Military

The military constitutes a major workforce in the nation. All over the world, the period of military service is a period of selfless service to the nation. It is a dignified profession for the personnel. However, the military personnel are engaged to serve for a certain period, thereafter, they are expected to retire into civil life just like their counterpart in the civil service. The life of military personnel during the service and after the service is not the same. Singh and De Noble (2003), observed that some of these retired military personnel continue to accept life as it is with income from pension allowance, accepting the individual fate. Some however, continue to search for new jobs to generate more income for themselves and their families. Over the years, the lives of retired military personnel had been shrouded in stories of woes due to unpaid retirement benefits and pensions. However, the present government has recognized the important contributions of retired military personnel and has been very sensitive to their plight in order to ameliorate their suffering. Various intervention strategies put in place include, prompt payment of allowances, provision of jobs to engage those that are agile and are still at the productive age and training in entrepreneurship.

Furthermore, the military established the Armed Forces Resettlement Centre (NAFRC) Oshodi, Lagos in the 70s to provide requisite pre-retirement entrepreneurial training to the ranks and file of the military. NAFRC is a tri-service Institution for the Army, Navy and Airforce which constitute the Armed Forces of Nigeria. Personnel were nominated to attend the institution for a 6 months course to the commencement of their disengagement/retirement from the Armed Forces. On arrival at NAFRC, these would be personnel (Trainees) are expected to choose a vocation in which he/she would be trained for the period of six months. The available vocational courses include Agriculture, Carpentry and Cabinet making, building/ civil work, electrical/electronics, mechanical, soap and cosmetics, fashion designing, Fine art & printing and Management. (Yusuf and Minai, 2016). Upon graduation, they are expected to establish their own businesses. Obi (2013) observed that many retired military personnel are involved in various businesses spreading across oil and gas, manufacturing, constructions, quarries, mechanized agriculture, poultry, educational services, and small-scale businesses among others. These retired personnel, according to Chandra (2014), are involved in different businesses world over and are directly or indirectly, generating employment and contributing to national development. Sadly enough, only few of them could be seen to be successful while many others are still jobless and wallowing in poverty as a result of not engaging in other sources of income. Their pitiable situation could have been caused by a number of psychological factors in individuals and the operating environment. Meanwhile, some of the programmes embarked upon by the Nigerian military to empower its personnel includes:

1. Establishment of Nigerian Armed Forces Resettlement Center (NAFRC) Oshodi to provide vocational training prior to their retirement.
2. Barracks Youth Empowerment programme
3. Pre-retirement workshop for personnel
4. Granting of staff loans
5. Establishment of vocational training centers in the barracks
6. Officers wives Association empowerment programme for members and wives of other ranks in the Army, Navy, and Airforce.
7. Agric-business programme/scheme.
8. Cooperative Association

Psychological Issues on Entrepreneurship in the Nigerian Military

The aforementioned programmes/schemes are measures put in place by the military authorities to ameliorate various constraints confronting retiring military personnel in Nigeria. However, some of these measures have not been able to have desired effects on the beneficiaries due to certain factors. Meanwhile, the following are psychological issues relating to entrepreneurship in the Nigerian military:

1. Making/inability to make appropriate choice(s) of entrepreneurial trade(s).
2. Lacking the competencies to engage in entrepreneurship
3. Lacking prerequisite entrepreneurial skills
4. Lacking financial power and support
5. Lacking social and environmental support
6. Lacking required mentorship
7. Lack of necessary knowledge and information for entrepreneurship growth.

A critical examination of the above enumerated factors shows that there are indeed psychological issues that retiring military personnel encountered in the course of their preparation, during the preparation for and while entering retirement. These factors mitigate against the peaceful retirement life of military personnel thereby leading to catastrophic retirement life. However, the place of counselling in assisting in solving most of these issues cannot be over emphasized.

English and English (1971) in a classical definition of counselling believed that the term 'counselling' best describes a relationship in which one person endeavours to help another to solve his/her adjustment problems. This could be said to be most appropriate and apt to the situation of retired military personnel who could be said to be passing through a period of adjustment. In the same vein, Akinboye (2003) says counselling practitioners help their client (counselles) improve their well-being, alleviate distress, resolve crisis, and increase their ability to be creative, innovative and make success-focused decisions where ever they exist. Therefore, this exposition about counselling by Akinboye could be said to have captured all that is needed for a retired military personnel to have an enjoyable life after service. Counselling is planned and professionally executed, modern counselling is the application of psychology to solve issues of psychological concern. Several studies (Idowu, 1995; Carrel & Carrel, 2006; Yahaya & Mustapha 2004; Ibijola, 2017) have confirmed the significant impacts of counselling. There are three (3) major categorization of counselling services: Educational counselling, personal-social counselling and career/vocational counselling. Educational Counselling involves provision of professional assistance in solving problems of learning, teaching and education generally. Osarenren (2011) noted that educational counselling focuses on issues pertaining to academic success and furtherance of education. It aims at helping individuals to realize their educational goals. On the other hand, Personal-Social Counselling: this deals with intra and interpersonal concerns. It focuses on personal, social and psychological concerns of individuals, this involves assisting individuals to acquire requisite skills and facilitate interactions with colleagues, co-workers and members of different communities. While Career/Vocational counselling involves provision of assistance to individuals on career related issues. Through this process, individuals are assisted to assess and understand their strengths and capabilities, interests and motivations. Osarenren (2011) noted that through vocational counselling individuals are enlightened about job requirements, duration of training, the emoluments, job prospects and hazard.

Although, counselling has been categorized as above, however they are all related and interwoven in that an intervention in one area could lead to further exploration of other aspects. Furthermore, all the three areas are quite germane to the overall development and growth of retired personnel. One of the strategies to improve entrepreneurial tendencies in the military is the entrenchment of entrepreneurial education. A question at this juncture is what is entrepreneurial education, what does it entail, what are its dynamics and to what extend can it bring a renewal of hope for retiring personnel. Entrepreneurial education is also refers to by some scholars as entrepreneurship education, enterprises education and entrepreneurial training. Bechard and Toulouse (1998) define entrepreneurial education as "a collection of formalized teachings that informs, trains, and educate anyone interested in participating in socio-economic development through a project to promote entrepreneurship awareness, business creation or small business development" However, Ross (1997) define entrepreneurship education in terms of creativity and innovation applied to social, governmental and business arenas.

According to David A Kirby (2004) entrepreneurship education refers to activities aimed at developing enterprising or entrepreneurial people and increasing their understanding and knowledge about entrepreneurship and enterprise. Azim and Al-Kahtani (2014) broadly identified entrepreneurship education to include two different elements or concepts:

1. A broader concept of education for entrepreneurial attitudes and skills, which involves developing certain personal qualities that may be applied in practice within the domain of self-employment, business initiation or employment in the large organization and is not directly focused on the creation of new business; and
2. A more specific concept of training in how to create a new business.

Jones and English (2004) define it as "a process of providing individuals with the ability to recognize commercial opportunities and the insight, self-esteem, knowledge and skills to act on them". Some researchers have perceived entrepreneurship education as a form of training for uncertain future (Kratko, 1997). The focus of this training is on fostering entrepreneurial attitude, skill, managerial attitudes, among others. Fayolle (2009) explained entrepreneurship education to include all activities aiming to foster entrepreneurial mindsets, attitudes and skills and covering a range of aspects such as idea generation, start-up, growth and innovation. Gautam and Sigh (2015) in a critical review of various works on entrepreneurship education as a discipline identified as follows:

1. It is a function of innovation
2. It is a function of fostering leadership
3. It is an organizational building function
4. It is a function of high achievement
5. It involves creation and operation of an enterprise
6. It is a process of creating value for customers by exploiting untapped opportunities
7. It is strong and positive orientation towards growth in wealth, knowledge and employment
8. It is concerned with attitudinal change, risk taking abilities and turning ideas into actions

Researchers have discovered that entrepreneurship involve inculcation of right attitudes, competencies and skills which need to be stimulated and developed early in the life of individuals through entrepreneurial education. Furthermore,

Researchers, Rico, Camara and Llamazares (2015), Nasr and Boujelbene (2014) have emphasized the importance and impact of early entrepreneurship education in promoting entrepreneurial attitudes and competencies. In line with this, Saheed, Taiwo and Alebiosu (2014) advocated that a specialized training programme in entrepreneurship should be organized to expose potential and existing entrepreneurs to risk taking strategies inherent in self-employment and wealth creation. However, little attention has been given to entrepreneurial education in Nigeria which could be said to be one of the factors responsible for lack of growth and premature collapse of most entrepreneurship and small scale businesses in the country. A situation whereby would be investors were granted loans without proper training and adequate exposure to various competencies and skills would definitely lead to collapse of such ventures. Although entrepreneurship training and education has been advocated at all settings of the society, little or nothing has been found in relation to the military setting in Nigeria. Inculcation of early entrepreneurship education at all levels in the Nigerian military would be of immense benefits to the military personnel and the Nigerian society as a whole. The aim of this is to adequately prepare the mindset of the personnel to post retirement lifestyle which is helping them to acquire the necessary competencies and skills needed to succeed as an entrepreneur. It is expedient therefore that a unified curriculum must be developed and implemented at all levels of unit training in the military. Factors such as level of unit training, education, rank structures must be taken into consideration when developing the training curriculum. For the other ranks, this early exposure would prepare them prior to their disengagement training at the Armed Forces Resettlement Centre, Oshodi.

Objectives and Components of Entrepreneurship Education

Intervention in the form of entrepreneurship education and training has become a common scenario in almost all countries, developed or developing (Azim, 2013). An entrepreneurship training and education programme is a process use to develop entrepreneur attitudes, skills and competencies in order to develop qualities required to create new business. Entrepreneurship education should be able to instill the entrepreneurial character of students, such as confidence, initiative and risk taking (Draycott et al, 2011). Consequently, Azim and Al-Kahtani (2014) summarize the objectives of entrepreneurship education programme as mentioned by different scholars as:

Table 1.

Study	Objective
Hills (1988)	• To increase the awareness and understanding of the process involved in initiating and managing a new business, and • To increase students' awareness of small business ownership as a serious career option.
Sexton and Kasarda (1992)	• Convince his/her student to become actively involved in entrepreneurship; • Understand the dynamic nature of the world of entrepreneurship; and • Slow down the reality shock of the real world by means of formal or informal tuition.
Garavan and O'Cinneide (1994)	• To acquire knowledge germane to entrepreneurship; • To acquire skill in the use of techniques, in the analysis of business situations, and in the synthesis of action plans. • To identify and stimulate entrepreneurial drive, talent and skills; • To undo the risk-adverse bias of many analytical techniques; to develop empathy and support for all unique aspects of entrepreneurship; • To devise attitudes towards change; • To encourage new start-ups and other entrepreneurial ventures.
Hisrich and Peters (1998)	• Develop various skills required by entrepreneurs; • Technical skills • Business management skills • Personal entrepreneurial skills
Roach (1999) at North Georgia Technical Institute:	• Knowledge of the characteristics of an entrepreneur; • Ability to recognize business opportunities; • Basic skills and knowledge to create an effective feasibility plan for a business venture; • Ability to identify the various business entry strategies available to entrepreneurs; and • Understanding of the skills needed and means available to collect the market information needed to evaluate the feasibility of a new business concept.
Carolyn Brown (2000)	• Learn to develop ideas • Prepare to start a business • Build a viable business
Ulla Hytti (2000)	• To learn to become an entrepreneur or to develop an individuals' own entrepreneurship. • To learn more about entrepreneurship, to get some information of entrepreneurship.
Vesper and Gartner (2001)	• Personal development • Enterprise development
Jereon Onstenk (2003)	• To build enterprising key skills • To grow the entrepreneur as manager • To develop the entrepreneur as entrepreneur.
Hytti and O'Gorman (2004)	• Learn about entrepreneurship • Learn to become entrepreneurial • Learn "how to" be an entrepreneur by listing how to start a business

Source: Azim and Al-Kahtani (2014)

Summary of the Objectives of Entrepreneur Education Programme

On the components of entrepreneurship education, Azim and Al-Kahtani (2014) suggest that programme aimed at developing entrepreneurship must be predominantly learner driven where the learner is an active agent. The main goal of the programme is to increase learner's awareness, to highlight the entrepreneurial path as a viable career option and to develop positive attitudes, entrepreneurial knowledge and skill. It is believed that if this foundation is imbibe in the military, would be entrepreneurs in a long term perspective, the Nigerian private sector would become more sustainable, human development would be highly supported and poverty alleviated. Redford, Margues and Vaz four indicators of curriculum in entrepreneurship education as:

Table 2.

Entrepreneur knowledge	Characteristics of the behavioral potentials of a person and their understanding of the key concepts associated with entrepreneurship.	Kourisky and Esfandiari, 1997 Hunt, 200; Peterman and Kennedy, 2003
Entrepreneurial skills	These skills reflect the combination of knowledge and experience gained which are necessary or useful in developing a successful business activity. In terms of this project, a set of skills related to entrepreneurial activity was selected, reflecting the construct of "self-efficacy" as a perception and confidence of the student in his abilities and in the control of his own success.	Alvarez & Jung, 2003; Bandura, 1977; Ehrlich et al. 2005; George et al, 2003; Lans et al. 2005; Moberg, 2013; Orton, 2007; Rosendahl Huber et al. 2012.
Entrepreneurial attitude	Perception of social norms and behavioural control, leading to the information of intensions.	McGee et al, 2009
Entrepreneurship Intention	Predisposed to act. A good predator of behavior, particularly the desire to start a new business, which usually requires a medium or long term approach.	Ajzen, 1991; Autio et al, 1997; Bird, 1992; Galloway & Brown, 2002; Fayolle, 2013; Klapper, 2004; Krueger et al, 2000; Linan & Chen, 2009; Noel, 2000; Peterman & Kennedy, 2003; Shapero (1982); Thompson, 2009.

Source: Redford, Margues, Vaz et al

Entrepreneurship Curriculum Programme Indicators

Based on the above, it is essential to implement the following in the military

1. The military is to provide enabling environment for entrepreneurship to thrive and relevant. This includes provision of adequate funding for personnel and their spouses to engage in entrepreneurship.

2. Entrepreneurship education and training should be incorporated into the military training curriculum at all levels of training. Training should be aimed at exposing personnel to various entrepreneurial strategies.
3. At the discharged point such as NAFRC, training curriculum for retiring personnel should incorporate case studies and business simulation techniques which will equip the personnel with the ability to be proactive, anticipate business related problems, set goals and objectives and be better prepared to face business challenges.
4. Early exposure of military personnel at all levels to various sources of information on business opportunities available within and outside the country.
5. Partnership with government and non-governmental agencies to develop and organize awareness programmes on entrepreneurship.
6. Establishment of micro-credit schemes and finance bank for military personnel.

Further psychological issues confronting the promotion of entrepreneurship in the military is the choice of entrepreneurial trade by military personnel. Research has shown that military personnel both while in service, during pre-retirement and after retirement are often at a cross road when faced with the choice of trade or business to engage in making the right and appropriate choices have been a major concern to most retiring military personnel. Meanwhile making an informed choice is highly essential and an important ingredient for positive adjustment in retirement. One of the fundamental roles of vocational counselling is to provide wide and extensive information and data to an individual so as to assist such individual to make a wise and informed choice. Counselling and vocational psychologists believe that choice of vocation, entrance into a career or occupation follow a theoretical model. These theories have emphasized the need to have the right people in the right occupation or career. These theories have addressed many intricate networks of factors that are responsible for individual's vocational or occupational choice. Some stressed some dominant factors such as background, sex, socio-economic reasons as some of the factors responsible for such choices. Some of the theories include Trait and factor theory, Economic theory, Accident theory, Socio-cultural theory, Predestination theory, Developmental theory, Decision theory. Few of these theories will be illustrated as follows:

Theories of Vocational Trade and Entrepreneurial Choice

Several theories have been developed by psychologists and practitioners to explain the factors and rationale behind the choice individuals made in respect to vocation, trade and by extension entrepreneurship. This is also applicable to the military as individual personnel is expected to make a choice of a vocation or trade after retirement from active military service. These theories or viewpoints have also been accountable for explanation on why people failed or succeed in the choice they made. Although it is impossible to discuss all these theories within the scope of this chapter however, attempts will be made to highlight the major ones. According to Awoyemi (2019), theories of vocational/career development and choice are divided into two (2) broad categories; Non- psychological theories and psychological theories. The non-psychological theories which include but not limited to socio-cultural theory, accident theory and predestation theory refer to the cultural level and rate of development of a particular society. They are set of theories that are in practice despite the lack of wide and global acceptability, validity and applicability. Thus a general view of these theories as illustrated by Awoyemi (2019) is as follows:

Non-Psychological Theories

Socio-Cultural Theory: - This theory emphasizes the influences of cultural background on career choice. It's of the view that the culture of an individual or a particular environment is largely considered or a strong determining factor in choice of career or trade. These cultural/environmental factors include family aspirators, attitudes, values, social class, one's sex, religion, orientation, locality, place of birth, kind of institution attended and the nature of the curricular context to which one is exposed on the choice of a career or trade (Gesinde and Awoyemi, 2001).

Accident Theory: - The theory attributes individual's choice of career or trade to chance factors. It simply illustrates that some people found themselves engaging in certain trade, career, business entrepreneurships by accident or chance without actually prepared for it or had prior knowledge of such trade. Accordingly to Gesinde (2001), this is a popular theory which has been regarded as the layman's explanation of how he entered his first occupation. Majority of Entrepreneurs cannot actively account for how they made their choice while most of them actually succumbed to factors beyond their control in making their choices.

Predestination: - The theory emphasizes the belief especially in the African setting, in the role of divine intervention in the choice of career or trade. It is a belief that every individual has a particular career or trade which has been approved by 'the divine', however individual needs to make some consultations to know what he or she has been destined to engage in. This explains why people in African setting usually consult the stars, soil and heads whenever issues relating choice of trade, career and occupations arises. Although this theory is popular, however there is no empirical evidence to verify its validity.

Economic Theory: - This theory can be credited to Smith and Mil (18th century). These classical economists emphasized the consideration of monetary and other material advantages as the major factor in the choice of trade, business or occupation.

This is to say that an individual will select an occupation which pays him or her better in terms of income and other fringe benefits. This is applicable in the Nigerian context where monetary gains is the major consideration for business engagement.

Psychological Theories on Vocational and Entrepreneurial Choice

There are quite a number of vocational theories that have received wide acceptability through scientific analysis, and conceptual framework, use of psychological principles, assessment, validity, reliability and empherical applicability (Awoyemi 2019). The collection includes development theory, personality theory, trait-factor, decision theory and self-concept theory.

Developmental Theory: - The theory is of the view that as individual growth and development is a continuous process in human beings, so also is choices in vocation and trade. The proponents believe that what one becomes in future in terms of vocation is not made suddenly in one day, rather the choice starts from the early childhood stage as the individual undergoes different stages of development in life. This is also applicable to military personnel. Their aspiration, competencies and abilities towards enterpreunship should be developed in the pre-retirement years. The proponent of the theory (Ginzberg, 1951) asserted that occupational choice is a developmental process, that is not single spurt but a series of decisions made over a period of years. They identified four sets of factors which ultimately end in a vocational choice. These include individual values, emotional factors, the amount and kind of education and the impact of reality through environmental pressures. Other proponents of development theory are Super and Tiedeman who identified critical developmental stages which an individual passes through from infancy, childhood, adolescence and adulthood in the course of choosing career and achieving vocational maturity. To these authors, the choice of a career or vocation is made as a result of series of experiences an individual encounters as he/she passes through the critical stages of fantasy, tentative and realistic.

Personality Type Theory: - Holland (1966) propounded the theory of personality type in career choice and development. He states that each and everyone has a stereotype personality that are psychologically and sociologically relevant to the individual. He named the six personality types as realistic, investigative, social, conventional, enterprises and artistic. He also created six basic types of work environments along the same personality types. According to him, people who choose to work in an environment similar to their personality type are more likely to be successful and satisfied. Holland provided a criterion that individuals can use to base their career decisions or by checking which personality type they fall in according to which best describes them. He believed that career success largely depends on the congruency between the person's personality and the work environment. In summary, Holland's theory predicts that individuals will choose careers or vocations which are consistent with their personal characteristics.

Trait and Factor Theory:- Frank Parsons is often regarded as the founder of vocational psychology (Zunker 2006) and his model for career decision making remains essential in the vision of career development and counselling (Hartung and Blustein, 2002). The theory sees vocational guidance as a process that requires rational decision-making in which individuals are matched to make the best fit with a specific career, trade or entrepreneur. The theory emphasizes three stages which individuals must pass through in making that choice. First, individual must have an understanding of himself/herself, his/her capabilities, aptitudes, interests and temperament. After this stage of self-analysis, he/she will analyse the trade or business, the opportunities, employment and prospect and all that the trades/ business require. Finally, he/she chooses the one that matches him best. Trait and Factor theory therefore indicates that the best way an individual can choose a trade business, career or occupation is to know him/her and the world of work, and thus integrate these two sets of peculiarities (knowledge) and make an informed decision. Counselling through the use of various psychological instruments (local and foreign) assists individuals to explore the two peculiarities.

Implications of Theories of Vocational Choice on Entrepreneurial Development in the Military

A critical examination of the various theories of vocational choices enumerated above reveals the following implications for entrepreneurial choice and development for military personnel's; Firstly, making a choice of entrepreneurial trade or vocation for military personnel or their spouse is a critical factor and remains a phenomenon of great concern for the personnel and his/her family. Furthermore, the success or otherwise of the enterprise depends largely on the types of choice he/she makes. Therefore, there is no doubt that personnel actually need professional counsellors' assistance to enable them make the appropriate and right choices. Secondly, to make the right decision in career or vocation follows a systematic and scientific procedure. The choice is not to be done haphazardly rather it should be done in scientific procedure which involves collection and analysis of veritable information and data through the use of standardized instruments and tests. Most of these are locally and foreign made and have been specifically designed for this specific purpose. Thirdly, early exposure to entrepreneurship is highly necessary to achieve success. Existing theories have illustrated the developmental nature of career decision and that it is not done in a day. Therefore, military personnel's exposure to entrepreneurship from the early stage of their military career would assist to acquire the necessary skills, competences and attitudes to be successful entrepreneurs after military service. This could be done through entrepreneurship education and relevant collaborations with the public and private sectors of the economy. Furthermore, employers in the military must provide an enabling environment for personnel to succeed as entrepreneurs. This support should be in form of physical, financial and psychological, among others.

Counselling Intervention Strategies for Handling Entrepreneurship in the Military.

According to Akinade (2006), counselling psychology is one of the fifty-three (53) branches of psychology and it is coded as Division 17 of psychology by the American Psychological Association, APA (APA, 2000). Counselling in itself, involves a number of procedures in assisting individuals in solving problems that arise in various aspects of their lives. Akinboye (2003) says counselling psychology of the 21st century could be seen as a specialty in the field of psychology where its practitioners (Counsellors) help counselles improve their well-being, alleviate distress, resolve crisis and increase their ability to be creative, innovative and make success focus decisions wherever they exist. Suffice to say that counselling it a relationship which utilizes psychological principles or frameworks to assist individual to become aware of himself and solve his/her various adjustive problems. This utilization of psychological principles make counselling to be scientific and base on validated and empirical models. There are quite a number of these principles and frameworks which have been empirically tested and accepted by practitioners and have therefore become models in counselling practice. Few of these that have been found to be relevant in assisting to promote entrepreneurial development among military personnel in Nigeria are hereby discussed:

One of these is the socio-cognitive framework or strategy. The socio-cognitive framework was initially developed as part of the social learning theory (Ashford & Le Croy, 2010). The framework was presented by Bandura in response to his dissatisfaction with the principles of behaviourism and psychoanalysis. Bandura (1977) argued that in these two theories, the role of cognition in motivation and the role of the situation are largely ignored. Social cognitive strategies illustrate how individuals do not simply respond to environmental influences but actively seek and interpret information (Nevid, 2009) Albert Bandura's socio-cognitive framework emphasizes how cognitive, behavioral, personnel and environmental factors interact to determine motivation and behaviour. According to Bandura human functioning is the result of the interaction of all three of these factors. The social cognitive strategy is composed of four processes of goal realization, self-observation, self-evaluation, self-reaction and self-efficacy. According to Bandura, these components are interrelated and each has an effect on motivation and goal attainment (Redmond,

2010). One of the basic features of entrepreneurship is goal setting. However, for the goal to be attained, these four important components are interwoven. These include self-observation, which involves continuous observation of behaviour when it occurs, self-evaluation involves comparing an individual's current performance with a desired performance of goal. Goal must be specific and important. However, if people have little regard for their goals, they will not evaluate performance. Self-reaction refers to individual reacting to its performance with the aim of improving on the present performance towards achieving set goals. The last component which at the same time most striking is the self-efficacy component. This is one's belief in the likelihood of goal completion, self-efficacy refers to people's judgements about their capability to perform particular tasks. It is what an individual believes he or she can accomplish using his or her skills under certain circumstances. This psychological framework is relevant for the growth of prospective military entrepreneur who needs high level of self-efficacy to navigate through the business of entrepreneurship. Meanwhile, the keyword here is motivation to achieve success.

Another strategy is the Rational-Emotive Behavioral Therapy (REBT). This psychological framework is of the view that humans get disturbed and malfunction mainly because of their erroneous and irrational beliefs, attitudes, values and philosophies. By application, this therapeutic strategy teaches military personnel how to solve their emotional problems by showing them how to dispute and surrender their self-defeating beliefs. It is otherwise known as ABC principles which shows how an individual acquires rational or irrational belief which is self-defeating, and rational and irrational ways of thinking and behaving. According to Ellis, it is never the things that happen to an individual that upset him or her rather it's individual perception of them. It is therefore Ellis's view that what causes happiness or unhappiness is man's perception of an attitude and reaction to an event around him and this disturbs the individual psychologically (Oladele, 2016). There are other intervention strategies which could not be discussed in this paper.

CONCLUSION

Career is a lifelong activity engaged by individuals. In the military, retirement from active military service is an opening door to be ushered into a new lease of life. One of the measures taken to assist personnel gets adjusted into civil life is the establishment of vocational training into viable entrepreneurial world. Other ranks are supposed to receive this training at NAFRC Oshodi while continuous seminars and workshops are put in place for the officers. However, there are psychological issues that must be tackled in order to effectively transit into entrepreneurship. This chapter therefore successfully illustrated these issues. It addresses the concept of entrepreneurship and its tendencies in the Nigerian military, objectives and components of entrepreneurship education which is being advocated to be given to personnel early enough and throughout the military career. In addition, various counselling intervention strategies for handling entrepreneurship issues have been illustrated.

REFERENCES

Afonja, A. A. (1999). *Entrepreneurship Education and enterprise culture lessons from other countries*. Paper presented at the National conference in Entrepreneurship Education in Nigeria Tertiary Institutions, Abuja, Nigeria.

Akinade, E. A. (2006). You, yes you too need counselling. An inaugural lecture delivered at the Lagos State University, Nigeria. Lagos State University Press.

Akinade, E. A. (2016). *Contemporary entrepreneurship and career development: A basic text for colleges, polytechnics and Universities*. Brightways Publishers.

Akinboye, J. O. (2003). Expanding professional and scientific issues in Counselling psychology. *Proceedings for the 26th annual conference of the Counselling Association of Nigeria (CASSON).*

Arthur, M. B., Lawrence, B. S., & Hall, D. T. (1989). *Handbook of career theory*. Cambridge University Press. doi:10.1017/CBO9780511625459

Ashford, J. B., & Lecroy, C. W. (2010). *Human behavior in the social environment: A multidimensional perspective* (4th ed.). Wadsworth, Cengage Learning.

Awoyemi, A. E. (2019). Vocational Counselling. In E. O. Egbochuku & I. C. S. Ifelunni (Eds.), *Counselling and human development in Nigeria*. Ambik Press.

Azim, M. T. (2013). Entrepreneurship training in Bangladesh: A case study on small and cottage industries training institute. *Life Science Journal, 10*(12s), 188–201.

Azim, M. T., & Al-Kahtani, A. H. (2014). Entrepreneurship education and training: A survey of literature. *Life Science Journal, 11*(1), 127–133.

Bandura, A. (1977). Self-efficacy: Towards a unifying theory of behavioural change. *Psychological Review, 84*(2), 191–215. doi:10.1037/0033-295X.84.2.191 PMID:847061

Berchard, J. P., & Toulouse, J. M. (1998). Validation of a Didactic model for the analysis of training objectives in entrepreneurship. *Journal of Business Venturing, 13*(4), 317–332. doi:10.1016/S0883-9026(98)80006-2

Carrel, S., & Carrel, S. (2006). Do lower student-to-Counsellor ratios reduce school disciplinary problem. *Economic Analysis and Policy*, *5*(1). Retrieved February 25th, 2017, from www.betpress.com/bejeap/conbribution/vol5/ISS/artII

Casson, M. (2003). *The entrepreneur: An economic theory* (2nd ed.). Edward Elgar. doi:10.4337/9781843765639

Chandra, S. (2014, May 24). Soldiers turn entrepreneurs. *Small Business and Entrepreneurship Journal.*

Dabalen, A., Oni, B., & Adekola, A. (2002). *Labour market prospect for University graduates in Nigeria.* World Bank.

De Montoya, M. L. (2000). Entrepreneurship and culture; the case of Freddy the strawberry man. In R. Suredburg (Ed.), *Entrepreneurship.* Oxford University.

Draycott, M., & Rae, D. (2011). Enterprise education in schools and the role of competency framework. *International Journal of Entrepreneurial Behaviour & Research*, *17*(2), 127–145. doi:10.1108/13552551111114905

Drucker, P.F. (1999). The discipline of innovation in review. In *Harvard Business Review on breakthrough thinking.* Boston: Harvard Business Review.

English, H. B., & English, A. (1971). *A comprehensive dictionary of psychological and psychoanalytic term.* Longman Green and Co.

Fayolle, A. (2009). Entrepreneurship education in Europe: Trends and challenges. *OECD LEED programme universities, innovation and entrepreneurship: good practice workshop.* Retrieved on February 6, 2015 from http://www.oecd.org/dataoecd/11/36/43202553.pdf

Gautam, M.K. (2015). Entrepreneurship education: Concept, characteristics and implications for teacher education. *Internal Journal of Education, 5*(1), 21-35.

Gesirde, S. A., & Awoyemi, A. E. (2001). *Vocational Development and adjustment.* External Studies Series. University of Ibadan, Ibadan Press.

Ginzberg, E. (1951). *Occupational choice.* Columbia University Press. doi:10.7312/ginz92170

Hartung, P. J., & Blustein, D. (2002). Reason, intuition and social justice: Elaborating on parsons' career decision-making model. *Journal of Counseling and Development*, *80*(1), 41–47. doi:10.1002/j.1556-6678.2002.tb00164.x

Hisrich, R. D. (1990). Entrepreneurship/Intrapreneurship. *The American Psychologist*, *45*(2), 209–222. doi:10.1037/0003-066X.45.2.209

Holland, J. L. (1966). *The psychology of vocational choice*. Walthan Massachusetts Gum and Company.

Ibijola, E. Y. (2017). Provision of student support services and its impact of quality university education. *British Journal of Education. Society and Behavioural Science*, *19*(2), 1–12.

Idowu, A. I. (1995). The role of guidance and counselling in the Development of Nigerian University students. *The Counsellor*, *13*(1), 72–78.

Jones, C., & English, J. (2004). A contemporary approach to entrepreneurship education. *Education + Training*, *46*(8-9), 416-23. doi:10.1108/00400910410569533

Kirby, D. A. (2004). Entrepreneurship education: Can business schools meet the challenge? *Education + Training*, *46*(8/9), 510–519. doi:10.1108/00400910410569632

Kuratko, D. F. (1997). *Entrepreneurship. International encyclopedia of business and management*. Routledge publishers.

Nasr, K. B., & Boujelbene, Y. (2014). Assessing the impact of entrepreneurship education. *Science Direct,* 713-715. www.sciencedirect.com

Nevid, J. S. (2009). *Psychology: Concepts and applications* (3rd ed.). Houghton Mifflin Company.

Obi, A. (2013). *The impact of military service on the successful operation of a business: A case study in Nigeria*. Academic Press.

Olu-Young, F. (2019). Entrepreneurship and youth empowerment in Nigeria: The national security imperative. In Strategic Lenses (Series 3). In Youth management and national security in Nigeria (pp. 175-191). National Defence College Nigeria.

Osarenren, N. A. (2011). Not advising but desirable alternatives: The work of the counsellor. An inaugural university of Lagos, Nigeria, Lagos: University of Lagos Press.

Redmond, B. F. (2010). *Self-efficacy theory: Do I think that I can succeed in my work. Work attitude and motivation.* The Pennsylvania State University, World Campus. Retrieved March 20, 2013 from http://cms.psu.edu

Rico, M.I.L., Camara, C.P., & Llamazares, M.C.E. (2015). Impacto de la educacion en el emprendimiento, making-of y analisis de tres grupos de discussion. *Pedagogia social*, (25), 221-250.

Saheed, G. A., Taiwo, A. A., & Alebiosu, S. O. (2014). Entrepreneurship education as panacea for sustainable economic development of Nigeria. *Journal of Research in Education and Society.*, *5*(1), 20–31.

Shane, S. (2003). *A general theory of entrepreneurship: The individual opportunity nexus*. Edward Elgar. doi:10.4337/9781781007990

Singh, G., & De Noble, A. (2003). Early retirees as the next generation of entrepreneurs. *Entrepreneurship Theory and Practice*, *27*(3), 207–226. doi:10.1111/1540-8520.t01-1-00001

Swedburg, R. (1993). Explorations in economic sociology. New York: Russell Sage Foundation.

Yahaya, L. A., & Mustapha, M. L. A. (2004). Efficacy of client-centered and rational-emotive behaviours therapics in reducing behavior among in-school adolescents in Ilorin, Nigeria. *International Journal of Instruction*, *8*(1), 61–74.

Yusuf, L., & Minai, M. S. (2016). Entrepreneurial training and career path of retired military personnel as entrepreneurs in Nigeria. *International Journal of Sciences, Basic and Applied Research*, *28*(3), 217–230.

Zinker, V. G. (2006). Career Counselling: A holistic approach (7th ed.). Thomas Brooks/Cole Publishing Co.

Chapter 9
Military Veterans "Sign Up" for Franchising:
Another Route to Entrepreneurship

Denise M. Cumberland
University of Louisville, USA

ABSTRACT

The franchise business model has proven particularly attractive to veterans. When former soldiers become franchisees, they sign up to follow the game plan of the franchisor, but they must apply their own personal aptitudes, skills, and training to ensure their entrepreneurial venture succeeds. This chapter explores the practitioner and academic literature to identify why franchising is attractive to veterans as well as how the franchise sector encourages those with prior military experience to enlist. The chapter also examines whether veterans are satisfied with their decision to become franchisees and identifies which franchise systems are rated "best" for veterans. Finally, the chapter offers thoughts about global research that is needed to help franchise systems be a gateway for veterans to pursue their dream of business ownership.

INTRODUCTION

Franchising, a multi-faceted form of entrepreneurship, has two types of entrepreneurs, the franchisor and the franchisee (Hoy & Shane, 1998). The founder of the franchise system (the franchisor) fits the traditional dictionary definition of an entrepreneur, the person who "organizes, manages, and assumes the risk of a business" (Merriam-Webster, n.d.). Franchisors also recruit individuals to purchase into their franchise

DOI: 10.4018/978-1-7998-6655-8.ch009

Copyright © 2021, IGI Global. Copying or distributing in print or electronic forms without written permission of IGI Global is prohibited.

system. Those who buy a franchise enter into a contractual relationship with the franchisor to operate the business and become the system's franchisees. While franchisees are not the inventors of the concept, they are entrepreneurs as they commit a certain amount of risk-taking and proactiveness to help ensure their business succeeds (DiPietro, Severt, Welsh, & Raven, 2008). After all, it is the franchisee's capital that is invested in opening their own unit or operation. Hence, the franchise business model creates opportunities on both sides of the relationship and is, in effect, an entrepreneurial partnership (Baucus, Baucus, & Human, 1996; Combs, Ketchen, Shook, & Short, 2011; Rosado-Serrano, Paul, & Dikova, 2018). This may explain why franchisors actively recruit franchisees with entrepreneurial spirit (Dada, Watson, & Kirby, 2012) and encourage franchisees to consider the business a personal venture (Gassenheimer, Baucus, & Baucus, 1996).

In the United States, there are over 745,000 business format franchised establishments (International Franchise Association [IFA], 2018), whereby franchisees pay fees for the right to offer, sell, or distribute goods or services under the brand name of the franchisor (Combs, Ketchen, Shook, & Short, 2011). According to data from the IFA, franchising accounts for $425.5 billion of the United States (U.S.) Gross Domestic Product (GDP) (IFA, 2018). Franchising is not, however, a sector confined to the U.S. On the international front, franchising has become a popular format for conducting business in numerous industries (Rosado-Serrano, Paul, & Dikova, 2018). Whether it is new franchisees entering established systems, small businesses and entrepreneurs turning to franchising as a growth platform, or the practice of conversion franchising, whereby independent businesses are rebranded to create a franchise system, the franchise business model is an attractive option for entrepreneurs.

Given the growth of franchising, it is not surprising that this type of entrepreneurial endeavor has sparked notice among those with prior military service. While numbers will vary by country, in the U.S., veterans account for 8% of the population (Bureau of Labor Statistics, 2020), and the IFA reports that one in every seven franchises in the U.S. is owned and operated by a veteran (IFA, 2018). Eric Stites, CEO of Franchise Business Review, a research and consulting organization that works in the franchising sector, reports that some 9% of U.S. franchisees have prior military service (personal communication). These veteran-owned franchise businesses employ millions and are integral to the economic vitality of their communities. Hence, as franchising expands globally, transitioning military and former armed service members will be an attractive talent pool for franchisors to enlist.

The appeal of veterans as a viable pool of prospective franchisees surfaced as far back as the early 1990s. In 1991, the IFA launched the VetFran Program to support former military who are interested in pursuing a franchise opportunity. There are now over 600 member companies participating in VetFran, representing every sector of the franchise community. The stated mission of VetFran is to "to educate both veterans and franchisors about the unique match between the skills and aptitude of entrepreneurial veterans and the demands and opportunities of being a franchisee" (The VetFran Program, n.d.). Furthermore, to facilitate veterans' transition into franchising, franchisors wishing to be a member of VetFran must offer a discount on the initial franchise fee to service members who were honorably discharged.

In this chapter, the author examines the practitioner and academic literature to identify why franchising is attractive to veterans, as well as how the franchise sector encourages those with prior military experience to enlist. The chapter also examines whether veterans are satisfied with their decision to become franchisees and identifies which franchise systems are rated "best" for veterans. Finally, the chapter offers thoughts about global research that is needed to help franchise systems be a gateway for veterans to pursue their dream of business ownership.

Throughout the chapter, the terms *military veterans*, *ex-military*, and *former service members* will be used interchangeably to refer to any person who served in a qualified military branch for their country. Transitioning military are those persons who are in the process of exiting the military and returning to civilian life.

VETERANS IN FRANCHISING

Why Is Franchising Attractive to Veterans?

Transitioning service members report one of their greatest stressors is securing employment when entering the civilian ecosystem (Minnis, 2014). Over the past decade, as more military veterans have transitioned back into civilian life, researchers have begun to investigate what influences, as well as what factors help facilitate transitioning military and veterans in their entrepreneurial quests (e.g., Bressler, Bressler, & Bressler, 2013; Chamberland, 2015; Hope, Christman, & Mackin, 2019; Polin & Ehrman, 2018). Some of this interest has been led or financed by the Office of Veteran Business Development, part of the U.S. Small Business Administration (Craig, 2015). The scholarly literature has even introduced nomenclature for this group, designating former military veteran entrepreneurs as "vetrepreneurs."

With respect to franchising, however, there is a more limited pool of empirical studies that have examined the motivators explaining why former military personnel pursue franchise ventures. In their phenomenological study of seven military veterans who became franchisees, McDermott and Jackson (2020) found the primary motivator was veterans' desire to be in control of their own destiny. Furthermore, these veterans were confident in their ability to lead others and believed that the military had prepared them for handling difficult situations. There was also a sense of comfort in pursuing business ownership under a franchise system, which relies on checklists, networking, and a hierarchical structure, all very familiar norms. The high confidence level of ex-military confirms Kerrick, Cumberland, and Choi's (2014) study, which found that veterans reported high entrepreneurial self-efficacy (ESE) scores both at the beginning and upon completion of an entrepreneurial training program. Hence, those who have served their country in the armed forces bring a high level of confidence that they can achieve their entrepreneurial goals.

Only one other study was located that examined why military veterans pursue the franchising business model. Using the Critical Incident Technique (CIT), Mires, Cumberland, and Berry (2020) interviewed eight veterans who had become franchisees in the last five years. These scholars found a distinct decision order was used during the decision-making process to become an entrepreneur. All eight veterans first decided to become entrepreneurs without knowing that they would eventually embrace franchising as their form of entrepreneurship. The decision to pursue self-employment was based on their desire for control, a desire to serve, and concern about their ability to fit into the corporate world. This confirms McDermott and Jackson's (2020) finding that former service members wish to control their own destiny. It reinforces Short, Zachary, and Ketchen's (2018) suggestion that for those who served, values transcend their tenure as a solider and become part of their personal ethos. Finally, the concern these veterans expressed about their "fit into corporate culture" supports Davis and Minnis's (2017) argument that veterans have "difficulties working in companies with less hierarchical structures or organizations that lack a clearly defined career path for them" (p. 10).

Mires, Cumberland, and Berry (2020) also found from their research that, unlike the emotional decision to pursue self-employment, the decision to become a franchisee was one of practicality. These ex-military members reported that they knew they did not have the idea, business model, or resources to start a new business venture independently. Hence, they selected the franchise business model as their path to entrepreneurship as it offered a business ready to go. Finally, the study indicated that for these veterans, the criteria for selection of a franchise system was based on the values of the franchisor, the culture in the organization, and the type of training that would be provided.

The number of studies to date on why military veterans sign up for franchising is limited, primarily qualitative in nature, and U.S. centric. This suggests the need for further research to confirm the findings that emotional reasons lead veterans towards entrepreneurship, while practical reasons encourage them to sign up for franchising.

Why Do Franchisors Pursue Veterans?

Companies offer numerous reasons for hiring veterans. While these reasons range from a sense of social responsibility to a desire to cultivate positive public sentiment, a study of 87 U.S. employers across 67 firms found that most were in pursuit of talented employees who could bring a broad range of technical skills and highly valued personal attributes to the organization (Harrell & Berglass, 2012). In the franchising sector, the IFA reports that 97% of franchisors believe veterans make excellent franchisees (Schenck, 2019). Much like the military, franchise operations depend on systems. Franchisors, like military commanders, expect their franchisees to follow procedures with precision to accomplish the mission and to do so with loyalty and respect for the unit. Ex-military members have the discipline, ability to lead, tolerance for risk, and ability to survive rigid system specifications that make them ideal franchisee candidates (McDermott, 2010). Hence, it comes as no surprise that articles in both the popular and trade press often suggest that military personnel are uniquely qualified to become successful franchisees (Mires, Cumberland, & Berry, 2020), another avenue for entrepreneurship.

Determining which prospective franchisees to allow into the franchise system is of critical importance (Ramirez-Hurtado, Rondan-Cataluna, Guerrero-Casas, & Berbel-Pineda, 2011). Good selection criteria can bring about positive results for the brand, while poor choices can result in lawsuits, encourage opportunistic behavior, diminish the brand, and negatively impact the franchise system's performance (Jambulingam & Nevin, 1999). Several practitioners and media sources offer advice on what traits and skills successful franchisees need (see Table 1).

Table 1. Practitioner and media sources: Top traits for franchisees

Franchise Direct	Franchise Gator	Entrepreneur Magazine
Top 10 Traits of a Good Franchisee	*Top 10 Traits of Successful Franchisees*	*8 Traits of a Successful Franchisee*
Reliable	Leadership	Motivated
Leadership	Risk-Taker	Big Thinker
Good Judgment	Learner	Chief Cheerleader
Learner	Adaptable	Optimist
Hard Worker	Takes Direction	People Person
Communicator	Team Player	Takes Direction
Networker	Financial Aptitude	Resilient
Financial Aptitude	Patient	Cool and Collected
Ability to Delegate	Results Driven	
Willing to Ask for Help	Passionate	

Sources: (Franchise Direct, 2019; Franchise Gator, 2016; Entrepreneur Magazine, 2012)

Scholars have also attempted to identify the characteristics and backgrounds that franchisors should seek when recruiting franchisees. Mohd and Ishan (2017) conducted a meta-analysis of the academic literature identifying the personal and business characteristics that have been found associated with successful franchisees. These scholars offered a high-level view, encapsulating broad attributes, including 1) entrepreneurial capacity, 2) professional experience, 3) motivation, and 4) financial capacity. Based on prior research, Ramirez-Hurtado, Rondan-Cataluna, Guerrero-Casas, & Berbel-Pineda (2011) provide a more granular review of personal traits ideal franchisees bring to the business (see Table 2).

Table 2. Scholarly research: Traits of ideal franchisees

Managerial Experience / Skills	Maturity Level / Demographics	Working Habits	Other
Management ability	Emotional stability	Willingness to work hard	Faithfulness to franchisor
Human relations ability	Self-esteem	Need to achieve	Support from family
Previous experience operating any business	Personal relations	Entrepreneurial	Personality
Previous experience operating a connected business	Age	Ability to adapt to changes	
Shrewdness	Education level	Creative	
Intelligence and practical skills	Financial status	Perseverance	
	Marital status	Ethical behavior	

Source: (Ramirez-Hurtado, Rondan-Cataluna, Guerrero-Casas, & Berbel-Pineda, 2011)

Ramirez-Hurtado, Paul, and Ditkova's (2011) empirical research of Spanish franchisors highlighted that, out of all of the above attributes, loyalty to the franchisor was the most important. Many of the traits listed in the tables above, especially loyalty and the willingness to work hard, would be characteristics aptly used to describe those who have served their country. In a case study of business franchises in Africa, Oshigbo (2014) argues that because veterans are "die-hard sticklers" for following procedures, they are able to command a higher level of staff productivity. Furthermore, the principles veterans' role model leads to dedicated and dependable workers (Oshigbo, 2014).

In their study of recruitment advertising targeting veterans, Short, Zachary, and Ketchen (2018) suggest that ex-military "possess a unique configuration of characteristics and skills that allow them to balance entrepreneurial characteristics with a commitment to a higher mission" (p. 7). In their study of Fortune 500 franchisors websites, these scholars examined the franchise recruitment sections and measured franchisors' level of entrepreneurial orientation (E.O.) rhetoric using a computer-aided content analysis. Characteristics associated with E.O. include innovativeness, risk-taking, and proactiveness (Wiklund & Shepherd, 2005). Short, Zachary, and Ketchen (2018) found that those franchisors targeting veterans with messages that encourage entrepreneurial behavior, including innovativeness and risk-taking, have more franchises than those franchisors who do not target veterans on their websites. This study highlights how franchise systems that focus on veterans' characteristics find a higher level of recruitment success.

Beyond personality characteristics and training, franchisors' interest in recruiting former service members could also stem from knowledge of governmental training and support programming available to transitioning military, favorable lending programs from banking institutions, and the vast cadre of service members and former service members who function as a support system. Given veterans listen and trust other veterans, this extensive, tight-knit network may facilitate customer acquisition as well as provide a future pool of franchisees. Furthermore, countries may struggle with franchisee recruitment. For example, Australia (Roberts, Frazer, Weaven, & Thaichon, 2020) and Poland (Gheribi, 2016) franchise systems are hindered by a shortage of suitable candidates. This suggests the need for recruitment from among groups such as those with a military background. Finally, franchisors may focus on recruiting former service members because they simply wish to capitalize on the successful track record military veterans have shown with respect to entrepreneurial endeavors (Hope, Oh, & Mackin, 2011; Moutray, 2007).

How Does the Franchise Industry Recruit Veterans?

A pivotal point in recruiting U.S. military personnel occurred when Don Dwyer, the franchisor of the Dwyer Group, founded a Veteran transition initiative after the Gulf War to educate veterans about entrepreneurship (Dragomaca, 2019). When the International Franchise Association (IFA) and Dwyer rolled out the VetFran Program in 1991, the goal was not only to educate veterans on how to investigate and become franchisees but also encourage franchisors to offer discounts and incentives to attract those service members exiting the military. The VetFran website offers the following rationale for franchisors to join VetFran:

Competition for entrepreneurial vets is heating up, and companies that aren't actively incentivizing and prioritizing veteran recruitment are missing out. Veteran franchisee recruitment is an important part of modern franchise growth and development strategies, and VetFran is your gateway to unlocking that potential (The VetFran Program, n.d.).

Franchisors must apply to become members of VetFran. There are two membership levels with different annual fees. The "premium tier" offers the franchise system more access to promotions and events. When a franchise system signs up to be a member of VetFran, their "star" rating is determined using the following criteria:

- *1-Star Franchisor Members*: Must offer a minimum 10% discount on the initial franchise fee, have operated as a franchise three or more years, and have a clean audit report.
- *2-Star Franchisor Members:* Must offer a minimum 15% discount on the initial franchise fee, have operated as a franchise for four or more years, have a clean audit report, have data in Item 19 of the Franchise Disclosure Document, and have at least 25 units in the franchise system.
- *3-Star Franchisor Members:* Must offer a minimum 20% discount on the initial franchise fee, have operated as a franchise for five or more years, have a clean audit report, have data in Item 19 of the Franchise Disclosure Document; have at least 50 units in the franchise system, have at least an 80% continuity rate over the past three years, and have at least one executive on staff who completed the IFA's Certified Franchise Executive training program. (Source: The VetFran Program, n.d.)

The Malaysian government's promotion of "franchise-preneurs" led Kharutin (2019) to analyze the core components used by franchise members of VetFran to attract those who have served in the military. Her effort began by examining the 593 franchisor companies registered with VetFran. Of that group, one hundred of those firms were recognized as the best franchisors in 2018 by *Military Times Best*. Kharutin then examined websites and Franchise Disclosure Documents (FDDs) of the top 50 of these 100 franchises to determine specific veteran incentive offers. She reported that while all franchise organizations offered financial inducements, some were based on percentages and others based on dollar amounts. When percent discounts were used on initial franchise fees, the majority of franchise organizations offered a discount between 10% to 15%. When dollar values were used, most reductions of fees were in the $2,500 to $7,500 range. One firm eliminated the initial fee for disabled veterans. Kharutin reported that a few systems waived royalty payments for veterans for the first year. Her analysis also provided a picture of what types of franchise systems specifically target veterans in the U.S. The most popular were in the home building, repair, and maintenance service sector. This was followed by franchise systems in the restaurant segment. Other sectors targeting veterans included landscaping services, cleaning services, and moving companies.

Other countries are also replicating VetFran. In 2018, VetFran was launched in the United Kingdom. Similar to the U.S. program, financial discounts are available to transitional military personnel and current veterans in the U.K. who want to own a franchise. In addition to 15% off the franchise fee for the initial base territory purchase, there are vendor incentives for those who qualify (www.bfa.org).

While franchisors vary in the type of incentives they offer to former service members, the recruitment tools they employ are similar. The most prominent marketing effort occurs on the franchise system's own website, where membership in VetFran is highlighted, or other wording is used that suggests the franchise is "military friendly." Some franchisors place advertising on websites focused on military issues. For example, four franchise systems (Signal 88 Security, JDog Carpet Cleaning and Junk Removal and Hauling, Cruise One: Dream Vacations, and Cruise Planners) are "sponsored advertisers" on *GI Jobs*. Web search engines that employ certain search words are standard marketing tools, particularly in geographic areas where military bases are located (R. Dragomaca, personal communication, April 21, 2020).

Are Veterans Satisfied With the Decision to Be Franchisees?

The franchise business model is an inter-organizational relationship in which conflict is inherent. The franchisor and franchisee are both economically dependent and contractually committed to each other, thereby creating conditions ripe for conflict to arise (Winsor, Manolis, Kaufmann, & Kashyap, 2012). In international markets such as South Africa, where homegrown brands have been expanding via franchising (Perrigot, 2017), franchisors must battle the assumption that franchisees are not adequately supported by their franchisors (van Wyk & De Jager, 2009). In general, the use of contracts to govern any relationship encourages opportunistic behavior, which is why partner trust is highlighted in the franchising literature as a critical factor to franchise success (Grace, Frazer, Weaven, & Dant, 2016; Ishak, Chuah, & Romle, 2016). Because of the potential for relationship issues to arise in the franchise system, scholars have spent significant time investigating franchisee satisfaction.

Morrison's seminal study on franchisee satisfaction (1997) found that satisfied franchisees are more likely to remain in the system, have stronger performance, express positive commitment, and have a good relationship with the franchisor. Research with respect to whether veterans are more likely to be satisfied or dissatisfied with being a franchisee, however, is more limited, and results are mixed. In a survey of 3,177 franchisees in the U.S. food sector, Kalargyrou, Aliouche, and Schlentrich (2018) found franchisee satisfaction is not impacted by veteran status. Rather, in their study of 58 restaurant franchise systems, the only demographic variable associated with franchisee satisfaction was education. Those franchisees with higher levels of education were less likely to be satisfied. Kalargyrou, Aliouche, and Schlentrich's (2018) study, however, did not specifically target veterans; rather, military status was one of numerous control variables. Franchisee satisfaction studies conducted for Franchise Business Review's clients revealed similar results. According to the CEO (Eric Stites), "from a satisfaction perspective, vets are equally satisfied as non-vets. There is no data from our pool across 258 franchise brands that vets are happier in franchising, or that they perform any better or worse than non-vets" (E. Stites, personal communication, April 22, 2020).

In their quantitative study of veterans' satisfaction with being franchisees, McDermott, Boyd, and Weaver (2015) hypothesized that franchise business owners who had served in the military were more likely to be satisfied than franchise business owners who had not served in the military. The study examined four U.S. franchise brands, randomly selected from three categories with high appeal to veterans: business and services, maintenance and cleaning, and home repair and improvement. All four brands were participants in the VetFran program, and all were mature franchise systems that had operated for 11+ years. A total of 249 franchisees responded to the survey about their satisfaction with their decision to become a franchisee. The survey measured life satisfaction, career satisfaction, job satisfaction, and total overall satisfaction. While these scholars found no significant differences in life, career, and overall satisfaction, they found franchisees who served in the military had a significantly higher level of job satisfaction [being a franchisee] compared to franchisees who had not served in the military. But, among the three business categories studied, it was only the home repair and improvement category where those with prior military service were significantly more satisfied than those who had not served.

The discrepancy in the findings of the two empirical studies that examined veterans' satisfaction to non-veterans' could be attributed to the selection of franchise sector examined. Kalargyrou, Aliouche, and Schlentrich's (2018) study was concentrated in the restaurant category and included a total of 58 franchise systems. Meanwhile, McDermott, Boyd, and Weaver's (2015) study focused on categories with high appeal to veterans and included only four franchise systems. Since the focus of these two studies was a comparison between those who served in the military and those who did not, the question still remains: In general, are veterans satisfied with their decision to become franchisees? Practitioner data from *Franchise Business Review's 2019 Special Report on Veterans in Franchising* reports that 88% of ex-military franchisees indicated that they enjoy operating their business, and 87% enjoy being part of their franchise system. Furthermore, across the 258 brands surveyed, most veterans indicated that buying a franchise was a good business decision for them, with 8 out of 10 of these veteran franchise owners indicating they respect and trust their franchisor and would recommend this franchise to another franchisee candidate.

In a follow-up study, McDermott and Jackson (2020) used qualitative inquiry to better understand how prior military experience influences franchisees' satisfaction. Leadership training in the military surfaced as a critical theme providing these ex-military franchisees with the confidence to pursue a second career as a franchisee. These veterans also highlighted the pre-defined system as a strength for franchising over other business models and "connected their ability to work well within a system to their prior military experience" (McDermott & Jackson, 2015, p. 777).

The only other veteran-specific study on franchising (Mires, Cumberland, & Barry) did not specifically investigate satisfaction, but did ask veterans about the advice they would offer other veterans considering this venture into entrepreneurship. Only one of the eight interviewed indicated they would have selected a different franchise. All of those interviewed, however, recommended that any veteran considering this investment speak with veteran franchisee owners before making a final decision.

Media articles in franchise and business journals frequently highlight successful and satisfied veteran franchisee owners. To date, however, the empirical literature examining veterans' satisfaction has yet to be fully explored. Since maximizing franchisee satisfaction and minimizing conflict is a goal of franchisors, greater understanding of whether veterans are satisfied after signing up and what factors influence veterans' satisfaction level would help franchisors understand how to manage this relationship.

What Franchise Brands Are Rated Best for Veterans?

Kirchner and Minnis (2018) define "military friendly" as "a process of providing transition support to military veterans through four pillars: (a) recruitment and hiring; (b) personal, professional, and career development; (c) community outreach; and (d) promotion of veteran hiring practices" (p. 103). The IFA fits this definition in that executive leadership of the IFA has actively encouraged franchisors to become members of VetFran, a unique program with clearly defined criteria for encouraging military veteran hiring initiatives. Furthermore, the IFA has been involved in veteran outreach programs, as well as lobbying efforts that promote veteran hiring.

With respect to how franchise systems serve veteran franchisees, the U.S. business and trade press, as well as U.S. military publications and websites, have provided rankings of "best franchises for veterans," including *Entrepreneur Magazine*, *Franchise Business Review*, *GI Jobs* and, *Military Times*. Because *GI Jobs* did not include the methodology for their ranking ("15 Hottest Franchises for Veterans", 2016), their list was not reviewed for commonalities. Of the other three rankings, only *Military Times* (Gross, 2018) included the total number of veteran-owned franchise units. Out of the Top 53 systems making the cut on *Military Times* list, there are six systems that report 20% or more of their franchisees have prior military service:

- Dream Vacations (32%)
- Ground Guys (28%)
- Pillar to Post Home Inspections (25%)
- Matco Tools (21%)
- Mr. Appliance (20%)
- Tailored Living (20%)

A comparison across the lists of the three rankings from *Entrepreneur Magazine* ("2019 top franchises for veterans ranking," 2019), *Franchise Business Reviews* ("Top Franchises for Veterans," 2019), and *Military Times* (Gross, 2018) to identify best franchises for veterans, reveals there are five brands that appear across all three sources. These franchise systems include the following:

- Budget Blinds
- Dream Vacations
- FastSigns
- Sport Clips Haircuts
- Two Men and a Truck

In the U.S., two franchise systems also market themselves exclusively to veterans:

1. JDog Junk Removal and Hauling and JDog Carpet Cleaning position their brand as "veteran and military family-owned and operated." Franchisees must be a veteran or military family member.
2. G Force is a franchise company that offers parking lot striping, pavement marketing, and sign installation. The franchise indicates their mission is to provide business ownership and employment opportunities to veterans.

Given that franchising can serve as a gateway for veterans to pursue entrepreneurial ventures, it is not surprising that U.S. franchise brands seek to enlist ex-military to the rank of franchisee. As veterans investigate these options, understanding what franchise organizations offer in terms of support after signing up is also critical. In her study to provide a guideline for Malaysia's franchise industry, Khairatun's (2019) proposed framework includes financial incentives as a key recruitment tool. She also suggests corporate support and corporate training be part of any veteran recruitment efforts undertaken by franchisors. Likewise, Cumberland (2017), in her review of subsidized educational training programs available to U.S. service members, suggests that entrepreneurial education can create more opportunities for veterans. However, she also argues that these training programs must be regularly assessed to determine if veterans are gaining the needed skills to successfully launch business ventures (Cumberland, 2017).

FUTURE RESEARCH DIRECTIONS

This chapter has some limitations, given that scholarly research regarding veterans in franchising is still in its infancy. The limited number of empirical studies provides avenues for future research streams. First, additional research is needed to understand why veterans sign up to be franchisees. Mires, Cumberland, and Berry (2020), using a qualitative lens, studied motivators citing Gilad and Levine's (1986) 'push' and 'pull' theory of entrepreneurial pursuit as a plausible explanation for why veterans sign up to be franchisees. These scholars call for more studies using a larger sample size to isolate which of the motivators most heavily influence veterans' decision making and to confirm or dis-confirm the decision-order process. They also call for more theory development to fully understand the phenomenon.

Second, there remain unanswered questions as to whether the military prepares individuals to successfully own and operate franchises. Since the literature has identified some of the commonalities of successful franchisees, future research could investigate the presence of these characteristics among veterans. Furthermore, research could follow the line of Avrahami and Lerner's (2003) study and attempt to understand whether specific types of military service influence the decision to become a franchisee. This information could be valuable from a recruitment standpoint as franchisors could tailor their message and possibly more narrowly target their efforts among the veteran population.

Third, while practitioner research does suggest veterans are highly satisfied with their decision to become franchisees, empirical studies are needed that control for selection of franchise systems as well as enable comparisons by franchise system size, sector, and number of veteran franchisees versus non-veterans. This type of research would address McDermott, Boyd, and Weaver's (2015) call to better understand which franchise system categories are the best fit for military veterans. It is also possible that brands with higher percentages of veteran franchisees differ from franchise systems with average to below-average percentages of ex-military. Qualitative research could be conducted to illuminate how those brands with high percentages of veteran franchisees operate and help franchisors understand what factors contribute to veteran franchisee satisfaction or dissatisfaction.

Fourth, from an action research perspective, initiatives could be developed that connect military veterans and entrepreneurship via the franchising route. As a business model, franchising can create opportunities for both skill development and reduce unemployment in emerging markets (Perrigot, 2017). In those countries where franchising associations operate, these organizations could replicate the International Franchise Association's VetFran program and encourage franchisors to consider financing incentives to those who served in the military. Governmental support and training that exists to assist military veterans as they engage in entrepreneurship could be expanded to incorporate curriculum on growth via the franchise business model. As Radipere (2012) argues, especially about higher education efforts in South Africa, instead of educating about entrepreneurship, academic institutions need to educate on how to be an entrepreneur. Additionally, in programs that teach entrepreneurship, military veterans' tuition could be subsidized (Kerrick, Cumberland, & Choi, 2016).

Finally, empirical research that identifies which recruitment incentives have the most appeal to transitioning military and veterans would be valuable. Franchisors would benefit from knowing which financial incentive packages to embrace, what types of training veterans prefer, and whether other types of corporate support, such as mentoring programs, would encourage ex-military to sign up.

CONCLUSION

Franchising appears to be a viable entrepreneurial path for military veterans on a global front. Veterans who become franchisees contribute to their respective economies, both as taxpayers and job creators. Furthermore, being an entrepreneur can create a sense of belonging, help veterans reintegrate and provide a way to be part of something bigger than oneself (Harrell & Berglass, 2012). As this chapter details, the franchise sector has shown significant interest with respect to recruiting military veterans, but the research on ex-military franchisees remains limited (Heinz, Freeman, Harpaz-Rotem, & Pietzak, 2017). Beyond the ability to provide franchise organizations with important data on attracting and meeting the needs of those with prior military service, research could help inform governmental and educational institutions on how to support veterans' entry into entrepreneurship via the franchising route.

REFERENCES

Avrahami, Y., & Lerner, M. (2003). The effect of combat service and military rank on entrepreneurial careers: The case of Israeli MBA graduates. *Journal of Political and Military Sociology*, *31*(1), 97–118.

Baucus, D. A., Baucus, M. S., & Human, S. E. (1996). Consensus in franchise organizations: A cooperative arrangement among entrepreneurs. *Journal of Business Venturing, 11*(5), 359–378. doi:10.1016/0883-9026(96)00055-9

Bressler, M. S., Bressler, L., & Bressler, M. (2013). A study of veteran-owned small businesses and the impact of military reserve call-ups since 9/11. *Academy of Entrepreneurship Journal, 19*(2), 1–22.

British Franchise Association. (2018, July 5). *Dwyer Group U.K. launches new franchising program to support military veterans resettlement.* https://www.thebfa.org/dwyer-group-uk-launches-new-franchising-program-to-support-military-veterans-resettlement/

Bureau of Labor Statistics. (2020, March 19). *Economic news release* (USDL-20-0452). U.S. Department of Labor. https://www.bls.gov/news.release/vet.nr0.htm

Chamberland, K. J. (2015). *Success factors of veteran-owned small businesses* [Doctoral dissertation, Walden University]. ScholarWorks. https://scholarworks.waldenu.edu/cgi/viewcontent.cgi?article=1572&context=dissertations

Combs, J. G., Ketchen, D. J. Jr, Shook, C. L., & Short, J. C. (2011). Antecedents and consequences of franchising: Past accomplishments and future challenges. *Journal of Management, 37*(1), 99–126. doi:10.1177/0149206310386963

Craig, J. (2015). Bounding veterans studies: A review of the field. In H. Nobles & M. Davitt (Eds.), *Race and/or Reconciliation: Proceedings of the Third Conference on Veterans in Society* (pp. 101–118). Virginia Tech. http://hdl.handle.net/10919/72939

Cumberland, D. M. (2017). Training and educational development for "Vetrepreneurs." *Advances in Developing Human Resources, 19*(1), 88–100. doi:10.1177/1523422316682948

Dada, O., Watson, A., & Kirby, D. A. (2012). Toward a model of franchisee entrepreneurship. *International Small Business Journal, 30*(5), 559–583. doi:10.1177/0266242610376078

Davis, V. E., & Minnis, S. E. (2017). Military veterans' transferrable skills: An HRD practitioner dilemma. *Advances in Developing Human Resources, 19*(1), 6–13. doi:10.1177/1523422316682961

DiPietro, R. B., Severt, D., Welsh, D. H. B., & Raven, P. V. (2008). Franchisee leadership traits vs. manager leadership traits: An exploratory study comparing hope, leadership, commitment, and service quality delivery. *The International Entrepreneurship and Management Journal*, *4*(1), 63–78. doi:10.100711365-007-0042-3

Dragomaca, R. (2019, July 30). Veteran franchisees on the front lines. *Franchising World*, *51*(7), 34-35. https://www.franchise.org/franchise-information/veterans/veteran-franchisees-on-the-front-lines

Elgin, J. (2012, April 24). 8 traits of successful franchisees. *Entrepreneur Magazine*. https://www.entrepreneur.com/article/223405

Entrepreneur. (n.d.). *2019 top franchises for veterans ranking*. https://www.entrepreneur.com/franchises/topfranchiseveterans

Gassenheimer, J. B., Baucus, D. B., & Baucus, M. S. (1996). Cooperative arrangements among entrepreneurs: An analysis of opportunism and communication in franchise structures. *Journal of Business Research*, *36*(1), 67–79. doi:10.1016/0148-2963(95)00164-6

Gherbi, E. (2016). Foreign and domestic food service business chains in Poland. *Management in Education*, *12*(2), 25–31.

Gilad, B., & Levine, P. (1986). A behavioral model of entrepreneurial supply. *Journal of Small Business Management*, *24*(4), 45–53.

Grace, A. R., Frazer, L., Weaven, S. K., & Dant, R. P. (2016). Building franchisee trust in their franchisor: Insights from the franchise sector. *Qualitative Market Research*, *19*(1), 65–83. doi:10.1108/QMR-09-2014-0085

Gross, N. (2018, February 16). 53 companies named to Military Times best: Franchises 2018 list. *Military Times*. https://rebootcamp.militarytimes.com/news/entrepreneurship/2018/02/16/53-companies-named-to-military-times-best-franchises-2018-list/

Harrell, M. C., & Berglass, N. (2012). *Employing America's veterans: Perspectives from businesses*. Center for a New American Society. https://www.benefits.va.gov/vow/docs/employingamericasveterans.pdf

Heinz, A. J., Freeman, M. A., Harpaz-Rotem, I., & Pietrzak, R. H. (2017). American military veteran entrepreneurs: A comprehensive profile of demographic, service history, and psychosocial characteristics. *Military Psychology*, *29*(6), 513–523. doi:10.1037/mil0000195 PMID:29290645

Hope, J., Oh, B., & Mackin, P. (2011). *Factors affecting entrepreneurship among veterans*. U.S. Small Business Administration, Office of Advocacy. https://www.sba.gov/sites/default/files/files/rs384tot.pdf

Hope, J. B., Christman, D. B., & Mackin, P. C. (2009). *An analysis of the effect of Reserve activation on small business*. U.S. Small Business Administration, Office of Advocacy.

Hoy, F., & Shane, S. (1998). Franchising as an entrepreneurial venture form. *Journal of Business Venturing*, *13*(2), 91–94. doi:10.1016/S0883-9026(97)00064-5

International Franchise Association. (2018). *Franchise Business Economic Outlook*. https://www.franchise.org/sites/default/.../Franchise_Business_Outlook_Jan_2018.pdf

International Franchise Association. (2018). *Franchising for veterans industry analysis 2019-costs and trends*. https://www.franchisehelp.com/industry-reports/franchising-for-veterans-industry-analysis-2018-cost-trends/

Ishak, K. A., Chuah, F. W., & Romle, A. R. (2016). The roles of trust in franchising relationship: The Malaysian franchisees' perspectives. *Middle East Journal of Scientific Research*, *24*(6), 2071–2078.

Jambulingam, T., & Nevin, J. R. (1999). Influence of franchisee selection criteria on outcomes desired by the franchisor. *Journal of Business Venturing*, *14*(4), 363–395. doi:10.1016/S0883-9026(98)00023-8

Kalargyrou, V., Aliouche, E. H., & Schlentrich, U. (2018). Antecedents and consequences of franchisee satisfaction in the U.S. restaurant industry. *Journal of Human Resources in Hospitality & Tourism*, *17*(1), 60–79. doi:10.1080/15332845.2017.1328261

Kerrick, S. A., Cumberland, D. M., & Choi, N. (2016). Comparing military veterans and civilians responses to an entrepreneurship education program. *Journal of Entrepreneurship Education*, *19*(1), 9–23.

Khairatun, S. N. (2019). Veterans initiatives in franchising framework. *Asia Proceedings of Social Sciences*, *4*(1), 107–110. doi:10.31580/apss.v4i1.622

Kirchner, M., & Minnis, S. (2018). Engaging military friendly in organizations: An empirical-based definition. *Journal of Veterans Studies*, *3*(2), 94–108. doi:10.21061/jvs.v3i2.49

McDermott, M. (2010). Do veterans make significantly more successful franchisees? A comparative study on the traits of veterans and successful franchisees literature review. In A. Kakouris (Ed.) *Proceedings of the 4th European Conference on Innovation and Entrepreneurship: ECIE* (p. 395). Academic Conferences Limited.

McDermott, M. J., Boyd, T. C., & Weaver, A. (2015). Franchise business ownership: A comparative study on the implications of military experience on franchisee success and satisfaction. *The Entrepreneurial Executive*, *20*, 9–30.

McDermott, M. J., & Jackson, J. (2020). A qualitative study: Military veterans and franchise ownership. *Qualitative Report*, *25*(3), 769–784.

Merriam-Webster. (n.d.). Entrepreneur. In *Merriam-Webster.com dictionary*. https://www.merriam-webster.com/dictionary/entrepreneur

Minnis, S. (2014). *A phenomenological exploration of combat veterans' experiences as they transition to civilian employment using higher education as career development* [Doctoral dissertation, Texas A & M University]. OAKTrust Digital Repository. http://hdl.handle.net/1969.1/152463

Mires, E., Cumberland, D. M., & Berry, A. (2020). Veterans serving the franchise sector: Exploring the appeal. *Small Business Institute Journal*, *16*(1), 24–43.

Mohd, Z. B., & Ishan, Z. B. M. (2017). Reevaluating successful franchisees characteristics. In *Social Sciences Postgraduate International Seminar (SSPIS)* (pp. 78-85). School of Social Sciences, USM.

Morrison, K. A. (1997). How franchise job satisfaction and personality affects performance, organizational commitment, franchisor relations, and intention to remain. *Journal of Small Business Management*, *35*(3), 39–67.

Moutray, C. M. (2007). Educational attainment and other characteristics of the self-employed: An examination using data from the panel study of income dynamics. In L. Niehm (Ed.), *USASBE 2008 Proceedings* (pp. 1731–1767). United States Association for Small Business and Entrepreneurship. doi:10.2139srn.1070835

Musial, S. (2016, August 22). Top 10 traits of successful franchisees. *Franchise Gator*. https://www.franchisegator.com/articles/4-essential-traits-of-a-franchisee-11183/

Oshigbo, T. O. (2014). The contributions of veterans in business and economy: Africa as a case study. In H. Nobles (Ed.), *Proceedings of the Second Conference on Veterans in Society: Humanizing the Discourse* (pp. 12–17). Virginia Tech. https://vtechworks.lib.vt.edu/handle/10919/56355

Perrigot, R. (2017). An exploration of franchising in Africa. In F. Hoy, R. Perrigot, & A. Terry (Eds.), *Handbook of research on franchising* (pp. 515–535). Edward Elgar Publishing. doi:10.4337/9781785364181.00037

Polin, B. A., & Ehrman, C. M. (2018). The curious relationship between military service and entrepreneurial intentions in Israel. *Armed Forces and Society*, *46*(3), 438–453. doi:10.1177/0095327X18789074

Radipere, S. (2012). South African university entrepreneurship education. *African Journal of Business Management*, *6*(44), 11015–11022. doi:10.5897/AJBM12.410

Ramirez-Hurtado, J., Rondan-Cataluna, F., Guerrero-Casas, F., & Berbel-Pineda, J. (2011). Identifying the franchisee profiles franchisors prefer. *Journal of Business Economics and Management*, *12*(4), 567–588. doi:10.3846/16111699.2011.599408

Roberts, R., Frazer, L., Weaven, S., & Thaichon, P. (2020). Understanding cultural diversity in franchising: Recommendations and implications for recruitment of migrant franchisees. In V. Ratten (Ed.), *Entrepreneurial Opportunities*. Emerald Publishing Limited. doi:10.1108/978-1-83909-285-520201006

Rosado-Serrano, A., Paul, J., & Dikova, D. (2018). International franchising: A literature review and research agenda. *Journal of Business Research*, *85*, 238–257. doi:10.1016/j.jbusres.2017.12.049

Schenck, J. R. (2019). Designed to give back: Franchise businesses are excellent opportunities for veterans to continue serving. *Franchising World*, *6*(51), 24–27.

Short, J. C., Zachary, M. A., & Ketchen, D. J. Jr. (2018). Entrepreneurial orientation rhetoric and franchise system size: The moderating role of military veteran recruitment. *Journal of Business Venturing Insights*, *10*, 1–10. doi:10.1016/j.jbvi.2018.e00097

Special report: 2019 top franchises for veterans. (2019, July). *Franchise Business Review*, 4, 10-13.

The VetFran Program. (n.d.). *VetFran*. https://www.vetfran.org/about-us/

Top 10 Traits of a Good Franchisee. (2019, January 30). *Franchise Direct*. https://www.franchisedirect.com/information/informationforfranchisees/top10traitsofagoodfranchisee/9/340/

van Wyk, G. J., & De Jager, J. W. (2009). Marketing orientation of franchisors. *African Journal of Business Management*, *3*(12), 907–914.

Wiklund, J., & Shepherd, D. (2005). Entrepreneurial orientation and small business performance: A configurational approach. *Journal of Business Venturing*, *20*(1), 71–91. doi:10.1016/j.jbusvent.2004.01.001

Winsor, R. D., Manolis, C., Kaufmann, P. J., & Kashyap, V. (2012). Manifest conflict and conflict aftermath in franchise systems: A 10-year examination. *Journal of Small Business Management*, *50*(4), 621–651. doi:10.1111/j.1540-627X.2012.00369.x

ADDITIONAL READING

AAFD Road Map to Selecting a Franchise (n.d.). Retrieved from https://www.aafd.org/buying-a-franchise/selecting-a-franchise/

Bisio, R., & Kohler, M. (2017). *The educated franchisee: The how-to book for choosing a winning franchise*. Hillcrest Publishing Group.

Judd, R. J., & Justis, R. T. (2008). *Franchising: An entrepreneur's guide*. Thomson.

Kaplan, M. I. (2017). *The prior-service entrepreneur: Veteran entrepreneurship and lean business start-up*. CreateSpace Independent Publishing.

Mathews, J. (2011). *Street smart franchising*. Entrepreneur Press.

O'Donnell, W. (2014). *Rise: The veteran's field manual for starting your own business and conquering the online economy*. Warrior Lodge Publishing.

Street Shares. (2020). The ultimate guide for veteran-owned businesses. Retrieved from https://go.streetshares.com/the-ultimate-guide-for-veteran-owned-small-businesses-download

KEY TERMS AND DEFINITIONS

Franchise Systems: Businesses that enter a legal contract with another party allowing that party to use the firm's name and operating system while providing the brand standards and training assistance in return for a monetary fee(s). The franchise business model enables expansion by leveraging others' capital for growth.

Franchisee: An entrepreneur or small business owner who has purchased the right and pays a fee to use an existing brand's trademark and operating system while upholding the standards set forth by the brand.

Franchisor: The specific brand that owns the trademark for the business. For a fee, the franchisor licenses the rights to the trademark and provides the operating platform to the franchisees. Typically, the franchisor provides training to franchisees to ensure they uphold the brand's standards.

International Franchise Association (IFA): A membership association for franchisors, franchisees, and franchise suppliers that serves as a global educational resource, as well as an advocate that protects and promotes the franchise business model.

Transitioning Military: A member of the military preparing to return to civilian life.

VetFran Program: An initiative of the IFA that provides resources for entrepreneurial veterans who are considering purchasing a franchise. The program offers membership on a tiered system to franchise systems willing to provide incentives to former military and/or their families.

Vetrepreneur: A military veteran who organizes and manages a business enterprise.

Chapter 10
Entrepreneurship and Intrapreneurship as Innovation Source in the Defense Industry and Military

Olcay Okun
https://orcid.org/0000-0002-7096-5794
Hasan Kalyoncu University, Turkey

Korhan Arun
Tekirdağ Namık Kemal University, Turkey

ABSTRACT

Many military-related innovation approaches can be followed, such as doctrinal, tactical changes, and innovations in the organizational structure of military units. These approaches examine innovation in its historical context and flow. Defense industries of the countries are an indicator of their power in the international arena and develop new war weapons, systems, and equipment with innovation. Innovations turn it into economic power. Militaries are the most important customers of the defense industries. From the design of the products to the feedback of the last user, the defense industry, and military are in mutual interaction. Military culture, which is shaped in the light of the experiences gained with blood on the battlefield and has its dynamics, is one of the main phenomena in the acceptance of innovations and shaping the culture of military innovation. In this chapter, the authors examine the contribution of the defense industry and military employees to innovation in these innovation processes and the organizational acceptance processes offered to the use of these innovations.

DOI: 10.4018/978-1-7998-6655-8.ch010

Copyright © 2021, IGI Global. Copying or distributing in print or electronic forms without written permission of IGI Global is prohibited.

INTRODUCTION

When the First World War ended, greater than ten million soldiers lost their lives, twenty million were injured, and most of them permanent, and tens of cities were ruined. In the Second World War, which started 21 years later, more than seventy million people died. These figures clearly show the extent of the devastating power of human beings, who started their struggle with nature by using sticks. Behind this, destructive power is increased scientific power. Dozens of chemists, physicists, and biologists; Like British admiral John Fisher, who said, “The war will be won thanks to new inventions,” he made brand new inventions in his field as a result of the financial resources provided by the managers who tried every way to win. These developments did not only remain on the battlefield but also became the ancestor of many studies that would advance humanity technologically. These two great wars, especially the 20th century and the post-war period, are responsible for the high point that science has reached today, as well as the disasters and destructions experienced by humanity.

Innovation and military concepts may seem separate perspectives. There are three main reasons for this (Posen, 1984). First, because of the process of institutionalization, innovation in military doctrine should be rare. It will only occasionally be sponsored by the military organization itself. Second, Innovations in military doctrine will be rare because they increase operational uncertainty. While innovation is in process, the organization’s standard operation procedures (SOPs) and training programs will be in turmoil. Third, military organizations often graft new pieces of technology on to old doctrines because a technology that has not been tested in war can seldom function by itself as the catalyst for doctrinal innovation. However, military innovations can occur for two main reasons. First, armed organizations do seem willing to learn from wars fought by their nations--with the weapons and perhaps the doctrine of the dominant nation or organization (in this paper NATO). Second, Military organizations are even better able to learn about technology by using it in their wars. In this case, Turkey has been fighting with many terrorist organizations until the 1980s.

Today, we live in an era where the latest technologies are used, and defense systems are being developed day by day. In the changing world order, the defense industries of the countries have become a leading indicator of their independence. The power of countries in the international arena is determined by the innovative products they develop in defense industries. Innovation is an important influence in shaping the economic future of a country. Innovation is the cornerstone of a sustainable economy, growth, and prosperity. In a globalizing world economy and an intensely competitive environment, countries must present differentiation, new products, services, or value-added processes to the market to sustain the defense industries. Therefore, budgets devoted to innovation in both public and private sectors are increasing in the world economies. In parallel, innovation, intrapreneurship, and innovation culture gain more importance for the defense industry and the natural customer of this industry. In today's world, where competitive changes are rapidly increasing, and innovative changes have become the routine of businesses, the added value of innovative activities to the military is a critical field of work in terms of their ability to compete and sustain their lives. For this reason, it is necessary to highlight the new thoughts of the soldiers and provide the culture of innovation and the process that affects the intrapreneurship.

The concept of innovation, which has a crucial role in gaining competitive advantage in today's organizations and sustaining the existence of businesses, can be understood and available in many ways in the military field. Some studies on military innovations distinguish between length and width of the process as revolutionary innovation and evolutionary innovation (e.g., Farrell & Terriff, 2002; Eckardt, 2015)). Many military-related innovation approaches, such as doctrinal changes, contextual changes, strategical changes, tactical changes, and innovations in the organizational structure of military units, can be followed. These approaches are mostly examined as historical flows and developments. In this section, innovation is examined from the organizational theory perspective. In this context, we will examine innovation as the new combat weapons, technological systems, and equipment that are subject to the innovation work of the defense industries of the countries where the military is the biggest customer. We will examine the contributions of those working in the military to these innovation processes and the organizational acceptance processes of these innovations that are offered for their use.

The purpose of the chapter is to reveal the relationship of intrapreneurship in the military with the culture of innovation. How the dynamics of intrapreneurship is implemented in the military will also be examined. With this section, the military is aimed to make significant contributions to department managers who are interested in innovation and entrepreneurship. Furthermore, it is aimed to provide conceptual information to researchers working in this field.

In this section, HAVELSAN, ROKETSAN, TAI, and ASELSAN companies, offering innovative products for Turkish and world defense industries will be examined, and examples of their creative products will be presented.

DEFENSE INDUSTRY AND ITS INTERACTION WITH MILITARY

The defense industry is an important layer of industrialization within the scope of the ecosystem. It can also be expressed as one of the most effective power factors of political and economic power. Countries with developed defense industry worldwide are economically and politically dominant. Technological competence is essential for the defense industry. This comes to life with R&D and technology production. The defense needs of the countries are shaped according to the strategic perceptions of the regions they are located in the world, their underground resources, and their proximity to the energy resources. Their perception of threats and whether they are regional or global powers, and they change in the strategies appropriate for the policies they pursue in line with the interests of the country. Depending on the worldwide and territorial crises, countries are planning defense spending. The world trade volume was calculated as 41 trillion 142 billion dollars, and 1,686 trillion dollars of this amount were realized as defense expenditures. Defense spending continued to fall in America and Western Europe and increased in Africa, Eastern Europe, Asia, and Oceania (TOBB, 2017). The world defense industry market volume was $ 94.5 billion. The top five countries in defense spending are the United States, the Republic of China, Saudi Arabia, Russia, and India. The expenditures of these countries are 610, 228, 69.4, 66.3, and 63.9 million dollars, respectively (SIPRI, 2017). Considering the development, defense industry product sales show a continuous upward trend.

Factors that accelerate defense spending in the world; countries' foreign policy targets are policies that contribute to real and felt threats, armed conflicts, and multilateral peacekeeping operations. Tensions between countries and wars of interest also push all countries to invest more in defense industries. The defense industry sector is one of the sectors that allocate the most resources to R&D activities worldwide. Defense industry R&D projects are costly investments. Since the laws and regulations of each country for the defense industry are different and the defense industry issues are confidential, it is very difficult to have clear information about the investments made in the defense industry R&D., However, R&D projects carried out in partnership with the state private sector can be followed. The basic principles of the governments for the establishment of the defense industry can be expressed as follows:

- It is a condition of the national independence of the countries,
- It is shaped and supported by the public sector,
- Confidentiality is provided by law,
- The supply of defense industry products is not subject to free trade rules.

Perhaps the most critical task of the social governments is to ensure the integrity and security of their countries by ensuring their nation survives. States keep their defense industries strong in line with their defense strategies against possible threats. General characteristics of the defense industry are listed below (Demirel, 2012):

- Requiring high technology sensitive production techniques,
- Require special quality standards,
- It requires trained manpower,
- Continuously requires the use of the best technologies and therefore substantially requires R&D activities,
- It requires high investment,
- Obligation to produce based on single buyer and limited need,
- It requires opening to foreign markets to ensure continuity,
- They have special conditions such as security and privacy.

There are significant differences from other sectors in general definitions, such as the strategic importance and scale of the defense industry. It is aimed to meet the needs of the military with the innovations realized by the defense industries. The prominent key features of the Defense Industry, which is defined differently from other sectors and is a very comprehensive sector, can be summarized as follows (OKA, 2012):

It is one of the most critical application tools of national security policies. Because the large-scale and fundamental products of the sector are composed of the defense tools and supports of the country, it can be defined as the main concrete tool of the national security policy.

- It is an important indicator of the level of talent in a country. The sector's R&D and innovation capacity, in other words, is one of the main indicators that directly affect the competitiveness level of the country due to the high technology-based sector content of the sector.
- It reflects the need for highly qualified human resources. Due to the sector's high technology-based information-intensive feature, qualified human resources (mostly defined as R&D personnel) employment is a priority.
- It is a high investment cost sector. Investment costs in the sector are relatively high compared to other sectors, both due to the large-scale and high-tech based product development and service delivery as well as the need for qualified human resources.
- It is one of the sectors where knowledge and investments are the fastest. The defense industry is an area where new technology is developed or high-level technology is applied. It is a sector with intense competition at the regional and international levels. Given that technology is advancing and changing very rapidly today, customer loyalty and sustainability in the market are short-term.
- The country and region are the focus of the protectionism-free trade conflict.
- It is excluded from international free trade agreements.

- It is the most critical sector that is subject to international goods, information, and technology transfer restrictions.

The defense industry is different from other industries and service sectors. The main reason for this difference is the interaction between the sector and the state. In the applications all over the world, the state relations with the sector are very intense in terms of supporting the investors and/or sector firms at a significant level. Most importantly, the biggest customer of the product developed and produced in the sector is the state institutions and organizations. It is a sector open to government intervention due to its sectoral characteristics such as the strategic importance, size, and investment costs of the defense industry.

The most important customer of the sector and the users of its products in the military. Products developed to meet military needs are put on the market, and the process of developing products and eliminating the deficiencies continues with the visits made by the R&D engineers of the enterprises or reports requested from the military units.

INNOVATION

It is possible to define innovation from different perspectives. Innovation can be defined as entrepreneurship oriented, focused on developing a new product and process, and focused on developing new ideas. Innovation is the potential for organizations to introduce new products/services or new production processes. Convention on the Organization for Economic Co-operation and Development (OECD, 2005) defines innovation under four headings.

- Product innovation: A new or significantly improved product or service. This includes significant improvements in specifications, components, and materials, software in the product, ease of use, or other functional features.
- Process innovation: A new or significantly improved production or delivery method. This includes important changes in techniques, equipment, and/or software.
- Marketing innovation: A new marketing method with significant changes in product design or packaging, product placement, product promotion, or pricing.
- Organizational innovation: A new organizational method in business practices, workplace organization, or foreign affairs.

Organizations want to gain or maintain a competitive advantage in existing or potential markets by discovering new opportunities through these four innovation types. Drucker (2002) argues that innovative ideas come from methodically analyzing seven areas of opportunity. There are four such areas of opportunity in a company or industry: unexpected events, inconsistencies, process needs, industry, and market changes. Apart from a company, there are three additional sources of opportunity in the social and intellectual environment: demographic changes, changes in perception, and new information. In this approach, innovation is a manageable process rather than an individual ability. The concept of innovation, which can be defined in different ways according to different perspectives, is gathered around the common features mentioned below (Ahmed & Shepherd, 2010).

- Innovation is creativity: Inventing a new product or service using resources such as people, time, and money is finding a way to think or do something new.
- Innovation is learning: focusing on using or supporting the product, service, or idea.
- Innovation is the result of the interaction of different events: It focuses on discrete events that affect the development of a single product, service, idea, or decision.
- Innovation creates a series of innovation orbits: It is a whole of innovation activities derived from the source, which facilitates the realization of the innovation portfolio.
- Innovation is change: Innovation is defined as all major and minor changes. Some innovations focus on small changes, while others focus on radical changes.
- Innovation is a process: Innovation is not a single activity; it is a series of activities that will result in an output.
- Innovation is a set of interactive processes, actors, and situations: Innovation consists of important factors such as institutional framework, socio-political networks, and talents.

Innovation is important in adding added value to the national economies. Innovation plays an essential role in economic development and growth. Innovative products and services will bring vitality to the domestic market and local businesses, as well as accelerate the development of economies with new opportunities in international trade (Wang & Kafouros, 2009). Innovation is gaining more importance, especially in the defense industry product market, which requires advanced technology. While emerging economies try to increase their competitiveness by acquiring and applying new technologies, the main players of the market try to maintain their competitive advantages with innovative products.

Innovation and R&D expenditures have doubled since 2000 in the world. The innovation, technology, and R&D expenditure of the world defense industry has been 2 trillion 66 billion dollars in SIPRI data (SIPRI, 2017). The USA ranks first with $ 527.5 billion, China ranks second with $ 429.5 billion, while the European Union ranks third with $ 346 billion. Global innovation and R&D investments are concentrated in G20 countries. Turkey is also among the world found that the share of expenditures on R & D G20 is around 92 percent. Besides, 94 percent of patent applications in the world are made in these countries (TOBB, 2017).

INNOVATION CULTURE

The globalized world defense industry is pushing organizations that offer innovative products in this field to adapt quickly to changes, or even to manage changes. The most crucial argument of the world defense industry is innovation. Defense industry actors need to create and maintain an innovation culture to sustain innovation, the key to the success of organizations. Creating an innovation culture where entrepreneurs will feel more comfortable will provide many useful new ideas to the organization.

The culture of an organization can be defined as a set of common habits, behaviors, and representations shared by its members. Organizational culture acts as social cement for the organization. It is also a powerful management tool that allows organizing members to act independently and consistently. "Innovation culture" is a special understanding of unity that makes innovative thinking natural within the organization and promotes innovation activities at the level of all employees. Some factors that support the culture of innovation are below. The culture of innovation has five dimensions (Chouteau et.al., 2018).

- Presence of innovative leaders and managers;
- Presence of innovative teams;
- Existence of innovative individuals;
- Organizational context conducive to innovation;
- A large number of easily accessible links from outside the organization.

There are norms within the organization that must be supported to develop a culture of innovation. Some of these norms are listed below (Russell, 1989).

- Being open to new ideas.
- Providing financial and moral support to individuals who produce new ideas.

- Encouraging taking the appropriate risk for new entrepreneurship activities Supporting creative attitudes and actions of individuals within the organization.
- Perceiving innovations and innovation activities as a strategic solution method for organizational problems. and to support the necessary exchange practices.
- To ensure the accessibility of both interdepartmental and intra-departmental information within the organization.
- To maintain communication at a required level, outside the organization, to individuals and groups related to innovative activities that may occur in the future.

The implementation and development of innovative work in the military are closely related to the organizational structure and innovation culture. Innovation is not an activity learned and implemented in a short time. Creating an organizational culture that supports innovation in the military can be achieved through the creation of intra-organizational entrepreneurship. For innovative work to be carried out effectively and efficiently in a business, all employees must interact and cooperate from the top to the bottom of the business related to innovative works. When businesses provide this interaction, the efficiency of innovative works will increase. Therefore, the culture of intrapreneurship and innovation has a major impact on the performance of businesses.

ENTREPRENEURSHIP AND INTRAPRENEURSHIP

Organizations need to develop innovative new projects to compete in the defense industry market, where developments are very fast. Entrepreneurship, which is understood as a process of designing a new project, has a close relationship with innovation. In the defense industry, concepts such as creativity, innovativeness, entrepreneurship, leadership, management ability, team building is a critical issue in organizations aiming to be competitive. In sectors where competition is intense, innovation is mostly understood as activities developed by entrepreneurship within the organization. From this point of view, entrepreneurship refers to the work developed in organizations that managers/entrepreneurs see as the mediators of innovation that contribute to an innovative and entrepreneurial organizational environment that is deeply related to the organizational culture as well as the changes in the profession and worker profile (Machado & Davim, 2020).

Five entrepreneurial functions can be defined as entrepreneurs who come out of the organizations and develop new ideas, ways of thinking, and different perspectives (Landström, 2010). Entrepreneur:

- Takes risk and manages risk
- Creates opportunities and is innovative
- Coordinates limited resources
- Waits for the opportunity
- An entrepreneur is a capitalist.

Intrapreneurship is the entrepreneurial behavior shown in existing organizations. Intrapreneurship is the development of new products and processes by creating an entrepreneurial culture in an organization. Intrapreneurship is the employee's desire to take responsibility to pursue new opportunities and stimulate creative change. Intrapreneurship with an innovative perspective, demonstrate their ability to perceive opportunities and turn opportunities into marketable ideas constantly, so they are the driving force of change (Naktiyok, 2004).

Intrapreneurship creates opportunities for innovation by enhancing their potential to compete by helping businesses adapt to their environment faster. Especially in the defense industry, which is developing amazingly fast and where competition is experienced fiercely, the Intrapreneurship capability of businesses will positively affect the capacity of enterprises to compete in the market.

Intrapreneurship is affected by environmental, organizational, and individual factors. It is difficult to see intrapreneurship behaviors in an organizational culture closed to new ideas and different perspectives or in an environment where managers with this narrow perspective exist. Individuals who are not willing to succeed, introverted, non-social, and focused on external control are also not expected to exhibit intrapreneurship behavior. Businesses that want to survive in the defense industry should be aware of the environmental, organizational, and individual factors of their intrapreneurial behavior (Şeşen, 2010).

INTRAPRENEURSHIP, ENTREPRENEURSHIP, AND INNOVATION

From today's intense competition environment, businesses seek to make a difference and gain a competitive advantage through their most important employees. Innovative services and products developed by business employees provide new expansions to businesses in the market. The only way to implement an innovative strategy; is through having intrapreneurial employees who can innovate, follow the opportunities around them, act proactively by taking risks when necessary. In this context, intrapreneurial behaviors are like the driving force of the long-term competitive superiority and, in a sense, with their innovative, proactive, risk-taking, autonomous, and based on individual networks (Şeşen, 2010).

The entrepreneur is an innovator that offers new combinations of resources with different perspectives in current conditions. The main feature of the entrepreneur is that he shows innovative behaviors. Entrepreneurs create value with a unique combination of resources to take advantage of an opportunity (Pinchot, 1985). In organizations, intrapreneurship and entrepreneurship are two main sources of innovation. Entrepreneurship can take place both inside and outside organization entrepreneurship is used to describe the entrepreneurship efforts of individuals operating outside the scope of an existing organization. At the same time, intrapreneurship refers to the entrepreneurial actions of employees in an existing organization (Sharma & Chrisman, 1999).

The main difference between Intrapreneurship and entrepreneurship clutches is the source of finance. Entrepreneurs must create the financial resources they need. An intrapreneur is financed by the businesses they work for. In this case, while the organization carries the financial risk that the intrapreneur is affiliated with, entrepreneurs carry this risk themselves (Shrader & Simon, 1997).

Intrapreneurs trust the support of their business. He usually takes over the management of a group of employees who can convince his project and complement each other. In many companies, intrapreneurship is integrated into the existing organizational structure and process organization of the current enterprise. Capital and other resources are provided by the enterprise. On the other hand, an intrapreneur puts his career at risk if he acts against his instructions or even a ban on his superior. If successful, the company will not receive any direct financial benefits because it is not the owner. Compared to the entrepreneur, he usually has fewer opportunities to influence his environment (Eckardt, 2015).

Considering the phenomenon of innovation and the context in which military organizations are taking place, military organizations should renew themselves by making innovations in peacetime to prepare for a war that will take place in violent brutality in an uncertain point in the future, yet to be made against an unidentified opponent and in difficult political conditions to predict (Murray & Millett, 1996). It is anticipated that innovations will be carried out mostly by intrapreneurs as defense industry investments require considerable financial resources. Besides, if the enterprise's vision is suitable for intrapreneurs, if new businesses are desired without leaving its colleagues, team spirit and safe business environment, if the business meets the necessary finance, the corporate image of the enterprise, its marketing channels, and the technology used supports the intrapreneurs by creating an innovation climate for the intrapreneurs (Pinchot,1985).

MILITARY DOCTRINE: INNOVATION CULTURE IN MILITARY

Innovation in the military has dual sides. First, authority and a clear structure of hierarchy make the armed forces to be an unsuitable place for genuine novel thinking. On the other hand, when a clever idea occurs, no one is better at utilizing it than military organizations (Adamsky, 2010; Adamsky & Bjerga, 2012; Haun, 2019). Military, namely doctrine as a specific term, turns out to be rather inept at encouraging inventiveness because, in terms of practical reasoning, armed forces only need to know whether something works – not why. However, units or personal are picked, trained, and use each invention per a given scheme. As a result, once the inventions are made, military doctrines are propelling these inventions into workable hardware and better ways of warfare.

NATO defines doctrine as "fundamental principles by which the military forces guide their actions in support of objectives. It is authoritative but requires judgment in application" (Gulyas, 2019). Doctrine's three basic elements can be encapsulated in a simple Figure 1. Theory can explain under assumptions about what leads to success, which entails an explanation of a general kind. Authority is telling how things should be done rather than describing how things are done by innovators (intrapreneurs). Lastly, doctrine, like culture, formalizes commonly held beliefs. So, they both should be rooted in the nation's beliefs and societal underpinnings that culture motivates intrapreneurs to act, and culture has negative and positive moderator power on that act.

Figure 1. Aspects of Doctrine (Adamsky & Bjerga, 2012; Høiback, 2013)

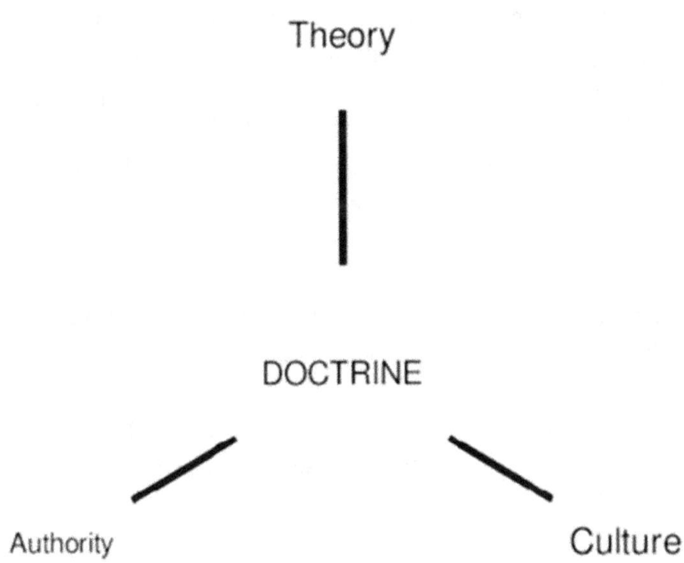

Rapid developments in science and technology in our age are one of the main sources of innovation in today's military. Nevertheless, how accurate would it be to see these rapid developments as the main source of innovation only? Technology, at most, determines the parameters of what is possible and creates the potential for military innovation. What generates innovation is the extent to which militarists recognize and understand the opportunities inherent in new combat vehicles, through organizational structures and power dissemination (Adamsky, 2010). While scientific and technological components are an important starting condition for innovation, the organizational structure of the military depends on the culture of innovation, the staff's entrepreneurial capacity, and the vision of the future war, predicted by the military. In other words, military innovation depends on doctrine because when the military does not practice war continuously, it needs shorter and often less ambiguous claims (Høiback, 2013). Because doctrine determines what can be expected from the finished product or service, but culture and authority decide what doctrine is.

Military culture can be defined as the sum of the intellectual, professional, and traditional values of military units. A military organization prone to innovation is an indispensable factor in the emergence of successful cultural innovations and the rapid adaptation to military innovations. The past is often filled with tradition that can hinder innovation. The reason for this is that the experiences gained with blood in the field of war are generally that innovations bring more loss of life during the war. Military cultures are more evident, especially in peacetime (Murray & Millett, 1996). The military organization institutionalizes the norms specific to national or military communities and produces permanent patterns of behavior. After institutionalization, norms are applied either by strong sanctions. Military organizational culture can facilitate or hinder innovations (Farrell & Terriff, 2002). For soldiers, innovation is not just a matter of talent and resources. Soldiers are communities on their own, with their sociology, history, values, and beliefs. Military culture is not just about individuals. Military culture is built on common history and principles of value. Operational and strategic concepts of "what works" in the military context are intertwined with social status and individual identity principles. The compatibility of innovation with organizational culture will enable it to be accepted faster (Hill, 2015).

- Fighting with Honor: The destructive effect of the innovative products on the battlefield (civilian loss, death form, etc.) is the perspective of the military organization from the perspective of religion, morality, and justice.
- Delegation of Authority: Delegation or centralization of the military organization's decision-making processes with subordinates.

- Standards in military material and tolerance to change of military material: new material, equipment, etc. of the military organization. a tendency to accept innovative products.

INNOVATION PRACTICES IN THE TURKISH MILITARY

SIPRI (2017), as countries that keep pace with the rapid development within the defense industry and can compete on the world defense market by offering innovative products to the market; Turkey, Brazil, South Korea, and India, were reported. Among the top 100 defense industry companies around the world, 4 American and 1 British company are in the top 5. South Korea while seven places on the list by the company from Turkey in 2017, our company has managed to enter the list 4. These firms are; ASELSAN, TAI, ROKETSAN, and STM. For a company to enter this list, its annual turnover should be over 300 million dollars. Turkey is a country producing and exporting technology. Using this advantage, it exports not only products but also technology to the world defense industry.

The Turkish defense industry policy pursues the main goal of developing products in the fields of production-design and R&D and acquiring the necessary infrastructure and technological and managerial capabilities. With the introduction of the private sector since the 2000s, significant investments have started in the fields of land and sea vehicles, electronics, and software. As of 2012, the Turkish Defense Industry increased its exports by 43 percent. Approximately 60 percent of land vehicles need at the moment met. The world's largest arms exporter after ten in the remaining 11 percent is now around 0.7 percent; Turkey's share is rising rapidly. If developments continue like this, our target to be among the top ten countries will be realized soon. Machinery Industry of Industry (MKE), the giant representative of the sector, meets 85 percent of the weapons and ammunition needs of the TAF with 250 kinds of military products, and exports to 40 countries. Other important institutions in this field are ASELSAN, TAI, HAVELSAN, and ROKETSAN.

Today, nearly 450 private companies are signing critical, innovative projects. ASELSAN pedestal mounted STINGER, 9600 frequency pulsed radio, ROKETSAN 122 mm multi-barrel rocket launcher, HAVELSAN simulator, and electronic warfare, TAI T.129 Atak Helicopter, Hürkuş, Anka unmanned aerial vehicles, and missile projects added to these are incredibly remarkable (TÜRKSAM, 2017).

The Turkish defense industry is in continuous development in recent years. The sector, which turns innovative ideas into products and presents them to the market, meets the needs of the Turkish Armed Forces and competes in foreign markets. Turkish Defense Industry companies are moving from being local actors to being global actors with their successful projects (modernization of Leopard tanks, Pedestal

Mounted Stinger, Storm Howitzer, missile systems, national main battle tank (Altay), etc.) (TOBB, 2017). Developments in the sector are closely monitored, both in businesses and non-governmental organizations such as the Union of Chambers and commodity exchanges of Turkey (TOBB), as well as through the Public Sector of Defense Industry Development and Support Administration (SAGEB), market research is conducted and information obtained is obtained. Innovative works are shared with private and public institutions.

ASELSAN

ASELSAN capability for innovation is one of the leading companies in the defense industry in Turkey is considered as the most important key to the company's success. In line with ASELSAN Strategic Goals, "Innovation Strategy" is defined, and innovation activities are carried out within this scope. To keep the innovation culture and environment alive and to improve constantly, all kinds of ideas are given importance and evaluated. Creating value-adding, creative and innovative ideas of employees within the organization are collected, evaluated continuously, and rewarded within the Idea Management System. Besides, theme-based idea competitions are organized, and valuable ideas are examined and awarded under different categories in these competitions. Innovative ideas produced through these competitions are transformed into innovation projects and implemented. Innovative ideas coming from outside the company are examined and evaluated by ASELSAN engineers (ASELSAN, 2020). ASELSAN supplies innovative products to the world defense industry market under the titles presented below.

- Military Communication Systems: Designing, producing, and integrating products and systems for military communication needs of the land, air, and sea elements.
- Public Security Communication Systems: Developing communication systems within the institution and/or inter-institution, especially the public security and health institutions providing public security services.
- Space Technologies: To develop satellite communication systems to provide a safe and uninterrupted communication opportunity between command control centers and tactical units.
- Crypto and Information Security Systems: Design and development for communication and communication systems and information technologies.
- Information Technology Systems: To realize the information technology projects needed in the military, public and civil fields at international standards and quality.

- Electro-Optical Systems: Thermal systems, laser rangefinder, laser marker, laser warning systems, day vision cameras, and image intensifier is the design and production of night vision devices.
- Navigation and Avionic Systems: It is the production of systems that enable military land, air, and sea vehicles to determine their position and orientation information under high precision and accuracy under all conditions.
- Naval Systems: The development of war and mission systems of naval platforms, system design, and system integration activities.
- Air Defense Weapon and Missile Systems: To design systems following the layered air defense concept, which is integrated with a high-performance sensor, command control, communication, and fire control systems.
- Command, Control, Communication, and Computer Systems: Designing Reconnaissance / Surveillance and intelligence systems.
- Unmanned Systems: Within the scope of this activity, development and production studies for "Unmanned Vehicles" and "Servo Systems" are carried out.
- Security Systems: border security, coast security, facility security, pipeline security, energy transmission lines security systems production, and development.
- Weapon Systems: Weapon systems that can be used in different platforms for land and sea combat are developed, produced, and offered to the service of the world armies with their original design and integration approach.
- Radar Systems: To meet the radar needs of the armed forces with advanced technology systems.
- Electronic Warfare Systems: It is the activities of system development and integration into the platform to protect the land, air, and sea platforms against electronic warfare and missile threats.

The organizational culture that supports innovation consists of a set of values that give importance to innovation, development, taking risks, being open to new ideas, adapting to new competitive conditions, and growing. The elements of the organizational culture that support innovation (Tidd & Bessant, 2011) and its comparison with ASELSAN are presented below.

Defense Technologies Engineering and Trade Inc. (STM)

System engineering, technical support, project management, technology transfer, logistics support services to Turkish Armed Forces and Defense Industry Directorate (SSB); was established in 1991 with the decision of the Defense Industry Executive Committee (SSİK) to perform its duties. STM offers engineering, technology, and consultancy services to the world defense industry market. In the field of engineering, air and sea platforms are developed, and innovative products are developed on cybersecurity, big data science, command and control information systems, and autonomous drone systems in technology.

Table 1. ASELSAN Organizational Innovation Culture Application

Component	ASELSAN Application
Shared vision, leadership, and the will to innovate	ASELSAN General Manager emphasizes that the pace of change is never the same as it is now and that the pace of future change will be faster than it is now. He says that the main dynamics of change for national and regional economies and societies, businesses in terms of technology with R&D and innovation, and that each unit is questioning this change and transformation. The impact of change on production is cost reduction, productivity, and market share increase, contributing to regional development, effects of changing process on production. One of the main goals of ASELSAN is to reduce the foreign dependency of the defense industry and to meet the need for domestic national products.
Appropriate structure	Global Product division structure
Exploratory Strategies	Ph.D. scholarship, hiring successful graduates, joint projects with universities, customer feedback, fairs, symposiums workshops
Exploitative strategies	R&D Centers, internal workshops
Key individuals	ASELSAN Technology Supreme Board members, external R&D service providers' members, IP out-licensing, patent and know-how owners, Idea Competitions, and Idea Competitions' winners.
Effective team working	Informal networking, Projects within the scope of the EUREKA Program, Publicly funded R&D Consortia's, and Co-operation with Universities.
High-involvement innovation	ASELSAN has approximately 4 thousand R&D personnel and spent $ 474 million in 2018 on R&D. According to the company's constitution, 50 percent of the turnover is devoted to R&D every year. In 2018, 54 universities were studied, and 126 projects were supported. The amount paid for university projects is 154.2 million dollars.
Creative climate	Integrated management system
External focus	ASELSAN sustains its production by NATO Quality Assurance Standards and international military standards for the products delivered to both domestic and international markets.

Defense Industries Research and Development Institute (SAGE)

SAGE was established in 1972 in Ankara. The Institute is a part of TUBİTAK - The Scientific and Technological Research Council of Turkey and specializes in the field of the defense industry. The main function of SAGE is to perform research and development activities for defense systems, including engineering and prototype production, starting with their fundamental research and conceptual design. Most of the projects are performed in coordination with related defense institutions. The mission of TÜBİTAK SAGE; to provide the defense industry with high competitiveness and value-added technology, products, and services through R&D. SAGE carries out projects with various partners by giving importance to international cooperation as much as national partnerships (SAGE, 2019). Some important military innovations developed by SAGE are below.

- Medium Range Ammunition Launched to the Surface: It is a long-range, air-to-surface turbojet-powered cruise missile that provides the target to be hit with great accuracy without entering the effective range of the air defense systems and can attack effectively against stationary surface targets and moving surface targets.
- Precision Guidance Kit: It is the owner guidance kit that converts the existing unguided 2000 lb Mk-84 general-purpose bombs and penetrating bombs into ammunition with intelligent and sensitive strike capability with ANS / KKS guidance system.
- Bozok: It is miniature ammunition that is thrown from the air to unmanned aerial vehicles.
- Penetrating Bomb: Designed to be used against the ground and underground targets. Sequencing with piercing warhead technology is the first concrete-piercing ammunition developed in Turkey.
- Winged Guiding Kit: A winged guiding kit that converts existing unguided 1000 lb MK83 and 500 lb MK82 general purpose bombs into long-range smart ammunition from air to land.
- Tendürek: It is a plastic-bonded thermobaric explosive containing more than 20% metal powder in its composition.
- Göktuğ: High-performance air-air missile systems for air superiority.

TAI

Turkish Aerospace Industries (TAI), Turkey's defense industry, was established in 1973 to reduce dependence on foreign sources. The company provides services in the development, modernization, production, system integration, and life cycle support processes of aviation and space industry systems. TAI aims to offer innovative products in the field of defense and aviation to the domestic and world markets. The company, which ranked 61st amongst aviation and space companies in the international arena in 2017, forms its strategies to reach a turnover of $ 10 billion in 2027. TUSAŞ, which is among the top 100 global players in the aviation and space industry, is organized within the six strategic business centers: Structural Group, Aircraft Group, Helicopter Group, Unmanned Aerial Vehicle (UAV) Systems Group, Space Systems Group, National Combat Aircraft (MMU) Group (TUSAS, 2019).

TAI follows the technologies of the future and the competencies that should be gained in line with the strategic goals of our defense industry with the technology roadmap. The roadmap, which is updated on an annual basis with the opinions of the field experts, is the basic planning tool that guides the R&D projects, university, and ındustry cooperation areas and academic study subjects carried out to achieve strategic goals. Some innovative projects developed by TAI are presented below.

- GÖKBEY: The first General Purpose Helicopter developed and produced with domestic facilities, GÖKBEY successfully realized its first flight on September 6, 2018, and it is predicted that it will start mass production in 2021.
- ATAK: Optimized for challenging "hot air-high altitude" missions with a heavy weapon load, ATAK Helicopter has been developed in line with national capabilities and capabilities to meet the needs of the Armed Forces' attack helicopter.
- T70 General Purpose Helicopter: TAI is the prime contractor and Sikorsky, ASELSAN, TEI, the subcontract Alp Aviation company, Sikorsky Aircraft company of which will be developed starting from the S70 the helicopter 109 T70 General Purpose Helicopter will be produced by production models under license in Turkey over the next 10 years.
- HÜRJET Jet Training and Light Attack Aircraft: It is designed to play a critical role by using superior performance features with its single-engine, tandem, and modern avionics suite cockpit. The armed variant of HÜRJET is a significant power factor in combat areas with its wide range of missions and superior payload capacity.
- GÖKTÜRK: It is the first high-definition earth observation satellite as the original is.
- ANKA: Medium Altitude Long Stay (MALE-Medium Altitude Long Endurance), UAV Program is a development project; It aims to complete the prototype and development tests by designing and developing three aircraft prototypes and ground systems.

ROKETSAN

Roketsan is a leading institution in the design, development, and manufacture of rockets and missiles. Today, Roketsan has more than 2,000 personnel and a total of 5.7 million m^2 of facilities, including 110,000 m^2 of indoor facilities in two separate campuses in Ankara; to design and produce rocket, missile, guided ammunition, and weapon systems of different features, their launch systems, and dispatch systems, rocket fuels, search warheads, guided and control systems, plug and warheads, mechanical parts, algorithms and software related to these systems, integrating land, air, and sea platforms, providing logistics support services, manufacturing ballistic protection (armor) systems of various platforms, developing satellite launch systems, ammunition sorting plant, ammunition improvement, development and renovation center and all kinds of artillery ammunition, tanks, Turnkey installation of firing test and evaluation center facilities where rocket and missile tests can be carried out within the framework of its activities (ROKETSAN, 2019).

HAVELSAN

HAVELSAN aims to be a pioneer in global competition with innovation and to keep the satisfaction of our customers and employees at the highest level by evaluating innovative idea's suggestions of our employees as well as our external stakeholders and establishing collaborations that will realize the ideas. HAVELSAN is looking for creative solutions that will increase performance and provide a route by taking into account the obstacles in the field to provide altitude data for use in Geographic Information Systems (GIS) products. Today, the use of map data has expanded; compatibility between information systems has emphasized the orientation to international open standards, and it has become important to create performance-based GIS solutions based on open sources. HAVELSAN aims to reach creative solutions in the field of GIS through two current issues and to reveal the values that can be created in the field of GIS (HAVELSAN, 2020). HAVELSAN is constantly in search of new technologies; it is working on artificial intelligence, big data, the Internet of things, augmented reality, autonomous systems, new-generation communication 5G technologies, cybersecurity. HAVELSAN conducts innovative idea campaigns with universities. For this purpose, an "Open Innovation Center" has been established in HAVELSAN for students to put their ideas into practice.

BMC

BMC Company is one of the half-century-long histories with Turkey's modern commercial and military vehicle production centers. In Turkey, the first foundry in the industry, the first diesel engine production, the first vocational training center, the first turbo car, the first domestic light commercial vehicles, the first environmentally-friendly natural gas buses, the first full low-floor buses, the first domestic production of tactical wheeled armored vehicles production The focus of this success of BMC is the experienced human resources and the R&D investments it has made since its establishment. By making regular investments in line with the expectations of military and commercial vehicle users in different fields from new product development to existing product improvements with the importance it attaches to research and development; it devotes a significant part of its turnover to R&D activities every year. BMC produces tactical wheeled vehicles, logistic support vehicles, armored vehicles, tanks, and new generation vehicles for military purposes. During the use of each vehicle, innovation activities are sustained through feedback from military units and visits to military units by the engineers of the company in certain periods.

FUTURE RESEARCH DIRECTIONS

When the current interests of the world defense industry are analyzed, it is evaluated that aviation and space defense advanced technological materials, information technologies, big data, space technologies, software analysis, and robotics, and automation will be the most innovative and R&D investments. It is important to concentrate the investments of the enterprises in these areas by working on the trends of the defense industry, especially these issues. In this context, research needs to be concentrated on these issues.

Guiding the innovations in the defense industry today, the military's instructions, military cultures, and the practices they implement to have been kneaded with the experience gained throughout history. The subject of commercializing military innovations can offer strong promises for researchers.

Threatening perceptions bring countries together and establish military organizations in the globalized world. How military organizations, e.g., NATO, affect innovations in the defense industry can also be an interesting topic.

Finally, how the intrapreneurs, which are taken out of the organizations themselves, are considered as an organizational variable and included in the management plans should be searched and turned into a systematic one.

CONCLUSION

Modern armies have been structured related to civil-military relations, and nation-building, nation structure, and larger military organizations (in this paper, NATO). From that point of view, two fundamental points stand out. First, certain attributes of modern military organizations are being defined by political-military integration and innovation. Second, some aspects of the structure of current nations or military organizations make it significant of authority, which has been exercised by civilians along the dimensions of military doctrine. Innovation in military doctrine can affect the likelihood of victory or defeat. The benefits of innovation can be judged, in part, in terms of its effect on integration. Innovation must be judged in terms of the general military and technological environment that military innovation consistent with the nations' political goals. Nevertheless, doctrines have cultural, managerial, and theoretical dimensions.

Concepts such as courage, glory, honor, absolute obedience, self-confidence, honesty are extraordinarily strong values and beliefs inherent in military service. The innovation culture of the military organizations and the innovations to be developed must be harmonized with the strong military culture. Innovations that upset this pattern of beliefs and values have little chance of success. One of the biggest responsibilities of strategic military leadership is to promote a context in which good ideas have the chance to turn into effective combat vehicles and methods.

Each country has military schools to meet the needs of its trained personnel. The main task of military schools is to train active staff with the qualifications that should be present in soldiers, with improved leadership qualities, gaining military referral and management skills, and having sufficient physical skills. The structure and curriculum of military training institutions that train military personnel to affect the direction of military innovation by shaping the professional military culture (Mullins, 2000). An innovative perspective to be given to military students in these schools will find application throughout their professional life.

The training and value system of military units is crucial for effective innovation. It is the staff that best analyze the lack of personnel, which are the first users of equipment and weapon systems, or the issues that need improvement. Leading personnel and subordinates with military values and professional values will be willing to convey innovative ideas about the equipment and weapon systems they are currently using, by following the innovations and technologies in the world.

Innovation is the tool for entrepreneurs to increase the potential of existing resources to create wealth or to create new wealth-producing resources. Entrepreneurship is a role that arises with the creation of appropriate organizational conditions rather than a personality trait. They occur with the correct roles and processes that intrapreneurs and management will reveal.

Organizations should have structured innovation management systems to ensure that the innovations developed are manageable organizational activity rather than the entrepreneurs involved in the innovation process play a key role.

Since the competitiveness of the defense sector is entirely based on innovation, R&D investments, and activities are important. R&D investments require great budgetary means. The main reason why the leading industrial enterprises in the sector are state-sponsored is the overcoming of the economic insufficiency with state support. Private-sector companies face considerable difficulties in financing

R&D investments and activities from financial institutions except for the abstract and uncertainty of equity.

In addition to the strategic product development and production demand for the armed forces' products that every country demands to have, the fact that the companies create demand in the market depends on innovation. The element that will facilitate the company's entry into the sector and ensure its sustainability is its innovative capacity, which has the power to create its demand (Gümüşdaş, 2010).

Policymakers should encourage research activities in the defense industry sectors, where there is a low foreign presence and is maintained with more national capabilities. Investments in innovation and entrepreneurship capability will provide countries with a competitive advantage in the defense industry market, which will enable their shares and economies to grow in this sector.

ACKNOWLEDGMENT

This research received no specific grant from any funding agency in the public, commercial, or not-for-profit sectors.

REFERENCES

Adamsky, D. (2010). The culture of military innovation: The impact of cultural factors on the Revolution in Military Affairs in Russia, the US, and Israel. Stanford University Press.

Adamsky, D., & Bjerga, K. I. (Eds.). (2012). *Contemporary military innovation: Between anticipation and adaption*. Routledge. doi:10.4324/9780203112540

Ahmed, P. K., & Shepherd, C. (2010). *Innovation management: Context, strategies, systems, and processes* (1st ed.). Pearson Prentice Hall.

ASELSAN. (2020). https://www.aselsan.com.tr/tr/inovasyon

Chouteau, M., Forest, J., & Nguyen, C. (2018). *Science, technology and innovation culture*. https://search.ebscohost.com/login.aspx?direct=true&scope=site&db=nlebk&db=nlabk&AN=1913571

Demirel, A. (2012). *Analysis of factors affecting the industrialization of the defense industry in Turkey* (Unpublished doctoral thesis). Turkish Military Academy, Defense Departments Institute, Department of Defense Management, Ankara.

Drucker, P. F. (2002). The Discipline of Innovation. *Harvard Business Review, 80*(8).

Eckardt, S. (2015). *Messung des Innovations- und Intrapreneurship-Klimas: Eine quantitativ-empirische Analyse*. Springer Fachmedien Wiesbaden., doi:10.1007/978-3-658-08882-8

Farrell, T., & Terriff, T. (Eds.). (2002). *The sources of military change: Culture, politics, technology*. Lynne Rienner Publishers.

Gulyas, Z. (2019). *NATO Glossary Of Terms and Definitions* (Edition 2019, Vol. AAP-06). NATO Standardization Office. https://standard.di.mod.bg/pls/mstd/MSTD

Gümüşdaş, E. (2010). *The Economics of the Defense Industry and Defense Spending in Turkey* (Unpublished Master's Thesis). University of Nigde.

Haun, P. (2019). Peacetime military innovation through inter-service cooperation: The unique case of the U.S. Air Force and Battlefield Air Interdiction. *The Journal of Strategic Studies*, 1–27. doi:10.1080/01402390.2018.1557053

HAVELSAN. (2020). https://inovasyon.havelsan.com.tr

Hill, A. (2015, Spring). Culture and the US Army: Military Innovation and Military Culture. *Parameters*, *45*(1), 94.

Høiback, H. (2013). *Understanding military doctrine: A multidisciplinary approach*. Routledge, Taylor & Francis Group.

Landström, H. (2010). *Pioneers in entrepreneurship and small business research*. Springer.

Machado, C., & Davim, J. P. (Eds.). (2020). *Entrepreneurship and Organizational Innovation*. Springer International Publishing. doi:10.1007/978-3-030-19289-1

Mullins, R. E. (2000). *Sharpening the Trident: The Decisions of 1889 and the Creation of Modern Seapower* (Ph.D. diss.). King's College London.

Murray, W., & Millett, A. R. (Eds.). (1996). *Military innovation in the interwar period*. Cambridge University Press. doi:10.1017/CBO9780511601019

Naktiyok, A. (2004). *İç Girişimcilik*. Beta Yayınları.

OECD. (2005). *Oslo manual. The measurement of scientific and technological activities. Proposed guidelines for collecting and interpreting technological innovation data* (2nd ed.). Paris: OECD/European Commission EUROSTAT. https://www.oecd.org/site/innovationstrategy/defininginnovation.htm

OKA. (2012). *Çorum Savunma Sanayi Sektörel Araştırma Raporu*. https://www.oka.org.tr/assets/upload/dosyalar/savunma-sanayi-arastirma-raporu-17-71.pdf

Pinchot, G. III. (1985). *Intrapreneuring*. Harper & Row.

Posen, B. (1984). *The Sources of Military Doctrine: France, Britain, and Germany between the World Wars*. Cornell University Press. Retrieved April 29, 2020, from www.jstor.org/stable/10.7591/j.ctt1287fp3

ROKETSAN. (2019). www.roketsan.com.tr

Russell, R. D. (1989). How Organisational Culture Can Help to Institutionalise the Spirit of Innovation in Entrepreneurial Ventures. *Journal of Organizational Change Management*, *2*(3), 7–15. doi:10.1108/09534818910005773

SAGE. (2019). http://www.sage.tubitak.gov.tr/tr/kurumsal/tubitak-sagenin-misyonu

Şeşen, H. (2010). *Öncülleri ve Sonuçları ile Örgüt İçi Girişimcilik: Türk Savunma Sanayinde Bir Araştırma, Doktora Tezi*. KHO Savunma Bilimleri Enstitüsü.

Sharma, P., & Chrisman, J. J. (1999). Toward a Reconciliation of the Definitional Issues in the Field of Corporate Entrepreneurship. *Entrepreneurship Theory and Practice*, *23*(3), 11–28. doi:10.1177/104225879902300302

Shrader, R. C., & Simon, M. (1997). Corporate Versus Independent New Ventures: Resource, Strategy, and Performance Differences. *Journal of Business Venturing*, *12*(1), 47–66. doi:10.1016/S0883-9026(96)00053-5

SIPRI. (2017). https://www.sipri.org/databases/milex

Tidd, J., & Bessant, J. R. (2011). Managing innovation: Integrating technological, market, and organizational change (4th ed.). Wiley.

TOBB. (2017). Turkey Defense Industry Sector Report. Academic Press.

Türksam, Y. (2017). http://turksam.org/turk-savunma-sanayine-bir-bakis-dun-ve-bugun

TUSAS. (2019). https://www.tusas.com

Wang, C., & Kafouros, M. I. (2009). What factors determine innovation performance in emerging economies? Evidence from China. *International Business Review*, *18*(6), 606–616. doi:10.1016/j.ibusrev.2009.07.009

KEY TERMS AND DEFINITIONS

Defense Industry: The defense industry is an important layer of industrialization within the scope of the ecosystem. It can also be expressed as one of the most effective power factors of political and economic power.

Entrepreneurship: Refers to the work developed in organizations that managers/entrepreneurs see as the mediators of innovation that contribute to an innovative and entrepreneurial organizational environment that is deeply related to the organizational culture as well as the changes in the profession and worker profile.

Innovation: Entrepreneurship oriented, focused on developing a new product and process, and focused on developing new ideas. Innovation is the potential for organizations to introduce new products/services or new production processes.

Innovation Culture: Special understanding of unity that makes innovative thinking natural within the organization and promotes innovation activities at the level of all employees. Some factors that support the culture of innovation are below.

Intrapreneurship: Entrepreneurial behavior shown in existing organizations.

Chapter 11
Military Enterprise and Entrepreneurship:
A Case Study of the Nigerian Armed Forces Resettlement Centre

Sanya Ojo
https://orcid.org/0000-0002-2585-9052
Nigerian Defence Academy, Nigeria

Mogbekeloluwa Oluyinka Fakokunde
Nigerian Defence Academy, Nigeria

ABSTRACT

The chapter investigates military enterprise and entrepreneurship through the prism of the Nigerian Armed Forces Resettlement Centre, Lagos. Through a mixed methodology, the chapter unveils innovative schemes and entrepreneurship culture in the centre. However, some tension exists between the military culture and entrepreneurship culture at the centre. Suggestions are offered to improve on the centre's service delivery. Generally, there is a need for NAFRC to further enhance its dynamic collaborative efforts, involve more in skills mapping of both its trainers and trainees, boost its mentoring capacity, and provide employment support through rigorous articulation of the value of retired military personnel to potential employers or funders. It is also suggested that NAFRC should liaise with other relevant stakeholders to support projects that deliver long-term solutions to the challenges faced by the retired military personnel community. The combination of all these activities will enable NAFRC to realise its vision and mission.

DOI: 10.4018/978-1-7998-6655-8.ch011

Copyright © 2021, IGI Global. Copying or distributing in print or electronic forms without written permission of IGI Global is prohibited.

INTRODUCTION

Retirement from the military service into civilian life can be very difficult for ex-Service personnel in many countries, especially in countries struggling with difficult economic conditions like Nigeria. In recognition of the sacrifices made by the military, many countries endeavour to fulfill their moral obligation to their ex-service personnel. The moral obligation is usually articulated in terms of the Armed Forces Covenant (Sparrow, 2008), which is a recognition of the need to develop effective approaches to meeting the social and economic needs of ex-service personnel. Thus, the Armed Forces Covenant represents the assurance of a nation to ensure that those who are serving or who have served in the Armed Forces, and their families, are treated fairly and reasonably resettled in retirement. Resettlement, a term the military uses for the shift back to civilian life, is characterised by a huge amount of significant life changes. Among the series of ways to increase the level of fulfilled resettlement procedure for ex-service personnel in Nigeria is entrepreneurship training for those leaving the Nigerian Armed Forces. Entrepreneurship training and skills acquisition are carried out in the Nigerian Armed Forces Resettlement Centre (NAFRC), Lagos. The Centre's mandate, among other things, is to enable retiring service personnel to integrate into civil society and enjoy post-service life. To actualise this, NAFRC came up with training objectives aimed at helping retirees establish their own businesses and to adequately prepare the retirees for gainful employment after retirement, as well as to prepare them psychologically for resettlement into civil life (Usman, 2011).

Moreover, like any other transition, retirement from the military into entrepreneurship presents some unique challenges. Though there exist some resettlement projects that help in the transition, there is not much analysis of their impact on veteran entrepreneurship. In the end, however, the appraisal of the quality of the intervention programmes can be important to ensure successful entrepreneurial outcomes among veteran entrepreneurs.

Essentially, this chapter seeks to highlight NAFRC activities in promoting veteran entrepreneurship and empowerment schemes for retiring military personnel. Thus, the main question this chapter will focus on is: To what extent is NAFRC fulfilling its mandates? Flowing from this question is a subordinate question: In what ways could NAFRC improve its services? The chapter is arranged into four sections. In section one the literature is reviewed, in section two the conceptual framework is examined. The methodology is laid out in section three, while section four is the finding and analysis. The last section discusses the recommendations and further studies.

Context Moderator

The majority of the Nigerian military personnel are the rank and file or Non-Commissioned Officers (NCOs) and many of them are likely to face greater economic disadvantages in retirement. The NCOs are individuals who, according to Ntiwunka (2012), wallow in abject poverty and generally have difficulties making ends meet because the income (pension) they depend on is meagre and not regular (Adekanye, 1999). Many of these individuals may be tempted to engage in criminal or anti-social activities after their disengagement from the military, thus, this group needs handholding and support. On that basis, the NCOs are the segment of RMP focused in this chapter/study, and the study was largely conducted in NAFRC facility in Lagos, which is uniquely positioned to serve the discernible niche segment.

Several nomenclatures are used in the literature to describe the phenomenon of retired military personnel. Some terms used include veteran, ex-Service personnel, and legionnaire. Although used interchangeably in many publications, the terms are not the same, and different countries have varying definitions of the word "veteran" (Burdett et al., 2013). For instance, in the UK, a veteran is defined as: "Anyone who has served for a least one day in Her Majesty's Armed Forces (Regular or Reserve) or Merchant Navy Seafarers and Fishermen who served in a vessel at a time when it was operated to facilitate military operation by HM Armed Forces" (Department of Health, 2008). In the USA, veterans are referred to as those who have served in the Armed Forces and are honourably discharged (Staskiel, 2020). Other perspectives refer to people who served for a long period in the Armed Forces or soldiers who have seen action, i.e., fought in a war.

In this chapter, retired military personnel (RMP), veteran, and ex-Service personnel will be used interchangeably just to stay as much as possible close to their original use in the literature they are extracted from. Finally, this chapter is part of a lager study on entrepreneurship and social empowerment of retiring military personnel commissioned by the Tertiary Education (TETFund), which the authors are involved in.

LITERATURE REVIEW

Study Background

The transition to retirement is often a combination of the anticipated and the unanticipated challenges. It is capable of generating major psychological issues that are sometimes ignored by those who paint a radiant picture of retirement (Osborne, 2012). Many retiring military personnel and their families are challenged by the transition to civilian life - particularly in securing employment, managing finances and health care, pursuing education, family reintegration, and negotiating with their new community (Robertson & Brott, 2017; Vogt et al., 2018). RMP may also experience symptoms of grief and stress in response to the perceived "loss of the military self" (Mobbs & Bonanno, 2018), and some studies (e.g. Interian et al., 2014) found that transition difficulty and stress are predictive of mental and physical health problems. While formal military retirement programmes are organised to provide support with planning and general logistics of transitions (Wolpert, 2000), research suggests that RMP (veterans) feel emotionally underprepared to manage the transition to civilian employment (Baruch & Quick, 2009). It is the case that the military does well when inducting civilian into the military but often perform poorly when training or preparing military personnel for civilian life such that many veterans struggle as they transit out of the military service (Zogas, 2017). Some researchers (e.g. Angrist, 1998; Smith-Osborne, 2013) have argued that RMP may not be able to achieve the desired life trajectory, compared to civilians of similar background and age.

Figure 1.

Nevertheless, many military retirement programmes prominently feature "entrepreneurship training" as part of their packages to empower retirees to grow as skilled entrepreneurs. For instance, the Nigerian Armed Forces Resettlement Centre (NAFRC), Lagos, mandated to provide necessary training geared towards preparing retiring servicemen/women for reintegration into civil life, has trained over 45,000 since its inception (Liman, 2019). The NAFRC trains retiring service personnel (non-commissioned officers) in vocational courses such as tailoring, plumbing, music, refrigeration and air-conditioning, barbing and hairdressing, electrical and electronics, electroplating and hydrographic as well as a bakery and many others. Ideally, service in the military often provides highly specific competencies that can be adapted as transferable expertise and knowledge for entrepreneurship (Smaliukienė, 2013). Military personnel are equipped with skills and know-how inherent in military training, which include risk management, performance under pressure and leadership - qualities that can be moderated and exploited as potent entrepreneurship skills and essential to effective venture management. According to Storlie (2010), ex-Service personnel acquired adapting skills such as directness, speed, assertiveness, team decision-making, and methodical approaches to problem-solving through military training. Consequently, veterans (i.e., in the USA) are at least 45% more likely to become self-employed than non-service individuals (i.e., people without military experience). Against the background of the increase in retirement among service members, many are interested in entrepreneurship (Maury et al., 2014).

Subsequently, several ex-Service personnel in Nigeria turn to entrepreneurship to earn income when they retire, however, according to Madichie and Ayasi (2018), the attrition rate in terms of failure is disquieting even though no official figure is available. Within the veteran entrepreneurship literature, there is a major gap in analysing the factors that affect entrepreneurship among veterans. Hope et al. (2011) analyse some general trends, including the general inverse relationship between the length of service and likelihood of self-employment post-transition. In Nigeria, however, reasons why ex-service men/women (RMP) fail in entrepreneurship, include lack of coordinated government assistance, lack of effective institutional support, and very few agencies exist to assist and promote military entrepreneurship (Madichie & Ayasi, 2018). Besides, Abubakar (2016) argues that entrepreneurship education for retired/retiring officers that could enhance their reintegration into civilian life is grossly lacking or inadequate. Abubakar (2016) also contends that the problem was not unconnected with the historical ineffective career management practice/administration of the Nigerian Military Force. Another problem is the lack of time and allowance for the officers to develop themselves individually while in service due to the nature of the military job. For example, the erratic work-life associated with a military career led to military personnel, on average, to spend less time with their families, have spouses who are less likely to work, and experience higher divorce rates (Angrist & Johnson, 2000). This unsettled work life could be a factor for inadequate preparedness for 'Civvies Street' and/or entrepreneurship.

Researchers, including Gentry et al. (2014) and Olokundun et al. (2014), point to the failure of entrepreneurship education and training in Nigeria. Reasons adduced for the failure include the claim that the method of teaching was not practical oriented and lacks real life experience. Also, there is the problem of inappropriate structuring of entrepreneurship curriculum. To underscore the failure of entrepreneurship training, Genty et al. (2014) identified the inadequacy underpinning the SMEDAN/NYSC Corpers' Entrepreneurship Development Programme (CEDP). Issues identified include flawed curriculum, lack of practical pedagogy, inadequate trainers' entrepreneurship background knowledge and lack of effective entrepreneurship training model to operate. Thus, the CEDP did not achieve the desired result as no change in behaviour and attitudes of the trainees (i.e., Youth Corpers) towards venture creation was realised.

Conceptual Review

In the context of this report, entrepreneurship is understood to be an aggregated concept. Hence, it is delineated as a context-dependent socio-economic process of discovering or creating, evaluating and exploiting new opportunities by individuals through which new business venture can be initiated such that value is generated to the society (Baron & Shane, 2008; Bruyat & Julien, 2000; Shane & Venkataraman, 2000). This all-encompassing contemporary understanding of entrepreneurship reflects the primary ways the concept manifests itself in peoples' lives and society beyond the orthodox meaning, thus, revealing its multi-dimensionality and complexity. Essentially, this perception provides a common ground for synthesising diverse approaches to understanding the concepts of entrepreneurship and entrepreneurship training.

Entrepreneurship training is anticipated to shape entrepreneurs or potential entrepreneurs through building up knowledge and skills for opportunity recognition and implementation and through acquiring different competences. Such competencies include proactiveness and self-confidence, a positive attitude to risk-taking and failure, and a perseverance disposition in general. Many of these qualities are already instilled in military personnel through their military training. In retirement, ex-servicemen/women bring with them qualities such as leadership, people management, determination and a strong work ethic amongst others. They are often better placed to thrive in team working and their experience in the Armed Forces will have left them with strong problem-solving skills. Ex-service personnel tend to be adaptable and are often highly efficient in a crisis. These are exceptional attributes that are useful in entrepreneurship (Cherry, 2020).

In the context of this chapter, entrepreneurship training is considered a form of social empowerment project from which ex-Service personnel derive benefits when they transit to civilian life. Thus, the sustainable livelihood approach served as the theoretical framework in which the study is anchored. A sustainable livelihood framework is valuable as it highlights the resources and assets (embracing social and material means) envisaged for survival. A livelihood (e.g., a business or employment) is deemed sustainable if it enables individual to survive and pull through stresses and shocks while maintaining or enhancing its capacities and resources in the long term without destabilising the ecological resource base (DFID, 1999). The essence of sustainable framework incorporates people's priorities, which must be at the heart of any project in order for them to feel committed to the project. The framework is adopted because it facilitates a new style of policy appraisal that departs from general prescriptions to context-specific approaches (Serrat, 2008).

The sustainable livelihoods framework, usually applied in development studies, is a way of thinking about the objectives, scope, and priorities for empowerment activities. It is grounded on evolving thinking about the way poor people live their lives and the importance of policies and institutions. The framework helps formulate empowerment and development activities that are people-oriented, responsive and participatory, multilevel, managed in partnership with the public and private sectors, dynamic, and sustainable. Moreover, the framework enables the identification of practical priorities for actions that are based on the views and interests of those concerned. Yet, the framework is not a panacea to all developmental challenges as it pays little attention to inequalities of power and underplays the fact that enhancing the livelihoods of one group can undermine those of another group (Serrat, 2008).

Nevertheless, the framework makes the connection between people and the overall enabling environment that influences the outcomes of livelihood strategies. It focuses the searchlight on the inherent potential of people in terms of their skills, social networks, access to physical and financial resources, and the ability to influence core institutions (Serrat, 2008). In addition, the sustainable livelihoods framework is unique as it stimulates and encourages reasoning from a new perspective and allows empowerment practitioners to look at contexts and relationships so that empowerment activities can become more process-oriented. Furthermore, the framework facilitates the need for the awareness of multiple entry points and encourages broader perspectives to issues.

The Nigerian Armed Forces Resettlement Centre

The Nigerian Armed Forces Resettlement Centre (NAFRC), Lagos, was started by the British colonial authorities as Vocational Resettlement Centre just after the World War II. In 1972 the Centre expanded to include the rehabilitation of disabled soldiers. A decade later the Centre's mandate evolved from "the" rehabilitation of demobilised soldiers to a resettlement centre (Liman, 2019; Usman, 2019) with an official name change to the Nigerian Armed Forces Resettlement Centre (NAFRC). From inception, the resettlement centre was charged with the responsibility of imparting skills relevant to the resettlement needs of ex-Servicemen. Over time, the initial mandate of the centre had evolved from that of rehabilitating and demobilising soldiers of war to that of resettling able-bodied soldiers who are about leaving active service. NAFRC, which has trained over 45,000 since its inception (Liman, 2019), help in enhancing retiring officers' capacity to productively reintegrate into the civil society upon retirement. The centre's mission is to consistently provide quality training, geared towards preparing Nigerian Armed Forces personnel to face the challenges of re-integrating into civil life.

NAFRC is one of the agencies under the supervision of the Nigerian Defence Headquarters, and is conventionally headed by a serving Air Force Officer of Air Vice Marshall (AVM) ranking. NARFC has five directorates; (a) administration (b) training (c) coordination (d) logistics (e) finance manned by directors. These directors, the commandant and deputy commandant formed the top hierarchy of the centre. All workshops and management wings are under the directorate of training. Each wing/department has a military Commanding Officer (CO) and a civilian Head of Department (HOD) running them. The workshops are where trainees receive vocational skill instructions such as electrical, automobile, bakery, photography, welder, carpentry, painting, etc. The departments under the management wing consist of general management, security and safety, entrepreneurship, information technology, waste management, and guidance and counselling. Trainees are required to select any vocational skill of their choice from the list of available resources; however, all trainees must attend the entrepreneurship class once a week. In the entrepreneurship class, trainees are taught basic entrepreneurial skills including the process of starting up a business (e.g. business plan writing, bookkeeping, etc.), business fundraising, business laws and regulations, etc.

Typically, each batch of trainees is trained for a six-month time cycle at the centre. However, the training cycle has been reduced to three months recently because of the need to comply with the COVID-19 pandemic protocols (social distancing rule has affected accommodation capacity and training arrangements). There have been concerted efforts by past and present commandants of NAFRC to bring innovation into the structure of the centre. For instance, the initial mandate of training retiring non-commissioned officers is under review and mid-level and senior officers have started to benefit from entrepreneurship training and skill acquisition at the centre (Usman, 2018). Moreover, the training programme is repackaged to enable mid-level and senior officer trainees to go back to their various units after their training at NAFRC and start some agricultural business whilst still in service (Wada, 2020). Also, for the first time in July 2020, NAFRC trained personnel from the Police, Nigerian Customs Service (NCS), Correctional Services, Immigrations, National Environment Management Authority (NEMA) and the Ministry of Finance, Defence, Foreign Affairs, among others (Usman, 2020). The inclusion of other security agencies and civilians is meant to provide a useful forum for the exchange of ideas, networking, as well as improve civil-military relationships (Wada, 2020). Furthermore, in response to the current security challenges (e.g., Boko Haram Terrorists) in Nigeria, NAFRC has expanded its "Training Curriculum to accommodate a wide range of contemporary national security issues". The training regime now includes "acquisition of skills in intelligence gathering to counter insurgency operations" (Liman, 2019: 58). NAFRC also signed a Memorandum of Understanding (MOU) with the Yaba College of Technology, Lagos to provide further training on security and enhance trainees' knowledge of the concept of security.

Figure 2. NAFRC Hydrographic/electroplating Workshop
Source: Fieldwork Picture File

Trainees receive management courses such as entrepreneurship and general studies, general management, security and safety practice, business plan and model, fundamentals of business laws and taxation, as well as human resource/supply chain management and Marketing. Vocational skills' training includes shoemaking, barbing, tailoring, laundering and weaving workshops. There are also facilities for training in fine arts and printing, soap and cosmetics, agriculture, woodwork, building and civil works, electrical and electronics, automobile mechanic, fabrication and welding, music, information technology, and food and beverages (Usman, 2018). Furthermore, trainees go for one-month industrial attachment in organisations/firms relevant to their training. Thus, NAFRC collaborates with external partners such as the Alliance Professional Resources Persons Limited, Empretech Nigeria Foundation, Enterprise Development Centre, Administrative Staff College, Yaba College of Technology, and the University of Lagos (Usman, 2018, 2019).

Figure 3. Snailery at NAFRC Agriculture Wing
Source: Fieldwork Picture File

By far, agriculture workshop/course has the largest number of trainees signing up for it (see Table 4). This is due, according to respondents (instructors), to the low capital input required to start agriculture business compared to many other vocations that involve high investments in terms of finance, equipment, and tools to set up. Another reason adduced for the high enrolment of trainees in agriculture classes is the concession given to serving military personnel to engage in agriculture. Serving military personnel are barred from participating in any enterprise outside soldiering.

Probably because of their larger numerical strength the Army group usually has the largest number of trainees most times at NAFRC (see Table 1). For example, in the 2017 batch, the Army had 281, the Nigerian Navy had 17 and the Nigerian Air Force had 105 (Usman, 2017). In 2018, the Nigerian Army had 262 personnel, the Nigerian Navy had 44, and the Nigerian Air Force had 14 retiring personnel (Usman, 2018). For Course 01/2020, 243 personnel were from the Nigerian Army, 100 from the Navy and 16 from the Nigerian Air Force (Usman, 2020). Yet, this is not always the case, for instance, at the Trainees Course 2/2011, out of a total number of 150 service personnel, 11 were from the Army, 17 from Air force and 122 from the Navy (Usman, 2011).

Figure 4. NAFRC Agriculture Wing Greenhouse
Source: Fieldwork Picture File

NAFRC instructors/trainers are equally given training once a week (i.e., every Thursday of the week) to keep them abreast of contemporary issues that have to do with their specialisation. Many respondents (trainers and HOD) confirm that in recent times, successful NAFRC commandant tried hard to outperform their predecessors in bringing innovation to the Centre. For instance, Air Vice Marshall (AVM) Liman brought in a lot of progressive changes including the establishment of a cattle ranch, launched an oven auto spraying workshop, inaugurated *Hope* Magazine (NAFRC publication), and series of road and building constructions (Yohana & Ugboaja, 2019). It was during AVM Lar's tenure that the government approved the expansion of the course to include non-military retirees from Ministries, Departments, and Agencies (MDAs). There is a plan to establish NAFRC Consults to coordinate and act as the business arm of the Centre (Lar, 2020). According to information gathered during the fieldwork, AVM Lar, the penultimate commandant, introduced the paint-making workshop where trainees are taught how to make different types of paints among other innovations. This paint-making enterprise produces paint for the use of the centre. Ultimately, the premises and most facilities at NAFRC are freshly painted and well maintained.

Figure 5. NAFRC's Paint – Product of the Paint-making Workshop
Source: Fieldwork Picture File

Table 1. Graduate by Service

Year Service	2011 (Course 2)	2017	2018	2020 (Course 01)
Army	11	281	262	243
Navy	122	17	44	100
Air Force	17	105	14	16

Sources: Usman, 2011; 2017; 2018; 2020

Table 2. NAFRC Departments and Workshops

Departments	Workshops				
Agriculture	Poultry	Fishery	Rabbitry	Ruminant	Snailery
Auto Mechanics	Mechanical Engineering	Battery Charging	Vulcanising	Car washing	Glass/Screen repair
Building and Civil Works	Bricklaying and construction	Plumbing and pipefitting	Painting and spraying		
Electrical and Electronics	Refrigeration and Air conditioning	Electrical Installation and Maintenance	Radio and Television		
Fabrication and Welding	Fabrication	Welding	Machining and Fitting	Foundry	
Fashion	Shoemaking	Barbing	Tailoring	Laundry	Weaving Hairdressing
Food and Beverages	Bakery	Cake Making and decoration			
Information Technology	Computer Appreciation	Hardware Maintenance	Networking and Internet	System Development and Design	
Management Courses	General Management	Security and Safety Practice	Entrepreneurial and General Studies		
Music	Playing Musical Instruments				
Printing and Fine Art	Printing	Fine Art	Ceramics	Photography	Creative Art
Soap and Cosmetics	Soap making	Cosmetics making	Domestics and Sanitary products		
Woodwork	Carpentry and Joinery	Furniture Design and Construction	Machine Woodwork		

Sources: *Hope* Magazine, 2019

METHODOLOGY AND APPROACH

This research was based on mixed methods, employing both qualitative and quantitative data collection techniques. Following purposive sampling, a review of quantitative data was used to collect information. The qualitative efforts included the following data collection tools: Interviews, observations, document review, these help to affirm trainees' satisfaction with NAFRC entrepreneurship and skills training intervention. Thus, the qualitative approach in this study assisted in delivering an interpretation of the participants' world through in-depth interview qualitative approach in which methods such as observations and interactive discussions are used. Six ex-trainees (all in Lagos) were interviewed initially, but later another set of seven was interviewed (two in Lagos and three in Kaduna). They were selected based on being representative of the past trainees. Eight heads of department (HOD), six Commanding Officers (COs), and eight instructors (trainers) were also interviewed. Eighty current trainees were given survey forms to fill and all returned except one. Consultation meetings, that is, two key informant interviews (administrators), six in-depth interviews (trainees) and four focus group discussions were conducted with the trainees (current and past trainees) to understand from them the relevance, efficiency, effectiveness, impact, and sustainability of the training programme (see Table 3). A desk review of relevant NAFRC documents (e.g., copies of *Hope* Magazine, telephone directories of ex-trainees, entrepreneurship and general management curriculums, and workshop manuals). Other stakeholders' interviews consisting of 3 civilian employees (working at NAFRC guest house, i.e., receptionist, caterer, and housekeeper) and two concessionaires (operate refreshment stands at the NAFRC Officers' Mess) were conducted to get the views of people who, though peripheral to the training regime, are very knowledgeable about the Centre's activities. Their inclusion helps to secure multiple perspectives and limit bias in line with Eisenhardt and Graebner's (2007: 28) suggestion to use "numerous and highly knowledgeable informants who view the focal phenomena from diverse perspectives".

The qualitative data was reviewed through existing secondary sources from newspaper reports, online news bulletins, progress reports and other relevant documents. Suffice it to declare that the focus of the research, from an entrepreneurship training perspective of ex-Service personnel, was firmly on those who were about to be discharged (retiring) and those already in retirement (retired). Probably due to the command chain structure of the military, all participants/respondents fully cooperated and were eagerly willing to provide needed information required by the researchers. The research process began with initial desk research and consultations, and this is followed by quantitative survey responses, qualitative interviews, and focus group discussions. Generally, the research design was in three stages as listed in the sub-section below.

STAGE 1: Desk Research and Pilot Interviews

This stage involved desk research in which researchers read previous literature on the subject. It also involved the conduct of exploratory semi-structured interviews with individuals that were well informed of the challenges entailed in military transition and resettlement and the entrepreneurship/skill training of ex-Service personnel. The aims of stage 1 were threefold. The first aim was to collect preliminary high-level information relevant to the study's research questions (to ensure that any key themes, insights, or questions were not ignored in the main study). The second aim was to establish a network of pertinent contacts in NAFRC and the target group communities (e.g., military formations) and the third aim was to gain access to apposite knowledge and information already available in different forms (e.g., reports, news items, and databases) in NAFRC and the target group communities. The semi-structured interviews provided knowledge that helps to further amplify the questionnaires used in the later stages of the research fieldwork. For instance, this helped to identify any issues in the proposed areas of questioning. The researchers were able to test (and adjusted as necessary) the relevance of the outlined themes through the interviews. The semi-structured interview design enabled the researchers to capture a wide range of themes and issues as possible so that issues that are yet to be detected in the desk-based research were not discounted.

Table 3. Qualitative Research

Characteristics of the Qualitative Study	
Period of the Study	28/10/2020 – 02/11/2020
Data Collection Method	Interview Focus Group discussions based on a predefined guide with topics of interest
Focus Group Size	Focus group 1 (28/10/20) = 10 participants (trainees) Focus group 2 (28/10/20) = 11 participants (trainees) Focus group 3 (29/10/20) = 6 participants (ex-trainees) Focus group 4 (01/11/20) = 6 participants (ex-trainees)
Number of Interviews	6 trainees 13 ex-trainees 8 Heads of Department 8 instructors/trainers 6 Commanding Officers 2 administrators 3 civilian employees (receptionist, caterer, and housekeeper) 2 Concessionaires (smoke-fish and smoked beef sellers at the Officers Mess)
The scope of the Qualitative Study	Impact of NAFRC training on participants' personal and professional development Relevance of NAFRC training Perception of participants Monitoring and evaluation of NAFRC training

Source: Fieldwork, 2020

STAGE 2: Questionnaire Survey and Semi-Structured Interviews

In stage 2, the researchers developed and conducted more semi-structured interviews and a questionnaire survey, performed mostly in parallel and based on the outputs from stage 1 above. The questionnaire survey was intended to gather demographic information from participants (with particular reference to age, time spent in the Service, education, experience while in Service, registered course, business location, etc.), along with a series of questions around the themes developed in stage 1. Both current and past trainees filled the questionnaires.

STAGE 3: Focus Groups

Stage 3 involved follow up focus groups, after the completion of the surveys and qualitative interviews and some initial thematic analysis were undertaken with participants (current and past trainees) who had also engaged with the questionnaire survey. The purpose of the focus group interviews was to triangulate and to test initial analysis and the conclusions produced in Stage 2, to minimise the likelihood of misinterpreting the findings and therefore reaching inaccurate conclusions. Both researchers shared some of the findings that had come out of the different sessions (also built on the core themes explored), and asked both current and past trainee participants to discuss them and the reasons behind them, as well as to explore common themes emerging from the interviews that the researchers were unable to explore due to the structure of Stage 2. This Stage 3 involved four focus group interviews as listed in Table 4. The focus group interviews were two-hour sessions each, and semi-structured according to questions and insight that had emerged under the research's core themes.

ANALYSIS AND FINDINGS

Consequently, from the data gathering processes described above, five general themes that crossed the data emerged. The five themes are: Disparities between the Services; New Initiatives and the Dialectics of Military Culture; Gap in Monitoring and Evaluation Processes; Challenging Business Environment; and Post Training Enterprise Funding Issues. The emerging key themes encapsulating the thrust of this chapter reflect the convergence of views of the research participants.

Table 4. Course 02/Stream 2/2020 Participants/Respondents

No	Gender	Business Experience	Rank	Years of Service	Type of Vocation	Education Level	Fund Source	NAFRC Experience	Training Material	Quality of training & facilities
1	Male	NO	Master Warrant	34.5	Agriculture			Excellent	Bit complex	Excellent
2	Male	YES	Flight Sergeant	-	Agriculture	SSCE	-	Excellent	Easily understandable	Excellent
3	Male	YES	Warrant Officer	35	Agriculture	City & Guilds	Personal	Good	Easily understandable	Excellent
4		NO	Sergeant	35	Agriculture	National Certificate of Education	Personal	Good	Easily understandable	Good
5	Male	NO	Master Warrant Officer	35	Agriculture	General Certificate of Education	Personal	Good	Bit complex	Good
6	Male	NO	Master Warrant Officer	35	Agriculture	General Certificate of Education	Personal	Good	Bit complex	Good
7	Male	NO	Master Warrant Officer		Consultancy	Post Graduate Diploma	Bank loan	Excellent	Bit complex	Fair
8	Male	YES	Sergeant	35	Agriculture	General Certificate of Education	Personal savings	Excellent	Easily understandable	Excellent
9	Male	NO	Petty Officer	20	Trade	Master of Science	Personal savings	Good	Relevant	Good
10	Male	NO	Petty Officer	20	Services (health)	1st degree	Personal savings	Good	Easily understandable	Excellent
11	Male	YES	Master Warrant Officer	35	Agriculture	Diploma	Personal savings	Good	Easily understandable	Good
12	Male	Yes	Master Warrant Officer	35	Consultancy	Diploma	Bank loan	Excellent	Easily understandable	Excellent
13	Male	NO	Master Warrant Officer	26	Agriculture	Post Graduate Diploma	Personal savings	Good	Relevant	Good
14	Male	NO	Warrant Officer	35	Consultancy	-	Personal savings	Good	Easily understandable	Good
15	Male	YES	Master Warrant Officer	35	Agriculture	-	-	Excellent	Easily understandable	Excellent

continues on following page

Table 4. Continued

No	Gender	Business Experience	Rank	Years of Service	Type of Vocation	Education Level	Fund Source	NAFRC Experience	Training Material	Quality of training & facilities
16	Male	NO	Warrant Officer	35	Agriculture	-	Personal savings	Excellent	Relevant	Excellent
17	Male	NO	Lance Corporal	35	Agriculture	SSCE	-	Good	Easily understandable	Excellent
18	Male	YES	Master Warrant Officer	35	Agriculture	GCE & WASC	grant	Excellent	Easily understandable	Excellent
19	Male	NO	Master Warrant Officer	34.5	Agriculture	WASC	Personal savings	Excellent	Easily understandable	Excellent
20	Male	YES	Assistant Corps Marshall	21	Consultancy	Bachelor of Science	Bank loan	Good	Easily understandable	Excellent
21	Male	NO	Petty Officer	16	Trade	Bachelor of Science	Personal savings	Good	Easily understandable	Good
22	Male	YES	Master Warrant Officer	35	Agriculture	Higher National Diploma	Personal savings	Excellent	Bit complex	Good
23	Male	NO	Master Warrant Officer	35	Agriculture	WASC	Personal savings	Excellent	Easily understandable	Excellent
24	Male	NO	Master Warrant Officer	35	Agriculture	General Certificate of Education	Personal savings	Excellent	Easily understandable	Excellent
25	Male	YES	Master Warrant Officer	35	Trade	General Certificate of Education	Personal savings	Good	Precise	Good
26	Male	YES	Master Warrant Officer	35	Trade	General Certificate of Education	Personal savings	Excellent	Bit complex	Fair
27	Male	NO	Master Warrant Officer	35	Trade	-	Personal savings	Good	Relevant	Good
28	Male	NO	-	35	-	Diploma	Personal savings	Good	Relevant	Good
29	Male	NO	Master Warrant Officer	35	Consultancy	Master of Business Administration	Personal savings	Good	Relevant	Good
30	Male	NO	Master Warrant Officer	-	Agriculture	Bachelor of Science	Personal savings	Excellent	Easily understandable	Good
31	Male	NO	Warrant Officer	35	Trade	GCE O/L	Personal savings	Excellent	Precise	Good

continues on following page

Table 4. Continued

No	Gender	Business Experience	Rank	Years of Service	Type of Vocation	Education Level	Fund Source	NAFRC Experience	Training Material	Quality of training & facilities
32	Male	No	Master Warrant Officer	-	Manufacturing	WASC	Manufacturing	Excellent	Relevant	Excellent
33	Male	No	Master Warrant Officer	35	Trade	-	Personal savings	good	Relevant	Good
34	Male	No	Staff Sergeant	35	Agriculture	G over class 3	Personal saving	Excellent	Easily understandable	Excellent
35	Male	No	Master Warrant Officer	-	Agriculture	GCE O/L	-	Excellent	Easily understandable	Excellent
36	Male	No	Master Warrant Officer	34	Manufacturing	Grade II/Associate	Personal savings	Good	Relevant	Good
37	Male	No	Master Warrant Officer	35	Agriculture	General Certificate of Education	Personal savings	Excellent	Easily understandable	Excellent
38	Male	No	Master Warrant Officer	34	Trade	WASC	Personal savings	Good	Easily understandable	Good
39	Male	No	Master Warrant Officer	35	Agriculture	Grade II Teacher	Crowdfunding	Excellent	Easily understandable	Good
40	Male	No	Warrant Officer	35	Trade	Bachelor of Engineering.	Personal savings	Excellent	Easily understandable	Excellent
41	Male	No	Master Warrant Officer	34+	Trade	Ordinary Level	Personal savings	Good	Easily understandable	Excellent
42	Male	No	Master Warrant Officer	35	Manufacturing	WASC	Personal savings	Excellent	Easily understandable	Excellent
43	Male	No	Master Warrant Officer	34.5	Water Production	Bachelor of Science	Manufacturing	Excellent	Relevant	Excellent
44	Male	No	Master Warrant Officer	35	Consultancy	WASC	Bank loan	Excellent	Relevant	Good
45	Male	No	Master Warrant Officer	35	Trade	Post Graduate Diploma	Personal savings	Excellent	Easily understandable	Excellent
46	Male	No	Master Warrant Officer	35	Agriculture	Advance Diploma	Bank loan	Good	Relevant	Good
47	Male	No	Staff Sergeant	35	Agriculture	School Certificate	Personal savings	Good	Easily understandable	Good
48	Male	No	Master Warrant Officer	34	Agriculture	Ordinary Level	Personal savings	Good	Relevant	Good

continues on following page

Table 4. Continued

No	Gender	Business Experience	Rank	Years of Service	Type of Vocation	Education Level	Fund Source	NAFRC Experience	Training Material	Quality of training & facilities
49	Male	No	Master Warrant Officer	34	Services/education	Artificer	Bank loan	Good	Relevant	Good
50	Female	No	Master Warrant Officer	34.4	Manufacturing	WASC	Personal savings	Excellent	Easily understandable	Excellent
51	Male	No	Warrant Officer	35	Agriculture	GCE (O/L)	Personal savings	Excellent	Easily understandable	Good
52	Female	No	Master Warrant Officer	35	Agriculture	O/L, Diploma	Personal savings	Excellent	Easily understandable	Excellent
53	Male	No	Master Warrant Officer	35	Agriculture	VTC	Personal savings	Good	Easily understandable	Good
54	Male	No	Master Warrant Officer	35	Agriculture	National Certificate of Education	Personal savings	Excellent	Easily understandable	Excellent
55	Male	Yes	Leading Seaman	34.5	Agriculture	WASC	-	Excellent	Easily understandable	Good
56	Male	No	Warrant Officer (Navy)	35	Barbing Salon	WASC	Personal savings	Excellent	Easily understandable	Excellent
57	Male	No	Master Warrant Officer	35	Online biz	MPA	Personal savings	Good	Easily understandable	Excellent
58	Female	No	POCA	20	Agriculture	Post Graduate Diploma	Friends/Family	Good	Easily understandable	Fair
59	Male	No	Petty Officer	19	consultancy	Bachelor of Science	Crowdfunding	Good	Relevant	Good
60	Male	Yes	Warrant Officer	35	Manufacturing	Grade II Certificate	Personal savings	Excellent	Easily understandable	Excellent
61	Male	No	Master Warrant Officer	35	Trade	General Certificate of Education	Personal savings	Excellent	Easily understandable	Good
62	Male	No	Master Warrant Officer	35	Agriculture	Advance Diploma	Personal savings	Excellent	Easily understandable	Excellent
63	Male	No	Master Warrant Officer	34.4	Agriculture	National Diploma	Personal savings	Excellent	Easily understandable	Excellent

continues on following page

Table 4. Continued

No	Gender	Business Experience	Rank	Years of Service	Type of Vocation	Education Level	Fund Source	NAFRC Experience	Training Material	Quality of training & facilities
64	Male	No	Staff Sergeant	35	Electrical services	Ordinary National Diploma	Personal savings	Good	Easily understandable	Good
65	Male	No	Master Warrant Officer	35	Agriculture	Master of Arts	Personal savings	Good	Easily understandable	Good
66	Male	No	Master Warrant Officer	34	Services	Bachelor of Science	Personal savings	Excellent	Easily understandable	Excellent
67	Male	No	Master Warrant Officer	35	Agriculture	National Certificate of Education	Personal savings	Good	Easily understandable	Good
68	Male	No	Master Warrant Officer	35	Manufacturing	WASC	Personal savings	Excellent	Easily understandable	Excellent
69	Male	No	Master Warrant Officer	34	Consultancy	General Certificate of Education	Personal savings	Good	Easily understandable	Excellent
70	Male	No	Staff Sergeant	35	Agriculture	Higher National Diploma	Personal savings	Good	Relevant	Good
71	Male	No	Master Warrant Officer	35	Trade	WASC	Personal savings	Good	Bit complex	Excellent
72	Male	No	Master Warrant Officer	34.4	Agriculture	WASC	Personal savings	Excellent	Easily understandable	Good
73	Male	No	Master Warrant Officer	35	Manufacturing	Diploma	Personal savings	Excellent	Easily understandable	Excellent
74	Male	No	Superintendent Route Commander	13	Manufacturing	LLB; LLM	Personal savings	Excellent	Easily understandable	Excellent
75	Male	No	Warrant Officer (Navy)	35	Agriculture	WASC	Personal savings	Good	Easily understandable	Excellent
76	Male	No	Master Warrant Officer	35	Trade	Ordinary Level	Personal savings	Excellent	Easily understandable	Excellent
77	Male	No	Superintendent Route Commander	24	Consultancy	Bachelor of Science	Bank loan	Excellent	Easily understandable	Excellent
78	Male	No	Master Warrant Officer	35	Agriculture	Teacher Grade II/ GCE O/L	Personal savings	Excellent	Relevant	Excellent

continues on following page

Table 4. Continued

No	Gender	Business Experience	Rank	Years of Service	Type of Vocation	Education Level	Fund Source	NAFRC Experience	Training Material	Quality of training & facilities
79	Male	No	Staff Sergeant	35	Agriculture	Post Graduate Diploma	Bank loan	Good	Relevant	Good
Ex- Trainees (All Male)										
Education	Business exp.	NAFRC Impact	Type of Business	Biz Registration/ type	Biz performance	Business location	Biz challenges	Access to Funding/source	Awareness of SMEDAN	Using professionals
BSc	Yes	Good	Agric/Transport	Yes, Ltd.	Just expanded	Ikoyi/Egbeda	Excessive family responsibility	No	No	lawyers
HND	No	Excellent	Nursing and medical care services	Yes, sole proprietor	Stagnated	Akute, Ogun State	Credit sales/ lack marketing experience	Yes; personal savings	No	No
BSc	No	Excellent	-	-	-	-	Funding	No	No	No
BSc	Yes	Excellent	Rentals of canopy/chairs	No	-	Sango Otta	Funding, maintenance cost	No	No	No
HND	Yes	Excellent	Cement distributor	Yes	Just expanded	Okene, Kogi State	High production cost	No	Yes	No
HND	Yes	Excellent	Clearing & Forwarding agency	Yes, Ltd	Just expanded	Tin Can Island Port	Lack of funding	No	No	No
Trainers										
No	Age	Years as trainer	Biz experience	Field of work	Previous experience	Gender	Education	Quality Ratings	Challenges	Recommendations
1	54	20	15 years	Woodwork	Teacher	Male	BSc	Good	Lack of tools and manpower	Hire more expert, buy more and better equipment
2	46	1	Navy Dockyard	Auto-mech wing	-	Male	Post Graduate	Fair	Lack of excursion experience for trainees	More time allocated for practical

Source: Fieldwork, NAFRC, 2020
WASC – West African School Certificate
GCE – General Certificate of Education
O/L – Ordinary Level

Disparities Between the Services

The researchers were notified of the different treatments obtained from the Services (i.e., Army, Navy, and Air Force). Mostly, trainees from the Nigerian Navy and the Nigerian Air Force appear to have some advantages over their colleagues from the Nigerian Army. For instance, some Air Force trainees from the Nigerian Air Force are allowed to come to NAFRC long before their retirement time. Such trainees go back to their units after their NAFRC training to continue with their jobs. This is not the case for trainees from the Nigerian Army. A common explanation for this is that the involvement of the Army in theatres of operations throughout the country exert pressure that leaves little room for creative deployment. As shown in Table 4, the trainees that have less than 34 or 35 years of service are not from the Nigerian Army.

New Initiatives and the Dialectics of Military Culture

The development projects in NAFRC are clear; from the neatly renovated class/lecture rooms to on-going refurbishment projects (painting, construction works, etc.) around the barrack. The zeal at which the NAFRC Commandants engage innovative schemes (e.g., commercialisation of NAFRC products) and programmes (e.g., new courses) is a testament to the commandants' desire to develop and ensure the centre remains true to its mandates. However, it seems some of the newly introduced courses/programmes emanated from the vision of the commandants. For example, the researchers found that the recently introduced painting workshop/course was the idea of the commandant. The utility of the paint workshop/course was highlighted by one of the respondents' statement: "The centre is saving a lot of money through the production of its paints, since there is always a paint job to be done all-year-round in the Centre". In essence, some workshop/course innovations are generated from the vision of the commandant (or the top hierarchy of NAFRC) and not driven by the needs of the trainees themselves. This could be one of the reasons for the absence of trainees in some workshops/courses; some workshops/courses have as low as one or two trainees enrolled. Consequently, it could be said that the introduction of new initiatives at NAFRC is not often driven by trainees' interest. The argument that many of the departments "have the potential to operate as full-fledged commercial outfits, generating income and self-sustaining" (Yohana & Ugboaja, 2019: 31) seems to gloss over the fact that NAFRC was not established as a profit-making institution. Successful ideas and innovations are customer-centric, that is, value creation or customer value has to be from the perspectives of the customers (in this case, the trainees).

However, Commandant as a source of value creation in NAFRC fits well into the narrative of the hierarchical top-down ordering system prevalent in the military tradition. The military is a closed social system where individual experiences of work, living, and emotional expression are controlled. Whilst on active duty, soldiers dutifully obey codes of military conduct at all times, on and off base, from the moment they enter the military until the moment they leave (Arkin, 1978). It is then understandable that successive NAFRC Commandants are often eager to initiate projects based on their sagacity and what they considered 'good' for the Centre.

Gap in Monitoring and Evaluation Processes

The process of monitoring and evaluating output in NAFRC seems fragile as the mechanisms for systematic collection of data for evaluation monitoring are weak. Although the Centre has a Course telephone directory for each cohort group, it is clear no coherent system of follow-up exists in the Centre. Some instructors do get in touch with some of their ex-trainees on a personal basis. For instance, the instructor at the bakery did confirm that he is in contact with a number of his ex-trainees, especially when they need his assistance in their enterprises.

Monitoring is not the same as evaluation. Monitoring programmes encompass the direct collection of data from relevant stakeholders to obtain a qualitative view of the programme outcomes. In contrast, evaluation is based on linking such outcomes with the specific features of the programme, taking into consideration the role of other factors that may influence monitored outcomes (OECD, 2018). Thus, evaluation is an organised determination of the merit, worth, and impact of a project/programme through the application of a set of benchmarks. It can help an organisation, design, project, programme, or any other initiative or intervention to measure any aim, achievable proposal/concept, or any alternative, to help construct knowledge about the value of social programs and in management decision (Shadish et al., 1991). Monitoring and evaluation (M&E) are needed to assess the training efficiency of NAFRC's entrepreneurship and skills training. M&E should also inform the design and mix of NAFRC training policies by identifying those features that lead to desirable outcomes. In essence, evaluation is fundamental to NAFRC's accountability.

Challenging Business Environment

Generally, the socio-economic and political environments in Nigeria are critical factors in initiating and processing productive ventures either by ex-Service personnel or civilians. Obviously, the economic and political environments in Nigeria have a significant influence on entrepreneurship and business in general. One of the main infrastructural problems cited by the respondents is the inadequate supply of electric power to do their business. This is understandable as Nigeria's incessant power shortage is well documented. Other infrastructural deficit highlighted are poor conditions of the roads, poor quality of workers, difficult access to bank loans, fragile safety and security environment, etc. In essence, the underdeveloped economic infrastructure, insecure environment (Ojo, 2017) could be blamed for the respondents' complaints in these regards. Entrepreneurs experience tough operating conditions as they struggle to overcome business obstacles.

Post Training Enterprise Funding Issues

Several respondents (trainees) lamented access to funding after the completion of their training at NAFRC. The general consensus is that the gratuity/emolument paid at retirement is often not adequate to resettled themselves and start a viable business at the same time. Many of the respondents admitted that getting a house to live with their families after discharge from the military is their first priority. Building or renting a house usually gulp the bulk of their gratuity with little left for starting a business.

RECOMMENDATIONS

Taken into considerations the findings, areas that require attention are listed and five main recommendations for improvement are suggested as follows:

Hypothecated Funding

A case is made for hypothecation tax collected from Defence Headquarters (DHQ) or from the Military Services (i.e., Army, Navy, and Air Force) to be spent on a specific area of military personnel welfare expenditure. This earmarked tax will provide a useful source of grant or affordable loan for retired military personnel who desire to go into business after leaving the military service. If guaranteed funding is available through a hypothecated tax (or taxes), retired military personnel who wishes to go into entrepreneurship may be able to overcome the negative cycle of rejection and/or high-interest rate (on loans) that many retired military entrepreneurs have complained about in the past and present.

Hypothecated fund could also be raised from other non-Military sources such as the financial industries (i.e., Banks and Insurance institutions), Lottery Fund, government agencies (e.g., the NNPC, FIRS), etc. The notion of hypothecation is not new in Nigeria as the Tertiary Education Trust Fund (TETFund) scheme operates on such principle successfully. The NAFRC should be a leading moral voice in the fulfilment of the military covenant, that is, Nigeria's duty of care to members of its armed forces.

Process Harmonisation

Referrals to NAFRC training programme was found to be inconsistent among branches of the military. The personnel of the Army are sent to NAFRC close to their retirement (i.e., after 34 to 35 years in the Service) compared to the Air Force and the Navy, whose personnel are sometimes sent to NAFRC long before their retirement. Those who came to NAFRC earlier have the opportunity of experiencing pre-retirement entrepreneurship training and have adequate time to prepare for retirement. This early referral approach should be replicated in the Nigerian Army and strengthened in the Navy and the Air Force respectively. Thus, NAFRC's management team should canvass for this system of early release for entrepreneurship training and skills acquisition for serving military personnel across the board.

Liaise With Key Service Providers

NAFRC intervention will be further enhanced if the Centre coordinates relationship with business fund providers such as Bank of Industry (BOI), Bank of Agriculture (BOA), Central Bank of Nigeria (CBN), and tap into the Government Enterprise and Empowerment Programme (GEEP) schemes (e.g., TraderMoni, FarmerMoni, MarketMoni, etc.). This relationship will help ease access to business fund for some NAFRC trainees after their training. Moreover, the GEEP could also be persuaded to create a special scheme tagged "SoldierMoni" exclusively for ex-Service personnel on the same basis as TraderMoni, FarmerMoni, and MarketMoni, which are directed at specific target groups.

Other funding sources could be Non-Governmental Organisations (NGOs), some of whom already have a system of assistance to ex-Service personnel. For instance, the National Personal Asset Acquisition Scheme (NAPASS), a social and economic empowerment program, provides affordable discounted, structure and flexible repayment spread in areas like housing, education, agriculture, health, transportation, and consumable items to ex-Service personnel (Freedom Sunrise News, 2019).

Application of Dynamic Internal Communication System

Constant dialogue between trainees and NAFRC management must be strengthened to bridge the information gap that may arise within the organisation from time to time. For instance, there appears to be a disconnection between the position of many of the trainees and that of the hierarchy of NAFRC concerning business funding. Whilst many trainees raised the issue of the inadequacy of fund to start or develop business ventures, the erstwhile commandant of NAFRC was quoted as cautioning "retirees against borrowing from banks or industries to start businesses, adding that the retirement benefits as provided by the administration of President Muhammadu Buhari were substantial to start businesses" (Wada, 2020). However, the commandant may have been quoted out of context or was referring to a specific situation that was not sufficiently captured in the statement. Nevertheless, constant internal dialogue promotes organisation cohesion and effectiveness. For example, some issues of concern for the trainees (e.g., provision of toilet facilities in some workshops or computer updating) could quickly be resolved with improvement in communication.

Understandably, military organisations have their peculiarities in term of internal information and communication management. But an astute information flow system that enables bi-directional information flow should be encouraged and carefully nurtured in NAFRC.

Customisation of Intervention

The career and training options individuals could choose from should be customised to suit each trainee following a discussion of personal finances, family adjustments, gratuity payments, age, health conditions, etc. The researchers found that whilst some trainees are concerned about issues of finance (for business or personal use), others are more concern about homeownership. Some have underlying health issues that occupied their minds and many are worried about age constraints in their choice of entrepreneurship or employment matters. Based on this finding, a more careful assessment procedure is needed to shift trainees according to individual needs and requirements. For instance, some trainees may not need to be at the Centre for the six-month duration (given their previous business experiences). Some trainees claimed they registered for NAFRC training programme so that the payment processes of their gratuity and entitlements will be faster. A careful career counselling and guidance regime tailored to take account of individuals' need nuances must be entrenched. This will enable resources to be optimally directed and maximise the benefits of NAFRC's intervention.

CONCLUSION

Transitioning from a structured, all-inclusive environment into a world full of choices and ambiguity can be overwhelming for military personnel. Retiring military personnel enter a phase of transition from the military to the civilian world. A major transition assistance programme is offered by the Nigerian Armed Forces Resettlement Centre (NAFRC) in Lagos. The Centre offers retiring Service members a six-month entrepreneurship and skills training as a social empowerment transition assistance programme. Invariably, NAFRC constantly improve on its service delivery and succeeding NAFRC Commandants have continued to introduce innovative ideas and projects to the Centre to enhance users' experience.

Though the entrepreneurship and skills training workshop/programme was only one step of military personnel's transition to becoming a veteran, it is an important piece to their future career success. Areas that require attention are pointed out and recommendations for improvement are suggested. The vision has been oriented towards ensuring that all ex-Service personnel and their families lead successful and fulfilled lives, and the mission preoccupied with ex-Service personnel making a successful and sustainable transition to civil life.

Despite its insightful findings, the issue of generalisability is a key weakness of this study since ex-Service personnel who partake in NAFRC entrepreneurship and skills training programme could be different from those who do not participate in the programme. The study's limited small sample size (i.e., ex-trainees) and the self-report measures presents a challenge to generalise findings to a wider veteran population. Nevertheless, research on the military's transition assistance programme is limited (Ziencik, 2020), hence, the study has the potential to contribute to the literature by providing an insight into the processes of returning military personnel into civilian life.

REFERENCES

AbubakarU. (2016). Career management of officers in the Nigerian Army (1970-2014). https://ssrn.com/abstract=2722249orhttp://dx.doi.org/10.2139/ssrn.2722249 doi:10.2139srn.2722249

Adekanye, J'B. (1999). *The retired military emergent power factor in Nigeria.* Ibadan: Heinemann Educational Book.

Angrist, J. D. (1998). Estimating the labor market impact of voluntary military service using social security data on military applicants. *Econometrica, 66*(2), 249–288. doi:10.2307/2998558

Angrist, J. D., & Johnson, J. H. IV. (2000). Effects of work-related absences on families: Evidence from the Gulf War. *Industrial & Labor Relations Review, 54*(1), 41–58. doi:10.1177/001979390005400103

Arkin, W., & Dobrofsky, L. R. (1978). Military socialization and masculinity. *The Journal of Social Issues*, *34*(1), 151–168. doi:10.1111/j.1540-4560.1978.tb02546.x

Baron, R. and Shane, S. (2008). *Entrepreneurship: a process perspective*. Thomson/South-Western.

Bruyat, C., & Julien, P. (2000). Defining the Field of Research in Entrepreneurship. *Journal of Business Venturing*, *16*(2), 165–180. doi:10.1016/S0883-9026(99)00043-9

Burdett, H., Woodhead, C., Iversen, A. C., Wessely, S., Dandeker, C., & Fear, N. T. (2013). "Are You a Veteran?" Understanding of the Term "Veteran" among UK Ex-Service Personnel: A Research Note. *Armed Forces and Society*, *39*(4), 751–759. doi:10.1177/0095327X12452033

Cherry, M. (2020). *Forewords: A Better Working Future for Ex-Service Personnel.* GoodPeople. Available at: https://s31949.pcdn.co/wp-content/uploads/GP_BWF_A4-Report_v13-interactive-Web-copy.pdf

DFID. (1999). Sustainable livelihoods guidance sheets. London: Department for International Development.

Eisenhardt, K. M., & Graebner, M. E. (2007). Theory building from cases: Opportunities and challenges. *Academy of Management Journal*, *50*(1), 25–32. doi:10.5465/amj.2007.24160888

Freedom Sunrise News. (2019). *NAPASS Brings Succour to Legionnaires*. Available at: https://www.freedomsunrise.com/2019/01/napass-brings-succour-to-legionnaires.html

Genty, K. I., Khairuddin, I., & Zaidatol, A. (2014). Exploring Entrepreneurship Education and Training on Venture Creation in Nigeria. *Elixir Management Arts*, *72*, 25710–25721.

Hope, J. B., Oh, B., & Mackin, P. C. (2011). *Factors affecting entrepreneurship among veterans small business research summary*. U.S. Small Business Administration, Office of Advocacy.

Hope. (2019). *NAFRC Magazine*. Publication of NAFRC.

Interian, A., Kline, A., Janal, M., Glynn, S., & Losonczy, M. (2014). Multiple deployments and combat trauma: Do home front stressors increase the risk for posttraumatic stress symptoms? *Journal of Traumatic Stress*, *27*(1), 90–97. doi:10.1002/jts.21885 PMID:24464407

Kanayo, O., Jumare, F., & Nancy, S. (2013). Challenges of micro finance access in Nigeria: Implication for entrepreneurship development. *Mediterranean Journal of Social Science*, *4*(6), 611-618. doi:.2013.v4n6p611 doi:10.5901/mjss

Lar, K. G. (2020). I want to make NAFRC a Vehicle for National Development. Hope, 2, 21-28.

Liman, A. S. (2019). From the Commandant's Desk. Hope, 1, 3.

Madichie, N. O., & Ayasi, K. (2018). Entrepreneurial opportunities and challenges for retired senior military officers in Nigeria. In African Entrepreneurship. Palgrave Studies of Entrepreneurship in Africa. Palgrave Macmillan. doi:10.1007/978-3-319-73700-3_7

Maury, R., Kemelgor, B., Cumberland, D., Church-Nally, M., & Kerrick, S. A. (2014). Military veterans marching towards entrepreneurship: An exploratory mixed methods study. *International Journal of Management Education*, *12*(3), 469–478. doi:10.1016/j.ijme.2014.05.006

Mobbs, M. C., & Bonanno, G. A. (2018). Beyond war and PTSD: The crucial role of transition stress in the lives of military veterans. *Clinical Psychology Review*, *59*, 137–144. doi:10.1016/j.cpr.2017.11.007 PMID:29180101

Ntiwunka, G. (2012). An assessment of the relevance of Adekanye's the retired military as emergent power factor in Nigeria to contemporary Nigeria. *Canadian Social Science*, *8*(2), 117–126.

OECD. (2018). *Monitoring and evaluation of SME and entrepreneurship programmes*. Available at: http://www.oecd.org/cfe/smes/ministerial/documents/2018-SME-Ministerial-Conference-Parallel-Session-6.pdf

Ojo, S. (2017). Interrogating returnee entrepreneurship in the Nigerian context. *Journal of Enterprising Communities: People and Places in the Global Economy*, *11*(5), 590–608. doi:10.1108/JEC-07-2016-0025

Olokundun, M., Hezekiah, F., Stephen, I., & Fred, I. (2014). An assessment of the taught entrepreneurship program in Nigerian secondary schools. *Merit Research Journal of Education and Review*, *2*(11), 257–275.

Osborne, J. W. (2012). Psychological effects of the transition to retirement. *Canadian Journal of Counselling and Psychotherapy*, *46*(1), 45–58.

Robertson, H. C., & Brott, P. E. (2017). *Military veterans' midlife career transition and life satisfaction.* Available at: https://tpcjournal.nbcc.org/military-veterans-midlife-career-transition-and-life-satisfaction/

Serrat, O. (2008). The sustainable livelihoods approach. In *Knowledge Solutions*. Springer.

Shadish, W. R. Jr, Cook, T. D., & Leviton, L. C. (1991). *Foundations of Program Evaluation: Theories of Practice*. Sage.

Shane, S., & Venkataraman, S. (2000). The Promise of Entrepreneurship as a Field of Research. *Academy of Management Review*, *25*(1), 217–227. doi:10.5465/amr.2000.2791611

Smaliukienė, R. (2014). Entrepreneurship opportunities after military career: Practice in Central and Eastern versus Western Europe. *Entrepreneurial Business and Economics Review*, *1*(4), 97–108. doi:10.15678/EBER.2013.010408

Smith-Osborne, A. (2013). Veterans administration health care policies as a protective mechanism supporting an expected life trajectory after military service. *Social Work in Public Health*, *28*(2), 81–96. doi:10.1080/19371918.2011.552038 PMID:23461344

Sparrow, A. (2008). *What is the military covenant?* Available at: https://www.theguardian.com/politics/2008/mar/04/defence.military

Staskiel, H. (2020). *The VA's Definition of "Veteran" – An In-Depth Look*. Available at: https://www.hillandponton.com/vas-definition-veteran-depth-look/

Storlie, C. (2010). *Combat to corporate: Applying military Spec Ops principles to business success*. Praeger.

Usman, E. (2011). *Armed Forces Resettlement Centre graduates 149 retiring servicemen*. Available at: https://www.vanguardngr.com/2011/12/armed-forces-resettlement-centre-graduates-149-retiring-servicemen/

Usman, E. (2017). *NAFRC trains 403 retiring soldiers*. Available at: https://www.vanguardngr.com/2017/12/nafrc-trains-403-retiring-soldiers/

Usman, E. (2018). *Military personnel retire says NAFRC Commandant*. Available at: https://www.vanguardngr.com/2018/06/320-military-personnel-retire-says-nafrc-commandant/

Usman, E. (2019). *35 middle cadre Military personnel undergo training on entrepreneurship, mgt.* Available at: https://www.vanguardngr.com/2019/01/35-middle-cadre-military-personnel-undergo-training-on-entrepreneurship-mgt/

Usman, E. (2020). *342 military officers retire in June*. Available at: https://www.vanguardngr.com/2020/06/342-military-officers-retire-in-june/

Vogt, D., Perkins, D. F., Copeland, L. A., Finley, E. P., Jamieson, C. S., Booth, B., Lederer, S., & Gilman, C. L. (2018). The veterans' metric initiative study of US veterans' experiences during their transition from military service. *BMJ Open*, *2018*(8), e020734. doi:10.1136/bmjopen-2017-020734 PMID:29895650

Wada, I. (2020). *Senate committee lauds Lar for judicious use of NAFRC funds.* Available at: https://guardian.ng/news/senate-committee-lauds-lar-for-judicious-use-of-nafrc-funds/

Wolpert, D. S. (2000). Military retirement and the transition to civilian life. In J. A. Martin, L. N. Rosen, & L. R. Sparacino (Eds.), *The military family: A practice guide for human service providers* (pp. 103–119). Praeger.

Yohana, C. I. D., & Ugboaja, O. (2019). Cover Story. Hope, 1, 33.

Ziencik, C. (2020). Transitioning from the Military to Higher Education: A Case Study of the Transition Assistance Program. *Journal of Veterans Studies*, *6*(2), 30–45. doi:10.21061/jvs.v6i2.178

Zogas, A. (2017, February). *US military veterans' difficult transitions back to civilian life and the VA's response.* Watson Institute International and Public Affairs. https://watson.brown.edu/costsofwar/papers/2017/us-military-veterans-difficult-transitions-back-civilian-life-and-va-s-response

KEY TERMS AND DEFINITIONS

Military Culture: Ethos and qualities that describe the norms and practices that are peculiar to the Military service.

Retired Military Personnel (RMP): People who are sometimes referred to as ex-Service personnel or veteran are individuals who served and were disengaged from military service.

Veteran Entrepreneurship: Refers to business ventures/enterprises created by retired military personnel.

Chapter 12
Nigerian Defence Academy and Military Entrepreneurship:
Challenges and Prospects

Bem Japhet Audu
https://orcid.org/0000-0002-2585-9052
Nigerian Defence Academy, Nigeria

Jamiu Yusuf Danga
Nigerian Defence Academy, Nigeria

ABSTRACT

This chapter specifically focuses on military entrepreneurship to explore the entrepreneurial activities of Nigerian Defence Academy Consult Ltd, focusing on problems and prospects of military institutions in Nigeria as spaces for entrepreneurial activities. By blending research on recent literature on military entrepreneurship, the chapter draws upon data from NDA Consult Ltd and interviews from consumers of NDA consult products. It is the case that military institutions are setting up various ventures through the incorporation of companies, and this has broad implications for military professionalism.

INTRODUCTION

Recent scholarship has studied factors that favour military entrepreneurship and the challenges facing such endeavours, but the entrepreneurship pursuit of military institutions has not been sufficiently explored. Although assessing some aspects of military entrepreneurship, these studies have overlooked military institutions and

DOI: 10.4018/978-1-7998-6655-8.ch012

Copyright © 2021, IGI Global. Copying or distributing in print or electronic forms without written permission of IGI Global is prohibited.

their activities in setting up enterprises in Nigeria, with the attendant possibilities and risks that follow such entrepreneurial schemes. For instance, Madichie and Ayasi (2018) have thoroughly examined entrepreneurial opportunities and challenges for retired senior military officers in Nigeria. Other literature on military entrepreneurship emphasizes the role of veterans in franchising, factors mediating the success or failure of military entrepreneurs (Kerrick & Cumberland *et al*, 2014). Many of these studies are mainly done in other climes, with few being focused on military entrepreneurship in Nigeria. The conclusions and assumptions are sometimes not applicable within the Nigerian context, for instance, franchising by retired military officers in Nigeria is rare, yet this dominates the literature by scholars elsewhere. This complicates our understanding of military entrepreneurship as a whole.

Despite the growing agency military institutions display in entrepreneurial activities, studies have not investigated military institutions in enterprises within their structure. Overall, existing literature considers military entrepreneurship in Nigeria as a post-service endeavor. This chapter specifically focuses on military entrepreneurship to explore the entrepreneurial activities of Nigerian Defence Academy, (NDA) Consult ltd, focusing on problems and prospects of military institutions in Nigeria as spaces for entrepreneurial activities. Specific questions addressed are: What is military entrepreneurship within the context of Nigeria? How does the Nigerian Defence Academy, Consult Ltd display a form of military entrepreneurship within military institutions? What are the problems, and prospects of military entrepreneurship in Nigeria? By blending research on recent literature on military entrepreneurship, this chapter draws upon data from NDA Consult ltd, and interviews from consumers of NDA Consult products. The findings of the paper contribute to the literature on military entrepreneurship in Nigeria.

Military Entrepreneurship in Nigeria

The literature on military entrepreneurship continues to grow, with different issues bothering on being debated. A major theme in the discourse is the nexus between military training and entrepreneurship, scholars argue that the trend of retired military personnel or military veterans engaging in entrepreneurship whether as start-ups or as franchisors can be linked to the many skills individuals acquire during military service (Lamidi & Minai, 2016; Smaliukienė, 2013; Wood, Bianchi, & Kucik 2012). Smaliukienė (2013) observes that such skills if well-developed can be transferred to entrepreneurship.

Kerrick and Cumberland *et al* (2014), for instance, examined how community-based entrepreneurship training programmes affect the frequency of military veterans in entrepreneurship, they found that attending structured courses in entrepreneurship leads to the active participation of veterans in entrepreneurship because it raises their awareness and networking skills and capacity (Kerrick & Cumberlandet *et al,* 2014: 471).

Some studies link military entrepreneurship with a lack of military professionalism. (Mani, 2000; Mulveron, 1999; Avant, 2005; Siddiqa-Agha, 2000). For instance, Mani (2007) studied several states in the developing world using typological theory in which several case studies in Asia and Latin America were observed, Mani (2016) concluded that military entrepreneurship is harmful to military professionalism as it weakens cohesion among the military personnel.

Entrepreneurship is an important factor in the national economy. Nigeria has been encouraging development in all ramifications especially, small and medium entrepreneurship have on health and the long-term growth of the national economy (Collins, Hangue. & Locke, 2004). The military in Nigeria has long been involved in entrepreneurial activities. The military has participated in the management of business enterprises in Nigeria, especially state-owned corporations, and other establishments both as serving personnel, at transitory stages of their military career, and as retirees. (Madichie & Ayasi, 2018; Lamidi & Minai, 2016) In recent years military institutions in Nigeria are directly establishing businesses in collaboration with civilian management to engage in various ventures. Although previous military involvement in entrepreneurship was facilitated by their control of political power before 1999, the return to civil rule has seen a rise in military involvement in entrepreneurship.

Nigerian military establishments have been paying close attention to global trends in entrepreneurial development since 1960; the military has been involved in entrepreneurship especially through the instrument of state power. The role of the military in political and economic control of Nigerian changed from 1966 as they became mainstream entrepreneurs who are responsible for running state corporations such as Nigeria National Petroleum Corporation to mention a few, however, the return to democracy in 1999 led to the military institution being rid of such direct involvement in entrepreneurial activities. (Siollun, 2019: 213)

The recent interest in military entrepreneurship within Nigeria connotes the active entrepreneurial involvement of both institution and individuals, in active service and retired service personnel in Nigeria has led to the incorporation of ventures through the corporate affairs commission (CAC). Some of this incorporation has been a form of a corporation, microfinance bank, and other SME such as tailoring and bakery. Some of these incorporations include Nigerian Army Post Exchange (NAPEX), Nigerian Army Properties Limited (NAPL), and Nigerian Army Small Scale Drug Manufacturing Unit (NASDMU). Others are the Nigerian Army Welfare Insurance Scheme (NAWIS), Post Service Housing Development (Ph.D.), and Post-Service Homes Savings and Loans (PHL). These businesses aim to maximize the profitability of various ventures and they have displayed resilience and profitability over time (Lamidi & Minai, 2016).

Lamidi and Minai (2016) observe that a major factor that mediates success by military entrepreneurs is their long years of training which has instilled discipline in them. For an entrepreneur wealth creation involves having a superior ability to face obstacles, opportunities, setbacks, and failures, hence physical and mental effort must prevail in any entrepreneurship endeavor.

There is a link between entrepreneurship and the military. An entrepreneur is a risk-taker, so is the military personnel. The entrepreneur sees opportunity where others see challenges, the military personnel is expected to confront the dangers head-on, where others are expected to flee. These factors prepare the military personnel for entrepreneurship, although the entrepreneurship potential of the military is often more often than not ignored or underdeveloped in Nigeria. Military entrepreneurship as a systematic academic pursuit is very recent. (Mani, 2007; Madichie & Ayase, 2018) What exists previously were studies on how retirees and officers' wives engaging in entrepreneurship ventures. For instance, wives of serving personnel collectively and individually involved in businesses such as ownership and maintenance of schools, superstores, and value-added services such as Consultancy.

Relatedly, ex-service personnel have shown great agency in entrepreneurship, through ownership of various business ventures in oil and gas, construction, agriculture, educational security services. (Madichie & Ayase, 2018) Retired military personnel also embark on businesses especially, with a seeming availability of capital in terms of pensions and gratuity, the aim of investing in businesses by retired military personnel are numerous, such as profit-making, staying active in the post-service period, and avoiding bankruptcy. (Madichie & Ayasie, 2018)

However, this study is concerned about military entrepreneurship in Nigeria with a focus on the Nigerian Defence Academy Consultancy services which was established in 2002 as an entrepreneurial development centre in the Nigerian Defence Academy, Kaduna. Since its establishment, the company has displayed a unique form of agency in military entrepreneurship that demands scrutiny.

Background to Nigerian Defence Academy Consultancy Limited

The Nigerian Defence Academy (NDA) is the foremost military training school in Nigeria founded in 1964 for the training of officer cadets of the Nigerian military (airforce, army, and the navy). Although the academy was so-named in 1964, the evolution of the academy can be traced to the 1959 Act of Parliament in Britain which established the Royal Military Forces Training College in Nigeria. This was later changed to Nigerian Training College and in 1963 it was further changed to Nigerian

Military Training College. However, in February 1964, the academy was renamed the Nigerian Defence Academy. NDA is saddled with the aim of training officer cadets in all facets of acquiring military skills necessary to become professionals in the tri-service (Navy, Army, and Airforce). Aside from the NDA serving as the fulcrum for the training of the Nigerian military officer cadre, namely Airforce, Navy, and Army, the academy has a short service wing that trains officer cadets for 9 months drawn from graduates seeking to become officers in the army (Idris, 2019).

The academy has witnessed a series of expansions that made entrepreneurship a viable option. First, in 1985 the academy became a degree-awarding institution, thereby expanding the scope of its activities from only military training to academic activities. The Nigerian Defence Academy Consultancy limited (NDA Consult) was established in 2002 with the mandate of pursuing profitable endevours on behalf of the academy (Nigerian Defence Academy Consultancy Ltd, 2012). However, until 2008, the NDA Consult was existing in name than in content or activities.

A major factor that changed the course of NDA Consult was the introduction of the school of postgraduate studies in 2008. This expansion to postgraduate studies initially boosted the activities in several ways, first; the Consult became the administrator of the school of postgraduate studies through the advertisement and registration of candidates for the postgraduate programmes of the school. The NDA Consult was responsible for the administration of two professional courses, Masters of Business Administration (MBA) and Masters in Advanced Strategic Studies (MIASS).

NDA Consult limited is funded by NDA headquarters and intervention grants from institutions such as Tertiary Education Trust Fund (TETFUND). When the Consult was registered with the Corporate Affairs Commission (CAC) of Nigeria in 2002, the specific ambition was to become a high-quality provider of Consultancy services especially in the management of security outfits. (Nigerian Defence Academy Consultancy Ltd, 2012) At that early stage of the Consultancy, there was a focus on providing services to organizations such as military establishments, government agencies, businesses, and the agricultural sector.

Clients were to be provided such services as security evaluation entrepreneurship and business incubation, surveillance installation, and operation among others. Several factors made this focus on security provisioning appealing to the heads of the Consult at the time. These include the utilization of military personnel, (retired and serving) as well as academics in the institution as resource persons.

What these early forays into service provisioning revealed was that there was inadequate knowledge of what the Consult should embark upon, there was a lack of professional management and this made the Consult almost redundant. Between 2002 and 2008, the Consult existed in name only. That early stage could be seen as an incubation period. (Nigerian Defence Academy Consultancy Ltd, 2012)

In addition to this, the NDA Consult established a water factory. The water factory produced sachet and bottled water for with the targets being those in and around the NDA vicinity. The administration of these two courses and the water factory formed the fulcrum of NDA Consult entrepreneurial activities. This situation proved untenable as the NDA Headquarters (NDA HQ) had to fund the NDA Consult for its continuous survival. (Nigerian Defence Academy Consultancy Ltd, 2012)

In 2012, the NDA Consult focused on entrepreneurial activities only, handing over the management of academic activities to the NDA Postgraduate School. Following this arrangement, the Consult employed more staff and expanded into human resource development through training of individuals in Information Communication Technology (ICT), cosmetics, and fashion designing. This strategy was effective, and the target groups included those living in and outside of Ribadu Cantonment, as well as the surrounding barracks, residents of *Hayi banki*, and *Kurmi Mashi* around the NDA *Ribadu* cantonment. The Consult equally took over the management of the transportation businesses around the cantonment as it is responsible for the management of the tricycle operators in the cantonment.

The NDA Consult is unique in several respects, first, it was not founded nor funded by individuals but the institution. This strategically positions the academy for entrepreneurial activities, as there exists a sizeable and serviceable population both within an immediate environment that can be targeted for various services such as hospitality services, skill development training, transport services, and educational support services. It is also an indication of the professional nature of the founding institution, which has helped its sustainability.

Given the growth of the NDA, it is not surprising that the NDA Consult has positioned itself to take advantage of the environment to expand its entrepreneurial services. Currently, the NDA Consult controls all the boarding lodges in the academy. These lodges include Ukpabi lodge and *Shelleng* lodge. Furthermore, the Consult has extended its services to vocational training, transportation confectionary, capacity development training, and facility management. (Nigerian Defence Academy Consultancy Ltd, 2012)

Nigerian Defence Academy changed its pattern of engagement by divesting from its initial forms of rendering services through professional academic programmes to producing consumer products such as confectionery, tailoring, and hairdressing. (Nigerian Defence Academy Consultancy Ltd, 2012) the Consult some advantages such as; it enjoys the NDA brand as a foremost military academy in Nigeria and Africa, and as an associate with a highly sought-after postgraduate school. It enjoys funding and resources from the academy headquarters. For instance, there was a recent construction of postgraduate lodges by the headquarters of the NDA, which was given to the Consult for management.

The NDA Consult enjoys a unique status of being a company in an academic institution, while still being recognized as an entrepreneurship development centre by funding agencies. Recently, the Tertiary Education Trust Fund (TETFUND) gave the NDA Consult expansion fund for the purchase of logistics such as buses for the marketing of their various products. (Nigerian Defence Academy Consultancy Ltd, 2012) This fund aided the expansion of the NDA to Consult by giving it new reach to target other markets such as the Mando Market that is close to the academy.

More so, the strategic location of NDA as an institution, close to a market, and 1 Division of the Nigerian Army and the enclosed barracks make the population available for targeted businesses. The skill acquisition branch of the NDA Consult seeks to specifically target the youthful population of the barrack. The importance of such a strategic location cannot be overemphasized; the presence of the 1 division barrack and the adjoining "Mammy market" creates outlets for the sale of NDA Consult products such as water, bread, and others. Although other consumers are available, this is the major market for the sale of NDA products; hence the barrack creates a sustainable market structure for the sale of the company's products.

Management of military entrepreneurship in Nigeria are often retained or controlled by the military institution such ventures are affiliated with. Siollun (2019) avers that tight controls over who leads military ventures are a source of conflict and friction that threatens efficient management of ventures in Nigeria's military establishments. When leaders are directly answerable to the military hierarchy it is capable of denying the business managers innovation and control. Decisions over management of the fund, whom to employ, and partnerships to pursue are regulated by military hierarchies.

In NDA Consult, the leadership is structured in a way that the NDA headquarters maintain the headship of the organization. The deputy commandant currently heads the board of directors and he is assisted by the academic provost. Other members of the board are the director of finance, director of administration, director of information communication technology, Academic Registrar, and Managing Director. Besides, only the academy provost and managing director are civilians on the board of directors.

The retention of the power to *hire and fire* by the commandant of the academy accounts for a major reason for the turnover of heads of the Consult since when it was established. For instance, there are have been at least eight different heads of Consult. This lack of security of a job at the management level is a bad business model for several reasons. While the number of heads of Consult may appear insignificant, it is quite important to maintain a measure of job security and continuity because, each coming head comes in with a different vision of how to run the Consult, there by leading to a lack of coherence and continuity with its attendant impact on profitability of the Consult.

Carol Deeb (2019) observed that incompetent management can impact a company's overall operations. The leadership of NDA Consult and are selected based on the consideration of the commandant and this does not permit competition and transparency. Appointing heads of Consult unilaterally by the NDA commandant does not complement the aim of the Consult, which is to be able to provide services locally and internationally. This practice constraints staff motivation, affects balanced budgeting and revenue collection; more so, the cost of training management to fit suitably well into the position. It is important to position the NDA Consult to be competitive by ensuring there is a strong corporate structure in place that can decide the next direction for the business ventures the Consult currently operates.

Therefore, the hierarchical structure of Consult does not permit such shared leadership. Since the appointment to the highest position of the Consult is done by the commandant, that lack of opportunity may be a lost a lost opportunity in staff motivation as the awareness of lack of upward movement may not lead to optimum productivity (Barba-Sanchez & Atienza-Sahuquillo, 2012).

In a discussion with the consumers of NDA products, especially the lodgers, there is the complain of unresponsive management of lodges.[1] For instance, routine repairs are hardly carried out by the Consult and when lodgers complain of faulty areas in the lodges, repairs are often incurred by them and not the Consult. Customer satisfaction is a standard factor in market intelligence (knowing where you are in the market place, as well as behaviours of others, such as the consumers). This helps to understand the latent needs of consumers appreciate and position the business to respond to such needs profitably, efficiently, and consistently.

However, NDA Consult displays certain behaviours because of its near-monopoly over facilities within the Ribadu cantonment where it is domiciled. The Consult leverages on the advantages it enjoys which is the secure environment its facilities are located and that factor keeps customers loyal regardless of how they are treated.

Although the NDA brand appears to be a strength, it has equally limited the Consult from diversifying to other profitable services this is because of the consideration of ensuring that the NDA brand does not incur any negative publicity that will put the entire academy in the spotlight. For instance, there is a huge prospect for the Consult to embark on training professional security operatives that are sourced (outsourcing) to banks and other institutions. This line of business has a prospect because getting specialized training needed for such a security outfit is easily achieved considering the presence of academic and serving and ex-personnel with requisite skills on the needed training for security personnel.

Challenges and Prospects of Military Entrepreneurship in Nigeria

Problems of military entrepreneurship: Military and entrepreneurship is a positive development in many respects; yet, it is bedeviled with several challenges. Military entrepreneurship is prone to corruption because of the absence of oversight. For instance, Christopher J. Coyne, Courtney Michaluk and Rachel Reese (2016) argue that the military sector is characterised by an entangled network of bureaucracy that rewards unproductive behaviours during peacetime that is intensified during wartimes as more resources are devoted to the sector, this process leads to unproductive entrepreneurship in military contracting. They argue that military entrepreneurship is often prone to corrupt attitudes of those involved in the sector, this is a major challenge in military entrepreneurship especially as there is a tendency for the absence of oversight.

Mani (2007) observes that military entrepreneurship impacts military professionalism. She argues that military entrepreneurship has the likelihood to undermine the professionalism, cohesiveness, and integrity of the military. This is because entrepreneurship tends to lure the military away from its core mandate. Mani's argument supposes that the more the military engages in entrepreneurial activities, there is a tendency for them to get involved in integrity eroding activities that imply cohesiveness, especially if it appears as if there are those benefitting from such entrepreneurial activities. Waste, fraud, and abuse have been associated with military entrepreneurship. In the NDA Consult, the commandant of the NDA reserves the right to appoint any person of his choice to the board of director and manager of the Consult. Previous appointments reflect the tendency to seek friends and loyalists to the Consult. Hence, the head of the Consult was and is still answerable to the commandant of the academy.

Similarly, by listening to the opinions of past and present members of staff of the NDA Consult who choose to be anonymous, one may reach the observe that the NDA Consult often depends on the commandant of the academy to release allocation or funds for projects that need to be embarked upon. The implication is that despite the potential profits that accrue to the Consult, it has no access to generated funds for the sake of reinvestment. Approval has to be sought and received from the commandant before any disbursement is carried out for investment purposes in the Consult, this model is unsustainable, slow, and have the tendency to take initiative away from the manager of the Consult, hence there are times when the water factory was unable to produce because funds had not been released to purchase necessary inputs such as bottles or sachets for production.

This reflects a major challenge to military entrepreneurship if military institutions are going to be in total control of the business venture, cronyism, and delay in taking administrative decision sets, thereby delaying, derailing, and stymieing adequate business initiative and reducing the productivity and profitability of the business.

A major challenge to military entrepreneurship especially within the context of Nigeria is what Madichie and Ayasi (2018: 142) explain as "cumbersome procedures" in which there is a relative difficulty in assessing credit facilities such as grants and loans. The problems associated with assessing credit in Nigeria are numerous, aside from high-interest rates which discourage borrowing, there is a tendency for lending agents such as banks to demand full proof collateral (Madichie and Ayasi, 2018: 142).

Another challenge of assessing credit is the relatively new and unexplored nature of military entrepreneurship. Most military entrepreneurs are new players in their chosen sector, thereby limiting their access to credit. Ahlberg and Anderson (2014) observe that the absence of asymmetric information about a business such as actual abilities and qualities of the business can lead to lenders refusing to offer credit the implication is that to offer credit. Hence, relative newness to an economic sector, military entrepreneurs are likely to be denied access.

Inadequate training by military entrepreneurs in line with the nature of business embarked upon is another reason why banks refuse credits (Mambula, 2002: 63). This is because such training gives the creditors confidence that requires expertise and competence have been attained and a proper understanding of the prospects and risks of such business venture undertaken are well known to the entrepreneur. This is also a general challenge with startups and SMEs in Nigeria. The absence of adequate training poses a challenge in assessing credits. Mambula described the specific way absence of training hinders SMEs thus:

Untrained small business managers handling complex ventures are not likely to be sufficiently competent in management, organization, and quality production to adhere to internationally competitive standards, and such SMEs therefore cannot survive without government protection from imports. There is also a lack of adequate information concerning areas of business in the sector generally. Most people with funds tend to use them in well-established sectors rather than seeking new production and new market niche (Mambula, 2002: 63).

The above assertion reflects the importance of training to SMEs and startups. Therefore, emphasis must be laid on the training of military entrepreneurs within the areas of businesses they are interested in, especially at the managerial level. This training should cut across the development of business plans, understanding the requirement for assessing loans, networking, and leveraging networks to assess information on grants among others.

There are specific aims entrepreneurial training achieve:

- training imbue in entrepreneurs the importance of reduction of waste;
- cost-effectiveness while ensuring quality;
- increase in market share as a result of customer satisfaction; goal setting and planning;
- building an entrepreneurial spirit that reflects increased self-confidence;
- persuasion and networking;
- efficient time management; information seeking;
- profitability as a result of increased sales;
- increase in market share through customer satisfaction;'
- innovation and marketing strategy;
- And establishing a good reputation in both qualities of goods and services offered to customers.

(Morris, Kuratko, & Covin, 2008; Liao, Welsch & Moutray, 2008; Minniti & Bygrave, 2001).

While it is easy to take these for granted as already existing, it is important to reaffirm the practice of these entrepreneurial skills to ensure avoidance of failure. Generally, such training is useful as they provide added skills and competence in a preferred field of business and this also increases the chances of obtaining credits. (Madichie and Ayasi, 2018: 142).

Prospects of Military Entrepreneurship in Nigeria

However, there is a huge prospect for military entrepreneurship, especially in Nigeria. Nigeria's population and the economy are growing rapidly. This portends options for profitable entrepreneurial development through innovations. Some of the alternatives of military entrepreneurship that can be pursued include expanding into agriculture, technology development, and manpower development such as training of civilian and military personnel especially in collaboration with local and international security companies that offer certification causes on security.

The training offered in military institutions includes leadership, innovation, and resilience, leveraging on such training can prepare military institutions and ex-servicemen for a career in entrepreneurship. Another aspect of military entrepreneurship is intrapreneurship where the military directly incorporates and controls aspects of an entrepreneurial institution as is the case of this study.

The potential for military entrepreneurship in Nigeria is high, the major responsibility lies on the military to be professional even while engaging in entrepreneurship, the issue of corruption and bureaucracy needs to be brought to the barest minimum if the drive towards entrepreneurship is to be sustained, this will ensure that the military retains its professional image while exploring opportunities in the corporate world.

Given the nature of the military, there is a need to find a balance that ensures that the military retains the initiative of its core mandate while actively pursuing entrepreneurial activities. There is evidence showing that military ventures need not necessarily affect professionalism, for instance, the successful management of various ranches owned by the Nigerian army shows the possibility of successful intrapreneurship given the right discipline.

CONCLUSION

The study found that NDA Consult Ltd has is an instance of the prospect of military entrepreneurship in Nigeria. The Consult leveraged the location, image, and control of the academy to carry out enterprises that have shown great prospects. This represents an opportunity for military institutions to explore an alternative avenue to entrepreneurship. One of the challenges of military entrepreneurship in Nigeria is the lack of exploratory studies on specific military institutions and their entrepreneurial drive. This attests to a wider issue of scanty literature in military entrepreneurship as an area of inquiry. It has been a common recurrence to treat military entrepreneurship as enterprises pursued by ex-service personnel. In Nigeria, military institutions are setting up various ventures through the incorporation of companies. This has consequences for the management of such ventures as the military institutions tend to seek retention of control while striving to achieve profitable ventures. This means that using the identity of the institutions for profit, again making a deviation from the core mandate of the military. This critical aspect of military entrepreneurship has broad implications for military professionalism. These areas need to be adequately researched if any proper understanding of how military institutions are impacted by their engagement in entrepreneurship is to be made.

REFERENCES

Ahlberg & Andersson. (2012). *How do banks manage the credit assessment to small businesses and what is the effect of Basel III? An n implementation of smaller and larger banks in Sweden* (Unpusblished Masters thesis). Jönköping International Business School.

Avant, D. D. (2005). *The Market for Force: The Consequences of Privatizing Security*. Cambridge University Press. doi:10.1017/CBO9780511490866

Barba-Sanchez, V., & Atienza-Sahuquillo, C. (2012). Entrepreneurial behavior: Impact of motivation factors on the decision to create a new venture. *Investigaciones Europeas de Dirección y Economía de la Empresa*, *18*(2), 132–138. doi:10.1016/S1135-2523(12)70003-5

Collins, C. J., Hanges, P. J., & Locke, E. A. (2004). The relationship of achievement motivation to entrepreneurial behavior: A meta-analysis. *Human Performance*, *17*(1), 95–117. doi:10.1207/S15327043HUP1701_5

Coyne, C. J., Michaluk, C., & Reese, R. (2016). Unproductive entrepreneurship in US military contracting. *Journal of Entrepreneurship and Public Policy*, *5*(2), 221–239. doi:10.1108/JEPP-12-2015-0037

Deeb, C. (2019). What happens to an organisation with bad management? https://smallbusiness.chron.com/happens-organization-bad-management-34749.html

DSW (Deutsche Stiftung Weltbeveolkerung). (2014). http://orange.ngo/wp-content/uploads/2018/06/Entreprenuership-Training-Manual.pdf

Edelman, L. F., Candida, G. B., Manolova, T. S., & Greene, P. G. (2010). Start-up motivations and growth intentions of minority nascent entrepreneurs. *Journal of Small Business Management*, *48*(2), 174–196. doi:10.1111/j.1540-627X.2010.00291.x

Idris, M. I. (2019). Professional Military Education for the Modern Officer: The Nigerian Experience. In Professional Military Education, A cross Cultural Survey. New York: Oxford.

Kerrick, S. A., Cumberland, D., Church-Nally, M., & Kemelgor, B. (2014). Military veterans marching towards entrepreneurship: An exploratory mixed methods study. *International Journal of Management Education*, *12*(3), 469–478. doi:10.1016/j.ijme.2014.05.006

Liao, J., Welsch, H., & Moutray, C. (2008). Start-up resources and entrepreneurial discontinuance: The case of nascent entrepreneurs. *Journal of Small Business Strategy*, *19*(2), 1.

Madichie, N. O., & Ayasi, K. (2018). Entrepreneurial opportunities and challenges for retired senior military officers in Nigeria. In *African Entrepreneurship*. Palgrave Studies of Entrepreneurship in Africa., doi:10.1007/978-3-319-73700-3_7

Maimaris, W., Hogan, H., & Lock, K. (2010). The impact of working beyond traditional retirement ages on mental health: Implication for public health welfare policy. *Public Health Reviews*, *32*(2), 532–548. doi:10.1007/BF03391615

Mambula, C. (2002). Perceptions of SME growth constraints in Nigeria. *Journal of Small Business Management*, *40*(1), 58–65. doi:10.1111/1540-627X.00039

Mani, K. (2007). Militaries in business. *Armed Forces and Society*, *33*(4), 591–611. doi:10.1177/0095327X06291348

Morris, M. H., Kuratko, D. F., & Covin, J. F. (2008). *Corporate entrepreneurship and innovation*. South-Western.

Nigerian Defence Academy Consultancy Ltd. (2012). *Company Profile*. Author.

Politis, D., & Gabrielsson, J. (2009). Entrepreneurs' attitudes towards failure. *International Journal of Entrepreneurial Behaviour & Research*, *15*(4), 364–383. doi:10.1108/13552550910967921

Siddiqa-Agha. (2000). *Power, Perks, Prestige and Privileges: Military's Economic Activities in Pakistan*. Paper presented at the International Conference on Soldiers in Business, Jakarta, Indonesia.

Smaliukienė, R. (2013). Entrepreneurship opportunities after military career: Practice in Central and Eastern versus Western Europe. *Entrepreneurial Business and Economics Review*, *1*(4), 97–108. doi:10.15678/EBER.2013.010408

Yusufa, L., & Minai, M. S. (2016). Military Personnel as Entrepreneurs in Nigeria. *International Journal of Sciences Basic and Applied Research*, *28*(3), 217–230.

ENDNOTE

1 Interview with Damilola Salami, Ashiru Dantata, Jemimah Otu, Post graduate students and lodgers in Ukpabi Lodge Nigerian Defence Academy, Kaduna, 28th September 2020. They were verbally asked to discuss their opinion about the service delivery of the NDA Consult Ltd.

Chapter 13
Transformation of Russian Military Enterprise in the Geopolitical During the Putin Era

Fei Wu
China Guangzhou Jinan University, China

ABSTRACT

Vladimir Putin's annual address as president in 2006 neatly summaries the reason why Russia had to press forward with long-overdue reforms of its armed forces. Two decades after the fall of the Soviet Union, Russia was still left with an oversized military organization built for large-scale mobilization and the demands of the Cold War, but highly ineffective for the type of conventional military conflicts that Russia was most likely to become involved in. The rationale behind Russia's reforms of the armed forces were thus clear long before the war in Georgia, which has often been pointed to as the reason why the reforms were launched in October 2008. President Vladimir Putin's current period runs out in 2024, when he is due to step down, according to the constitution. Given the fact that the current political system has been carefully crafted for almost 20 years, it is evident that there is uncertainty about its future. First, it no longer produces wealth for the population. For five years in a row, the real disposable income has been decreasing.

DOI: 10.4018/978-1-7998-6655-8.ch013

Copyright © 2021, IGI Global. Copying or distributing in print or electronic forms without written permission of IGI Global is prohibited.

INTRODUCTION

I remember the conversation with the then chief of the General Staff very well. ... In order to give an effective answer to the terrorists, we needed to gather a force numbering at least 65 000 men. But in all of the Ground Forces, there were 55 000 in battle-ready units, and these were scattered all over the country. An army of 1 million 400 thousand men, but there was no one who could go to war (Vladimir Putin's Annual Address to Parliament in 2006).

The quotation above, taken from Vladimir Putin's Annual Address as President in 2006, neatly summaries the reason why Russia had to press forward with long-overdue reforms of its Armed Forces. Two decades after the fall of the Soviet Union, Russia was still left with an oversized military organization built for large-scale mobilization and the demands of the Cold War. However, this military organization is highly ineffective for the type of conventional military conflicts that Russia was most likely to become involved in. The rationale behind Russia's reforms of its Armed Forces was thus clear long before the war in Georgia (Emerson, 2008), which has often been pointed to as the reason why the reforms were launched in October 2008. President Vladimir Putin's current period runs out in 2024 when he is due to step down, according to the Constitution. Given the fact that the current political system has been carefully crafted for almost 20 years, it is evident that there is uncertainty about its future. First, it no longer produces wealth for the population. For five years in a row, the real disposable income has been decreasing (IMEMO, 2019). Second, the legitimacy of the system could be questioned, since Putin's popularity figures are going down, and the surge from 2014–2015 has been eradicated.

War (indeed, the Soviet Union helped fuel conflict and instability), as well as, the communist ideology and groups that professed it lost their main backer with the fall of the Soviet Union. The demise of the Soviet Union also contributed, not only to weaken some African states, but resulted in the influx of arms on the global market. Thus, it was easy for disparate individuals and groups to carve out areas of influence under the barrel of the gun. Furthermore, in the U.S., private military companies (PMCs) (Westerlund & Norberg, 2016) emerged as a function of decades of decisions underscored by both the strategic requirement for resources and neoliberal thinking. The desired result is to reduce costs, gain efficiencies, and create economies of scale (Spearin, 2018).

This chapter focuses on the use of private military companies (PMCs) by the Russian state to achieve both its military and political objectives, through the Eurasian geopolitical space, in the international realm. The chapter is structured into four sections. Section one gives a background to the Russian military industrial complex and section two describes the Russian's military and state defense industries transformation. Section three analyzes the concept of geopolitics and the struggle for influence between Russia and the United States. Section four offers the discussion and concluding remarks.

THE RUSSIAN MILITARY INDUSTRIAL COMPLEX

Historically, the Russian defense industry has played an important role in Russian society. It has been argued that the Soviet Union did not have a military-industrial complex; rather it was one. By the 2000s, however, it was becoming increasingly misleading to refer to a Russian military-industrial complex in terms of a defense industry, armed forces and defense industry ministries operating as a single, integrated entity. Signs of deep dysfunctionality were increasingly apparent, and by 2016 the long-standing rifts between the defense leadership and the industry, as well as within the industry, were out in the open. The sector was no longer the state's primary focus; it had become dependent.

Since 2008, Russia's political leaders have intensified their efforts to steer the development of the country's defense industry. In addition to continued efforts to concentrate the defense industry in state-owned holding companies, a process begun in 2006–2007, the government has also sought to stimulate change from outside. The Russian defense industrial complex consists of approximately 1350 organizations. It employs about 2 million people, although not all of them work on military production (Pravitelstvo Rossii 2018). As a rule, and in comparison, with Western defense companies, Russian defense companies and organizations are more focused on defense production. A striking thing about the Russian defense industry is that there are very few small- and medium-sized enterprises, or SMEs.

The Ministry of Defense, with the backing of the president and prime minister, has been proactive in this process, using a carrot and stick approach. The defense industry has been sharply criticized for price rises, poor quality and unpunctual delivery as well as widespread corruption. The Ministry of Defense has also, and for the first time, placed orders for large materiel systems with foreign defense industries. Meanwhile, a substantial increase in domestic orders is being planned. Moreover, companies' profit margins on priority materiel are expected to increase. Domestic defense orders since 2007 have exceeded arms export contracts by 50 per cent. With the 2020 State Armament Programmed, government orders will become an even more important source of income for the Russian defense industry and thus a potentially stronger defense policy instrument.

Commercializing the Military: The Case of Private Military Companies (PMCs)

Private military companies (PMCs) are not something new in the modern world full of local conflicts and unstable regions. PMCs are usually considered as a commercial enterprise offering specialized services for the safeguarding or protection of any objects, as well as for demining, training, maintenance, elicitation, strategic planning, logistics and consulting (e.g., Tekingunduz, 2018). Private military companies are most often used where the task is beyond the power of civilian security companies, but for whatever reasons, it is impossible or impractical to involve a regular army. PMCs are not mercenaries, although both of them fight for money. However, mercenaries are banned by international laws while PMCs are considered legal (Tekingunduz, 2018). PMCs are also referred to as private security companies (PSCs) or private contractors, and PMCs and PSCs will be used interchangeably in this paper.

The records of Russian PMCs dated back to the 1990s when the first professed "Russian volunteers" went to fight in Yugoslavia. In that event, the exploit of Igor Strelkov-Girkin (an FSB officer) was noted. He was identified for the capture of Slavyansk in the Donbass, Ukraine, in the spring of 2014, and was also accused of involvement in the downing of the Malaysian Boeing MH17 in the sky over the Donbass on July 17, 2014 (InformNapalm, n.d).

It is doubtful if the Russians could be involved in the Yugoslavia hostilities of 1992 to 1995 without the authorization of the Russian leadership. It was recognized that "Russian volunteers" were constantly operating, using the tactics of reconnaissance and sabotage groups, on the territory of Bosnia. The fighting unit consisted of fighters from a St. Petersburg's security company named Rubicon who were aided by Russian Special Services and the Russian government. The use of PMC by Russia has also been noted in places such as Transnistria and Nagorno-Karabakh, Georgia, the Crimea, the Donbass, and Syria. The Kremlin sent mercenaries linked with the Special Services of the Russian Federation to those arenas of war under the guise of protecting Russia's interests (InformNapalm, n.d). Russia involvements in places mentioned above could be considered 'illegal' in the opinion of non-Russia commentators. Yet, it is worth stating that Russian military experts repeatedly appeared in various absolutely legal PMCs' operations. For instance, Russians are actively involved in protecting vessels against the Somali pirates' activities. Russia PMCs also worked with Western PMCs during the American campaign in Iraq; although, these were the foreign PMCs in which citizens of the Russian Federation participated as private individuals (InformNapalm, n.d).

Given the increasingly flexibility of PMCs, the Russian authorities saw the need to regulate the activities of PMCs so as, not only to legalize the participation of

Russians in private military companies, but would also enable the Kremlin to create PMCs legally to achieve its military and political goals outside of Russia.

RUSSIA MILITARY AND STATE DEFENSE INDUSTRIES TRANSFORMATION

One of the famous Russian PMCs is the Wagner Group, which is owned by Yevgeny Prigozhin, an oligarch connected to the Kremlin (he is also known as "Putin's chef"). However, several other groups exist. It appears that some PMCs were allowed to operate in Russia because of their close relationship with the President (Putin). This could serve as pointer to the unique nature of Russian PMCs (Borshchevskaya, 2019). Scholars have grouped Private Security Companies (PSCs) into categories based on the types of functions they perform. These functions range from analysis to the provision of goods and services to military forces, to acting as bodyguards. PMCs or private contractors are a different subset of PSCs and provide a very specific service - "kill or train others to kill" in foreign settings (Borshchevskaya, 2019). Russian PMCs overlap across different categories (e.g., militia, private contractors) when it comes to their activities, and at times also engage in mercenary behavior. PMCs largely hire military veterans usually those with a special-forces background, but not all individuals employed appear to have a Special Forces background. Some, for example, join PMCs in exchange for removal of their past criminal history. This is not the case with Western PMCs, where the system is more streamlined and transparent, and where PMCs tend to distance themselves from mercenary behavior (Borshchevskaya, 2019).

Moreover, the need for and use of PMCs arose differently in the West than in Russia. Before the end of the Cold war, Western nations perceived the state as the primary (though certainly not exclusive) employer of military power. The end of the Cold War changed that perception. When the Soviet Union collapsed, multiple small-scale conflicts broke out worldwide, while the global market flooded with excess military equipment and specialists (Borshchevskaya, 2019). Invariably, small conflicts and weapons flow flourished during the Cold war with increasing use of PMCs. According to Sukhankin (2019), the Kremlin could not challenge Western PMCs within the existing rules of the game, thus, it had to change "the principles of the game itself". Ambiguity and confusion are other unique features of Russian PMCs. PMCs are illegal under Russian law, specifically the Russian Constitution. Primarily, Article 13.5 prohibits "public associations" whose aims include "setting up armed units." Others had also indicated that article 71 of the Constitution defers matters of defense, security, war, and foreign policy to the state, although, this opinion may reflect an underlying fear that such groups could overwhelm the state.

After all, Western countries that utilize PMCs do so in full accordance of the law, and these laws give the state power to carry out matters of defense, security, and foreign policy (Borshchevskaya, 2019).

Indeed, PMCs clearly have links to the Kremlin, but they are not always controlled by the Russian state. This opacity provides the Russian state plausible deniability – this is another key unique feature of the Russian PMCs. However, it is not the only unique feature. Opacity fits the pattern of behavior of weak and corrupt authoritarian states, rather than great powers. It is uncertain how the illegality of PMCs contributes to plausible deniability for the Kremlin. But the illegality does help the state to maintain power dynamics and ensure loyalty within the rivalries of cronies around Putin. The notion of plausible deniability and how the illegality of PMCs is useful to Putin underscores a broader theme with regard to Russia - as it does not fit Western notions of great power or weak state behavior. Indeed, as historian Stephen Kotkin (2016) wrote, Russia has "almost always been a relatively weak great power." A strong state in the Western understanding of the term would not need to keep PMCs illegal in order to maintain its grip on power by hanging a sword of Damocles over rivaling groups. In this sense, the Kremlin's behavior with regard to PMCs is more characteristic of a mafia group than a strong state (Borshchevskaya, 2019).

In 2009, as part of major reforms of the Russian armed forces, several units were transferred from the Organization of the Main Intelligence Administration (Glavnoye Razvedyvatelnoye Upravlenie – GRU) to report directly to then-General Chief of Staff Nikolai Makarov. The next year, Makarov suggested publicly the use of PMCs "for delicate missions abroad . . . to avoid the humiliation of 2004," likely referring to the conviction in Doha over Yandarbiyev's murder (Kramik, 2016). The usage of PMCs by Russia was boosted in the Arab Spring and fighting in Syria and Libya with Putin openly supporting the use of PMCs in November 2012. It must be noted that Russia is not alone in the use of PMCs abroad; others include countries such as the U.S., Great Britain, and France (Kramik, 2016).

In early 2012, the general staff unveiled the Special Operations Forces Command (Командование сил специальных операций, КССО in Russian), and in March 2013, Valeriy Gerasimov officially announced the creation of Special Operations Forces (SOF, Силы специальных операций; ССО), as part of the Special Operations Forces Command, which are separate from other branches of the Russian armed forces. The prototype for the SOF appears to have been the units created in 2009-2010 mentioned earlier. Gerasimov said as part of the announcement, "Having studied the practice of the formation, training and use of special operations forces of the leading states of the world, the leadership of the Russian Ministry of Defense has also begun to create them." Indeed, Moscow appears to have modelled the unit in part after elite, Western SOF. However, Russia's SOF hires exclusively on contract (per

Russian definition of the term "contractor"), for officer positions. SOF operations, carried out usually in secret, are "under the direct control of senior military leaders or commanders-in-chief of the armed forces in theaters of war." The SOF has other unique features. According to Sukhankin (2019), they are "able to collaborate with local military formations," and are able to operate in smaller tactical groups, but without formal approval from the armed forces. The SOF are part of the story when it comes to understanding the origins of Russian PMCs under Putin, even as the SOF is formally part of the Russian armed forces. This model continued to expand and modify in the coming years.

Russian Defense Military Enterprise and Soft Power

Russia developed its main security and foreign policy doctrines and strategies throughout the 1990s. It is clear that the Russian threat assessment in the Military Doctrines has been consistent – with only a few variations – since the first draft of the 1993 Military Doctrine (Izvestiia 1993). In 1997, a concept of national security and an updated foreign policy concept were published (National Security Concept 1997; Foreign Policy Concept 1997). Although the Military Doctrine, in its initial year, took a more hard-liners' approach to Russian national security, focusing on external military threats to a greater extent than the other documents in 1997, by the year 2000, the anti-Western view had become persistent in the political debate.

Russian foreign policy has two overall long- standing objectives. The first is to be recognized as a Great Power in world affairs, comparable to the United States. According to the current National Security Strategy (2015), one of Russia's long-term strategic interests is to consolidate its "status as a leading world power, whose actions are aimed at maintaining strategic stability and mutually beneficial partnerships in a polycentric world". In a similar way, the Foreign Policy Concept (2016) talks about the country's need to consolidate its status as "a center of influence in today's world".

Since 2008, Russia's political leaders have intensified their efforts to steer the development of the country's defense industry. In addition to continued efforts to concentrate the defense industry in state-owned holding companies, a process begun in 2006–2007, the government has also sought to stimulate change from outside. The Ministry of Defense, with the backing of the president and prime minister, has been proactive in this process, using a carrot and stick approach. Yet, the defense industry has been sharply criticized for price rises, poor quality and unpunctual delivery as well as widespread corruption. The Ministry of Defense has also, and for the first time, placed orders for large materiel systems with foreign defense industries. Meanwhile, a substantial increase in domestic orders is being planned. Moreover, companies' profit margins on priority materiel are expected to increase. Domestic defense orders since 2007 have exceeded arms export contracts by 50 per cent. With the 2020 State Armament Programmed, government orders will become an even more important source of income for the Russian defense industry and thus a potentially stronger defense policy instrument.

After a period of high military spending, Russia's total military expenditure is now on a downward trend. It has fallen from over 5 per cent to 3.8–3.9 per cent of GDP, which represents a decrease, but this is still a high share compared to the other great powers, the US and China. This means that although Russia's spending in nominal terms is lower than that of its perceived potential adversaries, Russia continues to forsake a greater share of its GDP to at least maintain the higher level of military capability it has achieved thanks to the military reform, the GPV-2020 (Russian Defense Policy), and prioritizing defense spending over other public spending during a period of falling economic growth. A reason for ascribing lower priority to defense now is that the military reform and the GPV-2020 have produced visible results. During recent years, Russia has been able to demonstrate its status as a military great power at home and abroad. growth. Low growth hampers improvements in the population's living standard, which challenges the president's popularity rating, also another important priority. However, it is not through market reform that the president wants to restore growth; it is rather with administrative methods and by stipulating plan targets. A wide range of national projects has been created to accomplish ambitious goals regarding the economy's ranking internationally and the population's health and living standard. However, under present institutional arrangements, without economic reforms, it will be hard to raise growth sufficiently to achieve these goals.

Reforming the Russian Defense Architecture

At the annual evaluation meeting on 22 November 2011, the Russian minister of defense, Anatolii Serdiukov, declares that the task of transforming the Armed Forces (i.e., delivering a 'new look' Military) (Novyi Oblik), had been fulfilled. However, he also pointed to a number of tasks ahead. Despite the many problems and criticisms levelled against Serdiukov's reforms, the achievements so far are worth taking note of. Few believed that Serdiukov would be successful where earlier ministers of defense had failed, but three years after the reforms were launched, the results are impressive. In little more than three years, Russia has managed to downsize its bloated officer corps, to dismantle empty cadre units and to introduce a new command system as well as a new branch of arms. Although there are significant tasks ahead, there is every reason to note the scale and depth of the restructuring that has taken place inside Russia's Armed Forces.

The most recent large-scale military exercises, practicing and refining new concepts of employment of the Russian forces, serve as an illustration of the threat perceptions guiding the military transformation. They follow the pattern noted some time ago of exercises in Russia practicing offensive action in the West and defensive action in the East, and tally with the threat picture expressed during the Ladoga-2009 exercise by Chief of the Main Staff of the Ground Troops Lt-Gen Sergey Skokov - in the west, Russia has to contend with "innovative armies with non-contact forms and methods for using the latest forces and equipment", in the south, "irregular formations... [and] guerrilla warfare", and in the east, "a multi-million troop army using traditional approaches to the conducting of combat operations... with a great concentration of manpower and firing systems". Six months after this statement, Russia's new Military Doctrine emerged, containing a carefully nuanced treatment of NATO and a studied silence on the subject of China. Contrary to much media reporting at the time, the new Doctrine signed into law by President Medvedev in February 2010 does not describe NATO as a military threat to Russia. But specific NATO activities (in particular, the development of military infrastructure closer to the borders of Russia, and use of force globally 'in violation of international law') are noted as "military dangers" which could under certain circumstances lead to an immediate threat. At the forefront of Russian thinking in this respect are the Baltic States – within NATO but not subject to the restrictions of the un-adapted Conventional Forces in Europe (CFE) Treaty - and any potential new members for NATO that could be found around the Baltic rim.

In 2019, the Russian defense budget (in the federal budget what is classified as 'national defense') totaled 619.8 billion, corresponding to 2.9 per cent of GDP. Data on the defense budget and defense expenditure as a share of GDP are of interest, as they reflect how big a burden defense allocation are for the rest of the economy. Changes in this share also give us an idea of whether the Ministry of Defense and the defense lobby have grown stronger or weaker in the budget process, in which public expenditure is decided. Defense expenditure as defined in the Russian defense budget lay, on average, at a level of 2.7 per cent of GDP between 2009 and 2019. As the line 'Russia/Federal Budget', the defense budget share of GDP is expected to increase over the next two years and amount to 3.9 per cent in 2017.

The main cause of the rise in military expenditure as a share of GDP is the ongoing military reform and the fact that the state procurement of arms will increase. Arms procurement including research and development (R&D), which accounted for around 20 per cent of the defense budget in the early 2000s, was allocated almost 40 per cent of the defense budget in 2014. The plan is to increase this share to almost 60 per cent of the defense budget in 2018. The composition of the Russian defense budget is not easily discerned, since its breakdown into separate items of expenditure only becomes known when the budget is submitted to the Duma. However, many budget items are classified in this version, and researchers try to estimate their size. The Armed Forces is the largest item in the defense budget and amounted to 9 per cent of the federal budget in 2009 (2.3 per cent of GDP). If total military expenditure, as estimated from Russian budget data, is used as a basis, the Armed Forces account for the bulk, or almost 50 per cent of total military expenditure. A further 20 per cent goes to the Interior Ministry Troops and other troops outside the Armed Forces. Nuclear weapons, which are a major priority, accounted for 9 per cent and pensions and social provision, such as housing, for 6 and 7 per cent, respectively, in 2016.

The Ministry of Defense is in the process of reforming the state procurement system for weapons and equipment, which has been both corrupt and ineffective. According to Russia's chief military prosecutor, Sergei Fridinskii, 20 per cent of the defense budget disappears every year. Fake invoices, fraudulent dealings and bribes are commonplace, and some observers believe the losses caused by practices may be twice as large. Major delays caused by friction in the procurement process, disagreement over prices and the defence industry's limited ability to supply military equipment of the standard required by the Ministry of Defense are more the rule than the exception. Then President Dmitrii Medvedev called attention to these problems and took the defense industry to task for its failure to deliver in 2011. 29 Minister of Defense Serdiukov has sought to calm the industry's fears following this criticism by assuring it that no closures or major purchases abroad are planned.30 The Ministry of Defense, too, has been called to account for its failure to finalize orders in the first quarter of 2011. In July 2011, the ministry was still having trouble finalizing contracts for that year.

The pressure on prices from the defense industry together with the constant disagreements on prices led to that the Ministry of Defense established a special price department in 2011, in order to improve knowledge and transparency in relation to the price of military equipment. According to Serdiukov, disagreement over prices is one of the prime causes of delays in defense industry contracts.37 In some cases, the defense industry has had a guaranteed level of profit of up to 25 per cent, and given soft budget constraints in the form of large subsidies and favorable credits, the tendency has been to let all peripheral costs spill over in prices.

The large ineffective defense enterprises are still burdened by their own social service provisions (day-care centers, hospitals etc.) and other high external costs (such as extremely long development times and unfinished projects). The Ministry has tried to force these enterprises to phase out their social commitments and let them be taken over by local municipalities, but the municipalities are reluctant to shoulder these tasks. In October 2011, Serdiukov discussed the Ministry of Defense's 491 pre-schools with Medvedev, who sternly requested a list of the municipalities that were refusing to take them over, clearly intending to put pressure on the local authorities concerned. For 2011, the Ministry is requiring the industry to reduce its average level of profit from 15 per cent to 5 per cent. Enterprises producing priority equipment, however, are to be allowed to raise their margins to 25 per cent.40 Priority equipment refers to 200 products, including nuclear weapons, intercontinental ballistic missiles, cruise missiles and other advanced arms that are in high demand. A further change is a plan by the Ministry to boost pre-payments from 15–40 per cent to 80 per cent. This means that the enterprises will have less financing problems during production, but also that subcontractors should be paid sooner.

Government arms procurement comes under the Official Secrets Act, and details of the annual value and composition of procurements belong to the classified section of the federal budget. The lack of transparency has led researchers to add together data from different sources and produce their own estimates.42 Thanks to a statement by Viktor Zavarzin, head of the State Duma Defense Committee, data were made available in 2016 relating both to the 2010 defense budget and to the budget for 2014–2016.

THE CONCEPT OF GEOPOLITICS AND THE STRUGGLE FOR INFLUENCE BETWEEN RUSSIA AND THE USA

Both the historical and geographical aspects of the concept of geopolitics were developed in 1899, when the idea was originally proposed by the Swedish political scientist Rudolf Kjellen. It was the world view of Western imperialists who aimed to expand the European geographical sphere of influence to the rest of the world in order to seize more resources. It therefore indicates the hierarchical relationships in the European centralized ontology. The concept was extended by the Nazis to mean a fight for more territory. Given this expansionist context, the term "geopolitics" was out of favour until the US Secretary of State, Henry Kissinger, used it to define the global contest between the United States and the Soviet Union (O'Tuathail, 1998).

Geopolitics can be used as a theoretical research tool in the field of political rhetoric to make foreign policy decisions. From this diplomatic viewpoint, the word of geopolitics analytically frames the policy-making process in terms of national interests rather than ideology. During the Cold War period, Kissinger defined it as an approach that focused on the requirements of equilibrium, emphasizing the "balance of power". Secondly, the meaning of geopolitics assumes that geographical factors influence most national interests; this is taken for granted by policy-makers aiming to ensure global security and a military presence in various regions. Halford Mackinder has defined it as the exploitation of armed forces by economic wants and geographical opportunities to obtain political objectives (Gray & Sloan, 1999).

The dominant geopolitical view arose from the European-American experience and was then projected onto the rest of the world and into the future theory and practice of world politics. To think about the geopolitical framing of foreign policies is to recall the doctrines enunciated by various US presidents, from Monroe in

1823 through Truman in 1947, and G. W. Bush in 2002. The Monroe Doctrine initially involved three geopolitical imperatives relating to the US foreign policy: The Americas were closed to further European colonization; the United States must avoid becoming involved in wars in Europe; and the US government would regard efforts made by any European power to expand its empire into the Western hemisphere as a threat to the United States itself. During the Johnson and Reagan presidencies, this doctrine was invoked to justify the US military intervention in many parts of the Latin America. John Agnew has envisioned world politics by regarding the modern geopolitical imagination in multiple ways, rather than as a simple reflection of competing geopolitical and national interests and the "identities" of fetishized states (Agnew, 2003).

Ratzel's study of the way in which human society is shaped by the natural environment has not only led to the sub-field of political geography but has also fed into the study of strategic studies, both in its Anglo-American and Nazi manifestations. The historical trend was from smaller peripheral to larger continental states. Technological developments from the age of discovery had benefited both sea and land powers. Maritime technology had allowed the states of Western Europe to circumnavigate the physical barriers that had penned them in and turned the ocean from an obstacle to a highway. At the same time those at the Eastern margins—Russia—had succeeded in conquering the pivot area of central Asia (Ashworth, 2011).

Eurasia and Russian's Geopolitical Agenda

Eurasia encompasses most of the world's politically assertive and dynamic countries and all of the historical aspirants to global power stem from Eurasia. The world's most populous aspirants to regional hegemony, China and India, are in Eurasia, as are all the potential political or economic rivals to American dominance. Eurasia accounts for 75 percent of the world's population, 60 percent of its GNP, and 75 percent of its energy resources. Collectively, Eurasia's potential power overshadows even America's. Eurasia is the world's axial supercontinent. A power that dominated Eurasia would exercise decisive influence over two of the world's three most economically productive regions, Western Europe and East Asia. A glance at the map also suggests that a country dominant in Eurasia would almost automatically control the Middle East and Africa. With Eurasia now serving as the decisive geopolitical chessboard, it no longer suffices to fashion one policy for Europe and another for Asia. What happens with the distribution of power on the Eurasian landmass will be of decisive importance to America's global primacy and historical legacy (Brzezinski, 1997).

Eurasianism and geopolitics have become theoretical and doctrinal manifestations of the geomentality of Russia's foreign and security policy establishment. Political thinking about the importance of geographical space has strong intellectual and academic roots in Russia. The idea of Eurasianism emerged in 1920 and re-emerged in the 1990s. The decision on NATO enlargement helped Eurasianist ideas to emerge as the dominant doctrine in Russia's foreign and security policy. The NATO enlargement issue united Russia's political class in their opposition to this policy. The 1999 NATO-Yugoslavia war convinced the majority of Russians that Eurasians had always been right in their criticism of the West, NATO, and the Russian Liberals (Tchantouridze, 2001). Afterwards, the Russian authority has begun to adopt defensive realism to formulate its foreign and security policy. This direction has made the Russian president powerful, as several presidencies have resisted Western geopolitical expansion through NATO enlargement and economic sanctions against Russia. The distrust between the West and Russia have consolidated Eurasianism as a national identity and broadened its development in the East under the strategy of "Pivoting to Asia".

Realist and imperialist frames have dominated analyses of Russia's foreign policy under the leadership of Vladimir Putin. In one concept associated with defensive realism, Russia has been viewed as a status quo great power state seeking to preserve its position in the international system by maintaining the balance of power threatened by the US. From this standpoint, Russia's decision to annex Crimea stemmed from its desire to contain and balance the US. Prior Western activities, such as NATO's enlargement, prompted Russia's pushback when the opportunity presented itself. In another argument informed by offensive realism, Russia has been portrayed as a revisionist power harbouring aggressive intention and pursuing the goal of power-aggrandizement. According to the theory of offensive realism, Russia's decision to invade Crimea was rational and expected, as it allowed the Kremlin to acquire the requisite strategic control over a vital military security asset (Omelicheva, 2016).

Robert Dannenberg, Frank J. Cilluffo, and Sharon L. Cardash (2014) have argued that the Crimea event should be understood through a geopolitical analysis of Putin's Russia. Russia moved to annex Crimea; the speed and audacity of the action shook Eastern Europe and surprised the West. The West used economic sanctions to counterattack, resisting the influence of geopolitical change after the collapse of the USSR. Putin views sanctions as an opportunity to rebuild areas of the Russian economy that have suffered since the collapse of the Soviet Union and to reverse the increasing emphasis of the Russian economy on exporting commodities and importing manufactured goods. Putin wishes to use sanctions to change the world's macroeconomic paradigm. He has begun his own "Pivot toward Asia", finding an increasingly sympathetic audience in China. The Ukraine is the first step in Putin's campaign to reject the West culturally, economically, and strategically, in favour of a genuine and meaningful pivot toward the East. To make it all work, however, he needs China, Iran, and India—which is one reason why the Shanghai Cooperation Organization (SCO) is more important than people give it credit for. In any case,

Putin calculates that one important element in Russia's ability to withstand Ukraine-related sanctions is his personal relationship with Chinese President Xi Jinping, along with a series of economic and energy agreements. Finally, Putin is putting a lot of energy into building up the Eurasian Union as a regional counterpart to the EU and an instrument for Moscow to use to exert influence over its neighbours.

In other words, Russia's geopolitical strategy plays a key role in strengthening its power in the regions. The Black Sea gives Russia navy ports for its Black Sea Fleet and the ability to construct pipelines to Europe; these enhance Russia's influence on Europe and the Middle East and strengthen Russia's national security. Russia relies on this energy supply to support its federal budget. Energy is considered to be the most important strategic resource leveraging geopolitical influence. After the Crimean event, the Western block regarded Russia's actions as a form of aggression. For this reason, they launched a series of economic sanctions to pressure Russia. Western economic sanctions have strengthened the liberal ideological and military block but hampered the construction of Russia-EU gas pipelines and collaboration in other areas, such as fighting international terrorism. President Putin decided to boost his Asian strategy through a "Pivot to Asia" and has therefore promoted Russian geopolitical influence in the Asian Pacific Region. This strategy is helping Russia develop the economy of the Far East Region to integrate it better into North Eastern Asia, through which its path extends to South Asia. Russia has promoted its role in the Korean Peninsula and intensified the geopolitical wrestling among China, Japan, and the United States. Russia and China have used this new situation to work more closely together to map peace-route plans in international conflict regions. This approach could provide a similar arena for pursuing Russia-US relations.

The added external pressure on the Russian oil and gas industry stems from the increased EU and US sanctions announced on 12 September 2014, which specifically target Russia's energy, defence, and financial industries. The oil and gas sector is affected by the limited access to financing and by limitations on technology transfer for unconventional and offshore developments. While the sanctions have specifically focused on exploration and production from offshore and unconventional resources in Russia, their effect has spread through the entire oil and gas industry. In response to sanctions, the Russian government and industry operators have intensified their focus on partnerships with Asia-based interests. When the South Stream gas pipeline to Europe was cancelled, an immediate alternative for Russian gas was proposed by President Putin—a sub-sea pipeline under the Black Sea to deliver gas to Turkey. In addition to replacing the South Stream project with this Turkey-bound gas pipeline, Russia and China have signed a memorandum of understanding on 9 November to build another gas pipeline. The new pipeline, "Altai", will connect Russia's West Siberian fields to the Xinjiang Uyghur Autonomous Region of China. The pipeline will run to the West of the Power of Siberia ("Sila Sibiri") pipeline announced in May

2014, which connects East Siberian fields to China's Eastern provinces (GlobalData, 2014). The gas pipeline has guaranteed Russia-China relations and deepened the comprehensive strategic partnership of coordination.

DISCUSSION AND CONCLUSION

Assuming that the security policy situation remains unchanged, the most important factors determining the size of Russia's military expenditure are GDP growth and how well the Ministry of Defense and the defense lobby are able to negotiate in relation to other ministries and budget chapters in the federal budget process. Many scholars and analysts believe that confrontation between the United States and Russia will continue in the adversarial atmosphere created by recent events in the international arena such as the Ukraine crisis and Russiagate. Neither Russian nor US experts believe that Russia or the United States can afford to start a nuclear war, but both sides have to find ways to reduce the escalating tension by agreeing on concrete issues for negotiation and cooperation. The West regards the Ukraine crisis and Russiagate as examples of Russian aggressive geopolitical behaviour, ranging from economy-driven aggression to cybersecurity-based information warfare. The West therefore feels that Russia is challenging their national security; they need to counterattack against Russia's geopolitical ambitions through economic sanctions and military deterrence. This response is creating a new balance of power; it changed after the end of the Cold War and the start of NATO enlargement. The dilemma is that Russia has been too strong to compromise with the US in its geopolitical games, for example in the Ukraine and Syria. What price will the Biden administration pay to achieve normalization with Russia? Putin is very serious about overcoming difficulties related to economic sanctions and low energy prices through a geostrategy involving Asia and the Eurasian regions. The Russia-China strategic comprehensive partnership seems to have deepened in the face of US-Russian adversarial relations. This will give China a broader chessboard to implement its own geopolitical strategy under the "One-Belt-One Road" economic plan. Russia and China have consolidated their Eurasian strategies to counterattack the Western Liberal International order to meet their national interests and demands. If the United States cannot normalize relations with Russia, North Korea, Iran, and other states will develop nuclear weapons to guard against external threats in an unstable and uncertain world. US-Russia relations therefore determine global security more than any other international relationship. US and Russian experts on both sides have suggested resuming the dialogue to limit nuclear weapons; the balance of nuclear deterrence with the signing of periodic treaties to control the global security has created the present international order.

There is less space for Russia to concede. The next move on the chessboard depends on Trump's ability to stop the Russiagate investigation and cooperate with Russia.

From a foreign policy perspective, the Kremlin has concluded the PMC model is a useful tool. It will continue to experiment with PMCs as part of its competition with the West—a struggle in which the Kremlin will use any tool it has in its arsenal, without any concern for human rights, neither of its own citizens nor those of other countries. This means wherever Russian PMCs appear, the West should pay attention, even when the Kremlin denies any knowledge of these groups or downplays their importance. The revolution of the PMC model shows soft power of Putin's foreign policy in the Middle East and Africa, where Putin has worked to build leverage and connections with all major actors, rather than openly taking sides. PMCs are one tool of many in his arsenal.

The PMC model will evolve and expand insofar as the Kremlin sees it as successful in achieving foreign policy objectives. For Moscow, this means its focus on weakening the West in a zero-sum effort to prop up its own position. Analysts must study PMC groups in greater depth, examining their structure and operations, looking beyond their plausible deniability as the only explanation for their use. In the end, as PMCs play a larger role in the Kremlin's foreign policy, the West needs better solutions for countering Russian them.

REFERENCES

Головорезы с тесаками наперевес. (2018). https://lenta.ru/arti- cles/2018/02/21/chvk_interview/

Abrams, E. (2017). The trump national security strategy. *Council on Foreign Relations*. Retrieved from https://www.cfr.org/blog/trump-national-security-strategy

Agnew, J. (2003). *Geopolitics: Re-visioning world politics*. Routledge. Retrieved from https://books.google.com.tw/books?id=G8PKbsgXLNoC&printsec=frontcover&dq=geopolitics&hl=zh-TW&sa=X&ved=0ahUKEwijppW_7tnYAhXIWbwKHaXVD5sQ6AEINDAC#v=onepage&q=geopolitics&f=false

Allison, G. (2015). The Thucydides trap: Are the US and China headed for war? *The Atlantic*. Retrieved from https://www.theatlantic.com/international/archive/2015/09/united-states-china-war-thucydides-trap/406756/

Allison, G. (2017). America and Russia: Back to basics. *National interest*. Retrieved from https://nationalinterest.org/feature/america-russia-back-basics-21901

Ashworth, L. M. (2011). Realism and the spirit of 1919: Halford Mackinder, geopolitics and the reality of the League of Nations. *European Journal of International Relations, 17*(2), 208–286.

Borshchevskaya, A. (2019). *Russian Private Military Companies: Continuity and Evolution of the Model*. Retrieved from: https://www.washingtoninstitute.org/uploads/Documents/opeds/Borshchevskaya20191219-FPRI.pdf

Brzezinski, Z. (1997). A geostrategy for Eurasia. *Foreign Affairs, 76*(5), 50–64.

Cesa, M. (2009). Realist visions of the end of the Cold War: Morgenthau, Aron and Waltz. *British Journal of Politics and International Relations, 11*(2), 177–191.

Dannenberg, R., Cilluffo, F. J., & Cardash, S. L. (2014). *Putin's Russia: A geopolitical analysis.* HSPI Issue Brief 24, Homeland Security Policy Institute. Retrieved from https://cchs.gwu.edu/sites/cchs.gwu.edu/files/downloads/Issue%20Brief-Putin%27s%20Russia-%20A%20Geopolitical%20Analysis.pdf

Emerson, M. (2008). *Post-Mortem on Europe's First War of the 21st Century*. Centre for European Policy Studies. Retrieved from: http://aei.pitt.edu/9382/2/9382.pdf

Escobar, P. (2017). There will be no Russiaphobia reset. *Sputnik*. Retrieved from https://sputniknews.com/columnists/201704271053078743-there-will-be-no-russophobia-reset/

Gearan, A., & Mufson, S. (2017). Trump sets out national security strategy of "principled realism" and global competition. *Washington Post.* Retrieved from https://www.washingtonpost.com/politics/trump-sets-out-national-security-strategy-of-principled-realism-and-global-competition/2017/12/18/7edcb0be-e412-11e7-ab50-621fe0588340_story.html?utm_term=.2387b435ce47

Global Data Event Analysis. (2014). *Russian oil and gas landscape reshaped by geopolitics*. Global Data.

Gray, C. S., & Sloan, G. (1999). *Geopolitics, geography and strategy*. Routledge., Retrieved from https://books.google.com.tw/books?id=7BakAgAAQBAJ&printsec=frontcover&dq=geopolitics&hl=zh-TW&sa=X&ved=0ahUKEwijppW_7tnYAhXIWbwKHaXVD5sQ6AEIJTAA#v=onepage&q=geopolitics&f=false

InformNapalm. (n.d.). *Private Military Companies in Russia: Carrying Out Criminal Orders of the Kremlin*. Retrieved from: http://informnapalm.rocks/private-military-companies-in-russia-carrying-out-criminal-orders-of-the-kremlin

International Committee of the Red Cross (ICRC). (2009). *Montreux Document: On Pertinent International Legal Obligations and Good Practices for States Related to Operations of Private Military and Security Companies during Armed Conflict*. Geneva: ICRC. https://www.icrc.org/en/doc/assets/files/other/icrc_002_0996.pdf

Ivanov, I. (2018). Russia and Europe: From romanticism to pragmatism. *RIAC*. Retrieved from https://russiancouncil.ru/en/analytics-and-comments/analytics/russia-and-europe-from-romanticism-to-pragmatism/

Karaganov, S. (2017). A Cold War: A forecast for tomorrow. *Russia in global affairs*. Retrieved from http://eng.globalaffairs.ru/pubcol/A-Cold-War-A-Forecast-for-Tomorrow-19099

Khalilzad, Z. (2017). The path to US-Russia cooperation. *National interest*. Retrieved from https://nationalinterest.org/feature/the-path-us-russia-cooperation-21914

Khudoley, K. (2017). Russia and the US: The way forward. *Russia in global affairs 4*. Retrieved from http://eng.globalaffairs.ru/number/Russia-and-the-US-The-Way-Forward-19263

Kortunov, A. (2017a). Policy priorities in US-Russia relations. *RIAC*. Retrieved from https://russiancouncil.ru/en/activity/policybriefs/policy-priorities-in-us-russia-relations/

Kortunov, A. (2017b). A roadmap for US-Russia relations. *RIAC*. Retrieved from https://russiancouncil.ru/en/activity/publications/a-roadmap-for-u-s-russia-relations/

Kortunov, A. (2018a). How should Russia respond to an adversarial west? *RIAC*. Retrieved from https://russiancouncil.ru/en/analytics-and-comments/analytics/how-should-russia-respond-to-an-adversarial-west/

Kortunov, A. (2018b). Dialogue with US on nuclear-missile weapons is Russia's priority task. *RIAC*. Retrieved from https://russiancouncil.ru/en/analytics-and-comments/comments/dialogue-with-us-on-nuclear-missile-weapons-is-russia-s-priority-task/

Kotkin, S. (2016). Russia's perpetual geopolitics. Putin returns to the historical pattern. *Foreign Affairs*, *2016*(May/June). https://www.foreignaffairs.com/articles/ukraine/2016-04-18/russias-perpetual-geopolitics

Kramik, I. (2016). *Иностранные корни нового российского спецназа, Кто помогал Минобороны готовить зеленых человечков* [Foreign roots of new Russian Spetsnaz. Who helped Defense Ministry to prepare little Green Men]. Retrieved from: https://lenta.ru/articles/2016/12/20/specialforces/

Likhachev, V. (2017). Russia-EU energy relations. *RIAC*. Retrieved from https://russiancouncil.ru/en/activity/publications/russia-eu-energy-relations/

Locker, R. (2016). What's the arms race? A short history. *USA Today*. Retrieved from https://www.usatoday.com/story/news/politics/2016/12/23/whats-arms-race-short-history/95792412/

Macklem, P. (2008). Humanitarian intervention and the distribution of sovereignty in international law. *Ethics & International Affairs*, *22*(4), 369–393.

Mate, A. (2017). Russiagate is more fiction than fact. *The Nation*. Retrieved from https://www.thenation.com/article/russiagate-is-more-fiction-than-fact/

Morgenthau, H. J. (1973). *Politics Among Nations The Struggle for Power and Peace* (7th ed.). Mc Graw Hill Higher Education.

Myers, R. J. (1997). Hans Morgenthau's realism and American foreign policy authors. *Ethics & International Affairs*, *11*(1), 253–270.

Nye, J. S., Jr. (2015). *Is the American century over?* Wiley. Retrieved from https://www.wiley.com/en-us/Is+the+American+Century+Over%3F-p-9780745690063#

Nye, J. S., Jr. (2017). Will the liberal order survive? The history of an idea. *Foreign Affairs*. Retrieved from https://www.foreignaffairs.com/articles/2016-12-12/will-liberal-order-survive

O'Tuathail, G. (1998). Thinking critically about geopolitics. In *The geopolitics reader*. Retrieved from https://books.google.com.tw/books?id=VH2FAgAAQBAJ&printsec=frontcover&dq=geopolitics&hl=zh-TW&sa=X&ved=0ahUKEwijppW_7tnYAhXIWbwKHaXVD5sQ6AEILTAB#v=onepage&q=geopolitics&f=false

Omelicheva, M. Y. (2016). Critical geopolitics on Russian foreign policy: Uncovering the imagery of Moscow's international relations. *International Politics*, *53*(6), 708–726.

Podvig, P. (2011). *Russia's Nuclear Forces: Between disarmament and modernization, Proliferation Papers, Spring 2011*. Institute Français des Relations Internationals.

Reiter, D. (2014). Security commitments and nuclear proliferation. *Foreign Analysis*, *10*(1), 61–80.

Roberts, P. C. (2018). Russiagate turns on its originators. *Foreign Policy Journal*. Retrieved from https://www.foreignpolicyjournal.com/2018/01/09/russiagate-turns-on-its-originators

Rose, G. (2017). Introduction, from the anthology: What was the liberal world? *Foreign Affairs*. Retrieved from https://www.foreignaffairs.com/articles/2017-03-06/introduction

Russian use of private military and security companies-- the implications for European and Norwegian Security, Norwegian Defence Research Establishment (FFI). (2018). https://www.cmi.no/publications/file/6637-russian-use-of-private-military-and-security.pdf

Sears, N. A. (2017). What might Morgenthau have to say about the administration's emerging foreign policy? *National Interest*. Retrieved from https://nationalinterest.org/feature/trump-can-learn-morgenthaus-6-principles-political-realism-19481

Simes, D. (2017). Current mutual hostility threatens an explosive confrontation. *National Interest*. Retrieved from https://nationalinterest.org/feature/the-costs-ignoring-russia-21888

Spearin, C. R. (2018). Russia's Military and Security Privatization. *Parameters*, *48*(2), 39–49.

Strong, A. (2017). Trump promotes Reagan Era "peace through strength" in national security strategy. *CBN*. Retrieved from https://www1.cbn.com/cbnnews/national-security/2017/december/trump-promotes-reagan-era-peace-through-strength-in-national-security-strategy

Sukhankin, S. (2019). *Unleashing the PMCs and Irregulars in Ukraine: Crimea and Donbas*. Retrieved from: https://jamestown.org/program/unleashing-the-pmcs-and-irregulars-in-ukraine-crimea-and-donbas/

Tchantouridze, L. (2001). Awakening of spirits: Eurasianism and geopolitics in the foreign policy of Russia. Queen's University (Canada), ProQuest Dissertations Publishing, NQ63460, p. ii.

Tekingunduz, A. (2018). *Are private military contractors any different from mercenaries?* Retrieved from: https://www.trtworld.com/americas/are-private-military-contractors-any-different-from-mercenaries-20680

The Federal Council of Switzerland. (n.d.). *Federal Department of Foreign Affairs, Participating States of the Montreux Document*. https://www.eda.admin.ch/eda/en/home/foreign-policy/international-law/international-humanitarian-law/private-military-securi- ty-companies/participating-states.html

TNI Staff. (2017). A symposium on US-Russia relations in the age of Trump. *National Interest.* Retrieved from https://nationalinterest.org/feature/america-russia-permanent-confrontation-21891

United Nations. (n.d.). *Human Rights, Office of the High Commissioner, International Convention against the Recruitment, Use, Financing and Training of Mercenaries Adopted and opened for signature and ratification by General Assembly resolution 44/34 of 4 December 1989 Entry into force: 20 October 2001, in accordance with article 19.* Available at: https://www.ohchr.org/EN/ProfessionalInterest/ Pages/ Mercenaries.aspx

Westerlund, F., & Norberg, J. (2016). Military Means for Non-Military Measures: The Russian Approach to the Use of Armed Force as Seen in Ukraine. *Journal of Slavic Military Studies*, *29*(4), 581.

Wu, D. D. (2017). Russia-China relations reach a new high. *The Diplomat*. Retrieved from https://thediplomat.com/2017/07/russia-china-relations-reach-a-new-high/

KEY TERMS AND DEFINITION

Defense Military Enterprise: Represents activities/ventures (commercial and non-commercial) by the military and defense authorities.

Eurasian: Correspond to Russia's main geopolitical interests and aspirations to forge an ever-closer integration with those countries that it considers part of Eurasia, which is a geographical entity that combined the combined landmass of Europe and Asia.

Private Military Companies (PMCs): Denote private firms providing armed combat or security services for financial gain. Their services and expertise are usually analogous to those of governmental security, military, or police forces.

Soft Power: Refers to the capability of a country to employ co-optive influence rather than the command power to make others (countries) to do what it desires.

Chapter 14
Organizing for Innovation in the Armed Forces: A Logical Thinking Process Approach

Pedro B. Água
https://orcid.org/0000-0003-1886-9938
CINAV, Portuguese Naval Academy, Portugal

Anacleto Correia
https://orcid.org/0000-0002-7248-4310
CINAV, Portuguese Naval Academy, Portugal

ABSTRACT

Innovation is one of the main factors in driving any organization's effectiveness and sustainable competitiveness. Lack of innovation may affect organizations in several different ways, from lost opportunities for being more efficient, improve processes, and sometimes decrease of staff morale, with negative impact on development of organizational knowledge as well as values and culture. Innovation can also provide new forms of doing things, fuelling internal processes, either operational, logistical, or administrative ones. Highly innovative organizations usually make jobs more fulfilling, and ultimately contribute in making the world a better place. Therefore, driving innovation is crucial, and that needs an appropriate framework in order to promote the desirable involvement from the whole organization. By following a logical thinking process, one ends up at a pragmatic and more deployable model backed by cause and effect logics.

DOI: 10.4018/978-1-7998-6655-8.ch014

Copyright © 2021, IGI Global. Copying or distributing in print or electronic forms without written permission of IGI Global is prohibited.

INTRODUCTION

Innovation is one of the key drivers for any organization's effectiveness, improvement, competitiveness, and ultimately long-term sustainability. This applies equally to the Armed Forces, hereafter designated as the military organization, or to corporations at large.

Innovation is a broad concept which can be classified according to distinct reference frames. One can distinguish between different categories, for example product innovation and service innovation, which may have process innovation underneath. One can also distinguish according to the level of impact, for example (2) incremental innovation, the kind of innovation that is close to the concept to continuous improvement; (2) radical and disruptive innovation; or (3) recombination innovation – the kind of innovation that results from recombining existing products, services or processes into something new. The scope of this text is, however, about "organizing for innovation", which relates to organizational change that places the organization optimally to innovate. Corporations and firms have long been pursuing optimal forms of organizing for innovation. Today, military organizations almost everywhere are trying to change their organizational architectures in order to achieve such desirable paradigm, to become more innovative.

With so much at stake, senior military leaders need to place such subject on the top of their agendas to become more innovative. Military leaders across all branches face significant challenges, from constrained budgets to broaden scopes of responsibilities and operating, which demands a more proactive attitude, in a way not dissimilar from the modern corporation that competes in the marketplace (Charan, 2005, Nueno, 2016). This demands military leaders, similarly to corporate leaders, to step into subjects such as strategy development, risk management, and supporting the lower military ranks in a joint effort to improve organizational development - a subject that includes a need to rethink how to organise for innovation (Lorsch, 2012; Hill & Davis, 2017). For example, being diverse is a critical factor in fostering innovation across organizations.

Military leaders shall proactively monitor the diversity barometer score within the organizations they are responsible for. This is especially critical at upper echelons where it is important to prevent higher rank officers to surround themselves with professionals who mirror them. Such is particularly critical during times of tight budgets, when the "fixer" types of leaders may be put in charge (Tomaso, 2005). These "fixers", conversely to "growers", are typically designated to sort out performance problems in face of constrained budgets and the urgent need for corrective actions. However, fixers may be tempted to surround themselves by other "fixers", hence demotivating the raise of new ideas, initiatives and innovation across organizations

– such is especially critical in organizations which depend heavily on innovation, as would be the case of the military.

The approach taken in this text places a focus on organizing for innovation main drivers, where the whole organization is taken as a political system. Attention is drawn to four main governing areas, which will further support the development of a pragmatic and deployable model. Such model brings usefulness for academic circles and practitioners alike, therefore decreasing the gap between these two worlds. This comprehensive model follows a logical thinking process, which starts by identifying the problem – the need to increase the innovation capability of organizations – then progressing towards an effective way of architecting organizational factors that promotes innovation within the organization.

This chapter has four main parts, in addition to the introduction. section 2 presents some relevant background knowledge on the subject of organising for innovation, in order to sustain and bring sustainability to the military organization. section 2 introduces a holistic approach to organizations, by introducing the Business Policy Model (BPM) (Valero & Lucas,1991; Calleja & Melé, 2017). On the same section Miller & Wedell-Wedellsborg' innovation framework is introduced and blended with the business policy model, hence providing a holistic approach to innovation capability building within an organisation. By holistic, it is meant a systems view of organizations, and both concepts are interchangeable within the scope of this text.

The proposed methodological approach, based on Goldratt's Logical Thinking Processes (LTP) (Goldratt, 1994) is introduced within section 3. Direction is provided for practical strategy deployment, bringing into scene a strategy development approach (Mabin & Davies, 2010). Section 4 further develops the logical thinking model and introduces the resulting strategy. Section 5 provides some discussion and presents a way to make the developed innovation architecture more deployable in the field, as it is implicit that theoretical models are essential, however oftentimes they are not sufficient to make an effective change. This demands attention to deployment details and effective change management processes. Finally, some conclusions and key remarks about models, their validity and usefulness are presented.

This chapter is supported by several years of research on the intersection of three main domains – the Business Policy Model as a holistic approach to organizations, frameworks for organizing for innovation, and the Logical Thinking Process (Água & Correia, 2020a, 2020b).

ORGANIZING FOR INNOVATION

One possible definition of innovation is the creation value by doing new things or better processes (Miller & Wedell-Wedellsborg, 2013). Organizing for innovation, the subject of this text, is defined as the systemic arrangement through people which makes other people innovate by means of changing the environment they work in. Innovative organizations typically own a highly sought-after competitive edge, which is critical for the military organization in facing its many challenges, from highly technology battle fields to constraining operating budgets and the need to be more efficient.

Some authors argue that innovation is a subject that should not be left just under top management responsibility and their closer teams' attention, because, as such individuals are frequently under several types of short-term pressure, they may tend to place innovation at a lower priority level on their 'caring' lists (Deschamps & Nelson, 2014). For organizations where innovation is a critical feature, organizing for innovation should be placed high on the top management priority lists. Moreover, as top management across military organizations, get more involved and engaged with people, such senior officers may actually promote an effective innovation mindset, while getting an increasing amount of insight from their military units' capabilities when interacting with lower ranks across their organizations, regardless of being the army, the navy or the air force.

Higher rank officers have the responsibility for ensuring adequate effectiveness, performance, risk management, and growing competitive edges. As previously mentioned, military leaders' profile could be classified as one of two broad categories or stereotypes – *fixers* and *growers* – something that can dictate an organization's fate (Tomaso, 2005).

Fixer leaders are brought in to lead turnarounds among other difficult journeys on organizations. Grower type of leaders, however, are usually nominated, in order to prepare an organization to be more competitive for future challenges, and the development of such organizations' innovation capabilities is a key factor (Tomaso, 2005). In what innovation concerns, not every organization needs the same amount of effort. However, close attention is needed on both leaders´ profiles. Whenever an organizations' leader is a *fixer*, it is necessary to ensure that this leader doesn't compromise the organizations' long-term future by killing initiative and innovation. Conversely, if a given organizational leader is a *grower*, it is necessary to ensure that the organization is not taking 'too much' risk. Military assignments should optimally pay attention to such profiles when nominating military leaders for specific places.

Being aware of the need to pay close attention to the subject of organizing for innovation is a necessary condition, however not sufficient. A pragmatic approach to the subject needs a holistic approach together with a process that integrates the many organizational parts in a systemic way to reach a higher innovation maturity level.

THE BUSINESS POLICY MODEL AS A HOLISTIC APPROACH

Military organizations, as any kind of organizations, are systems. Systems can be defined as a grouping of parts that operate together for a common purpose (Forrester, 1968). Hence an adequate approach in dealing with them shall be by means of a "systems approach" as well. It is this systems approach that approaches military organizations in a holistic way, as no truly holistic approach would exist if one just focus on analyses of organizational parts.

Military leaders decide and act in a way to reach an organizational future that is desirably better than the present one, in relative terms. Organizational architecture and the creation of a desirable new organizational culture demands, first of all, to approach the whole organization, while ensuring that any potential non intended effects are minimized.

Christensen, Andrews & Bower (1978) did introduce the early roots of what may be regarded as a holistic approach to organizations - The *Business Policy* approach – which initially consisted of three main areas: (1) Corporate Strategy, (2) Executive Structure and (3) Incentive Systems.

Building on the works of Christensen, Andrews & Bower (1978), Valero & Lucas (1991), developed the *Business Policy Model*, which conceives the role of top management as making use of four main governing areas, together with the development of specific procedures that allow for detailed analysis, in order to guide decision-making and implementation of an organization's desired future. These four governing areas are: (1) The Business; (2) the Directing Structure; (3) Professional Commitment (incentive systems); and (4) the Institutional Configuration. Keeping these four dimensions distinguished is critical and useful to keep a holistic perspective (Calleja & Melé, 2017).

The Business means deciding how to carry out the particular content of the operations, tactics or activities that, when harmoniously related, allow the best possible evolution of the organization's effectiveness – which is critical across military organizations where national defence is at stake. Within the military organization's context, the business is a very specific endeavour which may refer to effectiveness or attaining specific goals, be it at land, sea or air.

Getting people to work together in alignment with the organization´s objectives is one of the main responsibilities of senior leadership. Therefore, through the creation of a *Directing Structure,* individuals at several distinct ranks are entrusted with specific parts of what needs to be done to proactively foster the organization effectively. Innovation is highly dependent on the way organizations are structured, organize and manage information; together with adequate autonomy and freedom of choice by taking into account the organization's objectives, values and culture.

Employing the *Professional Commitment,* senior military shall seek procedures which help people carry out their duties in a way that strengthens the professional commitment across the whole military organization. This means getting the people across the organization to take their duties professionally, contributing to the best of their creativity and ideas. Such criteria affect an organization's innovation culture and is impacted by that culture in turn. The military leader's main goal shall be to ensure a proper professional commitment from all people across the organization, in order for everyone to make a positive contribution to an organization-wide innovation culture.

A fourth governing area is the *Institutional Configuration*, which depends on three pillars: *Initiative, Money* (resources) and *Power* (Valero & Lucas, 1991). The Institutional Configuration is critical for organizational sustainability, as it impacts the important dimensions of *Initiative*, *Money* and *Power*, which may exhibit particular dynamics over time in order to ensure sustainability (Valero & Figueroa, 2011). Sustainability is a delicate subject whenever an organization starts a 'change strategy', as would be the case of having a military organization – Navy, Army or Air Force – engaging in an organizational transformation to achieve a more innovative culture.

Within this organizational framework *Money* dictates available resources needed to promote innovation initiatives while ensuring the ongoing armed forces operations training and equipment. The role of *Power* is critical as it may be an enabler, or sometimes a blocker to innovation initiatives, and it may indeed foster or restrain the number of organizational *Initiatives*. Driving organizational leaders' attention to these dimensions is critical to maximizing the level of innovation that flourishes across the military organization.

Because of its comprehensive approach, the Business Policy Model characterizes an organization as a system, which connects a humanistic conception of organizations with the organizations' mission as part of society- which the armed forces certainly are. Moreover, because creativity and innovative behaviours have close relationship with *intrinsic* motivation factors, this humanistic approach is critical for any organization wishing to improve their innovation culture. A summary is provided in Table 1 illustrating the potential crossings of the business policy model and the innovation subject.

AN INNOVATION MODEL

Effort has been placed on the subject of "how to make an organisation more innovative", through the blend of different frameworks and models, aiming at attaining optimal organizational architectures (Tushman & Nadler, 1986; Skarzynsky & Gibson, 2008; Miller & Wedell-Wedellsborg, 2013).

Table 1. The BPM (Business Policy Model) four areas and organizing for Innovation

Governance area	How innovation is related to the BPM four areas
The Business	The military organization's endeavour consists of providing defence services on a continuous basis, to attain the organization's mission during peacetime or wartime. It is therefore important to specify how it organizes its business, and how such is dependent on innovation across the organization. When considering the military organization, its business is strongly based on effectiveness and better ways of accomplishing it in face of the available resources.
The Directing Structure	The organization's command structure shall make explicit those responsible for executing specific duties. Hence, organizing for innovation affects the structure and at the same time gets affected by this same structure.
The Professional Commitment	One of the main duties of top rank leadership is to get people to work optimally in the pursuit of the organization's missions and objectives. Hence, adequate incentive mechanisms should be designed and put in place to ensure that the right extrinsic and intrinsic motivations are in place and aligned for achieving a more innovative military organization.
The Institutional Configuration	Initiative, Money, and Power are the three main dimensions of any organization's Institutional Configuration. They affect and get affected through the systemic interrelationships at play when promoting a new culture encompassing the whole military organization.

It is common to find a dichotomy between a model's usefulness and its comprehensiveness, which forces one to search for simpler but useful models. Sterman (2000, p. 846 & 890) argues that all models, mental or formal, are wrong in the sense that models are incomplete and partial representations of reality. Therefore, it is suggested that models cannot be fully validated in terms of their truth. Models, however, can be evaluated in what concerns their usefulness for purposes of decision-making support and policy design. This is the pursued positioning in this chapter.

Miller and Wedell-Wedellsborg (2013) presented an innovation model supported on five Critical Success Factors (CSF), when developing an innovation strategy aimed at reaching a better innovation culture, and is followed within this text. These key factors are: (1) Focus, (2) Connect, (3) Tweak, (4) Select, (5) "Stealthstorm".

These innovation critical success factors shall be all present within the military organization in order to ensure that the whole architecture holds (Figure 1). An effective innovation strategy shall specify how to attain such factors, their successive stages of development and how to overcome organizational obstacles to change in the pursuit of more innovative organizations.

In addition to the first five critical success factors, Miller & Wedell-Wedellsborg (2013), argue that 'persistence' is a necessary condition for organizations to achieve a higher innovative performance. Such is related to the fact that many reasonable and good ideas do not survive throughout implementation because they need a considerable persistence of effort during a reasonable amount of time and while facing challenges. This points to the fact that adequate incentive systems shall be designed and put in place.

Figure 1. The five pillars of an effective innovation model
Source: Authors' elaboration.

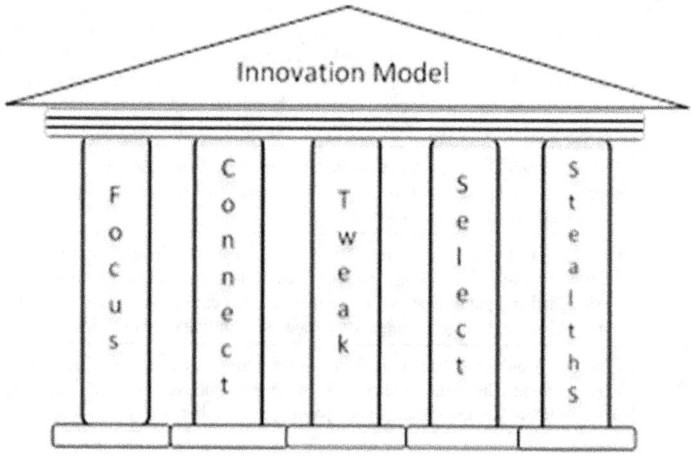

Those authors argue that even good ideas on their original form are usually poor and need further refinement; hence the need to be "tweaked" to get improved. Figure 2 suggests a potential interrelationship of such critical success factors (CSF1-6), in the way of supporting the attainment of a better innovation paradigm. For Miller and Wedell-Wedellsborg (2013; 2014) having good ideas is a starting point, a "necessary condition", however it is not a sufficiency condition. There is a need for a systemic way in governing innovation, which can only be achieved by understanding how the different critical factors interrelate among themselves, thus getting more (or less) effectiveness. Figure 2 also illustrates a potential dependency among the innovation main enabling factors.

Once established the relevance of this innovation model, and a holistic model of organizations, a process is required to support organizational leaders in developing their strategies and organizational policies aimed at transforming their organizations, military or otherwise.

A movement in the direction of a more innovative organization is a leadership process that demands some kind of "change strategy". A change strategy by its turn needs a suitable strategy development framework. The word 'development' suggests that the strategy process does not finish with the strategy formulation stage but shall continue with the deployment of the designed strategy, envisioning the "normalization of innovation" (Vilà, 2011 & 2012). Only then can the results of a better innovation organization be attained, a subject covered in the next section.

Figure 2. A Strategic Intermediate Objectives Map, relating critical factors and the goal
Source: Água & Correia, (2020a).

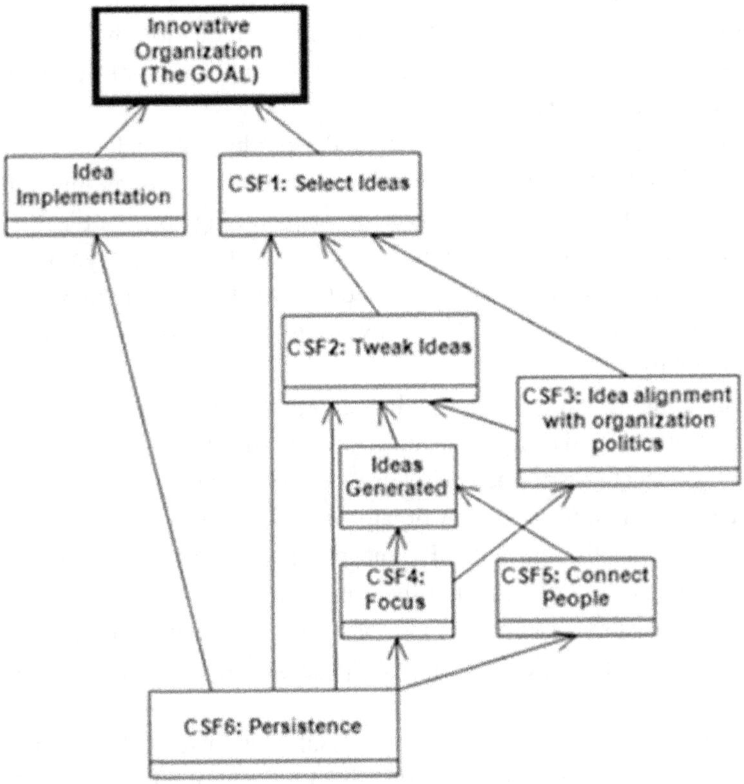

METHODOLOGICAL APPROACH

The Theory of Constraints (TOC) and the Logical Thinking Processes provide a cause-and-effect framework, which starts by a clear recognition of the strategic problem and the identification of the potential root causes in need for attention (Goldratt, 1994).

Contrasting to other approaches, perhaps statistical in nature, the chosen methodology makes use of logics. This is more critical the more complex is the problem or system to be managed, for instance, military or any other human organization. One of the most important thinking revolutions of the twentieth century suggested that we cannot completely understand the nature of a given system just by analysis, statistical or otherwise. Hence, another method is needed – synthesis.

Oftentimes, when trying to understand a system, the first thing an analyst do is trying to take its parts apart, when synthesis would advocate exactly the opposite. The followers of deductive approaches may be in disagreement at this point; however, it is worth remembering that all creativity, which is behind innovative ideas and innovation itself, come initially from forms of induction thinking. Deduction usefulness is not in question as it is important to "validate" (or refute) hypotheses, even if for a certain time horizon.

Sometimes analysts even suggest that the product of analysis is knowledge. Knowledge, however, is not always exactly the same as understanding. Oftentimes, knowledge leads to the know *how* it works, concerning some subject, process or procedure, but not necessarily know *why* it works. Giving up synthetic thinking for the merits of solely analysis has a price tag attached, as one may start missing understandability, which is especially relevant in organizational systems due to their inner complexity.

Systems thinking, which is essentially supported by cause-and-effect encompasses a blend of synthesis and analysis, leading towards an expansionism way of thinking instead of a reductionism doctrine (Forrester, 1961; Senge, 1990). For building increased understanding within any organizational system, one has to move towards larger systems, not the opposite. By means of synthesis, knowledge goes from wholes to the larger whole, and not the opposite – from wholes down to parts, as would be the case of an approach done solely from an analysis perspective. Hence, the justification to use a logical thinking process as a framework for developing understanding.

Causality implies determinism, and causality is ensured by means of logic. Aristotle´s logic first law implies that in a logical implication if the effects (consequences) are denied, one shall deny the cause. Therefore, it is a fundamental law of logic that non-determinism cannot ensure causality. The used logical approach, derived from the Logical Thinking Process, starts by questioning the nature of the problem - what is not right with the current organizational paradigm - and what shall be done in order to develop an adequate innovation model in organising for innovation.

THE LOGICAL THINKING PROCESS

Having the Business Policy Model as a background framework, one can start by questioning (1) *why change*? (reasons), then progressing by means of questioning (2) *what to change?* (3) *what to change to*? (4) and *how to cause the intended change*? For this to be done it is necessary to identify the Critical Success Factors (CSF) for reaching the organization's future innovation paradigm.

The process usually starts by characterizing the current organizational paradigm and identifying gaps and mismatches. Then create the necessary changes to allow for filling the found gaps, which will provide the basis for the design of a future reality tree – a type of cause-and-effect logical tree. Such logical tree, based on a chain of cause-and-effect, will bring clarity into the needed actions which may enable a more innovative organization, something that is ensured by the logical *sufficiency* of the associated conditional logics.

This approach finishes with two additional kinds of logical trees – *the prerequisite tree* (PRT) and the *Transition Trees* (TT); which are aimed at identifying organizational obstacles to change when implementing the developed strategy within military organizations. The Logical Thinking Process (Goldratt, 1994) offers a holistic approach by making use of the previously mentioned set of questions:

1. Why change?
2. What to change?
3. What to change to?
4. How to cause the change?

While the answer to the first question – *Why change?* – is clear by now, the remaining questions still need addressing, something which will be progressively dealt with below by following the sequence depicted in the following diagram (Figure 3).

Starting at the top left corner box forces military leaders to consider which innovation paradigm would they wish to build within their military organization. It is important to start with an aim in the future, as starting with the organization's current paradigm could produce an 'anchoring effect', that would potentially prevent more ambitious goals - an effect largely discussed in the literature on mind bias and decision making (Russo & Schoemaker, 1990; Hammond, Keeney, & Raiffa, 1998).

After this first step, military leaders should compare the envisioned future paradigm with their organization's current paradigm, to clearly identify the main gaps. After this step the process needs the creation of an adequate transformation that will end up at the design of a suitable innovation strategy, a set of specific tasks and intermediate objectives aligned with the overall goal. Next comes the planning, followed by the execution and deployment stages.

Finally, and regarding change as the normal state of affairs across many organizations, even the military ones, it is necessary to do some control on the validity of the whole new innovation architecture, by checking the effectiveness against the selected innovation's goals. This stage consists of a feedback control process which demands to start the same overall cycle all over again from the top-left corner, as per Figure 3.

Figure 3. The Constraint Management Model as a strategy development model (Mabin & Davies, 2010)

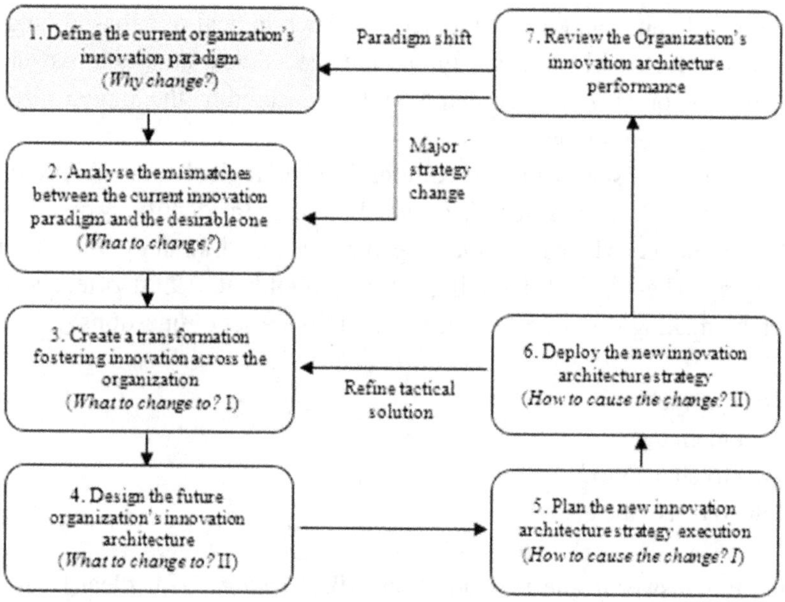

The strategy to attain the overall innovation architecture is developed through steps 1 to 5 and presented in the following section. Steps 6 and 7 are specific to any given military organization, or branch, and shall include specific implementation details that understandably fall off the scope of a general framework as this one.

RESULTING STRATEGY

The results from the described approach are obtained through the execution of the correct sequence of logical trees. Starting by the development of a Current Reality Tree (CRT), and by analysing the gaps between the organization´s current situation and the desirable one, one progresses towards the design of a Future Reality Tree (FRT), which by filling the founds gaps, will traduce itself into removing the "system's constraints", a central idea to the Theory of Constraints (Goldratt, 1994).

Having the background assumptions and dependencies from Figure 2 in mind, and taking a systems view of the organization by means of the Business Policy Model, the Logical Thinking Process approach next stage involves the drawing of a CRT, a current reality tree, whose objective is to identify and clarify what may be wrong within the current paradigm in what concerns organizational innovation capabilities (Figure 4). This tree develops from bottom up and there are some needed explanations to make it clearer. For instance, the statements UnDesirable Effects (UDE) in it, represent unwanted effects, which were triggered by the precedent chains of cause-and-effect logic. Also visible in the tree is the existence of "Root Causes" which will be explained in later stages of this process.

Figure 4. Current Reality Tree illustrating the organization perceived "current" situation regarding its innovation capabilities
Source: Authors' elaboration.

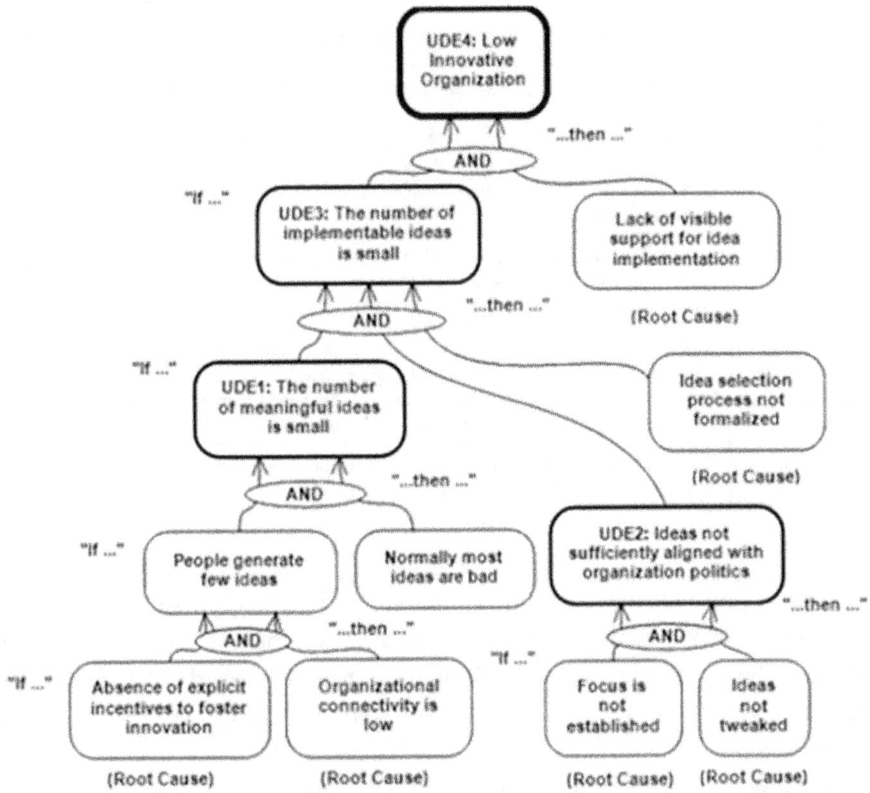

Focusing on the Current Reality Tree, the identified undesirable effects shall be eliminated on a one-by-one basis, by focusing on the identified root causes ("*What to change*?"), and by means of using the concept of "Evaporated Clouds"– a process of problem solving (Goldratt, 1994).

Next, one progresses towards "*What to change to*?" taking into account each of the four business policy areas in order to eliminate the identified undesirable effects. Such procedure will end at a future reality tree that describes how a more innovative organization would be achieved. To build this stage, there is a need to adequately address the identified root causes of problems as well as the respective underlying assumptions about how the whole organization functions, something which poses some relevant questions (Table 2).

Table 2. The BPM conceptual framework as a supporting tool in organizing for innovation

Governance area	Questions concerning governing areas vs. innovation	Action
The Business	Which necessary conditions shall be architected for a more innovative organization? How to increase the number of ideas across the organization? How to improve the quality of such ideas? How does one ensure alignment between ideas generated and organization's missions and strategy?	INJ 4 INJ 5 INJ 6
The Directing Structure	How will the military structure explicit those responsible for carrying out the specific tasks of fostering innovation and making it a normal organizational capability?	INJ 1 INJ 6
The Professional Commitment	How will people across the military organization be motivated, in order to generate and contribute with more innovative ideas? How do people become increasingly aware of the need for an innovation paradigm change across the whole organization?	INJ 2 INJ 3
The Institutional Configuration	How to institutionalise the new innovation model, establishing it as a perpetual organizational policy and cultural feature?	INJ 1

Figure 5 presents the developed Future Reality Tree, with several visible "injections" (INJ#), whose objective is to remove the system´s (undesirable) constraints, therefore changing the whole innovation model towards a better innovation paradigm, and closing the gap to its elected *Goal*. This is a logical tree that reads from top down to bottom.

It is visible a bowtie symbol ("MAG") which symbolizes a 'conjunction AND'. This characterizes a logical function where the effect is potentially magnified by the joint actions resulting from the related causes. A feedback loop is also visible on the right side of figure 5, which implies a reinforcing effect may actually support the goal.

Figure 5. Future Reality Tree. The rectangles represent INJection points, and the dotted lines represent a reinforcing feedback branch
Source: Água & Correia, (2020a).

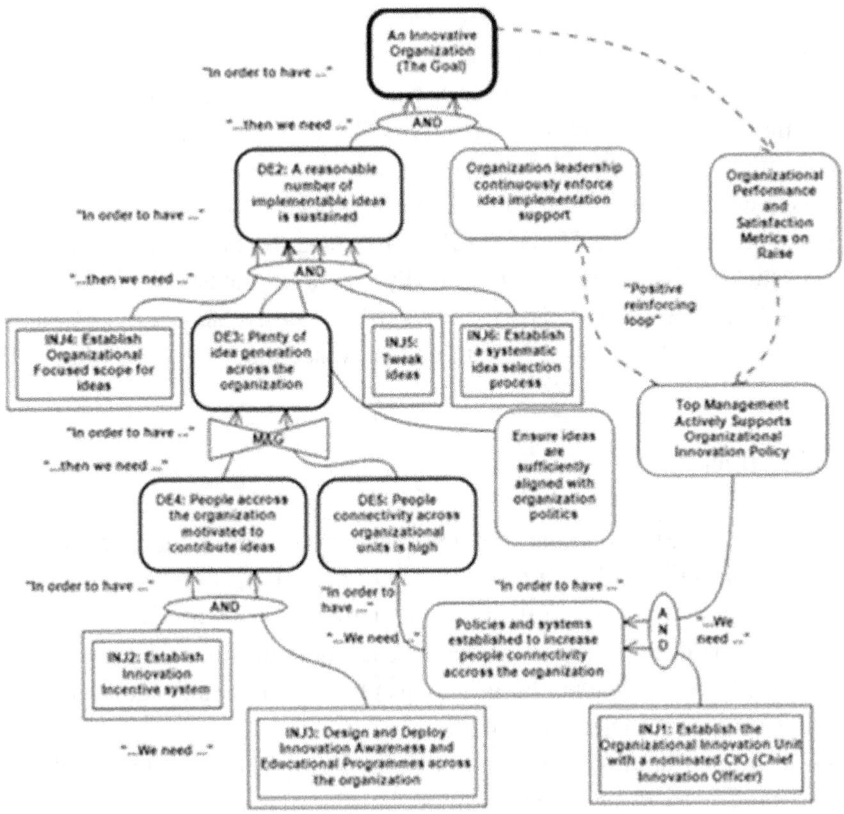

The FRT conveys a narrative where the actions taken – i.e., the "injections" (INJ#) - are enabling conditions which will drive the organization as a whole towards the intended goal of becoming more innovative. The identified actions are:

INJ1 – Establishment of an *Organizational Innovation Unit* headed by a selected Chief Innovation Officer (CIO), supported by an adequate team.

INJ2 – Establishment of an *Innovation Incentive System*, in order for people across the organization to be conscious of the potential benefits they may get by developing a proactive innovation mindset. This appeals to people's *extrinsic* motivation.

INJ3 - Design and deploy an *Innovation Awareness and Educational Programme* across the organization, to get people more integrated with the whole organization change process. This appeals to people's *intrinsic* motivations. Through awareness of the whole concept of innovation, people will be contributing to bring more ideas and innovation initiatives.

INJ4 - *Establish focus*, in order for people not only generate ideas, but ideas that are aligned and support the organization's strategy.

INJ5 – *Check and tweak ideas at early stages*, in a systematic way, so the number of valid and meaningful ideas is maximized.

INJ6 – Establishment of a systematic *idea selection system*, in order to ensure the organization filters or discards weaker or bad ideas sooner rather than later, hence minimizing waste of resources on such ideas. This is a critical and delicate stage as people might potentially become unmotivated by watching several of their ideas being discarded and might stop contributing new ones.

By making the Desired Effects (DE1 – 5) visible, the FRT provides an answer to the question (*What to change to?*). Finally, the fourth question – *How to cause the change*? – is then addressed by the *Prerequisite and Transition Trees* (Mabin & Davies, 2010), which is dealt with within the next section.

DISCUSSION

Several authors have been calling attention to the importance of not underestimating the natural resistance to change that occur in organizations as a crucial constraint (Kotter, 1996; Sull, Homkes, Sull, 2015). Actually, this is potentially an even more serious issue for military organizations as such organizations, regardless of the specific armed forces branches, have "strong cultures", rules and regulations which potentially may resist to new initiatives.

This section illustrates how progress is done throughout the logical thinking process approach. By using the cause-and-effect logical relationships and by clearly identifying *What to change?* and *What to change to?* one ends up at a set of necessary conditions. Such necessary conditions may not be enough solely on its own, however, to ensure sufficiency in reaching the desired innovation paradigm. In order to add value and be useful, it needs to further answer the question of *how to cause the change*? which in practice is part of the whole change management process.

In order to attain the desired innovation performance metrics *Pre-requisite trees* are used. Such logical trees ensure that the deployed strategy will drive the desired organizational transformation into the direction of a more innovative performance level by overcoming obstacles. Prerequisite trees are built with the objective in mind of ensuring that the 'strategic injections' (INJ) are implemented in practice in the smoothest fashion, and any potential obstacles to such deployment across the organization are removed. Six injections were identified within the context of the developed model, as illustrated in Figure 6. The hexagons shown in the figure signal potential obstacles that must be dealt with in order to successfully implement the intended changes.

Figure 6. The Prerequisite Trees shows how to overcome obstacles during the deployment stage
Source: Água & Correia, (2020a).

Additionally, in order to deploy the designed innovation strategy, the TOC Thinking Processes include a sixth kind of tree – the Transition Tree (TT) – which bridges into the world of project management, providing activity networks, and allowing for scheduling and planning in order to achieve a more efficient and effective implementation – a terrain familiar to the military.

Departing from the previous trees in order to design an activity map, the transition tree will have, as milestones, the injections illustrated in the previous prerequisite trees, which are achieved according to the most suitable sequence in order to support the whole organizing for innovation strategy – *the Goal* (Figure 7).

Figure 7. Transition Tree, where the bar sizes illustrate activities' duration
Source: Água & Correia, (2020b).

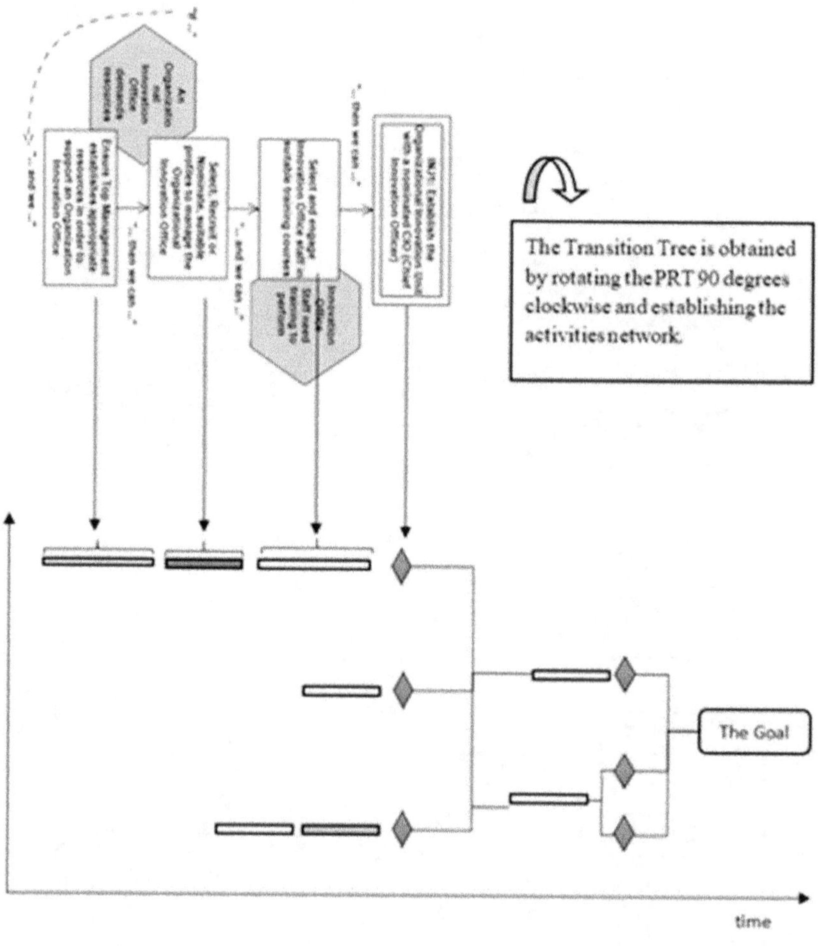

As an additional step, and drawing from the military culture, the developed solution for the strategic problem here discussed would benefit from checking all designed measures against the usual DOTMLPFI framework. The DOTMLPFI framework is a widely used model within military organisations in many countries, where any intended planning, strategy, tactics or actions are checked against several organizational variables: Doctrine, Organization, Training, Materiel, Leadership, Personnel, Facilities, and Interoperability. In this way it helps in bringing further awareness and clarification regarding any potential constraints (Lofgren, 2016). This checking is a guarantor of a more robust strategy, which may be refined as needed, hence maximizing the odds of successful implementation during the deployment stage.

CONCLUSION

This chapter calls attention for the need to organise for innovation within the armed forces as a source of effectiveness, performance and competitiveness. It urges senior military leaders to place innovation high on their agendas, and the urgency for proactively architecting a better innovation culture, in order to contribute to organizational effectiveness and sustainability. At the end, as shown from several historical episodes that occurred during wars, it may be an organization's creativity and innovation capabilities that may define its own fate during such challenging times. Oftentimes, and within the context of armed conflicts, it may usually dictate the success or failure, victory or defeat.

Organizing for innovation is an imperative and change is of critical importance. Before military leaders become able to promote a more innovative mindset within the organizations that they are responsible for, it is imperative to consider the concept of innovation models. Innovation could be classified as incremental, disruptive, or recombination. This text is in itself a sort of recombination innovation, as it blends knowledge belonging to several different models: organizing for innovation, taking an approach to the organization as a political system through the business policy model, and utilizing the logical thinking methodology. There is growing understanding, from the field of decision-making, that the simultaneous use of multiple models contributes to increase optimal decisions (Page, 2018). Hence, the overall approach followed within this chapter made use of several models in developing the overall strategy herein discussed. The presented approach interconnects three frameworks into a single one by making use of a systems approach and logics, supporting a change process aimed at building an organizational innovation model, which can further be managed, not only within the context of armed forces but with the due adaptations, to organizations at large.

A front-end approach is provided, on the subject of how to better organise for innovation, by means of an adequate innovation model that makes use of several key concepts, and which may be improved with further details specific to any particular organizational system – whole military organizations or parts of it – to accommodate specific realities, values and cultures and help support a raise on the level of organizational innovation capability – an urgent topic to be made normal in senior leaders' agendas. Among the main contributions a deployable model has been presented, which helps bridging between the academic and practitioners' worlds. Sometimes the search for the perfect solution is inefficient, and leaders, managers and field practitioners need practical solutions, something that quite often demands trading-off detail for practicality. In the same sense that architecture benefits from being developed in coordination with engineering, so does an innovation governance model may benefit if developed jointly or in complement with other approaches to strategy development.

There are several tangible actions or *take-aways* from this chapter which, *ceteris paribus*, shall improve military organizations performance in what innovation capabilities concerns, especially if taken in the most adequate sequence. Such actions are listed in the text as injections (INJ1-5), and should ensure the organization will evolve on an innovation maturity ladder, starting from its current paradigm, and progressing towards a progressively better innovation capability where culture and people's mindset change to a more innovative one – a paradigm were people are not afraid of contributing with more innovative ideas.

This model is useful enough in providing strategic guidance, by identifying several key areas where to focus attention, as well as the following suggested measures. As a first stage it suggests the need to design and deliver innovation short programmes across the several organizational units and echelons in order to create a proper level of awareness on the importance, possibilities and mechanisms of organizational innovation. Second, to progress from an organizational innovation awareness stage towards a higher maturity level, a tailor-made '*in-company*' programme may provide a considerable thrust toward the organizational innovation maturity goal. Fourth, with such organizational architecture for innovation in place, several programmes can be launched, as would be the case of an "idea (digital) platform" and "innovation selection and steering committees". Fifth, an innovation incentive system can be put in place in order to make innovation systematic. As motivation is always a factor in shaping people's mindset, such incentive system can be associated with the creation of "Innovation awards" and making innovation a key appraisal criterion for promotion advancement within the ranks.

REFERENCES

Água, P. B., & Correia, A. (2020a). Innovation governance in practice: A business policy approach. *Corporate Board: Role, Duties and Composition*, *16*(2), 54–64. doi:10.22495/cbv16i2art5

Água, P. B., & Correia, A. (2020b). Enabling factors in innovation governance: A business policy approach. In A. Kostyuk, M. J. C. Guedes, & D. Govorun (Eds.), *Corporate Governance: Examining Key Challenges and Perspectives* (pp. 194–201). Virtus Interpress.

Calleja, R., & Melé, D. (2017). Valero's "Enterprise Politics": A model of humanistic management and corporate governance. *Journal of Management Development*, *36*(5), 644–659. doi:10.1108/JMD-12-2015-0187

Charan, R. (2005). Boards that Deliver: Advancing Corporate Governance from Compliance to Competitive Advantage. Jossey-Bass Ed.

Christensen, C. R., Andrews, K. R., & Bower, J. L. (1978). Business Policy: Text and Cases (4th ed.). Irwin Ed.

Dechamps, J., & Nelson, B. (2014). *Innovation Governance*. John Wiley & Sons Ltd.

Forrester, J. W. (1961). *Industrial Dynamics*. Pegasus communications.

Forrester, J. W. (1968). *Principles of Systems*. Pegasus communications.

Goldratt, E. (1994). *It's Not Luck*. Gower Publishing Limited.

Hammond, J. S., Keeney, R. L., & Raiffa, H. (1998). The Hidden Traps in Decision Making. *Harvard Business Review*, (Sep–Oct), 1998. PMID:10185432

Hill, L., & Davis, G. (2017). The Board's New Innovation Imperative. *Harvard Business Review*, (Nov-Dec), 2017.

Kotter, J. P. (1996). *Leading Change*. Harvard Business School Press.

Lofgren. (2016). *NATO Capability Development Interoperability. The Three Swords Magazine*. https://www.jwc.nato.int/images/stories/_news_items_/2016/LT_GEN_Lofgren_interview.pdf

Lorsch, J. W. (2012). *The Future of Boards*. Harvard Business Review Press.

Mabin, V. J., & Davies, J. (2010). The TOC Thinking Processes. In The Theory of Constraints Handbook. McGraw-Hill.

Miller, P., Wedell-Wedellsborg, T. (2013). Clearing the Path to Innovation. *IESE Insight*, (16).

Miller, P., Wedell-Wedellsborg, T. (2014, Nov.). Get More Actionable Ideas from Your Employees. *Harvard Business Review*.

Nueno, P. (2016). *10 Trends for the Board of 2020*. IESE Publishing.

Page, S. E. (2018, Nov.). Why "Many-Model Thinkers" Make Better Decisions. *Harvard Business Review*.

Russo, J. E., & Schoemaker, P. J. H. (1990). Decision Traps. The Ten barriers To Brilliant Decision-Making and how to Overcome Them. New York: Fireside Ed.

Senge, P. (1990). *The fifth discipline*. Doubleday.

Skarzynsky, P., & Gibson, R. (2008). *Innovation to the Core: A Blueprint for Transforming the Way Your Company Innovates*. Harvard Business Review Press.

Sterman, J. (2000). *Business dynamics: Systems thinking and modeling for a complex world*. Irwin McGraw-Hill.

Sull, D., Homkes, R., & Sull, C. (2015, Mar.). Why Strategy Execution Unravels—and What to Do About It. *Harvard Business Review*.

Tomaso, R. M. (2005). *Bigger Isn't Always Better: The New Mindset for Real Business Growth?* AMACOM.

Tushman, M., & Nadler, D. (1986). Organizing for Innovation. *California Management Review*, *28*(3), 74–92. doi:10.2307/41165203

Valero, A., & Figueroa, E. T. (2011). La empresa de negócios y la alta dirección: Procedimientos politicos de gobierno (3rd ed.). Pamplona, Spain: Eunsa.

Valero, A., & Lucas, J. L. (1991). *Política de empresa: El gobierno de la empresa de negocios*. Pamplona, Spain: Eunsa.

Vilà, J. (2011). Innovative Culture: Values, Principles and Practices of Senior Executives in Highly Innovative Companies. Teaching Note SMN-681-E. IESE Publishing.

Vilà, J. (2012). Normalize Innovation to Transform Your Firm. *IESE Insight*, (14).

ADDITIONAL READING

Christensen, C. M., & Raynor, M. E. (2003). *The Innovator's Solution: Creating and sustaining successful growth*. Harvard Business School Press.

Dechamps, J., & Nelson, B. (2014). Innovation Leaders: How Senior Executives Stimulate, Steer and Sustain Innovation. West Sussex, UK: Jossey-Bass Ed.

Kotter, J. P. (2012). *Leading Change*. Harvard Business School Press.

Miller, P., & Wedell-Wedellsborg, T. (2013). *Innovation as Usual: How to help your people bring great ideas to life*. Harvard Business School Press.

Ries, E. (2011). The Lean Startup: How Today's Entrepreneurs Use Continuous Innovation to Create Radically Successful Businesses. New York: Currency Eds.

Skarzynski, P., & Gibson, R. (2008). *Innovation to the Core: A Blueprint for Transforming the Way Your Company Innovates*. Harvard Business Review Press.

Soliman, F. (2014). *Learning Models for Innovation in Organizations: Examining Roles of Knowledge Transfer and Human Resources Management.* IGI Global., doi:10.4018/978-1-4666-4884-5

Utterback, J. (1996). *Mastering the Dynamics of Innovation.* Harvard Business School Press.

KEY TERMS AND DEFINITIONS

Constraints: Any obstacle that prevents a system to achieve its intended goals.

Goal: The result or achievement toward which effort is directed.

Holistic Approach: The belief that the parts of something are intimately interconnected and explicable only by reference to the whole.

Innovation: The creation, development and implementation of a new product, process or service, improving efficiency, effectiveness or competitive advantage.

Logic: A form of correct reasoning, especially regarding making inferences.

Policy: A policy is a deliberate system of principles to guide decisions and achieve rational outcomes.

Problem Solving: The act of defining a problem; determining the cause of the problem; identifying, prioritizing, and selecting alternatives for a solution; and implementing a solution.

Structure: The arrangement of and relations between the parts or elements of something complex.

System: A grouping of parts that operate together for a common purpose.

Compilation of References

Abdulkareem, A. (2016). *Evaluation and Mitigation of Technical Losses on Power Lines: A Case Study of Nigeria 330-Kv NetworK*. Covenant University.

Abrams, E. (2017). The trump national security strategy. *Council on Foreign Relations*. Retrieved from https://www.cfr.org/blog/trump-national-security-strategy

Abreu, M., & Grinevich, V. (2013). The nature of academic entrepreneurship in the UK: Widening the focus on entrepreneurial activities. *Research Policy*, *42*(2), 408–422. doi:10.1016/j.respol.2012.10.005

AbubakarU. (2016). Career management of officers in the Nigerian Army (1970-2014). https://ssrn.com/abstract=2722249 orhttp://dx.doi.org/10.2139/ssrn.2722249 doi:10.2139srn.2722249

Academy. (2019). *Whole-life Costing of Asset: Compact Course on Principles of Asset Management*. London: Asset Management Academy.

Achumba, I. C., Ighomereho, O. S., & Akpor-Robaro, M. O. M. (2013). Security Challenges in Nigeria and the Implications for Business Activities and Sustainable Development. *Journal of Economics and Sustainable Development*, *4*(2), 79–99.

Adams, G. A., & Beehr, T. A. (Eds.), *Retirement: Reasons, processes, and results*. Springer.

Adamsky, D. (2010). The culture of military innovation: The impact of cultural factors on the Revolution in Military Affairs in Russia, the US, and Israel. Stanford University Press.

Adamsky, D., & Bjerga, K. I. (Eds.). (2012). *Contemporary military innovation: Between anticipation and adaption*. Routledge. doi:10.4324/9780203112540

Adebisi, J. F. & Gbegi, D. O. (2013). Effects of multiple taxations on the performance of small and medium scale business enterprises (A study of west Africa Ceramics Ajeokuta, Kogi State). *Mediterranean Journal of Social Sciences*, *4*(6), 324-334. doi:.2013.v4n6p323 doi:10.5901/mjss

Adekanye, J'B. (1999). *The retired military emergent power factor in Nigeria*. Ibadan: Heinemann Educational Book.

Adekanye, J'B. (1999). *The Retired Military Emergent Power Factor in Nigeria*. Ibadan: Heinemann Educational Book.

Adrienne, J., Heinz, A. J., Freeman, M. A., Harpaz-Rotem, I., & Pietrzak, R. H. (2017). American military veterans are nearly twice as likely to be self-employed compared to non-veterans, and are majority owners in nine percent of all businesses nationwide. *Military Psychology, 29*(6), 513–523. PMID:29290645

Afonja, A. A. (1999). *Entrepreneurship Education and enterprise culture lessons from other countries*. Paper presented at the National conference in Entrepreneurship Education in Nigeria Tertiary Institutions, Abuja, Nigeria.

Agnew, J. (2003). *Geopolitics: Re-visioning world politics*. Routledge. Retrieved from https://books.google.com.tw/books?id=G8PKbsgXLNoC&printsec=frontcover&dq=geopolitics&hl=zh-TW&sa=X&ved=0ahUKEwijppW_7tnYAhXIWbwKHaXVD5sQ6AEINDAC#v=onepage&q=geopolitics&f=false

Água, P. B., & Correia, A. (2020a). Innovation governance in practice: A business policy approach. *Corporate Board: Role, Duties and Composition, 16*(2), 54–64. doi:10.22495/cbv16i2art5

Água, P. B., & Correia, A. (2020b). Enabling factors in innovation governance: A business policy approach. In A. Kostyuk, M. J. C. Guedes, & D. Govorun (Eds.), *Corporate Governance: Examining Key Challenges and Perspectives* (pp. 194–201). Virtus Interpress.

Agwu, M. O., & Emeti, C. I. (2014). Issues, challenges, and prospects of small and medium scale enterprises (SMEs) in Port Harcourt city, Nigeria. *European Journal of Sustainable Development, 3*(1), 101–114. doi:10.14207/ejsd.2014.v3n1p101

Ahlberg & Andersson. (2012). *How do banks manage the credit assessment to small businesses and what is the effect of Basel III? An n implementation of smaller and larger banks in Sweden* (Unpusblished Masters thesis). Jönköping International Business School.

Ahmad, N., & Seymour, R. G. (2008). *Defining Entrepreneurial Activity: Definitions Supporting Frameworks for Data Collection*. OECD Statistics Working Paper. doi:10.2139srn.1090372

Ahmed, P. K., & Shepherd, C. (2010). *Innovation management: Context, strategies, systems, and processes* (1st ed.). Pearson Prentice Hall.

Aikhuomogbe, S. O. (2016). *Preparing employees for entrepreneurship in retirement: A case study* (Doctoral Dissertation submitted to Walden University). Retrieved on 18 May, 2020 from https://scholarworks.waldenu.edu/cgi/viewcontent.cgi?article=4017&context=dissertations

Ajibade, A. (2017). *Nigeria Imports 70M Generators*. The Nation. Asset Management.

Ajzen, I. (1991). The theory of planned behavior. *Organizational Behavior and Human Decision Processes, 50*(2), 179–211. doi:10.1016/0749-5978(91)90020-T

Akinade, E. A. (2006). You, yes you too need counselling. An inaugural lecture delivered at the Lagos State University, Nigeria. Lagos State University Press.

Akinade, E. A. (2016). *Contemporary entrepreneurship and career development: A basic text for colleges, polytechnics and Universities*. Brightways Publishers.

Akinboye, J. O. (2003). Expanding professional and scientific issues in Counselling psychology. *Proceedings for the 26th annual conference of the Counselling Association of Nigeria (CASSON).*

Akinnawo, T. (2013). *Framework and guidelines for entrepreneurship development as a sustainable employment generation strategy in Nigeria*. African Consulting Professionals Ltd.

Akinola, A. O., & Iordoo, D. A. (2013). The effect of Nigerian capital market on the micro, small and medium scale enterprises (MSMEs) in Nigeria. *Journal of Finance and Accounting*, *4*(7), 1–14.

Akintoye, S. A. (2011). The Economic Foundations of Ibadan in the Nineteenth Century. In Topics on Nigerian Economic and Social History. Ife: University of Ife Press Ltd.

Alarabe, A. (2008). On the road to institutionalising entrepreneurship education in Nigerian universities. *International Journal of Management Education, 7*(2), 23-45.

Alarape, A. A. (2014). Entrepreneurial orientation and the growth performance of small and medium enterprises in Southwestern Nigeria. *Journal of Small Business and Entrepreneurship, 26*(6), 553–577. doi:10.1080/08276331.2014.892308

Aliyu, S. M. (2013). An Assessment Of Women Entrepreneurship Performance In Nigeria. *Malaysian Management Journal, 17*, 1–12.

Allison, G. (2015). The Thucydides trap: Are the US and China headed for war? *The Atlantic*. Retrieved from https://www.theatlantic.com/international/archive/2015/09/united-states-china-war-thucydides-trap/406756/

Allison, G. (2017). America and Russia: Back to basics. *National interest.* Retrieved from https://nationalinterest.org/feature/america-russia-back-basics-21901

Anderson, A. R. (1998). Cultivating the Garden of Eden: Environmental entrepreneuring. *Journal of Organizational Change Management, 11*(2), 135–144.

Ango, Y. I. (2017). Entrepreneurship as an option for Nigerian retiring soldiers: A global review and lessons. In A. M. Ashafa & H. Jibrin (Eds.), *The Nigerian army in a democracy since 1999: A professional demonstration of military subordination to civil authority: Essays in honour of Lt. Gen. T.Y. Burutai* (pp. 615–625). Pyla-Mak Services Ltd.

Angrist, J. D. (1998). Estimating the labor market impact of voluntary military service using social security data on military applicants. *Econometrica, 66*(2), 249–288. doi:10.2307/2998558

Angrist, J. D., & Johnson, J. H. IV. (2000). Effects of work-related absences on families: Evidence from the Gulf War. *Industrial & Labor Relations Review, 54*(1), 41–58. doi:10.1177/001979390005400103

Anyadike, N., Emeh, I., & Ukah, F. O. (2012). Entrepreneurship development and employment generation in Nigeria: Problems and prospects. *Journal of Education and General Studies, 1*(4).

Arkin, W., & Dobrofsky, L. R. (1978). Military socialization and masculinity. *The Journal of Social Issues, 34*(1), 151–168. doi:10.1111/j.1540-4560.1978.tb02546.x

Arthur, M. B., Lawrence, B. S., & Hall, D. T. (1989). *Handbook of career theory*. Cambridge University Press. doi:10.1017/CBO9780511625459

ASELSAN. (2020). https://www.aselsan.com.tr/tr/inovasyon

Ashford, J. B., & Lecroy, C. W. (2010). *Human behavior in the social environment: A multidimensional perspective* (4th ed.). Wadsworth, Cengage Learning.

Ashforth, B. E., Kreiner, G. E., & Fugate, M. (2000). All in a day's work: Boundaries and micro role transitions. *Academy of Management Review*, *25*(3), 472–491. doi:10.5465/amr.2000.3363315

Ashworth, L. M. (2011). Realism and the spirit of 1919: Halford Mackinder, geopolitics and the reality of the League of Nations. *European Journal of International Relations*, *17*(2), 208–286.

Atchley, R. C. (1989). A continuity theory of normal aging. *The Gerontologist*, *29*(2), 183–190. doi:10.1093/geront/29.2.183 PMID:2519525

Auplat, C. (2006). *Do NGOs influence entrepreneurship?* Society and Business Review. doi:10.1108/17465680610706337

AuplatC. A. (2006). Do NGOs influence Entrepreneurship?: Insights from the developments of Biotechnologies and Nanotechnologies. *Society and Business Review*. https://www.researchgate.net/publication/228263059 doi:10.2139srn.1263584

AutoSmart. (2014). *Learn the Facts: Horsepower's Effect on Fuel Consumption*. Natural Resources Canada.

Avant, D. D. (2005). *The Market for Force: The Consequences of Privatizing Security*. Cambridge University Press. doi:10.1017/CBO9780511490866

Avlon, J. (2017). *The Military Industrial Complex is Real and it's Bigger than Ever*. Available at: https://www.thedailybeast.com/the-military-industrial-complex-is-real-and-its-bigger-than-ever

Avrahami, Y., & Lerner, M. (2003). The effect of combat service and military rank on entrepreneurial careers: The case of Israeli MBA graduates. *Journal of Political and Military Sociology*, *31*(1), 97–118.

Awoyemi, A. E. (2019). Vocational Counselling. In E. O. Egbochuku & I. C. S. Ifelunni (Eds.), *Counselling and human development in Nigeria*. Ambik Press.

Azim, M. T. (2013). Entrepreneurship training in Bangladesh: A case study on small and cottage industries training institute. *Life Science Journal*, *10*(12s), 188–201.

Azim, M. T., & Al-Kahtani, A. H. (2014). Entrepreneurship education and training: A survey of literature. *Life Science Journal*, *11*(1), 127–133.

Babangida, I. (2005). Quotes of a General: Selected Quotes of Major General Ibrahim Babangida. Lagos: Terry Publishers.

Babatunde, O. M., Adedoja, O. S., Babatunde, D. E., & Denwigwe, I. H. (2019). Off-grid hybrid renewable energy system for rural healthcare centers: A case study in Nigeria. *Energy Science & Engineering*, *7*(3), 676–693. doi:10.1002/ese3.314

Baechtold, M. (2011). Women warriors: Supporting female student veterans. *ASHE Higher Education Report*, *37*(3), 69–80. doi:10.1002/aehe.3703

Bah, E., & Fang, L. (2015). Impact of the business environment on output and productivity in Africa. *Journal of Development Economics*, *114*(C), 159–171. doi:10.1016/j.jdeveco.2015.01.001

Baliamoune-Lutz, M. (2007). *Entrepreneurship, reforms and development: Empirical evidence* (Working paper no. 38/2007). ICER.

Bandura, A. (1977). Self-efficacy: Towards a unifying theory of behavioural change. *Psychological Review*, *84*(2), 191–215. doi:10.1037/0033-295X.84.2.191 PMID:847061

Bankole, P. (2011). *The Entrepreneurship Challenge in Nigeria*. Retrieved August 27, 2011 from https://knowledge.wharton.upenn.edu/article.cfm?articleid=1675

Barba-Sanchez, V., & Atienza-Sahuquillo, C. (2012). Entrepreneurial behavior: Impact of motivation factors on the decision to create a new venture. *Investigaciones Europeas de Dirección y Economía de la Empresa*, *18*(2), 132–138. doi:10.1016/S1135-2523(12)70003-5

Barbosa, L. M., Monteiro, B., & Murta, S. G. (2016). Retirement adjustment predictors – a systematic review. *Work, Aging and Retirement*, *2*(2), 1–19. doi:10.1093/workar/waw008

Barnes-Farrell, J. L. (2003). Beyond health and wealth: attitudinal and other influences on retirement decision-making. In G. Adams & T. Beehr (Eds.), *Retirement: Reasons, processes, and results* (pp. 159–187). Springer.

Baron, R. and Shane, S. (2008). *Entrepreneurship: a process perspective*. Thomson/South-Western.

Baruch, Y., & Quick, J. C. (2009). Setting sail in a new direction: Career transitions of US Navy admirals to the civilian sector. *Personnel Review*, *38*(3), 270–285. doi:10.1108/00483480910943331

Bash, B. L. (1999). Leadership and Parochialism: An Enduring Reality. *Joint Force Quarterly*, *22*, 64.

Baucus, D. A., Baucus, M. S., & Human, S. E. (1996). Consensus in franchise organizations: A cooperative arrangement among entrepreneurs. *Journal of Business Venturing*, *11*(5), 359–378. doi:10.1016/0883-9026(96)00055-9

Baumol, W. J. (1990). Entrepreneurship: Productive, unproductive and destructive. *Journal of Political Economy*, *98*(5), 893–921.

Bawuah, K., Buame, S., & Hinson, R. (2006). Reflections on Entrepreneurship Education in African Tertiary Institutions. *Acts Commercial*, 1-8.

Beach, L. R., & Frederickson, J. R. (1989). Image theory: An alternative description of audit decision. *Accounting, Organizations and Society*, *14*(1-2), 101–112. doi:10.1016/0361-3682(89)90036-6

Becker, K., Fleming, J., & Keijsers, W. (2012). E-learning: Ageing workforce versus technology-savvy generation. *Education + Training, 54*(5), 385–400. doi:10.1108/00400911211244687

Beehr, T. A. (1986). The process of retirement: A review and recommendations for future investigation. *Personnel Psychology, 39*(1), 31–55. doi:10.1111/j.1744-6570.1986.tb00573.x

Bell, J. (2005). *Doing your Research Project: A guide for first-time researchers in Education, Health and Social Science* (4th ed.). McGraw.

Berchard, J. P., & Toulouse, J. M. (1998). Validation of a Didactic model for the analysis of training objectives in entrepreneurship. *Journal of Business Venturing, 13*(4), 317–332. doi:10.1016/S0883-9026(98)80006-2

Bergman, B., Burdett, H., & Greenberg, N. (2014). Service life and beyond—Institution or culture? *RUSI Journal, 159*(5), 60–68. doi:10.1080/03071847.2014.969946

Bertrand, M., & Schoar, A. (2003). Managing with style: The effect of managers on firm policies. *The Quarterly Journal of Economics, 118*(4), 1169–1208. doi:10.1162/003355303322552775

Bhattacharyya, S. (2006). Entrepreneurship and Innovation: How Leadership Style Makes the Difference? *Vikalpa, 31*(1), 107–115.

Bjørnskov, C., & Foss, N. J. (2020). Well-being and entrepreneurship: Using establishment size to identify treatment effects and transmission mechanisms. *PLoS One, 15*(1), e0226008. doi:10.1371/journal.pone.0226008 PMID:31940306

Black, S. E., & Strahan, P. E. (2002). Entrepreneurship and bank credit availability. *The Journal of Finance, 57*(6), 2807–2833. doi:10.1111/1540-6261.00513

Blass, F. R., & Ketchen, D. J. Jr. (2014). So, you want to be an entrepreneur? Lessons from the entrepreneurship bootcamp for veterans with disabilities. *Business Horizons, 57*(1), 5–9. doi:10.1016/j.bushor.2013.09.006

Bloom, N., Nahajan, A., Mckenzie, D., & Roberts, J. (2010). Why do firms in developing countries have low productivity. *The American Economic Review, 2*(2), 619–623. doi:10.1257/aer.100.2.619

Boldon, N. Y., Maury, R. V., Armstrong, N. A., & Van Slyke, R. (2016). *The State of Veteran Entrepreneurship Research: What We Know and Next Steps (Veteran Entrepreneurship Research, Paper No. 1)*. Institute for Veterans and Military Families, Syracuse University.

Borshchevskaya, A. (2019). *Russian Private Military Companies: Continuity and Evolution of the Model*. Retrieved from: https://www.washingtoninstitute.org/uploads/Documents/opeds/Borshchevskaya20191219-FPRI.pdf

Bozorgmehr, N. (2017). *Iran cracks down on Revolutionary Guards business network*. Available at: https://www.ft.com/content/43de1388-9857-11e7-a652-cde3f882dd7b

Bradburn, N. M. (1969). *The structure of psychological well-being*. Aldine.

Bressler, M. S., Bressler, L., & Bressler, M. (2013). A study of veteran-owned small businesses and the impact of military reserve call-ups since 9/11. *Academy of Entrepreneurship Journal, 19*(2), 1–22.

British Franchise Association. (2018, July 5). *Dwyer Group U.K. launches new franchising program to support military veterans resettlement.* https://www.thebfa.org/dwyer-group-uk-launches-new-franchising-program-to-support-military-veterans-resettlement/

Brock, W. A., & Evans, D. S. (1989). Small Business Economics. *Small Business Economics, 1*(1), 7–20. doi:10.1007/BF00389913

Brömmelhörster, J., & Paes, W.-C. (2004). *The Military as an Economic Actor: Soldiers in Business.* Palgrave Macmillan.

Bruyat, C., & Julien, P. A. (2001). Defining the field of Research in Entrepreneurship. *Journal of Business Venturing, 16*(2), 165–180. doi:10.1016/S0883-9026(99)00043-9

Brzezinski, Z. (1997). A geostrategy for Eurasia. *Foreign Affairs, 76*(5), 50–64.

Bulmer, S. (2013). Patriarchal confusion? *International Feminist Journal of Politics, 15*(2), 137–156. doi:10.1080/14616742.2012.746565

Burdett, H., Woodhead, C., Iversen, A. C., Wessely, S., Dandeker, C., & Fear, N. T. (2013). "Are You a Veteran?" Understanding of the Term "Veteran" among UK Ex-Service Personnel: A Research Note. *Armed Forces and Society, 39*(4), 751–759. doi:10.1177/0095327X12452033

Bureau of Labor Statistics. (2020, March 19). *Economic news release* (USDL-20-0452). U.S. Department of Labor. https://www.bls.gov/news.release/vet.nr0.htm

Burger, L., O'Neil, C., & Mahadea, P. (2005). The Impact of Previous Knowledge and Experience on the Entrepreneurial Attitude of Grade Learners. *South African Journal of Education, 25*(2), 29–94.

Busch, G. K. (2008). *The Chinese Military-Commercial Complex.* Available at: http://www.ocnus.net/artman2/publish/Editorial_10/The_Chinese_Military-Commercial_Complex.shtml

Byosiere, P., & Ingham, M. (2002). *Knowledge domains as driving force for competitive advantages: empirical evidence in a telecommunications MNC.* Strategic Management Society Conference. Paris Centre for Entrepreneurs. https://centreforentrepreneurs.org/cfe-research/the-military-entrepreneurship-manifesto/

Cahill, K. E., Giandrea, M. D., & Quinn, J. F. (2013). *New evidence on self-employment transitions among older Americans with career jobs.* Academic Press.

Cahill, K.E., Giandrea, M.D., & Quinn, J.F. (2013). *New evidence on self-employment transitions among older Americans with career jobs.* Academic Press.

Cai, S., & Ou, J. (2019). Does Managers' Military Experience Reduce Executive Compensation Stickiness? *Communication of Finance and Accounting*, (30), 16–21.

Calleja, R., & Melé, D. (2017). Valero's "Enterprise Politics": A model of humanistic management and corporate governance. *Journal of Management Development*, *36*(5), 644–659. doi:10.1108/JMD-12-2015-0187

Caplan, R. D. (1987, December). Person-environment fit theory and organizations: Commensurate dimensions, time perspectives, and mechanisms. *Journal of Vocational Behavior*, *31*(3), 248–267. doi:10.1016/0001-8791(87)90042-X

Caramela, S. (2017, November 27). *How to start a service-based business*. Retrieved on 18th May, 2020 from https://www.businessnewsdaily.com/8180-start-service-based-business.html

Carrel, S., & Carrel, S. (2006). Do lower student-to-Counsellor ratios reduce school disciplinary problem. *Economic Analysis and Policy*, *5*(1). Retrieved February 25th, 2017, from www.betpress.com/bejeap/conbribution/vol5/ISS/artII

Carrier, C. (1996). Intrapreneurship in small businesses: An exploratory study. *Entrepreneurship Theory and Practice*, *21*(1), 5–20.

Casson, M. (2003). *The entrepreneur: An economic theory* (2nd ed.). Edward Elgar. doi:10.4337/9781843765639

Cesa, M. (2009). Realist visions of the end of the Cold War: Morgenthau, Aron and Waltz. *British Journal of Politics and International Relations*, *11*(2), 177–191.

Chamberland, K. J. (2015). *Success factors of veteran-owned small businesses* [Doctoral dissertation, Walden University]. ScholarWorks. https://scholarworks.waldenu.edu/cgi/viewcontent.cgi?article=1572&context=dissertations

Chandra, S. (2014). Soldiers turn entrepreneurs. Small Business and Entrepreneurship Council.

Chandra, S. (2014, May 24). Soldiers turn entrepreneurs. *Small Business and Entrepreneurship Journal.*

Chandra, Y. (2018). Mapping the evolution of entrepreneurship as a field of research (1990–2013): A scientometric analysis. *PLoS One*, *13*(1), e0190228. doi:10.1371/journal.pone.0190228 PMID:29300735

Chappel, R., & Read, W. L. (1990). Definitions of Communications. In Introduction to Communication for Business and organizations. Ibadan: Spectrum Books Limited.

Charan, R. (2005). Boards that Deliver: Advancing Corporate Governance from Compliance to Competitive Advantage. Jossey-Bass Ed.

Chen, C. (2014). *The CiteSpace Manual*. http://cluster.ischool.drexel.edu/~cchen/citespace/CiteSpaceManual.pdf

Chen, C. (2006). CiteSpace II: Detecting and visualizing emerging trends and transient patterns in scientific literature. *Journal of the American Society for Information Science and Technology*, *57*(3), 359–377. doi:10.1002/asi.20317

Chen, C. (2016). *CiteSpace: Apractical guide for mapping scientific literature*. Nova Science Publishers, Inc.

Chen, C., & Song, M. (2019). Visualizing a field of research: A methodology of systematic scientometric reviews. *PLoS One, 14*(10), e0223994. doi:10.1371/journal.pone.0223994 PMID:31671124

Cherry, M. (2020). *Forewords: A Better Working Future for Ex-Service Personnel.* GoodPeople. Available at: https://s31949.pcdn.co/wp-content/uploads/GP_BWF_A4-Report_v13-interactive-Web-copy.pdf

Cherry, J. B. (2012). Charitable Organizations and Commercial Activity: A New Era - Will the Social Entrepreneurship Movement Force Change? *Journal of Business. Entrepreneurship & the Law*, *5*(2), 346–371.

Chibundu, E. (2006, September 29). How Nigerian SMEs can grow the economy. *Vanguard Newspaper*, p. 46.

China. com.cn. (2015). http://t.m.china.com.cn/convert/c_uPQQeDGz.html

Chinyem, V. (2018). *FG to retire 320 military personnel.* Available at: https://newsofnigeria.com/fg-to-retire-320-military-personnel/

Chouteau, M., Forest, J., & Nguyen, C. (2018). *Science, technology and innovation culture*. https://search.ebscohost.com/login.aspx?direct=true&scope=site&db=nlebk&db=nlabk&AN=1913571

Christensen, C. R., Andrews, K. R., & Bower, J. L. (1978). Business Policy: Text and Cases (4th ed.). Irwin Ed.

CNKI. (n.d.). http://www.oversea.cnki.net/rkns55/support/en/company.aspx

Cole, A. H. (1959). *Business enterprise in a social setting*. Harvard University Press.

Cole, R., & Sokolyk, T. (2016). Who needs credit and who gets credit? Evidence from the surveys of small business finances. *Journal of Financial Stability*, *24*(691), 40–60. doi:10.1016/j.jfs.2016.04.002

Collins, C. J., Hanges, P. J., & Locke, E. A. (2004). The relationship of achievement motivation to entrepreneurial behavior: A meta-analysis. *Human Performance*, *17*(1), 95–117. doi:10.1207/S15327043HUP1701_5

Collins, J. (1998). The complex context of American culture: A practitioner's view. *The Washington Quarterly*, *21*(4), 213–226. doi:10.1080/01636609809550359

Colombo Telegraph. (2014). *Increasing Military Involvement in Sri Lankan Business Ventures.* Available at: https://www.colombotelegraph.com/index.php/increasing-military-involvement-in-sri-lankan-business-ventures/

Combs, J. G., Ketchen, D. J. Jr, Shook, C. L., & Short, J. C. (2011). Antecedents and consequences of franchising: Past accomplishments and future challenges. *Journal of Management*, *37*(1), 99–126. doi:10.1177/0149206310386963

Connell, R. W. (1990). An iron man: The body and some contradictions of hegemonic masculinity. Sport, men, and the gender order: Critical feminist perspectives, 83-114.

Connell, R. W. (1995). *Masculinities*. Polity Press.

Cook, S. (2019). *Ex-forces entrepreneurs: How veterans can start and grow businesses*. Available at: https://startups.co.uk/ex-forces-entrepreneurs/

Cook, S. (2019). Ex-forces entrepreneurs: how veterans can start and grow businesses. *Startups*. https://startups.co.uk/ex-forces-entrepreneurs/

Cooper, A. D., & Beehr, T. A. (2015). Retirement and continuity theory. In N. Pachana (Ed.), *Encyclopedia of Geropsychology*. Springer. doi:10.1007/978-981-287-080-3_48-1

Cooper, L., Caddick, N., Godier, L., Cooper, A., & Fossey, M. (2016). Transition from the Military into Civilian Life: An Exploration of Cultural Competence. *Armed Forces and Society*. Advance online publication. doi:10.1177/0095327X16675965

Cornejo, C. (2008). Intersubjectivity as co-phenomenology: From the holism of meaning to the being-in-the-world-with-others. *Integrative Psychological & Behavioral Science*, *42*(2), 171–178. doi:10.100712124-007-9043-6 PMID:18196357

Coyne, C. J., Michaluk, C., & Reese, R. (2015). *Unproductive Entrepreneurship in U.S. Military Contracting*. GMU Working Paper in Economics No. 15-50. doi:10.2139srn.2667905

Coyne, C. J., Michaluk, C., & Reese, R. (2016). Unproductive entrepreneurship in US military contracting. *Journal of Entrepreneurship and Public Policy*, *5*(2), 221–239. doi:10.1108/JEPP-12-2015-0037

Craig, J. (2015). Bounding veterans studies: A review of the field. In H. Nobles & M. Davitt (Eds.), *Race and/or Reconciliation: Proceedings of the Third Conference on Veterans in Society* (pp. 101–118). Virginia Tech. http://hdl.handle.net/10919/72939

Crampton, N. (2019, August 1). *300 examples of business ideas to help you start a successful business*. Retrieved on 18 May, 2020 from https://www.entrepreneur.com/article/337316

Crampton, N. (2020). *Examples of manufacturing business ideas*. Retrieved on 18 May, 2020 from https://www.entrepreneur.com/article/335090

Cumberland, D. M. (2017). Training and educational development for "Vetrepreneurs." *Advances in Developing Human Resources*, *19*(1), 88–100. doi:10.1177/1523422316682948

Cumming, E., Dean, L. R., Newell, D. S., & McCaffrey, I. (1960). Disengagement: A tentative theory of aging. *Sociometry*, *23*(1), 23–35. doi:10.2307/2786135

Cunningham, J. B., & Lischeron, J. (1991). Defining Entrepreneurship. *Journal of Small Business Management*, 45–61.

Dabalen, A., Oni, B., & Adekola, A. (2002). *Labour market prospect for University graduates in Nigeria*. World Bank.

Dada, O., Watson, A., & Kirby, D. A. (2012). Toward a model of franchisee entrepreneurship. *International Small Business Journal, 30*(5), 559–583. doi:10.1177/0266242610376078

Dambazau, A. B. (2011). *Criminology and criminal justice*. Spectrum Books Ltd.

Dana, L. P. (2006). *Handbook of research on international entrepreneurship*. Edward Edgar.

Dannenberg, R., Cilluffo, F. J., & Cardash, S. L. (2014). *Putin's Russia: A geopolitical analysis*. HSPI Issue Brief 24, Homeland Security Policy Institute. Retrieved from https://cchs.gwu.edu/sites/cchs.gwu.edu/files/downloads/Issue%20Brief-Putin%27s%20Russia-%20A%20Geopolitical%20Analysis.pdf

David, C., & McClelland, D. C. (1961). *The achieving society*. Van Nostrand Company.

Davis, M. (2006). *Planet of Slums*. Verso.

Davison, W. (2013). *Ethiopian Military-Run Corporation Seeks More Foreign Partners*. Available at: http://nazret.com/blog/index.php/2013/02/18/ethiopian-military-run-corporation-seeks-more-foreign-partners

Davis, V. E., & Minnis, S. E. (2017). Military veterans' transferrable skills: An HRD practitioner dilemma. *Advances in Developing Human Resources, 19*(1), 6–13. doi:10.1177/1523422316682961

De Montoya, M. L. (2000). Entrepreneurship and culture; the case of Freddy the strawberry man. In R. Suredburg (Ed.), *Entrepreneurship*. Oxford University.

Dechamps, J., & Nelson, B. (2014). *Innovation Governance*. John Wiley & Sons Ltd.

Deeb, C. (2019). What happens to an organisation with bad management? https://smallbusiness.chron.com/happens-organization-bad-management-34749.html

Demers, A. (2011). When Veterans Return: The Role of Community in Reintegration. *Journal of Loss and Trauma, 16*(2), 160–179. doi:10.1080/15325024.2010.519281

Demirel, A. (2012). *Analysis of factors affecting the industrialization of the defense industry in Turkey* (Unpublished doctoral thesis). Turkish Military Academy, Defense Departments Institute, Department of Defense Management, Ankara.

Denzin, N., & Lincoln, Y. (2005). Introduction: The discipline and practice of qualitative research. In N. Denzin & Y. Lincoln (Eds.), *The SAGE handbook of qualitative research* (pp. 1–32). Sage.

DFID. (1999). Sustainable livelihoods guidance sheets. London: Department for International Development.

DiPietro, R. B., Severt, D., Welsh, D. H. B., & Raven, P. V. (2008). Franchisee leadership traits vs. manager leadership traits: An exploratory study comparing hope, leadership, commitment, and service quality delivery. *The International Entrepreneurship and Management Journal, 4*(1), 63–78. doi:10.100711365-007-0042-3

Dragomaca, R. (2019, July 30). Veteran franchisees on the front lines. *Franchising World, 51*(7), 34-35. https://www.franchise.org/franchise-information/veterans/veteran-franchisees-on-the-front-lines

Draycott, M., & Rae, D. (2011). Enterprise education in schools and the role of competency framework. *International Journal of Entrepreneurial Behaviour & Research, 17*(2), 127–145. doi:10.1108/13552551111114905

Drucker, P. F. (2002). The Discipline of Innovation. *Harvard Business Review, 80*(8).

Drucker, P.F. (1999). The discipline of innovation in review. In *Harvard Business Review on breakthrough thinking*. Boston: Harvard Business Review.

Drucker, P. F. (1985). *Innovation and Entrepreneurship*. Elsevier.

Drucker, P. F. (1985). *Innovation and entrepreneurship*. Harper & Row Publishers.

DSW (Deutsche Stiftung Weltbeveolkerung). (2014). http://orange.ngo/wp-content/uploads/2018/06/Entreprenuership-Training-Manual.pdf

Dunbar, C., Rodrigues, D., & Parker, L. (2001). Race, subjectivity, and the interview process. In J. Gubrium & J. Holstein (Eds.), *Handbook of interview research* (pp. 279–298). Sage Publications.

Dunne, J. P., & Sköns, E. (2010). *The Changing Military Industrial Complex*. Available at: https://www.researchgate.net/publication/46450061_The_Military_Industrial_Complex

Earl, J. K., Gerrans, P., & Halim, V. A. (2015). Active and adjusted: Investigating the contribution of leisure, health and psychosocial factors to retirement adjustment. *Leisure Sciences, 37*, 354–372.

Eckardt, S. (2015). *Messung des Innovations- und Intrapreneurship-Klimas: Eine quantitativ-empirische Analyse*. Springer Fachmedien Wiesbaden., doi:10.1007/978-3-658-08882-8

Edelman, L. F., Candida, G. B., Manolova, T. S., & Greene, P. G. (2010). Start-up motivations and growth intentions of minority nascent entrepreneurs. *Journal of Small Business Management, 48*(2), 174–196. doi:10.1111/j.1540-627X.2010.00291.x

Egbe-Okpenge, E. G., & Orhungur, M. M. (2012). Gender issues in entrepreneurial development in Benue state (Nigeria) and counselling implications. *Bulgarian Journal of Science and Education Policy, 6*(2).

Ehsan, L. (2010). The impact of retirement on psychological well-being in Canada. *Journal of Socio-Economics, 40*, 373–380.

Eisenhardt, K. M., & Graebner, M. E. (2007). Theory building from cases: Opportunities and challenges. *Academy of Management Journal, 50*(1), 25–32. doi:10.5465/amj.2007.24160888

Ekpo, U. N., & Bassey, G. E. (2016). An analysis of the economic consequences of infrastructural deficit in a developing economy: The case of electricity supply in Nigeria. *The International Journal of Social Sciences (Islamabad)*, *10*(1), 28–48.

Elder, G. H. Jr. (1995). The life course paradigm: Social change and individual development. In P. Moen, G. H. Elder Jr, & K. Lüscher (Eds.), *Examining lives in context: Perspectives on the ecology of human development* (pp. 101–139). Springer.

Elgin, J. (2012, April 24). 8 traits of successful franchisees. *Entrepreneur Magazine*. https://www.entrepreneur.com/article/223405

Emerson, M. (2008). *Post-Mortem on Europe's First War of the 21st Century*. Centre for European Policy Studies. Retrieved from: http://aei.pitt.edu/9382/2/9382.pdf

English, H. B., & English, A. (1971). *A comprehensive dictionary of psychological and psychoanalytic term*. Longman Green and Co.

Entrepreneur. (n.d.). *2019 top franchises for veterans ranking*. https://www.entrepreneur.com/franchises/topfranchiseveterans

Escobar, P. (2017). There will be no Russiaphobia reset. *Sputnik*. Retrieved from https://sputniknews.com/columnists/201704271053078743-there-will-be-no-russophobia-reset/

Esuong, P. J. (2013). *Intelligent investigation*. Willing Rose and Appleseed Publishing Company.

ETL. (2020). *ETL is a Great Place to Work*. Available at: https://www.etl.co.uk/

Etzkowitz, H. (1983). Entrepreneurial scientists and entrepreneurial universities in American academic science. *Minerva*, *21*, 1–21.

European Union. (2002). *Final report of the expert group "best procedure" project on education and training for entrepreneurship*. Brussels: European Commission.

ExcelFunctions.net. (n.d.). https://www.excelfunctions.net/excel-statistical-functions.html#:~:text=Excel%20Statistical%20Functions.%20Excel%20provides%20an%20extensive%20range,into%20categories%2C%20to%20help%20you%20to%20easily%20find

Fairlie, R. W., Karlan, D., & Zinman, J. (2015). Behind the gate experiment: Evidence on effects of and rationales for subsidized entrepreneurship training. *American Economic Journal. Economic Policy*, *7*(2), 125–161. doi:10.1257/pol.20120337

Fakehinde, O. B., Fayomi, O. S., Efemwenkieki, U. K., Babaremu, K. O., Kolawole, D. O., & Oyedepo, S. O. (2019). Viability of hydroelectricity in Nigeria and the future prospect. *Energy Procedia*, *157*, 871–878. doi:10.1016/j.egypro.2018.11.253

Fallon, N. (2020). *12 veteran-owned businesses making it big*. Retrieved on 18 May, 2020 from https://www.uschamber.com/co/good-company/growth-studio/veteran-owned-small-businesses

Farrell, T., & Terriff, T. (Eds.). (2002). *The sources of military change: Culture, politics, technology*. Lynne Rienner Publishers.

Fayolle, A. (2009). Entrepreneurship education in Europe: Trends and challenges. *OECD LEED programme universities, innovation and entrepreneurship: good practice workshop.* Retrieved on February 6, 2015 from http://www.oecd.org/dataoecd/11/36/43202553.pdf

Feldman, D. C. (1994). The decision to retire early: A review and conceptualization. *Academy of Management Review, 19*, 285–311.

Feyerabend, P. K. (1975). *Against Method.* New Left Books.

Fletcher, J. D., & Chatelier, P. R. (2000). *An Overview of Military Training. Institute for Defense Analyses.* Available at: https://apps.dtic.mil/dtic/tr/fulltext/u2/a408439.pdf

Fodd, W. (1993). *Constructing Questions for Interviews and Questionnaires: Theory and Practice in Social Research.* Cambridge University Press. doi:10.1017/CBO9780511518201

Force A.P.T. (2010). *A Primer for Emergency Physicians in Pre-Retirement Years.* Author.

Forrester, J. W. (1961). *Industrial Dynamics.* Pegasus communications.

Forrester, J. W. (1968). *Principles of Systems.* Pegasus communications.

Foster, M., & Meinhard, A. (2000). *Revenue diversification among Canadian voluntary organizations: A response to the external environment.* Centre for Voluntary Sector Studies Working Paper Series, Working Paper No. 16, Toronto: Ryerson University.

Franchise Business Review. (2014). *Veterans in Franchising.* Available at: https://www.franchise.org/sites/default/files/201906/VetFran%20Progress%20Report%202014.pdf

Freedom Sunrise News. (2019). *NAPASS Brings Succour to Legionnaires.* Available at: https://www.freedomsunrise.com/2019/01/napass-brings-succour-to-legionnaires.html

Gallegos, G. B. (2004). *Transparencia del presupuesto de defensa en Ecuador.* Working Paper. Buenos Aires: RESDAL Proyecto Transparencia. www.resdal.org/presupuestos/caso-ecuador.pdf

Gassenheimer, J. B., Baucus, D. B., & Baucus, M. S. (1996). Cooperative arrangements among entrepreneurs: An analysis of opportunism and communication in franchise structures. *Journal of Business Research, 36*(1), 67–79. doi:10.1016/0148-2963(95)00164-6

Gautam, M.K. (2015). Entrepreneurship education: Concept, characteristics and implications for teacher education. *Internal Journal of Education, 5*(1), 21-35.

Gbandi, E. C., & Amissah, G. (2014). Financial options for small and medium enterprises (SMEs) in Nigeria. *European Scientific Journal, 10*(1), 327–340.

GCF. (2018). *Becoming the Best: The Government Commercial Function will be the best commercial function in the UK.* Available at: https://jobs.jobvite.com/gcf/

Gearan, A., & Mufson, S. (2017). Trump sets out national security strategy of "principled realism" and global competition. *Washington Post*. Retrieved from https://www.washingtonpost.com/politics/trump-sets-out-national-security-strategy-of-principled-realism-and-global-competition/2017/12/18/7edcb0be-e412-11e7-ab50-621fe0588340_story.html?utm_term=.2387b435ce47

Genty, K. I., Khairuddin, I., & Zaidatol, A. (2014). Exploring Entrepreneurship Education and Training on Venture Creation in Nigeria. *Elixir Management Arts*, *72*, 25710–25721.

George, L. T. (1993). Sociological perspective on life transitions. *Annual Review of Sociology*, *19*(1), 353–373. doi:10.1146/annurev.so.19.080193.002033

Gesirde, S. A., & Awoyemi, A. E. (2001). *Vocational Development and adjustment*. External Studies Series. University of Ibadan, Ibadan Press.

Gherbi, E. (2016). Foreign and domestic food service business chains in Poland. *Management in Education*, *12*(2), 25–31.

Gilad, B., & Levine, P. (1986). A behavioral model of entrepreneurial supply. *Journal of Small Business Management*, *24*(4), 45–53.

Giles, L. (1910). *Sun Tzu on the Art of War*. Luzac and Company.

Gintaras, B. (2012). Academic entrepreneurship: Barriers and fears versus wishes and opportunities. *International Journal of Technology Management & Sustainable Development*, *11*(3), 231–244.

Ginzberg, E. (1951). *Occupational choice*. Columbia University Press. doi:10.7312/ginz92170

Global Data Event Analysis. (2014). *Russian oil and gas landscape reshaped by geopolitics*. Global Data.

GlobalSecurity.org. (2019). *Ecuador - Defense Industry*. Available at: https://www.globalsecurity.org/military/world/ecuador/industry.htm

Goel, R. K., & Saunoris, J. W. (2018). Military spending and entrepreneurship: Spatial effects of cross-country spillovers. *Managerial and Decision Economics*, *39*(3), 363–373.

Goldratt, E. (1994). *It's Not Luck*. Gower Publishing Limited.

Goodman, L. A. (1961). Snowball sampling. *Annals of Mathematical Statistics*, *32*(1), 148–170. doi:10.1214/aoms/1177705148

Goyal, Y. (2011). Inefficient Parastatal Agencies and the Growing Modern Food Market in India: The need for Private Participation. *Asian Journal of Public Affairs*, *3*(2), 48–66.

Grace, A. R., Frazer, L., Weaven, S. K., & Dant, R. P. (2016). Building franchisee trust in their franchisor: Insights from the franchise sector. *Qualitative Market Research*, *19*(1), 65–83. doi:10.1108/QMR-09-2014-0085

Gray, C. S., & Sloan, G. (1999). *Geopolitics, geography and strategy*. Routledge., Retrieved from https://books.google.com.tw/books?id=7BakAgAAQBAJ&printsec=frontcover&dq=geopolitics&hl=zh-TW&sa=X&ved=0ahUKEwijppW_7tnYAhXIWbwKHaXVD5sQ6AEIJTAA#v=onepage&q=geopolitics&f=false

Green, E. (2016). *Why Does the United States Give So Much Money to Israel?* Retrieved from: https://www.theatlantic.com/international/archive/2016/09/united-states-israel-memorandum-of-understanding-military-aid/500192/

Greenwood, R., & Suddaby, R. (2006). Institutional Entrepreneurship in Mature Fields: The big five accounting firms. *Academy of Management Journal*, *49*(1), 27–48. doi:10.5465/amj.2006.20785498

Greller, M. M., & Stroh, L. K. (2003). Extending work lives: are current approaches tools or talismans? In G. A. Adams & T. A. Beehr (Eds.), *Retirement: Reasons, processes, and results* (pp. 115–135). Springer.

Griswold, J. (2017). *Mission Entrepreneur: Applying Lessons from Military Life to Create Success in Business Startups*. Mango Publishing Group.

Gross, N. (2018, February 16). 53 companies named to Military Times best: Franchises 2018 list. *Military Times*. https://rebootcamp.militarytimes.com/news/entrepreneurship/2018/02/16/53-companies-named-to-military-times-best-franchises-2018-list/

Gulyas, Z. (2019). *NATO Glossary Of Terms and Definitions* (Edition 2019, Vol. AAP-06). NATO Standardization Office. https://standard.di.mod.bg/pls/mstd/MSTD

Gümüşdaş, E. (2010). *The Economics of the Defense Industry and Defense Spending in Turkey* (Unpublished Master's Thesis). University of Nigde.

Gunelius, S. (2011). *30-minute social media marketing: Step-by-step techniques to spread the word about your business*. McGraw-Hill.

Gustman, A. L., & Steinmeier, T. L. (1986). A Structural Retirement Model. *Econometrica*, *54*(3), 555–584.

Hagen, E. E. (1956). *The process of economic development (A revision of elements in a theory of economic development)*. Center for International Studies.

Hale, J. (2017). *Military Culture and Translating it to the Civilian Workplace*. Available at: https://www.dvidshub.net/news/237637/military-culture-and-translating-civilian-workplace

Halpern, M. (1963). *The Politics of Social Change in the Middle East and North Africa*. Princeton University Press.

Hammond, J. S., Keeney, R. L., & Raiffa, H. (1998). The Hidden Traps in Decision Making. *Harvard Business Review*, (Sep–Oct), 1998. PMID:10185432

Hancock, D. R., & Algozzine, B. (2006). *Doing case study research: A practical guide for beginning researchers*. Teachers College Press.

Hanson, J. L., Balmer, D. F., & Giardino, A. P. (2011). Qualitative research methods for medical educators. *Academic Pediatrics*, *11*(5), 375–386. doi:10.1016/j.acap.2011.05.001 PMID:21783450

Harness, T. (2009). Research Methods for the Empirical Study of Strategic Human Research Management. *Qualitative Market Research*, *12*(3), 321–336. doi:10.1108/13522750910963836

Harrell, M. C., & Berglass, N. (2012). *Employing America's veterans: Perspectives from businesses*. Center for a New American Society. https://www.benefits.va.gov/vow/docs/employingamericasveterans.pdf

Hartung, P. J., & Blustein, D. (2002). Reason, intuition and social justice: Elaborating on parsons' career decision-making model. *Journal of Counseling and Development*, *80*(1), 41–47. doi:10.1002/j.1556-6678.2002.tb00164.x

Hasik, J. (2016). Defense Entrepreneurship: How to Build Institutions for Innovation Inside the Military. *Joint Force Quarterly*, *81*(2), 112–117.

Haun, P. (2019). Peacetime military innovation through inter-service cooperation: The unique case of the U.S. Air Force and Battlefield Air Interdiction. *The Journal of Strategic Studies*, 1–27. doi:10.1080/01402390.2018.1557053

HAVELSAN. (2020). https://inovasyon.havelsan.com.tr

Heijmans, P. (2019). *UN Calls for Sanctions Against Firms Owned by Myanmar Military*. Available at: https://www.bloomberg.com/news/articles/2019-08-05/un-calls-for-sanctions-against-firms-owned-by-myanmar-military

Heinz, A. J., Freeman, M. A., Harpaz-Rotem, I., & Pietrzak, R. H. (2017). American military veteran entrepreneurs: A comprehensive profile of demographic, service history, and psychosocial characteristics. *Military Psychology*, *29*(6), 513–523. doi:10.1037/mil0000195 PMID:29290645

Henry, C., Hill, F., & Leitch, C. M. (2003). Education and Training for Aspiring Entrepreneurs: The Issue of Effectiveness. Ashgate Publishing.

He, S., & Li, C. W. (2016). Human capital, management quality and the exit decisions of entrepreneurial firms. *Journal of Financial and Quantitative Analysis*, *51*(4), 1269–1295. doi:10.1017/S0022109016000363

Higate, P. (2001). Theorizing continuity: From military to civilian life. *Armed Forces and Society*, *27*(3), 433. doi:10.1177/0095327X0102700306

Higate, P. (2003). 'Soft clerks' and 'hard civvies': Pluralizing military masculinities. In P. Higate (Ed.), *Military masculinities: Identity and the state* (pp. 27–43). Praeger.

Higgins, D. (1978). *A Dialectic of Centuries: Notes Towards a Theory of The New Perspectives on the Humanities*. University of Wisconsin Press.

Higgs, R. (2006). Depression, War, and Cold War: Studies in Political Economy: Studies in Political Economy. Oxford University Press.

Hill, A. (2015, Spring). Culture and the US Army: Military Innovation and Military Culture. *Parameters*, *45*(1), 94.

Hill, L., & Davis, G. (2017). The Board's New Innovation Imperative. *Harvard Business Review*, (Nov-Dec), 2017.

Hisrich, R. D. (1990). Entrepreneurship/Intrapreneurship. *The American Psychologist*, *45*(2), 209–222. doi:10.1037/0003-066X.45.2.209

Hisrich, R. D., Peters, M. P., & Shepherd, D. A. (2017). *Entrepreneurship* (10th ed.). McGraw-Hill Education.

History.com Editors. (2018). *Military-Industrial Complex*. Available at: https://www.history.com/topics/21st-century/military-industrial-complex

Hjorth, D., & Steyaert, C. (Eds.). (2009). *The Politics and Aesthetics of Entrepreneurship*. Edward Elgar.

Hobfoll, S. E. (2002). Social and psychological resources and adaptation. *Review of General Psychology*, *6*(4), 307–324.

Høiback, H. (2013). *Understanding military doctrine: A multidisciplinary approach*. Routledge, Taylor & Francis Group.

Holland, J. L. (1966). *The psychology of vocational choice*. Walthan Massachusetts Gum and Company.

Hope, J., Oh, B., & Mackin, P. (2011). *Factors affecting entrepreneurship among veterans*. U.S. Small Business Administration, Office of Advocacy. https://www.sba.gov/sites/default/files/files/rs384tot.pdf

Hope. (2019). *NAFRC Magazine*. Publication of NAFRC.

Hope, J. B., Christman, D. B., & Mackin, P. C. (2009). *An analysis of the effect of Reserve activation on small business*. U.S. Small Business Administration, Office of Advocacy.

Hope, J. B., Oh, B., & Mackin, P. C. (2011). *Factors affecting entrepreneurship among veterans small business research summary*. U.S. Small Business Administration, Office of Advocacy.

Hope, J. B., Oh, B., & Mackin, P. C. (2011). *Factors Affecting Entrepreneurship among Veterans Small Business Research Summary*. U.S. Small Business Administration, Office of Advocacy.

Hope, J. B., Oh, B., & Mackin, P. C. (2011). *Factors affecting entrepreneurship among veterans*. SAG Corporation.

Hoy, F., & Shane, S. (1998). Franchising as an entrepreneurial venture form. *Journal of Business Venturing*, *13*(2), 91–94. doi:10.1016/S0883-9026(97)00064-5

Hudson, R. (2005). *Economic Geographies: Circuits, Flows and Spaces*. Sage.

Human Rights Watch. (2007). *Indonesia: Reform of Military Business: A Human Rights Watch Background Briefing*. Retrieved from https://www.hrw.org/news/2007/02/16/indonesia-reform-military-business

Huntington, S. P. (1996). *Political Order in Changing Societies*. Yale University Press.

Hwang, H., & Powell, W. W. (2006). Institutions and entrepreneurship. In H. Hwang & W. W. Powell (Eds.), *The handbook of entrepreneurship* (1st ed., pp. 179–210). Springer Publishing.

Ibijola, E. Y. (2017). Provision of student support services and its impact of quality university education. *British Journal of Education. Society and Behavioural Science*, *19*(2), 1–12.

Idowu, A. I. (1995). The role of guidance and counselling in the Development of Nigerian University students. *The Counsellor*, *13*(1), 72–78.

Idris, M. I. (2019). Professional Military Education for the Modern Officer: The Nigerian Experience. In Professional Military Education, A cross Cultural Survey. New York: Oxford.

Igwe, Madichie, & Newbery. (2019). Determinants of livelihood choices and artisanal entrepreneurship in Nigeria. *International Journal of Entrepreneurial Behavior & Research.*

IMANI. (2011). *IMANI Report: The Dangers of Military Commercialisation in Ghana.* Available at: https://www.modernghana.com/news/344019/imani-report-the-dangers-of-military-commercialis.html

InformNapalm. (n.d.). *Private Military Companies in Russia: Carrying Out Criminal Orders of the Kremlin.* Retrieved from: http://informnapalm.rocks/private-military-companies-in-russia-carrying-out-criminal-orders-of-the-kremlin

Interian, A., Kline, A., Janal, M., Glynn, S., & Losonczy, M. (2014). Multiple deployments and combat trauma: Do home front stressors increase the risk for posttraumatic stress symptoms? *Journal of Traumatic Stress*, *27*(1), 90–97. doi:10.1002/jts.21885 PMID:24464407

International Committee of the Red Cross (ICRC). (2009). *Montreux Document: On Pertinent International Legal Obligations and Good Practices for States Related to Operations of Private Military and Security Companies during Armed Conflict.* Geneva: ICRC. https://www.icrc.org/en/doc/assets/files/other/icrc_002_0996.pdf

International Crisis Group. (2016). *Nigeria: The Challenge of Military Reform.* Crisis Group Africa Report N°237. Available at: https://www.refworld.org/pdfid/5756664c4.pdf

International Franchise Association. (2018). *Franchise Business Economic Outlook*. https://www.franchise.org/sites/default/.../Franchise_Business_Outlook_Jan_2018.pdf

International Franchise Association. (2018). *Franchising for veterans industry analysis 2019-costs and trends.* https://www.franchisehelp.com/industry-reports/franchising-for-veterans-industry-analysis-2018-cost-trends/

Isaac, E., Visser, K. J., Frederick, C., & Brijlal, P. (2007). Entrepreneurship education and training at the further education and training (FET) level in South Africa. *South African Journal of Education, 27*, 613–629.

Ishak, K. A., Chuah, F. W., & Romle, A. R. (2016). The roles of trust in franchising relationship: The Malaysian franchisees' perspectives. *Middle East Journal of Scientific Research, 24*(6), 2071–2078.

Ivanov, I. (2018). Russia and Europe: From romanticism to pragmatism. *RIAC*. Retrieved from https://russiancouncil.ru/en/analytics-and-comments/analytics/russia-and-europe-from-romanticism-to-pragmatism/

Jain, S., George, G., & Maltarich, M. (2009). Academics or entrepreneurs? Investigating role identity modification of university scientists involved in commercialization activity. *Research Policy, 38*, 922–935.

Jambulingam, T., & Nevin, J. R. (1999). Influence of franchisee selection criteria on outcomes desired by the franchisor. *Journal of Business Venturing, 14*(4), 363–395. doi:10.1016/S0883-9026(98)00023-8

Jiang, H. B. (2015). A review of the quality of full-text databases of three major Chinese periodicals. *Modern Intelligence, 35*(9), 84-88. doi:10.3969/j.issn.1008-0821.2015.09.016

Jolly, R. (1996). *Changing step; From military to civilian life: People in transition*. Brassey.

Jones, C., & English, J. (2004). A contemporary approach to entrepreneurship education. *Education + Training, 46*(8-9), 416-23. doi:10.1108/00400910410569533

Kalargyrou, V., Aliouche, E. H., & Schlentrich, U. (2018). Antecedents and consequences of franchisee satisfaction in the U.S. restaurant industry. *Journal of Human Resources in Hospitality & Tourism, 17*(1), 60–79. doi:10.1080/15332845.2017.1328261

Kanayo, O., Jumare, F., & Nancy, S. (2013). Challenges of micro finance access in Nigeria: Implication for entrepreneurship development. *Mediterranean Journal of Social Sciences, 4*(6), 611–618. doi:10.5901/mjss.2013.v4n6p611

Kanter, R. (1983). *The Change Masters: Innovation and Entrepreneurship in the American Corporation*. Simon and Shuster.

Kao, J. (1989). *Entrepreneurship, Creativity and Organization*. Prentice-Hall.

Karaganov, S. (2017). A Cold War: A forecast for tomorrow. *Russia in global affairs*. Retrieved from http://eng.globalaffairs.ru/pubcol/A-Cold-War-A-Forecast-for-Tomorrow-19099

Kayode, K. B., & Ilesanmi, A. O. (2014). Determinants of factors influencing capacity of small and medium enterprises (SMEs) in employment creation in Lagos State, Nigeria. *International Journal of Financial Research, 5*(2), 133–141. doi:10.5430/ijfr.v5n2p133

KCH. (2017). *About Us*. Available at: https://www.kchcommercial.com/about-us/

Kedia, S. (2019). *With this organisation's help, Indian army veterans are becoming entrepreneurs*. Available at: https://yourstory.com/socialstory/2019/03/indian-army-veterans-turn-entrepreneurs-8icuu43y47

Kerrick, S. A., Cumberland, D. M., & Choi, N. (2016). Comparing military veterans and civilians responses to an entrepreneurship education program. *Journal of Entrepreneurship Education*, *19*(1), 9–23.

Kerrick, S. A., Cumberland, D., Church-Nally, M., & Kemelgor, B. (2014). Military veterans marching towards entrepreneurship: An exploratory mixed methods study. *International Journal of Management Education*, *12*(3), 469–478. doi:10.1016/j.ijme.2014.05.006

Khairatun, S. N. (2019). Veterans initiatives in franchising framework. *Asia Proceedings of Social Sciences*, *4*(1), 107–110. doi:10.31580/apss.v4i1.622

Khalilzad, Z. (2017). The path to US-Russia cooperation. *National interest.* Retrieved from https://nationalinterest.org/feature/the-path-us-russia-cooperation-21914

Khudoley, K. (2017). Russia and the US: The way forward. *Russia in global affairs 4*. Retrieved from http://eng.globalaffairs.ru/number/Russia-and-the-US-The-Way-Forward-19263

Kimball, A. (2015). *Long-term Historical Reflection on the Rise of Military-Industrial, Managerial Statism or "Military-Industrial Complexes"*. Available at: https://pages.uoregon.edu/kimball/MIC.htm

Kim, J. E., & Moen, P. (2002). Retirement transitions, gender, and psychological well-being a life-course: Ecological model. *The Journals of Gerontology. Series B, Psychological Sciences and Social Sciences*, *57*(3), 212–222. PMID:11983732

Kincheloe, J. L., & McLaren, P. (2005). Rethinking critical theory and qualitative research. In N. Denzin & Y. Lincoln (Eds.), *The Sage Handbook of Qualitative Research* (3rd ed., pp. 303–342). Sage Publication.

Kirby, D. A. (2004). Entrepreneurship education: Can business schools meet the challenge? *Education + Training*, *46*(8/9), 510–519. doi:10.1108/00400910410569632

Kirchner, M., & Minnis, S. (2018). Engaging military friendly in organizations: An empirical-based definition. *Journal of Veterans Studies*, *3*(2), 94–108. doi:10.21061/jvs.v3i2.49

Kirzner, I. M. (1973). *Competition and Entrepreneurship*. University of Chicago Press.

Knight, F. H. (1961). *Risk uncertainty and profit* (2nd ed.). Kelley.

Kortunov, A. (2017a). Policy priorities in US-Russia relations. *RIAC*. Retrieved from https://russiancouncil.ru/en/activity/policybriefs/policy-priorities-in-us-russia-relations/

Kortunov, A. (2017b). A roadmap for US-Russia relations. *RIAC*. Retrieved from https://russiancouncil.ru/en/activity/publications/a-roadmap-for-u-s-russia-relations/

Kortunov, A. (2018a). How should Russia respond to an adversarial west? *RIAC*. Retrieved from https://russiancouncil.ru/en/analytics-and-comments/analytics/how-should-russia-respond-to-an-adversarial-west/

Kortunov, A. (2018b). Dialogue with US on nuclear-missile weapons is Russia's priority task. *RIAC*. Retrieved from https://russiancouncil.ru/en/analytics-and-comments/comments/dialogue-with-us-on-nuclear-missile-weapons-is-russia-s-priority-task/

Kotkin, S. (2016). Russia's perpetual geopolitics. Putin returns to the historical pattern. *Foreign Affairs, 2016*(May/June). https://www.foreignaffairs.com/articles/ukraine/2016-04-18/russias-perpetual-geopolitics

Kotter, J. P. (1996). *Leading Change*. Harvard Business School Press.

Kramik, I. (2016). *Иностранные корни нового российского спецназа, Кто помогал Минобороны готовить зеленых человечков* [Foreign roots of new Russian Spetsnaz. Who helped Defense Ministry to prepare little Green Men]. Retrieved from: https://lenta.ru/articles/2016/12/20/specialforces/

Krippendorff, Ä. (2004). *Content analysis: An introduction to its methodology* (2nd ed.). Sage Publications.

Kuratko, D. F. (1997). *Entrepreneurship. International encyclopedia of business and management*. Routledge publishers.

Kvale, S. (1996). *Interviews: An introduction to qualitative research interviews*. Sage Publications.

Lai, L., Gong, Y., & Ma, Y. (2016). Managers' Military Experience, Financing Preference and Business Performance. *Management World*, (8), 126–136.

Lai, L., Gong, Y., Xia, X., & Ma, Y. (2017). Managers' Military Experience and Company M&A. *Japan and the World Economy*, (12), 141–164.

Landstrom, H. (1998). The roots of entrepreneurship research. *Conference Proceedings*.

Landström, H. (2010). *Pioneers in entrepreneurship and small business research*. Springer.

Lar, K. G. (2020). I want to make NAFRC a Vehicle for National Development. Hope, 2, 21-28.

Lee, S. H., Peng, M. W., & Barney, J. B. (2007). Bankruptcy law and entrepreneurship development: A real options perspective. *Academy of Management Review*, *32*(1), 257–272. doi:10.5465/amr.2007.23464070

Lee, T. K., & Chu, W. Y. (2013). How entrepreneurial orientation, environmental dynamism, and resource rareness influence firm performance. *Journal of Management & Organization*, *19*(2), 167–187. doi:10.1017/jmo.2013.33

Leipold, J. D. (2014). *Is the Army a business?* Available at: https://www.army.mil/article/126882/is_the_army_a_business

Liao, F., Han, H., & Chen, L. (2018). Does Executives' Military Experience Improve Internal Control Quality? Empirical Evidence from Listed Companies in China. *Auditing Research*, (6), 121–128.

Liao, J., Welsch, H., & Moutray, C. (2008). Start-up resources and entrepreneurial discontinuance: The case of nascent entrepreneurs. *Journal of Small Business Strategy*, *19*(2), 1.

Likhachev, V. (2017). Russia-EU energy relations. *RIAC*. Retrieved from https://russiancouncil.ru/en/activity/publications/russia-eu-energy-relations/

Liman, A. S. (2019). From the Commandant's Desk. Hope, 1, 3.

Locker, R. (2016). What's the arms race? A short history. *USA Today*. Retrieved from https://www.usatoday.com/story/news/politics/2016/12/23/whats-arms-race-short-history/95792412/

Lofgren. (2016). *NATO Capability Development Interoperability. The Three Swords Magazine*. https://www.jwc.nato.int/images/stories/_news_items_/2016/LT_GEN_Lofgren_interview.pdf

Lorsch, J. W. (2012). *The Future of Boards*. Harvard Business Review Press.

Lugo-Galicia, H. (2018). *Maduro turns Venezuela military officers into businessmen to quell discontent*. Available at: https://www.miamiherald.com/news/nation-world/world/americas/venezuela/article210233099.html#storylink=cpy

Lumpkin, G. T., & Dess, G. G. (1996). Clarifying the Entrepreneurial Orientation Construct and Linking it to Performance. *Academy of Management Review*, *21*(1), 135–172.

Lytle, M. C., Foley, P. F., & Cotter, E. W. (2015). Career and retirement theories: Relevance for older workers across cultures. *Journal of Career Development*, *42*(3), 185–198. PMID:26101455

Mabin, V. J., & Davies, J. (2010). The TOC Thinking Processes. In The Theory of Constraints Handbook. McGraw-Hill.

Machado, C., & Davim, J. P. (Eds.). (2020). *Entrepreneurship and Organizational Innovation*. Springer International Publishing. doi:10.1007/978-3-030-19289-1

Macklem, P. (2008). Humanitarian intervention and the distribution of sovereignty in international law. *Ethics & International Affairs*, *22*(4), 369–393.

Madichie, N. O., & Ayasi, K. (2018). Entrepreneurial Opportunities and Challenges for Retired Senior Military Officers in Nigeria. In L. P. Dana, V. Ratten, & B. Honyenuga (Eds.), *African Entrepreneurship. Palgrave Studies of Entrepreneurship in Africa* (pp. 131–151). Palgrave Macmillan. doi:10.1007/978-3-319-73700-3_7

Maimaris, W., Hogan, H., & Lock, K. (2010). The impact of working beyond traditional retirement ages on mental health: Implication for public health welfare policy. *Public Health Reviews*, *32*(2), 532–548. doi:10.1007/BF03391615

Mambula, C. (2002). Perceptions of SME growth constraints in Nigeria. *Journal of Small Business Management*, *40*(1), 58–65. doi:10.1111/1540-627X.00039

Mani, K. (2007). Militaries in business. *Armed Forces and Society*, *33*(4), 591–611. doi:10.1177/0095327X06291348

Mani, K. (2011). Military Entrepreneurship: Patterns in Latin America. *Latin American Politics and Society*, *53*(3), 25–55.

Mares, D. R. (1998). Civil-military relations, democracy, and the regional neighborhood. In D. R. Mares (Ed.), *Civil-Military Relations*. Westview Press.

Mate, A. (2017). Russiagate is more fiction than fact. *The Nation*. Retrieved from https://www.thenation.com/article/russiagate-is-more-fiction-than-fact/

Maynard, C., & Blalock, A. (1977). The Welfare State within the Military. *Journal of Sociology and Social Welfare*, *4*(8), 494–521.

McDermott, M. (2010). Do veterans make significantly more successful franchisees? A comparative study on the traits of veterans and successful franchisees literature review. In A. Kakouris (Ed.) *Proceedings of the 4th European Conference on Innovation and Entrepreneurship: ECIE* (p. 395). Academic Conferences Limited.

McDermott, M. J., Boyd, T. C., & Weaver, A. (2015). Franchise business ownership: A comparative study on the implications of military experience on franchisee success and satisfaction. *The Entrepreneurial Executive*, *20*, 9–30.

McDermott, M. J., & Jackson, J. (2020). A qualitative study: Military veterans and franchise ownership. *Qualitative Report*, *25*(3), 769–784.

Meinhard, A., Moher, L., & Fitzrandolph, S. (2004). *Case Studies of Commercial Ventures in Nonprofit Organizations: Determining Probability for Success.* Centre for Voluntary Sector Studies Working Paper Series, Working Paper No. 27, Toronto: Ryerson University.

Melman, S. (1970). *Pentagon Capitalism: The Political Economy of War*. McGraw Hill.

Melman, S. (1985). *The Permanent War Economy*. Simon and Schuster.

Mercier, G. (2010). *Indonesia: The Dangerous Business Empire of The Military*. Available at: http://newsjunkiepost.com/2010/01/12/indonesia-the-dangerous-business-empire-of-the-military/

Meredith, O. (1983). *The practice of entrepreneurship*. International Labour Office.

Merriam-Webster. (n.d.). Entrepreneur. In *Merriam-Webster.com dictionary*. https://www.merriam-webster.com/dictionary/entrepreneur

Mid-Atlantic Research, Inc. (1984). *Profiling Entrepreneurial Veterans*. U.S. Small Business Administration, Office of Advocacy.

Miller, P., Wedell-Wedellsborg, T. (2013). Clearing the Path to Innovation. *IESE Insight*, (16).

Miller, P., Wedell-Wedellsborg, T. (2014, Nov.). Get More Actionable Ideas from Your Employees. *Harvard Business Review*.

Ministry of National Defense of the People's Republic of China (MOD). (2018). *China's Regulations on the Discipline of the People's Liberation Army*. http://www.mod.gov.cn/topnews/2018-04/18/content_4809753.htm

Ministry of Veterans Affairs of the People's Republic of China (MVA). (2019). http://www.mva.gov.cn/gongkai/zfxxzdgkml/fgzc/gfxwj/201903/t2019321_23376.html

Minnis, S. (2014). *A phenomenological exploration of combat veterans' experiences as they transition to civilian employment using higher education as career development* [Doctoral dissertation, Texas A & M University]. OAKTrust Digital Repository. http://hdl.handle.net/1969.1/152463

Mires, E., Cumberland, D. M., & Berry, A. (2020). Veterans serving the franchise sector: Exploring the appeal. *Small Business Institute Journal*, *16*(1), 24–43.

Mobbs, M. C., & Bonanno, G. A. (2018). Beyond war and PTSD: The crucial role of transition stress in the lives of military veterans. *Clinical Psychology Review*, *59*, 137–144. doi:10.1016/j.cpr.2017.11.007 PMID:29180101

Mohd, Z. B., & Ishan, Z. B. M. (2017). Reevaluating successful franchisees characteristics. In *Social Sciences Postgraduate International Seminar (SSPIS)* (pp. 78-85). School of Social Sciences, USM.

Morgenthau, H. J. (1973). *Politics Among Nations The Struggle for Power and Peace* (7th ed.). Mc Graw Hill Higher Education.

Morris, M. H., Kuratko, D. F., & Covin, J. F. (2008). *Corporate entrepreneurship and innovation*. South-Western.

Morrison, K. A. (1997). How franchise job satisfaction and personality affects performance, organizational commitment, franchisor relations, and intention to remain. *Journal of Small Business Management*, *35*(3), 39–67.

Moser, C. (1994). The Informal Sector Debate, Part 1: 1970-1983. In C. A. Rakowski (Ed.), *Contrapunto: The Informal Sector Debate in Latin America* (pp. 11–29). State University of New York Press.

Moutray, C. M. (2007). *Educational attainment and other characteristics of the self-employed: an examination using data from the panel study of income dynamics*. Hudson Institute Research Paper, (07-06).

Moutray, C. M. (2007). Educational attainment and other characteristics of the self-employed: An examination using data from the panel study of income dynamics. In L. Niehm (Ed.), *USASBE 2008 Proceedings* (pp. 1731–1767). United States Association for Small Business and Entrepreneurship. doi:10.2139srn.1070835

Mowery, D., Nelson, R., Sampat, B., & Ziedonis, A. (1999). The effects of the Bayh-Dole Act on U.S. university research and technology transfer. In L. Branscomb, F. Kodama, & R. Florida (Eds.), *Industrializing knowledge* (pp. 269–306). MIT Press.

Mullins, R. E. (2000). *Sharpening the Trident: The Decisions of 1889 and the Creation of Modern Seapower* (Ph.D. diss.). King's College London.

Mulvenon, J. (2001). *Soldiers of Fortune*. M.E. Sharpe.

Muratore, A. M., & Earl, J. K. (2015). Improving retirement outcomes: The role of resources, pre-retirement planning and transition characteristics. *Ageing and Society*, *35*, 2100–2140.

Muratore, A. M., Earl, J. K., & Collins, C. G. (2014). Understanding heterogeneity in adaptation to retirement: A growth mixture modeling approach. *International Journal of Aging & Human Development*, *79*, 131–156. PMID:25536703

Murray, W., & Millett, A. R. (Eds.). (1996). *Military innovation in the interwar period*. Cambridge University Press. doi:10.1017/CBO9780511601019

Murtala, S. S. (2005), Entrepreneurship development policy: A renewed perspective for achieving economic development in Nigeria. A paper presented at the Inaugural National conference organised by the Academy of Management Nigeria.

Musial, S. (2016, August 22). Top 10 traits of successful franchisees. *Franchise Gator*. https://www.franchisegator.com/articles/4-essential-traits-of-a-franchisee-11183/

Muto, M., & Yamano, T. (2009). Impact of mobile phone coverage expansion on market participation: Panel data evidence from Uganda. *World Development*, *37*(12), 1887–1896. doi:10.1016/j.worlddev.2009.05.004

Myers, R. J. (1997). Hans Morgenthau's realism and American foreign policy authors. *Ethics & International Affairs*, *11*(1), 253–270.

Naguib, R. (2012). *Boycott them: Activists raise awareness about military's economic empire*. Retrieved from https://www.egyptindependent.com/boycott-them-activists-raise-awareness-about-militarys-economic-empire/

Naktiyok, A. (2004). *İç Girişimcilik*. Beta Yayınları.

Nasr, K. B., & Boujelbene, Y. (2014). Assessing the impact of entrepreneurship education. *Science Direct,* 713-715. www.sciencedirect.com

Nevid, J. S. (2009). *Psychology: Concepts and applications* (3rd ed.). Houghton Mifflin Company.

Nicholson, J. W. (2019). *Veterans Are the Future of America's Startups, And Nonprofit Leaders Can Help Them Succeed*. Available at: https://www.forbes.com/sites/forbesnonprofitcouncil/2019/11/05/veterans-are-the-future-of-americas-startups-and-nonprofit-leaders-can-help-them-succeed/#6f22065e61d4

Nigeria - South Africa Chamber of Commerce. (2016). *Security Challenges in Nigeria and the Implications for Business Activities and Sustainable Development*. Available at: http://nsacc.org.ng/security-challenges-in-nigeria-and-the-implications-for-business-activities-and-sustainable-development/

Nigerian Defence Academy Consultancy Ltd. (2012). *Company Profile*. Author.

Nigerian Defence Academy. (2018). *Our History*. Available at: https://www.nda.edu.ng/#news/item/277

Nigerian Electricity Regulatory Commission. (2015). *Multi-Year Tariff Order (MYTO): 1st February 2016 to 2024 (Ikeja DISCO)*. Nigerian Electricity Regulatory Commission.

Nigerian Electricity Regulatory Commission. (2019). *Power Generation in Nigeria*. Nigerian Electricity Regulatory Commission.

Nigerian Finder. (2020, May 18). *100 small scale businesses ideas in Nigeria*. Retrieved from https://nigerianfinder.com/small-scale-business-ideas-in-nigeria/

Niwattanakul, S., Singthongchai, J., Naenudorn, E., & Wanapu, S. (2013). Using of Jaccard Coefficient for keywords similarity. *Proceedings of the International MultiConference of Engineers and Computer Scientists (IMECS)*.

Njorge, C. W., & Guthunga, J. M. (2013). The effect of entrepreneurial education and training of small and medium size enterprises in Githungari District-Kenya. *International Journal of Education and Research*, *1*(8), 1–22.

Ntiwunka, G. (2012). An assessment of the relevance of Adekanye's the retired military as emergent power factor in Nigeria to contemporary Nigeria. *Canadian Social Science*, *8*(2), 117–126.

Ntiwunka, G. (2012). An Assessment of the Relevance of Adekanye's The Retired Military as Emergent Power Factor in Nigeria to Contemporary Nigeria. *Canadian Social Science*, *8*(2), 117–126.

Nueno, P. (2016). *10 Trends for the Board of 2020*. IESE Publishing.

Nyambura, J. N. (2014). An analysis of entrepreneurship aspects of current training programs conducted on practicing micro and small enterprises (MSEs): A case study of Roysambu. *International Journal of Academic Research in Business & Social Sciences*, *4*(10), 1–15. doi:10.6007/IJARBSS/v4-i10/1224

Nye, J. S., Jr. (2015). *Is the American century over?* Wiley. Retrieved from https://www.wiley.com/en-us/Is+the+American+Century+Over%3F-p-9780745690063#

Nye, J. S., Jr. (2017). Will the liberal order survive? The history of an idea. *Foreign Affairs*. Retrieved from https://www.foreignaffairs.com/articles/2016-12-12/will-liberal-order-survive

Nzelibe, G. C. (2006). *Entrepreneurship and management of small scale business*. Optimal Publishers.

O'Tuathail, G. (1998). Thinking critically about geopolitics. In *The geopolitics reader*. Retrieved from https://books.google.com.tw/books?id=VH2FAgAAQBAJ&printsec=frontcover&dq=geopolitics&hl=zh-TW&sa=X&ved=0ahUKEwijppW_7tnYAhXIWbwKHaXVD5sQ6AEILTAB#v=onepage&q=geopolitics&f=false

Obi, A. (2013). *The impact of military service on the successful operation of a business: A case study in Nigeria.* Academic Press.

Obokoh, L. O., & Asaolu, T. O. (2012). Examination of relationship between financial market liberalization and the failures of small and medium sized enterprises in Nigeria. *International Business Research, 5*(1), 182–193. doi:10.5539/ibr.v5n1p182

Odia, J., & Odia, A. A. (2013). Developing entrepreneurial skills and transforming challenges into opportunities in Nigeria. *Journal of Educational and Social Research, 3*, 289–299. doi:10.5901/jesr.2013.v4n3p289

OECD. (2005). *Oslo manual. The measurement of scientific and technological activities. Proposed guidelines for collecting and interpreting technological innovation data* (2nd ed.). Paris: OECD/European Commission EUROSTAT. https://www.oecd.org/site/innovationstrategy/defininginnovation.htm

OECD. (2018). *Monitoring and evaluation of SME and entrepreneurship programmes.* Available at: http://www.oecd.org/cfe/smes/ministerial/documents/2018-SME-Ministerial-Conference-Parallel-Session-6.pdf

Oghojafor, E. A., Kuye, O. L., Sulaimon, A. A., & Okonji, P. S. (2009). Empowering Nigerian Youths For National Economic Development: The Role of Entrepreneurship Education. *Journal Of Research In National Development, 7*(2). Advance online publication. doi:10.4314/jorind.v7i2.50945

Ojo, S. (2013). *Diaspora entrepreneurship: A study of Nigerian entrepreneurs in London* (PhD thesis). University of East London. Available at: http://hdl.handle.net/10552/3506

Ojo, S. (2017). Interrogating returnee entrepreneurship in the Nigerian context. *Journal of Enterprising Communities: People and Places in the Global Economy, 11*(5), 590–608. doi:10.1108/JEC-07-2016-0025

Ojo, S., & Nwankwo, S. (2017). Diaspora and Transnational Entrepreneurship: A Conceptual Exploration. In S. Ojo (Ed.), *Diaspora and Transnational Entrepreneurship in the Global Contexts* (pp. 1–23). IGI Global. doi:10.4018/978-1-5225-1991-1.ch001

OKA. (2012). *Çorum Savunma Sanayi Sektörel Araştırma Raporu.* https://www.oka.org.tr/assets/upload/dosyalar/savunma-sanayi-arastirma-raporu-17-71.pdf

Oliyide, O. (2012). Law, credit risk management and bank lending to SMEs in Nigeria. *Commonwealth Law Bulletin, 38*(4), 673–695. doi:10.1080/03050718.2012.707350

Olokundun, M., Hezekiah, F., Stephen, I., & Fred, I. (2014). An assessment of the taught entrepreneurship program in Nigerian secondary schools. *Merit Research Journal of Education and Review, 2*(11), 257–275.

Olomola, A. S. (2015). *Driving agricultural transformation with the power of information and communication technology: the performance of Nigeria's growth enhancement support scheme.* NSSP Working Paper 30. Washington, DC: International Food Policy Research Institute (IFPRI).

Olson, M. (2000). *Power and Prosperity*. Basic Books.

Olu-Young, F. (2019). Entrepreneurship and youth empowerment in Nigeria: The national security imperative. In Strategic Lenses (Series 3). In Youth management and national security in Nigeria (pp. 175-191). National Defence College Nigeria.

Omelicheva, M. Y. (2016). Critical geopolitics on Russian foreign policy: Uncovering the imagery of Moscow's international relations. *International Politics*, *53*(6), 708–726.

Opara, J. O. (2011). Factors constraining the growth and survival of SME in Nigeria: Implications for poverty alleviation. *Management Research Review*, *34*(2), 156–171. doi:10.1108/01409171111102786

Osarenren, N. A. (2011). Not advising but desirable alternatives: The work of the counsellor. An inaugural university of Lagos, Nigeria, Lagos: University of Lagos Press.

Osborne, J. W. (2012). Psychological effects of the transition to retirement. *Canadian Journal of Counselling and Psychotherapy*, *46*(1), 45–58.

Osborne, J. W. (2012). Psychological Effects of the Transition to Retirement. *Canadian Journal of Counselling and Psychotherapy*, *46*(1), 45–58.

Oshigbo, T. O. (2014). The contributions of veterans in business and economy: Africa as a case study. In H. Nobles (Ed.), *Proceedings of the Second Conference on Veterans in Society: Humanizing the Discourse* (pp. 12–17). Virginia Tech. https://vtechworks.lib.vt.edu/handle/10919/56355

Owuala, E. I., & Obokoh, L. O. (2008). Tackling Youth Restiveness in the Niger Delta Region of Nigeria through Entrepreneurship. *Journal of Enterprising Communities, People and Places in Global Economy*, *2*(2), 168–179.

Oyinlola, O. T., Ajiboshin, I. O., Raimi, L., Raheem, S., & Igwe, C. N. (2013). Entrepreneurship for sustainable economic growth in Nigeria. *Journal of Sustainable Development Studies*, *2*(2).

Ozioma-Eleodinmuo, P. (2015). Analysis of entrepreneurship policy for small and medium scale enterprise in Aba, Abia State Nigeria. *Journal of Economic Development, Management, IT, Finance and Marketing*, *7*(1), 47–60.

Padilla, A., Coyne, C.J., Michaluk, C., & Reese, R. (2016). Unproductive entrepreneurship in US military contracting. *Journal of Entrepreneurship and Public Policy*.

Page, S. E. (2018, Nov.). Why "Many-Model Thinkers" Make Better Decisions. *Harvard Business Review*.

Parker, S. C. (2018). Entrepreneurship and economic theory. *Oxford Review of Economic Policy*, *34*(4), 540–564. doi:10.1093/oxrep/gry013

Perera, M. H. S. B., Premarathna, W., & Welamedage, I. (2017). *Entrepreneurial aspirations and expectations of Sri Lanka military veterans*. Retrieved on 18 May, 2020 from http://ir.kdu.ac.lk/handle/345/1726

Perrigot, R. (2017). An exploration of franchising in Africa. In F. Hoy, R. Perrigot, & A. Terry (Eds.), *Handbook of research on franchising* (pp. 515–535). Edward Elgar Publishing. doi:10.4337/9781785364181.00037

Phillips, U. U. (2019). Security management and private security outfits in Nigeria. *International Journal of Social Sciences and Management Research, 5*(1).

Pilon, A. (2017, February 2). *50 Small business manufacturing ideas*. Retrieved on 18 May, 2020 from https://smallbiztrends.com/2017/02/manufacturing-business-ideas.html

Pinchot, G. III. (1985). *Intrapreneuring*. Harper & Row.

Podvig, P. (2011). *Russia's Nuclear Forces: Between disarmament and modernization, Proliferation Papers, Spring 2011*. Institute Français des Relations Internationals.

Polin, B. A., & Ehrman, C. M. (2018). The curious relationship between military service and entrepreneurial intentions in Israel. *Armed Forces and Society, 46*(3), 438–453. doi:10.1177/0095327X18789074

Politis, D., & Gabrielsson, J. (2009). Entrepreneurs' attitudes towards failure. *International Journal of Entrepreneurial Behaviour & Research, 15*(4), 364–383. doi:10.1108/13552550910967921

Posen, B. (1984). *The Sources of Military Doctrine: France, Britain, and Germany between the World Wars*. Cornell University Press. Retrieved April 29, 2020, from www.jstor.org/stable/10.7591/j.ctt1287fp3

Pranger, T., Murphy, K., & Thompson, J. (2009). Shaken World Coping with Transition to Civilian Life. *Canadian Family Physician Medecin de Famille Canadien, 55*, 159–161. PMID:19221074

Puffer, M. S., Mccarthy, D., & Satinsky, M. D. (2018). *Hammer and Silicon*. Cambridge University Press. doi:10.1017/9781108120302

Pursell, C. (1972). *The military-industrial complex*. Harper & Row Publishers.

Putta, S. S. (2014). Improving entrepreneur's management skills through entrepreneurship training. *Journal of Commerce & Management Thought, 5*(3), 459–474. doi:10.5958/0976-478X.2014.00334.6

Quan, X., Cu, W., & Xu, X. (2019). Executives' Military Experience and Corporate Earnings Management: A New Perspective on the Military-Civilian Integration Strategy. *Finance & Trade Economics, 40*(1), 98–113.

Quan, X., Cu, W., & Yin, H. (2019). Military Service Experiences of Top Management, Management Style and Corporate Innovation. *Nankai Business Review*, (6), 140–151.

Quan, X., Xu, X., & Cai, W. (2018). Does Executives' Military Experience Affect Audit Fees: A New Perspective Based on Organizational Culture. *Auditing Research*, (2), 80–86.

Radipere, S. (2012). South African university entrepreneurship education. *African Journal of Business Management, 6*(44), 11015–11022. doi:10.5897/AJBM12.410

Ramirez-Hurtado, J., Rondan-Cataluna, F., Guerrero-Casas, F., & Berbel-Pineda, J. (2011). Identifying the franchisee profiles franchisors prefer. *Journal of Business Economics and Management*, *12*(4), 567–588. doi:10.3846/16111699.2011.599408

Ray, S., & Heaslip, K. (2011). Canadian military transitioning to civilian life: A discussion paper. *Journal of Psychiatric and Mental Health Nursing*, *18*(3), 18. doi:10.1111/j.1365-2850.2010.01652.x PMID:21395911

Redlich, F. (1964). The German Military Enterpriser and His Work Force': A Study in European Social and Economic History (2 Vols.). Wiesbaden.

Redmond, B. F. (2010). *Self-efficacy theory: Do I think that I can succeed in my work. Work attitude and motivation.* The Pennsylvania State University, World Campus. Retrieved March 20, 2013 from http://cms.psu.edu

Reeuwijk, K. G., de Wind, A., Westerman, M. J., Ybema, J. F., van der Beek, A. J., & Geuskens, G. A. (2013). All those things together made me retire: Qualitative study on early retirement among Dutch employees. *BMC Public Health*, *13*(1), 516–524. doi:10.1186/1471-2458-13-516 PMID:23714371

Reiter, D. (2014). Security commitments and nuclear proliferation. *Foreign Analysis*, *10*(1), 61–80.

Reuters. (2018). *From war room to boardroom. Military firms flourish in Sisi's Egypt.* Available at: https://www.reuters.com/investigates/special-report/egypt-economy-military/

Rezaei, S., Goli, M., & Dana, L.-P. (2014). Beyond legal entrepreneurship: The case of Austria. *International Journal of Entrepreneurship and Small Business*, *21*(2), 202–215. doi:10.1504/IJESB.2014.059473

Rico, M.I.L., Camara, C.P., & Llamazares, M.C.E. (2015). Impacto de la educacion en el emprendimiento, making-of y analisis de tres grupos de discussion. *Pedagogia social*, (25), 221-250.

Roach, M. (2017). Encouraging entrepreneurship in university labs: Research activities, research outputs, and early doctorate careers. *PLoS One*, *12*(2), e0170444. doi:10.1371/journal.pone.0170444 PMID:28178270

Roberts, P. C. (2018). Russiagate turns on its originators. *Foreign Policy Journal.* Retrieved from https://www.foreignpolicyjournal.com/2018/01/09/russiagate-turns-on-its-originators

Robertson, H. C., & Brott, P. E. (2017). *Military veterans' midlife career transition and life satisfaction.* Available at: https://tpcjournal.nbcc.org/military-veterans-midlife-career-transition-and-life-satisfaction/

Robertson, H. C., & Brott, P. E. (2017). *Military Veterans' Midlife Career Transition and Life Satisfaction.* Available at: https://tpcjournal.nbcc.org/military-veterans-midlife-career-transition-and-life-satisfaction/

Roberts, R., Frazer, L., Weaven, S., & Thaichon, P. (2020). Understanding cultural diversity in franchising: Recommendations and implications for recruitment of migrant franchisees. In V. Ratten (Ed.), *Entrepreneurial Opportunities*. Emerald Publishing Limited. doi:10.1108/978-1-83909-285-520201006

Rockefeller, M. L. (2016). Why The Military Is The Best Entrepreneurship Training Program In America. *Forbes*.

ROKETSAN. (2019). www.roketsan.com.tr

Roland, A. (2009). The Military-Industrial Complex: lobby and trope. In A. J. Bacevich (Ed.), *The Long War: A New History of U.S. National Security Policy Since World War II* (pp. 335–370). Columbia University Press.

Rosado-Serrano, A., Paul, J., & Dikova, D. (2018). International franchising: A literature review and research agenda. *Journal of Business Research*, *85*, 238–257. doi:10.1016/j.jbusres.2017.12.049

Rose, G. (2017). Introduction, from the anthology: What was the liberal world? *Foreign Affairs*. Retrieved from https://www.foreignaffairs.com/articles/2017-03-06/introduction

Rosen, S. J. (1973). *Testing the theory of the military-industrial complex*. Lexington Books.

Ross, E. (2015). *Life after war: veterans turned successful entrepreneurs*. Available at: https://www.theguardian.com/small-business-network/2015/mar/03/war-veterans-successful-entrepreneurs-military

Russell, R. D. (1989). How Organisational Culture Can Help to Institutionalise the Spirit of Innovation in Entrepreneurial Ventures. *Journal of Organizational Change Management*, *2*(3), 7–15. doi:10.1108/09534818910005773

Russian use of private military and security companies-- the implications for European and Norwegian Security, Norwegian Defence Research Establishment (FFI). (2018). https://www.cmi.no/publications/file/6637-russian-use-of-private-military-and-security.pdf

Russo, J. E., & Schoemaker, P. J. H. (1990). Decision Traps. The Ten barriers To Brilliant Decision-Making and how to Overcome Them. New York: Fireside Ed.

SAGE. (2019). http://www.sage.tubitak.gov.tr/tr/kurumsal/tubitak-sagenin-misyonu

Saheed, G. A., Taiwo, A. A., & Alebiosu, S. O. (2014). Entrepreneurship education as panacea for sustainable economic development of Nigeria. *Journal of Research in Education and Society.*, *5*(1), 20–31.

Salami, C. G. E. (2011). Entrepreneurial interventionism and challenges of youth unemployment in Nigeria. *Global Journal of Management and Business Research*, *II*(7), 4–25.

SanJuan, E. (2011). Mapping knowledge domains combing symbolic relations with graph theory. *Processing of the International Conference on Knowledge Discovery and Information Retrieval (SSTM-2011)*, 519-528. DOI: 10.5220/0003721105190528

Sankaran, S., & Battisto, J. (2018). *Financing Their Future: Veteran Entrepreneurs and Capital Access*. Available at: https://www.fedsmallbusiness.org/veteran-entrepreneurs-and-capital-access

Schaper, M., & Volery, T. (2004). *Entrepreneurship and small business: A Pacific Rim perspective*. John Wiley and Sons Australia Ltd.

Schenck, J. R. (2019). Designed to give back: Franchise businesses are excellent opportunities for veterans to continue serving. *Franchising World*, *6*(51), 24–27.

Schlossberg, N., Waters, E., & Goodman, J. (1995). *Counseling adults in transition*. Springer.

Schumpeter, J. A. (1949). Economic Theory and Entrepreneurial History, Change and the Entrepreneur. Harvard University Press.

Schumpeter, J. A. (1934). *The theory of economic development: An inquiry into profits, capital, credit, interest and business cycle*. Harvard University Press.

Sears, N. A. (2017). What might Morgenthau have to say about the administration's emerging foreign policy? *National Interest*. Retrieved from https://nationalinterest.org/feature/trump-can-learn-morgenthaus-6-principles-political-realism-19481

Seibert, T. (2010). *Turkey's military has a stake in 60 companies*. Available at: https://www.thenational.ae/world/europe/turkey-s-military-has-a-stake-in-60-companies-1.557015

Senge, P. (1990). *The fifth discipline*. Doubleday.

Serrat, O. (2008). The sustainable livelihoods approach. In *Knowledge Solutions*. Springer.

Şeşen, H. (2010). *Öncülleri ve Sonuçları ile Örgüt İçi Girişimcilik: Türk Savunma Sanayinde Bir Araştırma, Doktora Tezi*. KHO Savunma Bilimleri Enstitüsü.

Shadish, W. R. Jr, Cook, T. D., & Leviton, L. C. (1991). *Foundations of Program Evaluation: Theories of Practice*. Sage.

Shane, S. (2003). *A general theory of entrepreneurship: The individual opportunity nexus*. Edward Elgar. doi:10.4337/9781781007990

Shane, S. (2004). *Academic Entrepreneurship: University Spinoffs and Wealth Creation*. Edward Elgar Publishing Limited.

Shane, S., & Venkataraman, S. (2000). The Promise of Entrepreneurship as a Field of Research. *Academy of Management Review*, *25*(1), 217–227. doi:10.5465/amr.2000.2791611

Shao, J., & Wu, S. (2018). Military Experience of Managers and Government Subsidies: From Dual Perspectives of Corporate Philanthropy and Redundant Employees. *Journal of Shanghai University of Finance and Economics*, *20*(3), 63–78.

Sharma, P., & Chrisman, J. (1999). Toward a Reconciliation of the Definitional Issues in the Field of Corporate Entrepreneurship. *Entrepreneurship Theory and Practice*, *23*(3), 11–27. doi:10.1177/104225879902300302

Sheingate, A. D. (2003). Political entrepreneurship, institutional change, and American economic development. *Studies in American Political Development*, *17*(2), 185–203. doi:10.1017/S0898588X03000129

Short, J. C., Zachary, M. A., & Ketchen, D. J. Jr. (2018). Entrepreneurial orientation rhetoric and franchise system size: The moderating role of military veteran recruitment. *Journal of Business Venturing Insights*, *10*, 1–10. doi:10.1016/j.jbvi.2018.e00097

Shrader, R. C., & Simon, M. (1997). Corporate Versus Independent New Ventures: Resource, Strategy, and Performance Differences. *Journal of Business Venturing*, *12*(1), 47–66. doi:10.1016/S0883-9026(96)00053-5

Siddiqa, A. (2007). *Military Inc.: Inside Pakistan's Military Economy*. Pluto Press.

Siddiqa-Agha. (2000). *Power, Perks, Prestige and Privileges: Military's Economic Activities in Pakistan*. Paper presented at the International Conference on Soldiers in Business, Jakarta, Indonesia.

Simes, D. (2017). Current mutual hostility threatens an explosive confrontation. *National Interest*. Retrieved from https://nationalinterest.org/feature/the-costs-ignoring-russia-21888

Singh, G., & DeNoble, A. (2003). Early retirees as the next generation of entrepreneurs. *Entrepreneurship Theory and Practice*, *27*(3), 207–226. doi:10.1111/1540-8520.t01-1-00001

SIPRI. (2017). https://www.sipri.org/databases/milex

Skarzynsky, P., & Gibson, R. (2008). *Innovation to the Core: A Blueprint for Transforming the Way Your Company Innovates*. Harvard Business Review Press.

Slaughter, S., & Leslie, L. (1997). *Academic Capitalism: Politics, Policies and the Entrepreneurial University*. Johns Hopkins University Press.

Slavnic, Z. (2010). Political economy of informalization. *European Societies*, *12*(1), 3–23.

Smaliukienė, R. (2014). Entrepreneurship Opportunities after Military Career: Practice in Central and Eastern versus Western Europe. *Entrepreneurial Business and Economics Review*, *1*(4), 97–108. doi:10.15678/EBER.2013.010408

SmallBusiness.com. (2018). *Americans Rank Military and Small Business as Nation's Two Most Trusted Institutions*. Available at: https://smallbusiness.com/about-small-businesses/americans-trust-in-small-business/

SMEDAN. (2013). *SMEDAN and national bureau of statistics collaborative survey: Selected findings 2013*. Abuja: SMEDAN. Retrieved from Small and Medium Enterprises Development Agency of Nigeria: http://nigerianstat.gov.ng

Smith, S. (2020). *Most Military and Government Jobs Pay Less Than the Private Sector*. Available at: https://www.thebalancecareers.com/historic-military-pay-raises-3354557

Smith-Osborne, A. (2013). Veterans Administration health care policies as a protective mechanism supporting an expected life trajectory after military service. *Social Work in Public Health*, *28*(2), 81–96. doi:10.1080/19371918.2011.552038 PMID:23461344

Sobota, J. (2017). *Veteran-owned businesses and their owners: Data from the U.S. Census Bureau's Survey of Business Owners*. U.S. Small Business Administration Office of Advocacy.

Sofat, P. (2016). Human resource management in the armed forces: Transition of a soldier to a second career. IDSA Monograph Series No. 54.

Soriano, D. R. (2017). Small business and entrepreneurship: their role in economic and social development. *Entrepreneurship & Regional Development*, *29*(1-2), 1-3. doi:10.1080/08985626.2016.1255438

Sottile, J. (2017). *America's Military-Industrial Addiction*. Retrieved from: https://consortiumnews.com/2017/12/01/americas-military-industrial-addiction/

Sparrow, A. (2008). *What is the military covenant?* Available at: https://www.theguardian.com/politics/2008/mar/04/defence.military

Spearin, C. R. (2018). Russia's Military and Security Privatization. *Parameters*, *48*(2), 39–49.

Special report: 2019 top franchises for veterans. (2019, July). *Franchise Business Review*, 4, 10-13.

Staskiel, H. (2020). *The VA's Definition of "Veteran" – An In-Depth Look*. Available at: https://www.hillandponton.com/vas-definition-veteran-depth-look/

Steinfioff, D., & Burgers, J. (1993). *Small business fundamentals*. McGraw Hill International.

Stepan, A. (1971). *The Military in Politics: Changing patterns in Brazil*. Princeton University Press.

Sterman, J. (2000). *Business dynamics: Systems thinking and modeling for a complex world*. Irwin McGraw-Hill.

Steven, H., & Gumpert, D. E. (2002). The heart of entrepreneurship. *Harvard Business Review*, (June-July), 77–85.

Stevenson, H., Roberts, M., & Grousback, H. (1985). *New Business Ventures and the Entrepreneur*. Richard D. Irwin.

Steyaert, C., & Hjorth, D. (Eds.). (2003). *New Movements in Entrepreneurship*. Edward Elgar.

Steyaert, C., & Hjorth, D. (Eds.). (2006). *Entrepreneurship as Social Change*. Edward Elgar.

Storlie, C. (2010). *Combat to corporate: Applying military Spec Ops principles to business success*. Praeger.

Storlie, C. (2010). *Combat to Corporate: Applying Military Spec Ops Principles to Business Success*. Praeger.

Strange, R. E. (1984). Retirement from the service: The individual and his family. In F. W. Van Praag, M. (2003). Business survival and success of young small business owners. *Small Business Economics*, *21*(1), 1–17.

Strong, A. (2017). Trump promotes Reagan Era "peace through strength" in national security strategy. *CBN.* Retrieved from https://www1.cbn.com/cbnnews/national-security/2017/december/trump-promotes-reagan-era-peace-through-strength-in-national-security-strategy

Sukhankin, S. (2019). *Unleashing the PMCs and Irregulars in Ukraine: Crimea and Donbas.* Retrieved from: https://jamestown.org/program/unleashing-the-pmcs-and-irregulars-in-ukraine-crimea-and-donbas/

Suleiman, A. S. (2006). *The business entrepreneur: Entrepreneurial development and small enterprises.* Entrepreneurship Academy Publishing.

Sull, D., Homkes, R., & Sull, C. (2015, Mar.). Why Strategy Execution Unravels—and What to Do About It. *Harvard Business Review.*

Swedburg, R. (1993). Explorations in economic sociology. New York: Russell Sage Foundation.

Taiwo, O. (2013). Employment choice and mobility in multi-sector labor markets: Theoretical model and evidence from Ghana. *International Labour Review*, *152*(3–4), 469–492.

Tang, A. (2015). *Business, military, government seize land for rubber in Myanmar: rights group.* Retrieved from: https://www.reuters.com/article/us-myanmar-rights-land/business-military-government-seize-land-for-rubber-in-myanmar-rights-group-idUSKBN0MM1N120150326

Tchantouridze, L. (2001). Awakening of spirits: Eurasianism and geopolitics in the foreign policy of Russia. Queen's University (Canada), ProQuest Dissertations Publishing, NQ63460, p. ii.

Tekingunduz, A. (2018). *Are private military contractors any different from mercenaries?* Retrieved from: https://www.trtworld.com/americas/are-private-military-contractors-any-different-from-mercenaries-20680

Thang, V. H. (2017). The restructuring and improved performance of military-run enterprises. *National Defense Journal.* Available at: http://tapchiqptd.vn/en/theory-and-practice/the-restructuring-and-improved-performance-of-militaryrun-enterprises/10726.html

The Federal Council of Switzerland. (n.d.). *Federal Department of Foreign Affairs, Participating States of the Montreux Document.* https://www.eda.admin.ch/eda/en/home/foreign-policy/international-law/international-humanitarian-law/private-military-securi- ty-companies/participating-states.html

The Millennium Report (2016). *Who Owns and Controls the Military-Industrial Complex?* Available at: http://themillenniumreport.com/2016/03/who-owns-and-controls-the-military-industrial-complex/

The VetFran Program. (n.d.). *VetFran.* https://www.vetfran.org/about-us/

Thisday. (2016, December 11). *Armed forces retire: 507 trained military retirees for post service life*. Retrieved on 18 May, 2020 from https://www.thisdaylive.com/index.php/2016/12/11/armed-forces-retire-507-train-military-retirees-for-post-service-life/

Tidd, J., & Bessant, J. R. (2011). Managing innovation: Integrating technological, market, and organizational change (4th ed.). Wiley.

TNI Staff. (2017). A symposium on US-Russia relations in the age of Trump. *National Interest*. Retrieved from https://nationalinterest.org/feature/america-russia-permanent-confrontation-21891

TOBB. (2017). Turkey Defense Industry Sector Report. Academic Press.

Tomaso, R. M. (2005). *Bigger Isn't Always Better: The New Mindset for Real Business Growth?* AMACOM.

Top 10 Traits of a Good Franchisee. (2019, January 30). *Franchise Direct*. https://www.franchisedirect.com/information/informationforfranchisees/top10traitsofagoodfranchisee/9/340/

Toth, R. (2012). Entrepreneurial human capital and entrepreneurial dynamics: evidence from natural experiment. *Economics*. https://www.semanticscholar.org/paper/Entrepreneurial-Human-Capital-and-Entrepreneurial-a-Toth/10d60012b1eebd6730070778fdbd4bbdc325dac0

Tucker, J. D., Chang, H., Brandt, A., Gao, X., Lin, M., Luo, J., Song, P., Sun, K., & Zhang, X. (2011). An Empirical Analysis of Overlap Publication in Chinese Language and English Research Manuscripts. *PLoS One*, *6*(7), e22149. doi:10.1371/journal.pone.0022149 PMID:21765946

Tuoi tre. (2017). *Vietnam's deputy defense minister on why military must engage in business activities*. Available at: https://tuoitrenews.vn/business/41955/vietnam-deputy-defense-minister-on-why-military-must-engage-in-business-activities

Türksam, Y. (2017). http://turksam.org/turk-savunma-sanayine-bir-bakis-dun-ve-bugun

TUSAS. (2019). https://www.tusas.com

Tushman, M., & Nadler, D. (1986). Organizing for Innovation. *California Management Review*, *28*(3), 74–92. doi:10.2307/41165203

U. S. Small Business Administration. (n.d.). https://www.sba.gov/content/facts-veterans-and-entrepreneurship

U.S. Small Business Administration. (2013). *Small business development centers (SBDCs)*. Retrieved from https://www.sba.gov/content/small-businessdevelopment-centers-sbdcs

Udeozor, V. (2016). *Evaluating Compulsory Entrepreneurship Education Across Private And Public Higher Education Institutions in Nigeria*. Available at: http://irep.ntu.ac.uk/id/eprint/38446/1/1239809_udeozor.pdf

United Nations. (n.d.). *Human Rights, Office of the High Commissioner, International Convention against the Recruitment, Use, Financing and Training of Mercenaries Adopted and opened for signature and ratification by General Assembly resolution 44/34 of 4 December 1989 Entry into force: 20 October 2001, in accordance with article 19*. Available at: https://www.ohchr.org/EN/ProfessionalInterest/ Pages/Mercenaries.aspx

United States Census Bureau. (2007). *Veteran-owned businesses and their owners*. Data from the Census Bureau's Survey of Business Owners. Retrieved from https://www.sba.gov/sites/default/files/393tot.pdf

Urbano, D., & Aparicio, S. (2016). Entrepreneurship capital types and economic growth: International evidence. *Technological Forecasting and Social Change*, *102*, 34–44. doi:10.1016/j.techfore.2015.02.018

Usman, E. (2011). *Armed Forces Resettlement Centre graduates 149 retiring servicemen*. Available at: https://www.vanguardngr.com/2011/12/armed-forces-resettlement-centre-graduates-149-retiring-servicemen/

Usman, E. (2016, June 23). DHQ retires 464 Military personnel. *Vanguard Nigeria Newspaper*.

Usman, E. (2017). *NAFRC trains 403 retiring soldiers*. Available at: https://www.vanguardngr.com/2017/12/nafrc-trains-403-retiring-soldiers/

Usman, E. (2018). *Military personnel retire says NAFRC Commandant*. Available at: https://www.vanguardngr.com/2018/06/320-military-personnel-retire-says-nafrc-commandant/

Usman, E. (2019). *35 middle cadre Military personnel undergo training on entrepreneurship, mgt*. Available at: https://www.vanguardngr.com/2019/01/35-middle-cadre-military-personnel-undergo-training-on-entrepreneurship-mgt/

Usman, E. (2020). *342 military officers retire in June*. Available at: https://www.vanguardngr.com/2020/06/342-military-officers-retire-in-june/

Valero, A., & Figueroa, E. T. (2011). La empresa de negócios y la alta dirección: Procedimientos politicos de gobierno (3rd ed.). Pamplona, Spain: Eunsa.

Valero, A., & Lucas, J. L. (1991). *Política de empresa: El gobierno de la empresa de negocios*. Pamplona, Spain: Eunsa.

van Crefeld, M. (1977). *Supplying War: Logistics from Wallenstein to Patton*. Cambridge University Press.

van Solinge, H. (2014). Who opts for self-employment after retirement? A longitudinal study in the Netherlands. *European Journal of Ageing*, *11*(3), 261–272. doi:10.100710433-013-0303-7 PMID:28804332

Van Solinge, H., & Henkens, K. (2000). Adjustment to and satisfaction with retirement: Two of a kind? *Psychology and Aging*, *23*(2), 422–434. doi:10.1037/0882-7974.23.2.422 PMID:18573015

Van Vuuren, J. J., & Groenewald, D. (2007). A critical analysis of the influence of start-up factors in small businesses and entrepreneurial ventures in South Africa. *Acta Commercii*, *7*(1), 269–280. doi:10.4102/ac.v7i1.39

van Wyk, G. J., & De Jager, J. W. (2009). Marketing orientation of franchisors. *African Journal of Business Management*, *3*(12), 907–914.

Vaziri, S. A., Hosseini, S. E., & Jafari, A. (2014). The Impact of entrepreneurship education on entrepreneurial skills of university graduates. *International Conference on Arts, Economics and Management (ICAEM'14)*. Retrieved on 25 December, 2020 from http://icehm.org/upload/9718ED0314050.pdf

Vego, M. (2013). On Military Creativity. *Joint Forces Quarterly*, (70), 83-90.

Venkatachalam, V. B., & Waqif, A. A. (2005). Outlook on integrating entrepreneurship in management education in India. *Decision (Washington, D.C.)*, *32*(2), 57–71.

Vigoda-Gadot, E., Baruch, Y., & Grimland, S. (2010). Career transitions: An empirical examination of second career of military retirees. *Public Personnel Management*, *39*(4), 379–404. doi:10.1177/009102601003900405

Vilà, J. (2011). Innovative Culture: Values, Principles and Practices of Senior Executives in Highly Innovative Companies. Teaching Note SMN-681-E. IESE Publishing.

Vilà, J. (2012). Normalize Innovation to Transform Your Firm. *IESE Insight*, (14).

VOA. (2017). *Military-linked Business Enterprises Dominate in Cuba*. Available at: https://www.voanews.com/americas/military-linked-business-enterprises-dominate-cuba

Vogt, D., Perkins, D. F., Copeland, L. A., Finley, E. P., Jamieson, C. S., Booth, B., Lederer, S., & Gilman, C. L. (2018). The Veterans Metric Initiative study of US veterans' experiences during their transition from military service. *BMJ Open*, *2018*(8), e020734. doi:10.1136/bmjopen-2017-020734 PMID:29895650

Vombatkere, S. G. (2015). Is the 'babu' scared of veterans' skills? *Indian Defence Review*, 31. Retrieved on 25 December, 2020 from http://www.indiandefencereview.com/isthe- bab-scared-of-veterans-skills/

Vroom, V. H. (1964). *Work and motivation*. Jossey-Bass.

Wada, I. (2020). *Senate committee lauds Lar for judicious use of NAFRC funds*. Available at: https://guardian.ng/news/senate-committee-lauds-lar-for-judicious-use-of-nafrc-funds/

Waldman Associates & REDA International. (2004). *Entrepreneurship and Business Ownership in the Service-Disabled Veteran Community*. U.S. Small Business Administration, Office of Advocacy.

Walia, A. (2013). *Eisenhower and Kennedy Blow: The Whistle: The Military Industrial Complex*. Available at: https://www.collective-evolution.com/2013/02/15/eisenhower-and-kennedy-blow-the-whistle-the-military-industrial-complex/

Wang, C., & Kafouros, M. I. (2009). What factors determine innovation performance in emerging economies? Evidence from China. *International Business Review*, *18*(6), 606–616. doi:10.1016/j.ibusrev.2009.07.009

Wang, M., Henkens, K., & van Solinge, H. (2011). Retirement adjustment: A review of theoretical and empirical advancements. *The American Psychologist*, *66*(3), 204–213. doi:10.1037/a0022414 PMID:21341882

Wang, M., & Shultz, K. S. (2010). Employee retirement: A review and recommendations for future investigation. *Journal of Management*, *36*(1), 172–206. doi:10.1177/0149206309347957

Wang, Y., & Xu, K. (2019). Conservative or Radical: The Influence of Managers' Military Experience on the Company's Risk-Taking. *Foreign Economics & Management*, *41*(9), 17–30.

Wang, Y., & Xu, Ye. (2020). Does Military Experience of Managers Affect Corporate Governance? Evidence from China's Listed Companies. *Management Review*, *32*(1), 153–165.

Weber, M. (1905). The Protestant Ethic and the Spirit of Capitalism. London: Unwin Paperbacks.

Westerlund, F., & Norberg, J. (2016). Military Means for Non-Military Measures: The Russian Approach to the Use of Armed Force as Seen in Ukraine. *Journal of Slavic Military Studies*, *29*(4), 581.

Westwood, M. (1999). *Career transition program for Canadian peacekeeping veterans*. Veterans Affairs Canada.

Westwood, M., Black, T., & McLean, H. (2002). A Re-entry Program for Peacekeeping Soldiers: Promoting Personal and Career Transition. *Canadian Journal of Counselling*, *36*, 221–232.

Wiklund, J., & Shepherd, D. (2005). Entrepreneurial orientation and small business performance: A configurational approach. *Journal of Business Venturing*, *20*(1), 71–91. doi:10.1016/j.jbusvent.2004.01.001

Wilson, E. (2008). *The military millionaires who control Pakistan Inc*. Available at: https://www.spectator.co.uk/2008/01/the-military-millionaires-who-control-pakistan-inc/

Winsor, R. D., Manolis, C., Kaufmann, P. J., & Kashyap, V. (2012). Manifest conflict and conflict aftermath in franchise systems: A 10-year examination. *Journal of Small Business Management*, *50*(4), 621–651. doi:10.1111/j.1540-627X.2012.00369.x

Wolpert, D. S. (2000). Military retirement and the transition to civilian life. In J. A. Martin, L. N. Rosen, & L. R. Sparacino (Eds.), *The military family: A practice guide for human service providers* (pp. 103–119). Praeger.

Woo, C. Y., Cooper, A. C., & Dunkelberg, W. C. (1988). Entrepreneurial Typologies: Definitions and Implications. In Frontiers of Entrepreneurship Research. Babson College.

Woodward, R., & Jenkings, N. (2011). Military identities in the situated accounts of British military personnel. *Sociology*, *45*(2), 252–268. doi:10.1177/0038038510394016

Worldometer. (2020). *Nigeria Population (Live).* Available at: https://www.worldometers.info/world-population/nigeria-population/

Wu, D. D. (2017). Russia-China relations reach a new high. *The Diplomat*. Retrieved from https://thediplomat.com/2017/07/russia-china-relations-reach-a-new-high/

Xinhua Press. (2019). *Most beautiful veterans' urge ex-service personnel to contribute more to China's development.* http://www.chinadaily.com.cn/a/201901/23/WS5c47d7f5a3106c65c34e6072.html

Xue, J.F. (2011). Structural reform of military establishment should coordinate with the level of social and economic development. *Military Economic Research*, 2.

Yahaya, L. A., & Mustapha, M. L. A. (2004). Efficacy of client-centered and rational-emotive behaviours therapics in reducing behavior among in-school adolescents in Ilorin, Nigeria. *International Journal of Instruction*, *8*(1), 61–74.

Yanos, R. (2004). *Perception of adjustment to civilian life among recently retired airforce officers.* Available from: https://drum.lib.umd.edu/bitstream/1903/2321/1/umi-umd-2126.pdf

Year Book, S. I. P. R. I. (2008). *Armaments, Disarmaments and International Security*. Oxford University Press.

Yin, R. K. (2012). *Applications of case study research.* Sage.

Yohana, C. I. D., & Ugboaja, O. (2019). Cover Story. Hope, 1, 33.

Yusufa, L., & Minai, M. S. (2016). Military Personnel as Entrepreneurs in Nigeria. *International Journal of Sciences Basic and Applied Research*, *28*(3), 217–230.

Yusuf, L., & Minai, M. S. (2016). Entrepreneurial training and career path of retired military personnel as entrepreneurs in Nigeria. *International Journal of Sciences, Basic and Applied Research*, *28*(3), 217–230.

Zerbe, W. J., & Paulhus, D. L. (1987). Socially desirable responding in organizational behavior: A recognition. *Academy of Management Review*, *12*(2), 250–264. doi:10.5465/amr.1987.4307820

Ziencik, C. (2020). Transitioning from the Military to Higher Education: A Case Study of the Transition Assistance Program. *Journal of Veterans Studies*, *6*(2), 30–45. doi:10.21061/jvs.v6i2.178

Zikmund, W. G., Babin, B. J., Carr, J. C., & Griffin, M. (2010). *Business research methods.* Wadsworth.

Zinker, V. G. (2006). Career Counselling: A holistic approach (7th ed.). Thomas Brooks/Cole Publishing Co.

Zogas, A. (2017, February). *US military veterans' difficult transitions back to civilian life and the VA's response.* Watson Institute International and Public Affairs. https://watson.brown.edu/costsofwar/papers/2017/us-military-veterans-difficult-transitions-back-civilian-life-and-va-s-response

Головорезы с тесаками наперевес. (2018). https://lenta.ru/arti- cles/2018/02/21/chvk_interview/

About the Contributors

Sanya Ojo holds a PhD in Entrepreneurship. He is an accomplished entrepreneur with forty years' experience. This informs his research interests in diaspora/ethnic entrepreneurship, international business strategy and management. He has the privilege of mobility in career choices, exploring options critically, establishing educational preferences, and placing bets on multiple knowledge paths, as a consequence of his capacity to benefit from high-end knowledge and research. Currently, he operates a goal-oriented consultancy in business and entrepreneurship both in practice and the academic field. He is a Fellow of Higher Education Academy (FHEA) and a Senior Lecturer at the Nigerian Defence Academy, Kaduna, Nigeria. As an award-winner, he has published in reputable academic journals and resources.

* * *

Bem Japhet Audu is a lecturer in the Department of History and War Studies, and Research Fellow, Centre for the Study of Leadership and Complex Military Operations, Nigerian Defence Academy, Kaduna, Nigeria. He earned his PhD in History (International Studies) at the prestigious Nigerian Defence Academy, Kaduna in 2016. He also studied M.A. History (2012) and M.A. International Relations and Strategic Studies (2007) as well as B.A. History (2003) at Benue State University, Makurdi. He has published many scholarly articles in local and international journals and contributed chapters in books. One of his notable books is; Wars and Changing Patterns of Inter-Group Relations in the Middle Benue Valley, c.1300-1900 (2018).

Pedro B. Água is a Professor of General Management at the Portuguese Naval Academy. He has authored several articles and book chapters, while continuing his research in the field of cutting-edge technology, industrialization, innovation and business policy and regularly teaches such. Professor Água has over twenty-five years of experience across high technology endeavours, from defence to telecommunications and oil and gas industry, combining his extensive professional and business background with teaching. Andre holds a Ph.D. in Management and Engineering awarded by the University of Lisbon.

Korhan ARUN received a BA in mathematics from Hacettepe University (Turkey) and an M.B.A in Total Quality Management from Dokuz Eylul University in 2003 and a Ph.D. in Organization and Management from Ataturk University (Turkey) in 2008. He is an assistant Professor of Organization and Management at the University at Namik Kemal University (Tekirdag/Turkey). His current research and teaching interests include leadership, power and influence, organization and management development. Dr. Arun worked at the government agencies for 15 years. In addition, he had an advisor position for NATO (KFOR/ Kosovo Force) in 2012. He has been involved in several projects to improve leadership in the Turkish Army while he is in the editorial board of many journals indexed in web of science and SCOPUS.

Anthony Chukwu - BA, MA (Ibadan); PhD (Leipzig, Germany), is a philosophy generalist who recently taught at Seneca College in Canada. His research interests include: Analytical Philosophy, African Philosophy, Epistemology, Logic and, Social and Political Philosophy. He is current working on procedural Uses and Abuses of Reason in Complex Military Operations. A military operation presupposes an engagement on the basis of rules that are founded on practical use of reason and rooted in law and ethical consideration. But, while in combat situations, military exigency trumps reason and the need to neutralize a threat at all cost takes precedence over rationality and morality. Yet, humane and ethical considerations would reject a situation of anything goes——especially abuse of reason, and others: abuse of right, abuse of law, etc.——that ensues. The situation of litany of abuses created by military operations not only conflicts with, but vitiates the rational and practical uses of reason. To this extent, he is currently exploring ways to center rationality and formal moral reasoning in the discourse of procedural complex military operations.

Anacleto Correia is a professor of Information Systems at the Portuguese Navy Academy. He holds a Ph.D. in Computer Science, a M.Sc. in Statistics and Information Management, a B.Sc. degree in Management, and also a B.Sc. in Naval Sciences from the Portuguese Naval Academy. His research interests are focused on requirements and software engineering, process modelling, data mining, machine learning, and business engineering. Professor Correia has more than 15 years of industry experience, leading projects and architecting large scale software projects, and is the author of several scientific papers in journals and conference proceedings.

Denise M. Cumberland is an Associate Professor in the Master of Science in Human Resources and Organization Development Program at the University of Louisville. Her research interests include governance, entrepreneurship, leadership, and training within global organizations, franchise firms and the nonprofit sector. She has authored eight book chapters and has over 30 journal articles in publications such as Human Resource Development Review, Leadership and Organization Development Journal, Human Resource Development International, Human Resource Development Quarterly, Nonprofit Management & Leadership, and Teaching and Learning in Medicine.

Jamiu Danga is an Asst Lecturer and a PhD candidate of the Nigerian Defence Academy.

Mogbekeloluwa Oluyinka Fakokunde is a Brigadier General in the Nigeria Army. He is presently the Director Quality Assurance in Nigerian Defence Academy, Kaduna and also a Senior Lecturer in the department of Psychology of the same institution.

Wu Fei is General Editor of US New York Journal "Communication and Public Diplomacy" (Online) ISSN 2578-4277 (Print) ISSN 2578-4269. A Professor at China Guangzhou Jinan University, WU is a columnist and writer for several major Hong Kong and international newspapers and magazines and has published more than 20 books in China, Hong Kong, and Taiwan. He also is a commentator for several television channels that have a combined audience of 20 million viewers in China mainland and Hong Kong. Wu Fei is an alumna of the US East West center, and membership in the international studies association and Visiting Researching Fellow at Georgetown University (2010 and 2012). Between 2011 and 2012, he served two times as panel chair at the ISA Montreal and San Diego conference. He received several awards at IAFIE annual conferences in 2017, 2018 and 2019 IAFIE at west Virginia \Australian Sydney\New York. Professor Wu Fei also acts as Analyst for Voice of America\Radio free Asia\France 24 English\Russian Sputnik\Hongkong TVB\China CCTV. His research interests include International Communication, Public Diplomacy, and International Relations.

Yang Gao studied at Shanghai Maritime university for BA, Renmin University of China and University of Westminster for MA, and studying at Jilin University for Doctor of Laws. He works as Research Fellow of China Center for Contemporary World Studies, Adjunct Research Fellow of Institute for Global Cooperation and Understanding, Peking University and MA Tutor of Central University of Finance and Economics. He focuses on the Sino-American relationship, Great power strategy and the risks and challenges of the Belt and Road Initiative(BRI).

Hua Geng is a teacher at the School of Language, Literature and Law, Xi'an University of Architecture and Technology, China. Her research interests include innovation and entrepreneurship, college students' entrepreneurship, internationalization of SMEs, entrepreneurship and China's Belt and Road Initiative (BRI), foreign linguistics and applied linguistics, and practicability of college students' English competence. She has attended international meetings: International Conference on Education Science and Management Engineering (ESME) and International Workshop on Education Technology and Computer Science and published correlative papers. She has also worked as a project leader of S&T Fund for Young Researchers in her university XAUAT.

Yu Hongjun, born in Nong'an County of Jilin province. He studied at Northeast Normal University for BA and MA and Renmin University of China for Doctor of Laws. He worked as a senior visiting scholar in Russia's Dun Rostov University in the 1990s. He works as an Adjunct Professor of Renmin University of China, International College of Defence Studies,NDU,PLA,China.He is also a Doctoral Tutor of Renmin University of China. Yu Hongjun is a former professional diplomat. He used to be Vice Minister of International Department of the CPC Central Committee, President of China Center for Contemporary World Studies (CCCWS) and Member of Foreign Affairs Committee of the CPPCC National Committee. He served as Chinese Extraordinary and Plenipotentiary Ambassador to Uzbekistan. He is Vice President of Chinese People's Association for Peace and Disarmament (CPAPD). He is also appointed as Special Expert of Lecture Room of the Public Department of theCPC Central Committee, Senior Research Fellow of the Academy of Contemporary China and World Studies of China Foreign Languages Publishing Administration, Expert of People's Daily Overseas Thinktank, and Special experts in the talent pool of CPPCC.

Qingan Huang is a Professor at the International Business School, Guangdong University of Finance & Economics, China. He is the founding dean of this school. He also serves as a Senior Lecturer in Strategic Management at Royal Docks School of Business & Law, University of East London. His research interests include internationalization of SMEs, marketing, strategic leadership, entrepreneurship and China's Belt and Road Initiative (BRI). He regularly presented his projects at the AoM and SMS annual meetings. He published papers in International Marketing Review, Journal of Business Ethics, International Journal of Entrepreneurial Behavior & Research and edited book chapter.

Sagir Lawan (rtd) is currently a Senior Lecturer in the Department of Electrical Electronic Engineering Nigerian Defence Academy. Sagir Lawan is an author, teacher, career coach, veteran, and an expert in the field of Telecommunication and Electronic Engineering. During his career he assisted thousands of service members in their searches for employment, placing more than 500 in their new jobs. Prior to civilian life, he graduated from the Brunel University London, Obafemi Awolowo University Ile-Ife Nigeria and Nigerian Defence Academy. He served as a communication signal officer with the UN in Sudan and Sierra Leone and participated in many military operations in Nigeria. He teaches telecommunication, management and strategic security studies course. He also gives seminars on entrepreneurship career and job change, writes about the career transition process, and continues to counsel current and former military personnel on entrepreneurship.He is a regular contributor to many reputable International and local journals. Sagir lives in Kaduna with his wife and children. He is an active member Nigerian Veterans community Veterans Sagir enjoys reading, play Badminton and Scrabble.

Olcay Okun graduated from Turkish Military Academy and received a Ph.D. in Organization and Management from Hasan Kalyoncu University (Turkey). He is a colonel at Turkish Military Forces Head Quarters. His research focuses on identifying and understanding key pathways involved throughout the development of organizational management, leadership, strategic management, and organizational behavior. He had an advisor positions for NATO. He has been involved in several projects to improve leadership in the Turkish Army while he has much scientific research in web of science and SCOPUS.

Usman A Tar (PhD) Professor of Political Science and Defence Studies and distinguished endowed Chair of Defence and Security Studies at the Nigerian Defence Academy, and Director of the Academy's flagship Centre for Defence Studies and Documentation (CDSD). Prof Tar has held faculty positions in Africa, United Kingdom and Republic of Iraq. He is a Member of the Board of Social Science Research Council's African Peacebuilding Network (SSRC/APN), New York, USA. Prof Tar was a member of the Nigerian Presidential Committee to review Nigeria's National Defence Policy (2017), and presently a member of the Nigerian Federal Ministry of Defence Think Tank on National Security. He was formerly, Associate Research Fellow at John and Elnora Ferguson Centre for Africa Studies (JEFCAS) at the University of Bradford, UK. He was also an Assistant Professor at the Department of Politics and International Relations and Director of Postgraduate Studies at the University of Kurdistan-Hewler, Northern Iraq. Prof Tar is the author of *The Politics of Neoliberal Democracy in Africa* (London/New York: IB Tauris, 2009); *Globalization in Africa: Perspectives on Development, Security, and the Environment* (Lexington Books, Lanham MD, USA, 2016); *Defence Transformation and the Consolidation of Democracy in Nigeria* (Kaduna: Academy Publishers, 2018); and *New Architecture for Regional Security in Africa: Counter-Terrorism and Counter-Insurgency in the Lake Chad Basin* (Lexington Books, Lanham MD, USA, 2020). Prof Tar has consulted, or consults, for the *Westminster Foundation* *for Democracy* (WFD, Nigeria), *United Nations Development Programme* (UNDP, Nigeria), *United States Institute for Peace* (Nigeria Office) and *Konrad Adaneur Stiftung* (German Development Fund, Nigeria). He also serves as visiting professor and external examiner to several institutions of higher learning in Nigeria and overseas. Address: Centre for Defence Studies and Documentation, Nigerian Defence Academy, Kaduna. email: uatar@nda.edu.ng

Sharkdam Wapmuk (PhD) is an Associate Professor with the Department of Defence and Security Studies, Nigerian Defence Academy, Kaduna. Formerly, Senior Research Fellow and Ag. Director of Research and Studies, Nigerian Institute of International Affairs (NIIA), Lagos. Member, Nigerian Political Science Association (NPSA) and Nigerian Society of International Affairs (NSIA). Editor, African perspectives on ACP-EU Relations (with Sesay, A and Ugwuanyi, C.A.), Lagos: Nigerian Institute of International Affairs, 2020; Editor, Civil Society and National Security in Nigeria: A strategic analysis (with Kalu, E. N.), Lagos and Dallas: Concept Publications, 2020; Editor, Culture and Nigeria's Foreign Relations in a Globalizing World (Edited with Louis Eriomala), Abuja: National Institute for Cultural Orientation -NICO, 2020; Editor, Nigeria's Foreign Policy under the Administration of President Muhammadu Buhari: 2015-2019 (Bukar Bukarambe, Osita A. Agbu, and Tola Ilesanmi), Lagos: Nigerian Institute of International Affairs, 2020; Editor, Perspectives on Contemporary Nigerian Politics and International Relations: Essays in Honour of Professor Warisu Oyesina Alli (Edited with Usman A. Tar and Efem Nkam Ubi). Lagos and Kaduna: NIIA and NDA, 2020; Editor, Gas Flaring in the Niger Delta: The Internal and External Dimensions (Edited with Bukar Bukarambe and Osita Agbu). Lagos: Nigerian Institute of International Affairs, 2020. Former Editor, Nigerian Forum: A Journal of Opinion on World Affairs, published by the NIIA. Research Consultant for Humanitarian Dialogue (HD) – UNDP, 2015; Samuel Hall FZE (Think Tank) -2017; Samuel Hall FZE (Think Tank) and International Organisation for Migration (IOM) -2018. He serves as Resource Person to several academic institutions in Nigeria. He has published numerous articles in journals and contributed book chapters on Nigerian foreign policy, security, cooperation and integration, Africa-India relations, think-tanks.

Benzhao Yang is an Associate Professor at Northwestern Polytechnical University (NPU), China & Vice President at NPU Science Park. He also serves as a visiting scholar at Royal Docks School of Business & Law, University of East London. His research interests include knowledge management, Technology transfer, internationalization of SMEs, marketing, entrepreneurship .He regularly presented his projects at annual meetings of entrepreneurship and technology transfer. He published papers in Journal of Northwestern Polytechnical University, Science and Technology Management Research, Statistics and Decision and International Conference on Engineering Management and Service Sciences (EMS).

Gao Yang, studied at Shanghai Maritime university for BA, Renmin University of China and University of Westminster for MA, and studying at Jilin University for Doctor of Laws. He works as Research Fellow of China Center for Contemporary World Studies, Adjunct Research Professor of Institute for Global cooperation and Understanding, Peking University and MA Tutor of Central University of Finance and Economics. He focuses on the Sino-American relationship, Great power strategy and the risks and challenges of the Belt and Road Initiative (BRI).

Index

R

S

T

V

Recommended Reference Books

IGI Global's reference books can now be purchased from three unique pricing formats:
Print Only, E-Book Only, or Print + E-Book.
Shipping fees may apply.

www.igi-global.com

ISBN: 978-1-7998-1048-3
EISBN: 978-1-7998-1049-0
© 2020; 605 pp.
List Price: US$ 285

ISBN: 978-1-5225-8933-4
EISBN: 978-1-5225-8934-1
© 2020; 667 pp.
List Price: US$ 295

ISBN: 978-1-7998-0357-7
EISBN: 978-1-7998-0359-1
© 2020; 451 pp.
List Price: US$ 235

ISBN: 978-1-7998-0070-5
EISBN: 978-1-7998-0071-2
© 2020; 144 pp.
List Price: US$ 175

ISBN: 978-1-5225-6980-0
EISBN: 978-1-5225-6981-7
© 2019; 339 pp.
List Price: US$ 235

ISBN: 978-1-5225-5390-8
EISBN: 978-1-5225-5391-5
© 2018; 125 pp.
List Price: US$ 165

Do you want to stay current on the latest research trends, product announcements, news, and special offers?
Join IGI Global's mailing list to receive customized recommendations, exclusive discounts, and more.
Sign up at: **www.igi-global.com/newsletters.**

Publisher of Peer-Reviewed, Timely, and Innovative Academic Research

IGI Global
PUBLISHER of TIMELY KNOWLEDGE

www.igi-global.com Sign up at www.igi-global.com/newsletters facebook.com/igiglobal twitter.com/igiglobal

Ensure Quality Research is Introduced to the Academic Community

Become an Evaluator for IGI Global Authored Book Projects

The overall success of an authored book project is dependent on quality and timely manuscript evaluations.

Applications and Inquiries may be sent to:
development@igi-global.com

Applicants must have a doctorate (or equivalent degree) as well as publishing, research, and reviewing experience. Authored Book Evaluators are appointed for one-year terms and are expected to complete at least three evaluations per term. Upon successful completion of this term, evaluators can be considered for an additional term.

If you have a colleague that may be interested in this opportunity, we encourage you to share this information with them.

IGI Global Author Services

Providing a high-quality, affordable, and expeditious service, IGI Global's Author Services enable authors to streamline their publishing process, increase chance of acceptance, and adhere to IGI Global's publication standards.

Benefits of Author Services:

- **Professional Service:** All our editors, designers, and translators are experts in their field with years of experience and professional certifications.
- **Quality Guarantee & Certificate:** Each order is returned with a quality guarantee and certificate of professional completion.
- **Timeliness:** All editorial orders have a guaranteed return timeframe of 3-5 business days and translation orders are guaranteed in 7-10 business days.
- **Affordable Pricing:** IGI Global Author Services are competitively priced compared to other industry service providers.
- **APC Reimbursement:** IGI Global authors publishing Open Access (OA) will be able to deduct the cost of editing and other IGI Global author services from their OA APC publishing fee.

Author Services Offered:

English Language Copy Editing
Professional, native English language copy editors improve your manuscript's grammar, spelling, punctuation, terminology, semantics, consistency, flow, formatting, and more.

Scientific & Scholarly Editing
A Ph.D. level review for qualities such as originality and significance, interest to researchers, level of methodology and analysis, coverage of literature, organization, quality of writing, and strengths and weaknesses.

Figure, Table, Chart & Equation Conversions
Work with IGI Global's graphic designers before submission to enhance and design all figures and charts to IGI Global's specific standards for clarity.

Translation
Providing 70 language options, including Simplified and Traditional Chinese, Spanish, Arabic, German, French, and more.

Hear What the Experts Are Saying About IGI Global's Author Services

*"Publishing with IGI Global has been **an amazing experience** for me for sharing my research. The **strong academic production** support ensures quality and timely completion."* – **Prof. Margaret Niess, Oregon State University, USA**

*"The service was **very fast, very thorough, and very helpful** in ensuring our chapter meets the criteria and requirements of the book's editors. I was **quite impressed and happy** with your service."* – **Prof. Tom Brinthaupt, Middle Tennessee State University, USA**

Learn More or Get Started Here:

For Questions, Contact IGI Global's Customer Service Team at cust@igi-global.com or 717-533-8845

IGI Global
PUBLISHER of TIMELY KNOWLEDGE
www.igi-global.com

IGI Global
PUBLISHER of TIMELY KNOWLEDGE
www.igi-global.com

Celebrating Over 30 Years of Scholarly Knowledge Creation & Dissemination

InfoSci®-Books

A Database of Nearly 6,000 Reference Books Containing Over 105,000+ Chapters Focusing on Emerging Research

InfoSci®-Books Database

The **InfoSci®-Books** is a database of nearly 6,000 IGI Global single and multi-volume reference books, handbooks of research, and encyclopedias, encompassing groundbreaking research from prominent experts worldwide that spans over 350+ topics in 11 core subject areas including business, computer science, education, science and engineering, social sciences, and more.

Open Access Fee Waiver (Read & Publish) Initiative

For any library that invests in IGI Global's InfoSci-Books and/or InfoSci-Journals (175+ scholarly journals) databases, IGI Global will match the library's investment with a fund of equal value to go toward **subsidizing the OA article processing charges (APCs) for their students, faculty, and staff** at that institution when their work is submitted and accepted under OA into an IGI Global journal.*

INFOSCI® PLATFORM FEATURES

- Unlimited Simultaneous Access
- No DRM
- No Set-Up or Maintenance Fees
- A Guarantee of No More Than a 5% Annual Increase for Subscriptions
- Full-Text HTML and PDF Viewing Options
- Downloadable MARC Records
- COUNTER 5 Compliant Reports
- Formatted Citations With Ability to Export to RefWorks and EasyBib
- No Embargo of Content (Research is Available Months in Advance of the Print Release)

**The fund will be offered on an annual basis and expire at the end of the subscription period. The fund would renew as the subscription is renewed for each year thereafter. The open access fees will be waived after the student, faculty, or staff's paper has been vetted and accepted into an IGI Global journal and the fund can only be used toward publishing OA in an IGI Global journal. Libraries in developing countries will have the match on their investment doubled.*

To Recommend or Request a Free Trial:
www.igi-global.com/infosci-books
eresources@igi-global.com • Toll Free: 1-866-342-6657 ext. 100 • Phone: 717-533-8845 x100

IGI Global
PUBLISHER of TIMELY KNOWLEDGE
www.igi-global.com

www.ingramcontent.com/pod-product-compliance
Lightning Source LLC
LaVergne TN
LVHW080603300926
849162LV00005B/1033